More and Better Jobs in South Asia

South Asia Development Matters

More and Better Jobs in South Asia

Reema Nayar, Pablo Gottret, Pradeep Mitra,
Gordon Betcherman, Yue Man Lee,
Indhira Santos, Mahesh Dahal, and
Maheshwor Shrestha

THE WORLD BANK
Washington, D.C.

ISBN (paper): 978-0-8213-8912-6
ISBN (electronic): 978-0-8213-8913-3
DOI: 10.1596/978-0-8213-8912-6

Library of Congress Cataloging-in-Publication Data
More and better jobs in South Asia / World Bank.
    p. cm.— (South asia development matters)
  Includes bibliographical references.
  ISBN 978-0-8213-8912-6 — ISBN 978-0-8213-8913-3 (electronic)
  1. Labor market—South Asia. 2. Labor policy—South Asia. 3. Employment—South Asia. 4. South Asia—Economic policy. 5. South Asia—Economic conditions. I. World Bank.
  HD5812.57.A6M67 2011

                                                                331.120954—dc23

Cover photo: Ray Witlin, The World Bank
Cover design: Bill Pragluski, Critical Stages, LLC

Contents

Boxes

Figures

Tables

Foreword

It is my great pleasure to introduce the inaugural issue of South Asia Development Matters. *More and Better Jobs in South Asia* is timely because of its relevance to the region's 490 million young people who can make South Asia the region of the future. Despite having one of the lowest female participation rates in the developing world, South Asia will add at least one million people to its labor force every month. The significant additions to the labor force could be a demographic dividend or a curse, which is why this report is so important: the key to future peace and poverty reduction in South Asia is the creation of enough good-quality jobs in the decades to come. Future generations will thank this one for using this opportunity to create an environment for progressively better jobs, which are the only sustainable pathway out of poverty.

The South Asia Development Matters series will be published annually under the supervision of Kalpana Kochhar, Chief Economist for the South Asia Region. I hope the series will promote dialogue and debate with all our partners, not only policy makers but also civil society organizations, academic institutions, development practitioners, and the media. This series will serve as a vehicle for voicing an in-depth synthesis of economic and policy analysis on key development topics for South Asia.

Next year we will address the theme of inequality, the challenges faced by individual countries in South Asia, and the ways in which inequality can be addressed so that countries can grow and develop with equity. I hope that the knowledge gathered in the South Asia Development Matters series will benefit the entire region and that it promotes debate and builds consensus of all those who care about stimulating development and eradicating poverty in South Asia.

I would like to thank the team members for their high-quality product. They were able to tackle a very difficult issue in a way that examined technical quality, with great openness to views from different professional streams. This was a tough topic, and they have produced important recommendations to promote policy debate.

Isabel Guerrero
Vice President, South Asia Region
The World Bank

Preface

More and Better Jobs in South Asia launches the series South Asia Development Matters. When selecting the first topic in the series, we had no doubt that it should focus on jobs. South Asian countries will add 1.0 million to 1.2 million new entrants to the labor force every month for the next two decades and will contribute about 40 percent of the total new entrants to the global working-age (15–64) population. It is not surprising that we decided to focus our attention on the changes in policies necessary to create a larger number and higher quality of jobs. Identification and implementation of these policies are central to South Asia's employment challenge of absorbing the growing number of entrants to the labor force at rising levels of productivity.

Recent global events have helped shine a brighter light on this issue. According to the International Labour Organization, as many as 30 million people worldwide lost their jobs as a result of the 2008 crisis. Youth unemployment is especially high, and inequality has increased in many countries around the world. As recent events during the "Arab Spring" in the Middle East and North Africa demonstrate, joblessness and inequality can trigger political instability and unrest. Closer to home, labor is the most important, if not the only, asset of the poor.

South Asia, despite impressive growth and poverty reduction over the past two decades, remains home to more than half a billion poor people, large numbers of whom have little or no education and suffer from poor health. Part of the reason is that South Asia has some of the worst nutrition indicators in the world. Research clearly shows that a person's cognitive development begins in the early years of life, long before formal schooling begins. Nutrition and early childhood development have a strong positive relationship with educational achievement and significant payoffs for lifetime learning and labor market productivity. The challenge of generating more productive jobs is intensified because most of the countries in the region are still in conflict or have only recently emerged from it and many people face serious problems related to access to opportunities based on gender, caste, and socioeconomic status.

More and Better Jobs in South Asia attempts to answer three questions:

- Has South Asia been creating an increasing quantity and quality of jobs?

- What are the determinants of the quality of job creation and what is the employment challenge going forward?
- What demand- and supply-side bottlenecks need to be eased to meet South Asia's employment challenge in the face of intensifying demographic pressure?

Although details vary by country, overall there is reason for cautious optimism. Over the past two decades, the region has created more jobs—at a rate largely comparable to growth in the working-age population—and better jobs, in terms of higher pay for wage workers, lower poverty for self-employed workers, and reduced risk of low and uncertain income for the most vulnerable group of workers. Yet, there is no room for complacency because the challenges are big. Not only do a larger number of jobs need to be created, but the jobs also need to be more productive and make workers less vulnerable. Our study shows that creating a larger number of more productive jobs for a growing labor force calls for a multisectoral reform agenda that includes improving access to electricity for firms across all sectors in urban and rural settings, dealing decisively with issues of governance and corruption, improving access to land and transport links between town and country, improving nutrition in early childhood, equipping workers with skills relevant for the world of work, and reorienting labor market regulations and programs to protect workers rather than jobs.

This book is divided into seven chapters. Chapter 1 is an overview. Chapter 2 reviews South Asia's recent track record with regard to the quantity and quality of job creation. It traces the relationship of such job creation mostly to overall economic growth and attempts to answer what needs to be done to meet South Asia's employment challenge. Chapter 3 discusses the key features of labor markets in South Asia, including where the better jobs are, who holds them, and the implications for the employment challenge ahead. Chapter 4 reviews the business environment constraints affecting, in particular, those firms that have expanded employment and discusses policy options for overcoming the most binding business constraints in South Asia. Chapter 5 analyzes the dimensions of the education and skills challenge in the region and discusses policy priorities for improving the quality and skills of graduates of education and training systems. Chapter 6 reviews the role of labor market policies and institutions in encouraging job creation and protecting workers in the formal and informal economy and discusses possible directions for labor market policies, including options to increase the access of informal sector workers to programs that help them manage labor market shocks and improve their future earnings potential. Finally, chapter 7 reviews the key constraints to job creation and the policy priorities for creating more and better jobs in conflict-affected areas.

Kalpana Kochhar
Chief Economist, South Asia Region
The World Bank

Acknowledgments

More and Better Jobs in South Asia is the first in a series of flagship reports conceived and launched by Isabel Guerrero, Regional Vice President of the South Asia Region. It is the product of a collaborative effort by many professionals and institutions from both inside and outside the World Bank.

The report was prepared by a team led by Reema Nayar and Pablo Gottret, under the direction of Kalpana Kochhar, Chief Economist of the South Asia Region. The core team comprised Pradeep Mitra, Yue Man Lee, Indhira Santos, Gordon Betcherman, Mahesh Dahal, and Maheshwor Shrestha. Wendy Carlin, Amit Dar, Lakshmi Iyer, Toby Linden, and Mark Schaffer made significant contributions to specific chapters.

Many people provided written inputs and contributions on various issues. Early think pieces and background papers were prepared by T. N. Srinivasan, Barry Bosworth, Peter B. Hazell, Derek Headey, Alejandro Nin Pratt, Derek Byerlee, David Robalino, Ashish Narain, Ernest Sergenti, Pierella Paci, David Margolis, Mario Di Filippo, Tanja Lohmann, Tenzin Chhoeda, Mark Dutz, Hong Tan, Stephen O'Connell, Lucia Madrigal, and Meera Mahadevan. The report also draws on specific contributions or analytical pieces by Shaghil Ahmed, Harold Alderman, Sudeshna Ghosh Banerjee, Hai Anh Dang, Puja Vasudeva Dutta, Madhur Gautam, Rana Hasan, Benjamin Herzberg, Ina Hoxha, Kalim Hyder, Karl Jandoc, Maria Jos, Samir KC, Somik Lall, Peter Lanjouw, Norman Loayza, David McKenzie, Claudio Montenegro, Martin Moreno, Rinku Murgai, Denis Nikitin, Sheoli Pargal, Harry Patrinos, Zhiheng Png, Shumaila Rifaqat, Hiroshi Saeki, Mehnaz Safavian, Vibhor Saxena, Claudia Ines Vasquez, Jessica Villegas, Tomoko Wada, and Karar Zunaid. The team also benefited from papers prepared by colleagues at various institutions in the region, including Nazneen Ahmed, Rushidan Rahman, R. Shamsunnahar, and Mohamad Yunus (Bangladesh Institute of Development Studies); Farzana Munshi (BRAC University, Dhaka); Bibek Debroy (Center for Policy Research, New Delhi); Koushik Dutta (independent consultant); Ramani Gunatilaka (adjunct research fellow, Faculty of Business and Economics, Monash University); Amrita Dutta, Ann George, Dev Nathan, Preet Rustagi, Alakh Sharma, and Ravi Srivastava (Institute of Human Development, New Delhi); and Nisha Arunatilake, Roshini Jayaweera, and Anushaka Wijesinha (Institute of Policy Studies, Colombo).

The team benefited from advice and comments from Eliana Cardoso and Andrew Steer (former Chief Economists of the South Asia Region), Martin Rama, Michal Rutkowski, and Marcelo Selowsky. Arup Banerji, Emmanuel Jimenez, and Ana Revenga were peer reviewers for the report. The team is grateful for the contributions of participants at various panel discussions and brainstorming sessions. They include Janamitra Devan, Tamar Manuelyan Atinc, Shanta Devarajan, Ariel Fiszbein, Ernesto May, John Henry Stein, Roberto Zagha, Rachid Benmessaoud, Ellen Goldstein, Nicholas Kraft, Susan Goldmark, Asli Demirgüç-Kunt, Kaushik Basu, Nadeem Haque, Michael Walton, Dilip Mukherji, Siddiqur Osmani, Manish Sabharwal, Binayak Sen, and the late Suresh Tendulkar. The team gratefully acknowledges comments and assistance from Faizuddin Ahmed, D. H. C. Aturupane, Roshan Darshan Bajracharya, Dan Biller, Andreas Blom, John Blomquist, Jose Roberto Calix, Eliana Carranza, Anthony Cholst, Maria Correia, Halil Dundar, Simeon Ehui, Ejaz Syed Ghani, Sangeeta Goyal, Mary Hallward-Driemeier, Zahid Hussain, Nalin Jena, Dean Mitchell Jolliffe, Sanjay Kathuria, Ayesha Khan, Gladys Lopez-Acevedo, Eric David Manes, Nkosinathi Mbuya, Julie McLaughlin, Cem Mete, Hanid Mukhtar, Karthik Muralidharan, Somil Nagpal, Hassan Naqvi, Claudia Nassif, Naveed Naqvi, John Newman, Thomas O'Brien, Robert Palacios, Dilip Parajuli, Giovanna Prennushi, Jasmine Rajbhandary, Dhushyanth Raju, Mansoora Rashid, Susan Razzaz, Silvia Redaelli, Francis Rowe, Deepa Sankar, Tahseen Sayed, Hisanobu Shishido, Venkatesh Sundararaman, and T. G. Srinivasan. Many individuals from a variety of research, policy, and academic institutions and international development agencies in Bangladesh, India, Nepal, and Pakistan participated in and provided extremely useful insights at consultation meetings held in the countries. Unfortunately, it is not possible to name them individually here.

The report would have not been possible without the able assistance of Izabela Anna Chmielewska, Julie-Anne Graitge, Marjorie Kingston, and Elfreda Vincent. The team also gratefully acknowledges financial support from the Multi-Donor Trust Fund for Trade and Development, the Poverty and Social Impact Analysis (PSIA), and the World Bank Research Committee. Aziz Gökdemir, Patricia Katayama, Andrés Meneses, Santiago Pombo-Bejarano, and Janice Tuten of the World Bank's Office of the Publisher coordinated the editing, design, production, and printing of this book.

Abbreviations

ANTA	Australian National Training Authority
CDC	community development council
CPI	Competitiveness Partnership Initiative
CSSP	Community School Support Program
DDR	disarmament, demobilization, and reintegration
EPZ	export processing zones
FATA	Federally Administered Tribal Areas
FPD	Financial and Private Sector Development
GDP	gross domestic product
GET	Global Education Trend
GHTDP	Great Himalaya Trail Development Programme
G–PSF	Government–Private Sector Forum
GW	gigawatts
IFC	International Finance Corporation
ILO	International Labour Organization
MCTEE	Ministerial Council for Tertiary Education and Employment
MGNREGA	Mahatma Gandhi National Rural Employment Guarantee Act
MSME	micro and small and medium-size enterprise
MW	megawatt
NATO	North Atlantic Treaty Organization
NCEUS	National Commission for Enterprises in the Unorganised Sector
NGO	nongovernmental organization
NSDC	National Skills Development Corporation
NSP	National Solidarity Program
NTFP	nontimber forest produce
NWFP-KP	North West Frontier Province (Khyber Pakhtunkhwa)
OECD	Organisation for Economic Co-operation and Development
PAF	Poverty Alleviation Fund
PPP	public-private partnership
PPP	purchasing power parity

PRI	Panchayati Raj Institutions
PSDC	Penang Skills Development Centre
SEZ	special economic zone
TEWA	Termination of Employment of Workmen Act
TFP	total factor productivity
UCDP/PRIO I	Uppsala Conflict Data Program and Centre for the Study of Civil War at the International Peace Research Institute
UNESCO	United Nations Education, Scientific and Cultural Organization
UNICEF	United Nations Children's Fund
WHO	World Health Organization

Note: All dollar amounts are U.S. dollars (US$) unless otherwise indicated.

Key Messages

Message 1: South Asia has created many, mostly better jobs.

- Job creation in South Asia averaged almost 800,000 a month between 2000 and 2010. The rate of employment growth broadly tracked that of the working-age (15–64) population. Open unemployment is low.
- Real wages rose for wage workers, and poverty declined for the self-employed as well as all types of wage workers. Wages and poverty are the primary criteria for improved job quality that guide the analysis in this book. A reduced risk of low and uncertain income for the most vulnerable group of workers is a secondary criterion for improved job quality. It could be monitored only in India, where it is satisfied.
- The improvement in job quality has been associated with accelerating economic growth in Bangladesh and India since the 1980s. In Nepal, where growth has been slow for several decades, massive out-migration in response to limited opportunities at home has improved labor market prospects for those who remain. Workers' remittances have reduced poverty across a wide swath of households.

Message 2: The region faces an enormous employment challenge, but its demography can work in support of the reforms needed to meet it.

- An estimated 1.0–1.2 million new entrants will join the labor market every month over the next few decades—an increase of 25–50 percent over the average number of entrants between 1990 and 2010. The employment challenge for the region is to absorb these new entrants into jobs at rising levels of productivity.
- Aggregate productivity growth in South Asia over the last three decades was driven by an extraordinary surge in the growth of total factor productivity (TFP) (a combination of changes in the efficiency with which inputs are used and changes in technology). Its contribution was larger than in the "miracle" growth years of high-performing East Asian economies (excluding China). Going forward, rapidly growing countries in South Asia need to sustain and slow-growing countries to ignite growth by easing constraints to physical and human capital accumulation. Higher rates of factor accumulation, alongside more typical rates of TFP growth, which will vary according to country circumstances, will allow the region to absorb new entrants to the labor force at rapidly rising levels of labor productivity.

- Aggregate TFP growth should also increase through a faster reallocation of labor from agriculture to industry and services, where TFP growth is higher. Reallocation across sectors needs to be complemented by moving labor out of lower-productivity firms in manufacturing and services, where the overwhelming majority of South Asians who are employed in these sectors work, into higher-productivity firms within those sectors. Reallocation across and within sectors will require physical capital accumulation (in electricity, for example, the lack of reliable supply of which is reported by job-creating firms as an obstacle to their operation). It will also require investment in human capital to provide workers with the skills necessary to access better jobs.

- The "demographic transition"—the period during which the number of workers grows more rapidly than the number of dependents—can provide a tailwind in support of policy reform for the next three decades in much of South Asia, as the resources saved from having fewer dependents provides a "demographic dividend." This dividend can be used for high-priority physical and human capital investments necessary to absorb the growing number of entrants into the labor force at rising wages and more productive self-employment. The dividend can be reaped, however, only if a policy framework is in place that can channel the extra savings into priority investments (including, for example, an efficiently intermediating financial sector and a business environment conducive to firms' carrying out those investments). In the absence of such a framework, productivity will grow slowly or remain stagnant, and the dividend will go uncashed. The window of demographic opportunity is expected to close around 2040 for all countries except Sri Lanka, where it closed around 2005, and Afghanistan, where it will stay open beyond 2040. The demographic transition will eventually give way to old age dependency, as the share of the elderly in the population increases.

- Continuance of high economic growth, which has been an important driver of improved job quality, is not assured. Globally, correlations of country growth rates across decades are low. Thus policy reforms required to ease bottlenecks to improving job quality are needed, irrespective of whether there is a demographic dividend, in order to maintain and increase the pace of creation of better jobs, even in lower growth environments. The window of demographic opportunity lends urgency to the agenda, since policies take time to bear fruit.

Message 3: Creating more and better jobs for a growing labor force calls for a reform agenda that cuts across sectors.

- Investing in reliable electricity supply is critical. South Asian firms of all types—rural and urban, formal and informal—rate electricity as a top constraint to operations. Reported power outages are consistent with reported severity: Afghanistan, Bangladesh, and Nepal have some of the highest reported outages in the world. The gap between demand and supply of electricity is large. Reforms need to manage the required expansion of capacity efficiently and improve the financial and commercial viability of the power utilities. They involve a combination of investment and reform of governance in the sector—both are critical.
- Formal urban firms cite corruption in interactions with the state, especially in transactions involving tax administration and utilities, as an important constraint to their operations.
- Informal urban firms in India report inad-

equate access to land among their leading constraints. Rural-based industry and service firms in Bangladesh, Pakistan, and Sri Lanka report as a top constraint inadequate transport, which inhibits their access to markets that would make them less dependent on local demand.

- Agriculture will continue to be the largest employer in much of South Asia for the foreseeable future. Boosting TFP growth in the sector through accelerated diversification into cash crops and high-value activities will require investment in key public goods. Investment in agricultural research and development has much higher returns than power, fertilizer, and credit subsidies.
- Education reform and action before children enter school are key. Poor nutrition in early childhood, where South Asia has the weakest indicators in the world, impairs cognitive development before children get to school, reducing the payoff from subsequent educational investments. Policy makers must also strengthen the quality of learning at all levels to equip tomorrow's workers, not only with academic and technical skills, but also with the behavioral, creative thinking, and problem-solving skills employers increasingly demand.
- Moving away from protecting jobs to protecting workers is essential for formal sector job creation in India, Nepal, and Sri Lanka. Enterprise managers in the urban formal sector report labor regulations as being a more severe constraint to the operation of their business than is the case for countries at their levels of per capita income. High costs of dismissing regular workers are, in effect, a tax on hiring them. Reforms to encourage job creation in the formal economy should lower these costs, which protect a minority of workers. These reforms must go hand in hand with reforms that strengthen labor market institutions and programs that formal and informal sector workers can use to help them adjust to labor market shocks and improve their future earnings potential. Building incrementally on existing schemes is likely the best way forward.

Overview | 1

This book investigates how more and better jobs can be created in South Asia.[1] It does so for two reasons. First, this region will contribute nearly 40 percent of the growth in the world's working-age (15–64) population over the next several decades. It is important to determine what needs to be done to absorb them into employment at rising levels of labor productivity. Second, creating more productive jobs—with jobs defined to include all wage work and self-employment—is the most reliable route out of poverty for a region that is home to more than 40 percent of the world's absolute poor.[2]

The book addresses three major questions.

- Has South Asia been creating an increasing number of jobs and better jobs?
- What determines the quality of job creation, and what is the employment challenge going forward?
- What demand- and supply-side bottlenecks need to be eased to meet South Asia's employment challenge in the face of intensifying demographic pressure?

South Asia's track record

This section examines South Asia's track record in creating jobs. It looks at the quantity of jobs, the quality of jobs, and labor mobility.

Job quantity

Employment grew in South Asia over the past decade, broadly tracking growth in the working-age (15–64) population (figure 1.1). Lack of safety nets precludes high rates of open unemployment, which averaged a little over 3 percent in the region. Thus employment growth tends to broadly mirror growth in the labor force. As the proportion of the working-age population that is in the labor force changes slowly, the growth of the labor force tends to track that of the working-age population. Together these observations imply that employment growth can be expected to broadly reflect that of the working-age population.

Among five of the larger countries in the region, employment growth since 2000 was highest in Pakistan, followed by Nepal and Bangladesh, India, and Sri Lanka. Total employment in South Asia (excluding Afghanistan and Bhutan) rose from 473 million in 2000 to 568 million in 2010, creating an average of just under 800,000 new jobs a month.

FIGURE 1.1 **Annual growth in working-age population, employment, and labor force in selected South Asian countries**

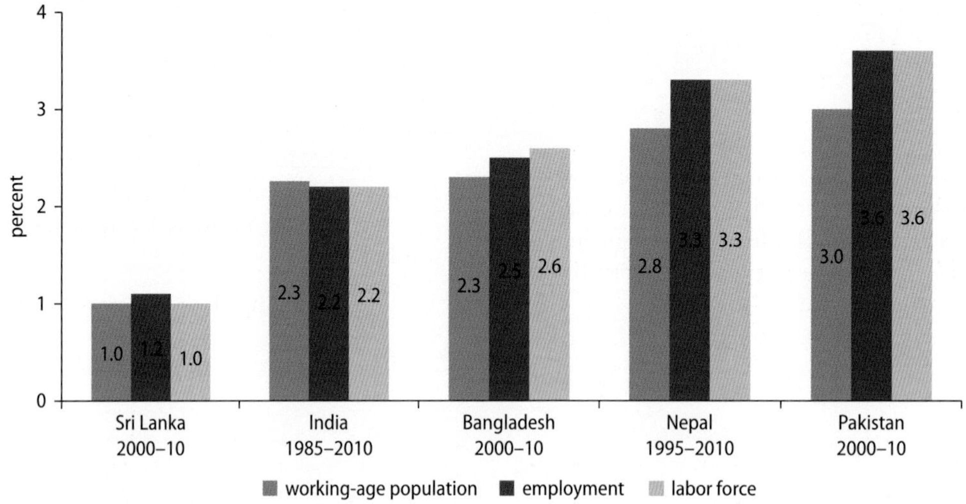

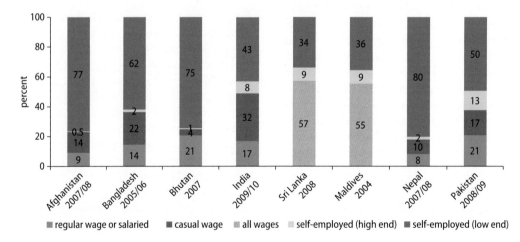

Sources: Authors, based on data on working-age population from UN 2010 and data on employment and labor force from national labor force surveys.

FIGURE 1.2 **Distribution of employment by type in South Asia, by country**

Source: Authors, based on data from national labor force and household surveys.
Note: The data for Maldives and Sri Lanka do not allow the separation of wage employment into regular wage or salaried workers and casual laborers.

In all countries except Maldives and Sri Lanka, the largest share of the employed are the low-end self-employed (figure 1.2).[3] Nearly a third of workers in India and a fifth of workers in Bangladesh and Pakistan are casual laborers. Regular wage or salaried workers represent a fifth or less of total employment.

Job quality

South Asia has created better jobs, defined primarily as those with higher wages for wage workers and lower poverty levels for the self-employed and secondarily as jobs that reduce the risk of low and uncertain income for the most vulnerable group of workers. By these measures, results have been positive:

- Real wages for wage workers—both casual and regular wage or salaried—grew 0.1–2.9 percent a year during various subperiods between 1983 and 2010 for which comparisons can be made (figure 1.3).
- A higher proportion of self-employed workers (on whom information on earnings is not available) are now in households above the national poverty line in Bangladesh, India, Nepal, Pakistan, and Sri Lanka. This figure is used as a proxy for improving job quality for this segment of the labor force (figure 1.4).[4] Increasing proportions of casual and regular wage or salaried workers in Bangladesh, India, and Nepal and all wage workers in Pakistan and Sri Lanka are also now in households that are above the poverty line. Indeed, poverty rates for all types of workers during all time periods show a decline when the data are disaggregated by location (rural or urban) or gender. Thus, the primary criterion for better jobs is satisfied.
- In India over the period 1999/2000 through 2009/10, there was a decline

in the average number of months for which all casual laborers were without work despite looking for it (figure 1.5). Thus, the secondary criterion for better jobs—that they should reduce the risk of low and uncertain incomes for the most vulnerable—has been met in India. This is not necessarily the case in other countries in South Asia. (For a discussion of these criteria and the way in which they are used to rank jobs by quality, see annex 1C.)

Notwithstanding the variation in wages and poverty rates across employment types and their changes over time, there is a stable pattern of association between poverty and the type of employment that has been maintained over time. Regular wage or salaried workers have the highest wages and lowest poverty rates; the self-employed have higher poverty rates; and casual workers, especially in agriculture, have the lowest wages and highest poverty rates (see annex 1C).

The proportion of workers in different employment types has remained largely unchanged over time (figure 1.6). At this level of aggregation, better jobs have been created mainly as a result of increasing

FIGURE 1.3 Average annual increases in mean real wages in selected countries in South Asia

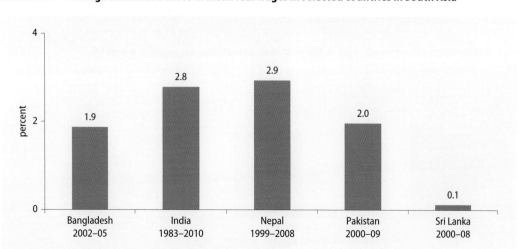

Source: Authors, based on data from national labor force and household surveys.

FIGURE 1.4   Percentage of workers in households below the poverty line in selected South Asian countries, by employment status

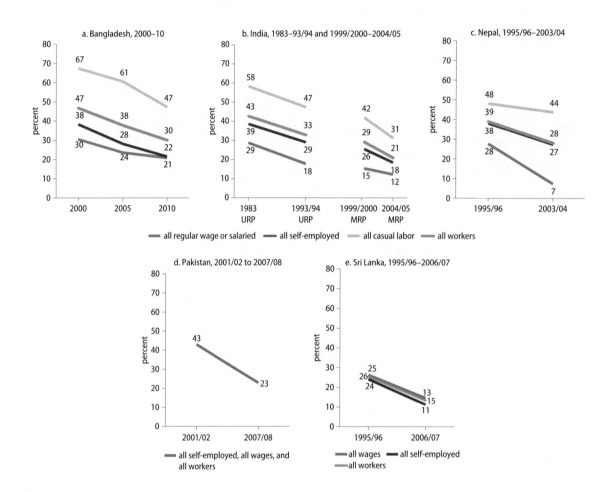

Source: Authors, based on data from national labor force and household surveys.
Note: URP = uniform recall period (the period in which respondents were asked to recall all consumption items over the same recall period [for example, 7 days]).
MRP = mixed recall period (the period need not be the same for all items, [for example, 7 days for some and 365 days for others]). Figures are for workers age 15–64.

FIGURE 1.5   Average number of months without work in the past year, casual laborers in India, by sector, 1999/2000–2009/10

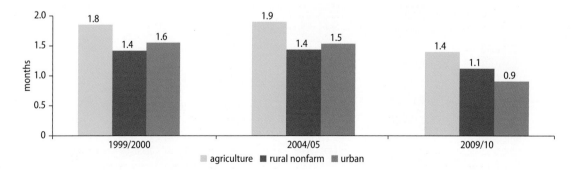

Source: Authors, based on data from Indian labor force and household surveys.
Note: Figures are for workers age 15–64 who were available for work during at least part of the month.

FIGURE 1.6   **Distribution of rural and urban workers in selected South Asian countries, by employment type**

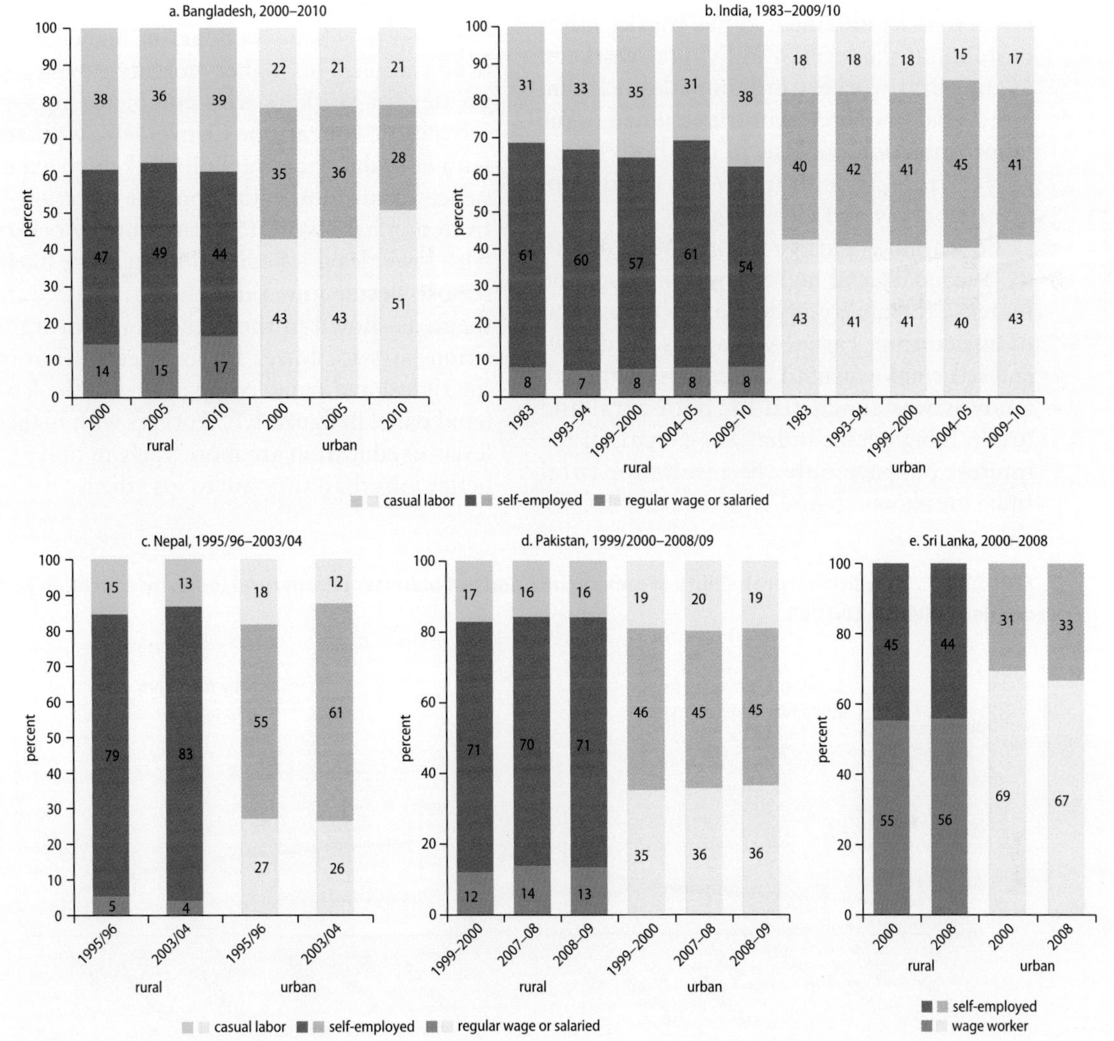

Source: Authors, based on data from national labor force and household surveys.
a. Data from the Bangladesh Household Income and Expenditure Surveys (HIES) were used to calculate worker poverty rates. The share of workers by employment type in the HIES differs from the share in the Bangladesh labor force surveys. The difference is likely to be partly driven by how female employment is captured, with female participation rates in the HIES less than half those reported in the labor force survey. Therefore, the changes in the share of workers by type in Bangladesh from the HIES should be interpreted with caution. For example, between 2005 and 2010 the significant increase in the share of regular wage or salaried work in urban areas was driven largely by changes in the female urban workforce reported in the HIES 2005 and HIES 2010.
b. Although there is variation in the shares of casual labor and self-employment in rural areas in India, there is no persistent increase or decline in the shares throughout the whole period (for example, the increase in casual labor between 2004/05 and 2009/10 mostly reversed the decline between 1999/2000 and 2004/05); the share of regular wage or salaried workers remained constant throughout the 25-year period.

quality within jobs rather than reallocation of the labor force across employment categories.

Looking across broad sectors, wages in industry and services are higher than in agriculture. Thus, the rural nonfarm economy offers better jobs than agriculture. Improvement in job quality has been associated with increasing shares of industry and services in employment, which includes a growing share of the rural nonfarm economy in rural employment.

Labor transitions

The broad constancy in the share of workers across employment types masks labor mobility at the level of individual workers. Many rural workers in Bangladesh, India, and Nepal (the three countries studied in the labor transition analysis in this book) have moved from agriculture to the rural nonfarm economy and vice versa.

Education is closely tied to labor mobility. Secondary and higher levels of education increase the ability of workers to move out of agriculture, casual wage jobs, and low-end self-employment to better jobs. Although analysis was conducted for both rural and urban Bangladesh, India, and Nepal, in the interest of space only the results for rural India are shown (figure 1.7).

Rural workers who were in agriculture in the first period were more likely to make the transition to a better job—to nonfarm work—if they had secondary or higher levels of education. This higher mobility is typically greater for workers who completed upper-secondary education. Conversely, workers with less education were more likely to experience a transition in the opposite direction—from nonfarm work to agriculture. Workers with lower levels of education are more likely to lose better jobs than they are to secure them, as shown in the higher levels of transition bars for lower levels of education in the right-hand panel compared with the left-hand panel in figure 1.7. Workers with higher levels of education are more likely to move to better jobs than they are to lose them.

FIGURE 1.7   **Conditional probability of moving into and out of better jobs in rural India, by education and gender, 2004/05–2007/08**

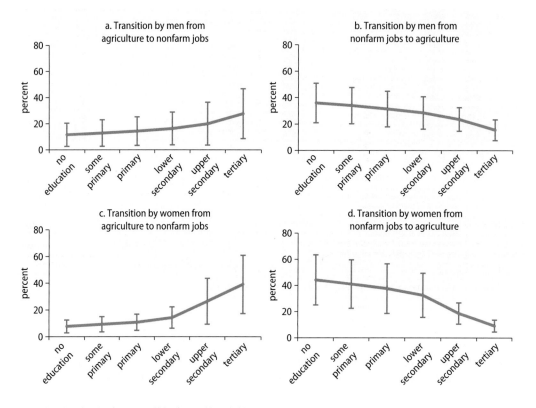

Source: Authors, based on data from national labor force and household surveys.
Note: The probability of transition is conditional on being in a specific type of employment in the first period (e.g., panel a shows the estimated probability that a rural male worker who was in agriculture in the first period is working in a nonfarm job in the second period). The probability differs by the level of education of the worker. Upper and lower bounds of the estimated probabilities are shown. The blue lines are drawn through the midpoints of the bounds.

Determinants of job quality and the employment challenge

Improving job quality for most segments of the labor force can usually occur only in a growing economy. South Asia has seen an acceleration of growth in gross domestic product (GDP) per capita over the three decades since 1980; its growth has been second only to that of East Asia (figure 1.8). But growth experiences have varied within South Asia (figure 1.9). Growth in GDP per capita accelerated, particularly since the 1980s, in Bangladesh and India. It stagnated in Nepal and was marked by volatility around a broadly declining trend over the last four decades in Pakistan. Sri Lanka witnessed an acceleration of growth over the last five

FIGURE 1.8   Annual growth in GDP per capita, by region, 1960s–2000s

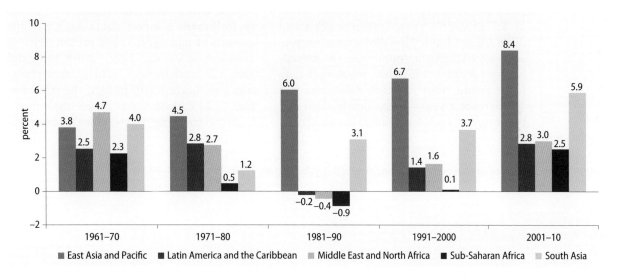

Source: Authors, based on data from World Bank 2011c.

FIGURE 1.9   Annual growth in GDP per capita in South Asia, by country, 1960s–2000s

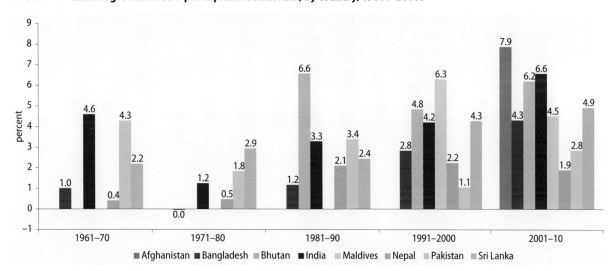

Source: Authors, based on data from World Bank 2011c.
Note: Growth in the earliest available decade for Afghanistan, Bhutan, and Maldives is not based on data for the entire decade because data for the entire decade were not available. Thus Afghanistan 2001–09 is based on 2003–09, Bhutan 1981–90 is based on 1982–90, and Maldives 1991–2000 is based on 1996–2000.

decades, except for a dip in the 1980s, and it managed to avoid the slowdown or stagnation of the 1970s that affected the other countries in the region.

Sources of growth

The marked acceleration in growth in South Asia has allowed better jobs to be created. Among industrial and all developing regions except China, aggregate labor productivity (GDP per worker) grew fastest in South Asia, at 3.7 percent a year, between 1980 and 2008 (figure 1.10). This performance represents a striking turnaround from the preceding two decades (1960–80), when aggregate labor productivity in South Asia grew just 1.6 percent a year—more slowly than any other region, including Sub-Saharan Africa.

Growth in aggregate labor productivity can be decomposed into two factors:

- "Extensive" growth, comprising growth in physical capital per worker (capital deepening) and growth of human capital per worker (education)
- "Intensive" growth, comprising growth in total factor productivity (TFP), a measure of the efficiency with which inputs are combined to produce output.

This decomposition indicates that growth in TFP made a larger contribution to the growth of aggregate labor productivity in South Asia during 1980–2008 than did physical and human capital accumulation (see figure 1.10). In fact, the contribution of TFP growth was higher than in the high-performing East Asian economies

FIGURE 1.10   **Sources of annual growth in labor productivity, by region, 1960–80 and 1980–2008**

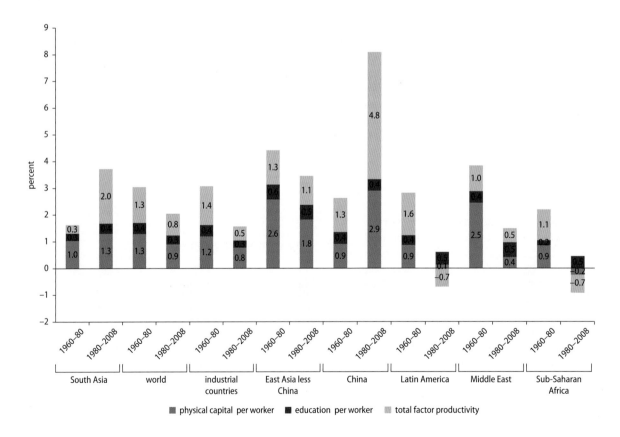

Source: Bosworth 2010.

FIGURE 1.11   **Sources of annual growth in labor productivity in selected countries in South Asia, by country, 1960–80 and 1980–2008**

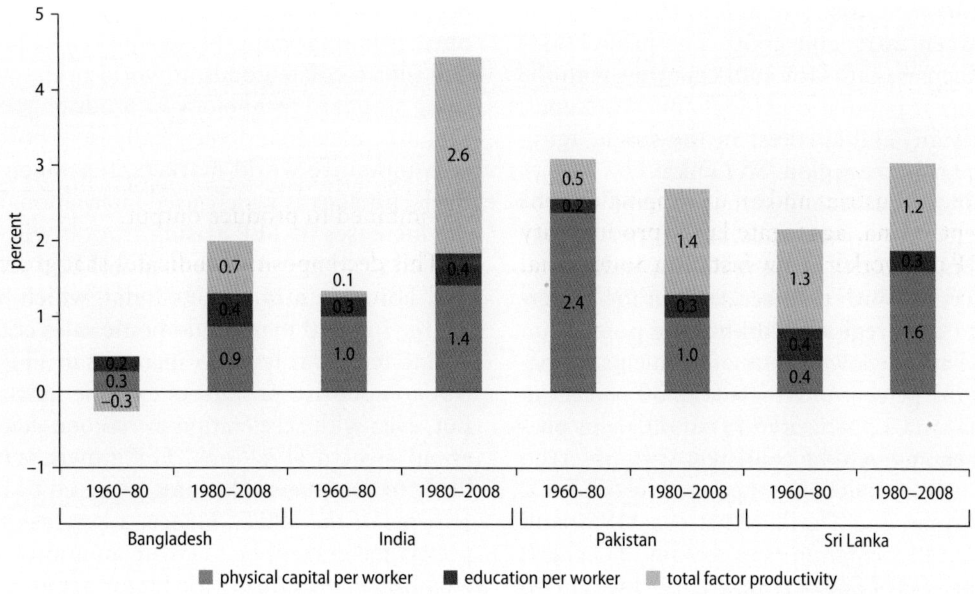

Source: Bosworth 2010.

excluding China during their "miracle" growth years.[5]

The sources of growth varied across countries (figure 1.11). In Bangladesh, education accounted for a fifth of the growth in aggregate labor productivity. Growth of TFP was more important in India, reflecting its increased exposure to external and internal competition brought about by trade liberalization and deregulation. Capital deepening played a significant role in India and Pakistan. But whereas its contribution rose in India after 1980, it fell sharply in Pakistan, accounting for the relative importance of TFP growth there. Capital deepening was more important in Sri Lanka, where the share of investment in GDP nearly doubled following its "big bang" opening up in 1977.

Job quality has not been associated with accelerated economic growth everywhere in the region. In Nepal, for example, growth in per capita GDP remained at about 2 percent a year during the last three decades. It was the massive out-migration

of workers—estimated at at least a third of all working-age men—that contributed to the reduction in labor supply and led to rising real wages for those left behind (World Bank 2010). Declining poverty, which is used as a proxy for improving job quality, owes less to growth in Nepal than to the inflow of worker remittances, estimated at nearly a quarter of GDP.

The employment challenge

The pressure to create better jobs will intensify very substantially over the next few decades. In its medium-fertility scenario, the United Nations projects that the region's current population of 1.65 billion will increase 25 percent by 2030 and 40 percent by 2050. Given the region's generally youthful population, the working-age population is projected to increase even more (35 percent by 2030 and 50 percent by 2050).

Two scenarios reveal the job creation implications of these demographic changes.

In the first, there is no increase in female labor force participation rates from current levels. In this scenario, South Asia adds nearly 1 million entrants a month to the labor force between 2010 and 2030. The proportionate increases are largest in countries with the youngest populations (Afghanistan, Nepal, Pakistan) and smallest in the single aging country in the region (Sri Lanka).

Under the second scenario, female labor participation rates increase 10 percentage points by 2030 in Bangladesh, India, and Pakistan, which together account for 95 percent of the region's working-age population and have the lowest rates of female participation (31 percent in Bangladesh, 30 percent in India, and 22 percent in Pakistan). (This phenomenon would be consistent with observed behavior in Indonesia, the Republic of Korea, Malaysia, and Thailand between 1960 and 2000.) Participation rates remain unchanged in the rest of South Asia. Nearly 1.2 million new entrants a month join the labor force between 2010 and 2030, intensifying labor market pressure in Bangladesh, India, and Pakistan. These projections imply a huge increase over the just under 800,000 entrants a month that joined the labor force between 1990 and 2010.

Can high economic growth, which has been the major driver of improving job quality in some South Asian countries, be expected to continue over the next few decades? The historical evidence from around the world shows on the contrary that growth rates are highly unstable over time: the cross-decade rank correlation of growth rates per capita for 94 countries across five decades is a mere 0.1–0.4—and correlations with time periods more than two decades apart are typically negligible.[6] The rarity of sustained growth is underlined by the fact that since 1950, per capita GDP has grown at a rate of 7 percent or more—the rate required to double living standards every 10 years—in only 13 countries, 9 of them in East Asia (World Bank 2008b).

Looking forward, productivity growth in the region will need to rely more on factor accumulation (physical capital deepening and human capital accumulation) and less on the extraordinary growth of TFP seen in the last three decades.[7] As the region has become more open to the international economy, it is importing better-quality capital and intermediate goods at world prices and using standard technology to produce goods that are either sold domestically or exported in competitive world markets. Inasmuch as the technology is widely used internationally, the increases in TFP arising from it will be limited to what is routine in global best practice. For a country such as India, which has a large internal market, domestic sales could lead to temporarily larger increases in TFP as less competitive producers exit the market. But, even with acceleration in "second-generation" structural reforms, TFP growth is not likely to continue at the rates triggered by the reforms of the 1990s. Hence, a key task for policy makers will be to create an improving enabling environment for factor accumulation (physical capital deepening and human capital formation), which, alongside more routine rates of TFP growth, can deliver rising wages and declining poverty.

Aggregate TFP growth could also be increased as a result of a faster reallocation of labor out of low-productivity agriculture. The contribution of reallocation to TFP growth has been substantially greater in East Asia than in South Asia (figure 1.12). Reallocation accounted for two-thirds of aggregate TFP growth in Thailand between 1977 and 1996, a period during which the share of agriculture in employment fell nearly a third. The contribution of reallocation to TFP growth in China between 1978, when reforms started, and 1993 was nearly one-third. During this period, the share of agriculture in employment fell more than a fifth.[8] In contrast, reallocation contributed 15 percent to aggregate TFP growth in Pakistan and 20 percent in India between 1980 and 2008, during which time the share of agriculture fell just under a fifth in both countries.

The creation of better jobs also requires that labor be moved more rapidly not only out of agriculture into industry and services but also out of lower-productivity into

FIGURE 1.12   **Sources of annual growth in total factor productivity in China, India, Pakistan, and Thailand, by sector and reallocation effects**

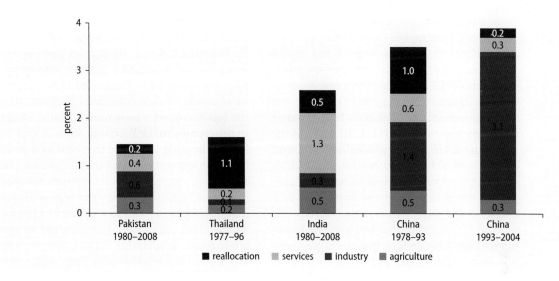

Sources: Authors, based on data from Bosworth 2005, 2010; Bosworth and Collins 2008.
Note: The contribution of reallocation during a decade is calculated as aggregate TFP growth minus the sum over the three sectors of TFP growth weighted by the share of the sector in GDP at the beginning of the decade.

FIGURE 1.13   **Median wage and value added per manufacturing worker in India, by firm size and type, 2005**

(percentage of median wages/value added per worker in formal firms with 200 or more employees)

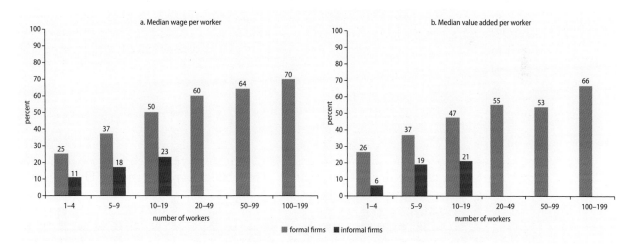

Sources: Authors, based on data on formal firms from the Annual Survey of Industries and data on informal firms from the National Sample Survey manufacturing surveys.
Note: Formal firm with 200 or more employees = 100 percent.

higher-productivity firms within industry and services. Wage differentials between smaller and larger firms are particularly marked in India's manufacturing sector, where both output and wages per worker in formal

firms employing one to four workers average one-quarter the levels of firms employing more than 200 workers (figure 1.13).[9]

Output per worker and wages are also much lower in informal firms than in formal firms within the same size class. In informal firms with one to four workers, these measures are just 25–50 percent of those of formal firms the same size. The difference probably reflects both the higher capital intensity and the higher skill levels at larger firms versus smaller ones and at formal firms versus informal firms of the same size. Firm-size productivity differentials exist in other countries, but they are particularly high in India compared with East Asia.

Although output per worker and wages at larger, formal firms are higher, more than 80 percent of employment in manufacturing in India is in micro firms (firms with 1–4 workers) and small firms (firms with 5–49 workers), a situation that has persisted over time (figure 1.14). In fact, half of employment is in own-account manufacturing enterprises that do not hire any wage workers. The concentration of employment in micro and small firms is even higher in services, where 96 percent of workers are in firms that employ

fewer than 50 people. As in manufacturing, the size distribution of firms did not change between 2001 and 2006.

Notwithstanding its declining share of employment, agriculture will continue to be the largest employer among the three broad sectors in most of South Asia for some time. For this reason, it is important that agricultural productivity be increased to ensure that the quality of jobs be improved for workers in the sector (box 1.1).

Accelerating the exit from agriculture to industry and services and enabling industrial and service sector firms to expand, become more productive, and thus pay higher wages requires urgent action on a number of fronts. The limited educational attainment of the labor force, inadequate infrastructure, and low capital intensity of most firms imply that realizing higher TFP growth through the intersectoral and intrasectoral reallocation of labor will require substantial investment in human and physical capital.

FIGURE 1.14   **Share of manufacturing employment in India, by firm size and type, 1994–2005**

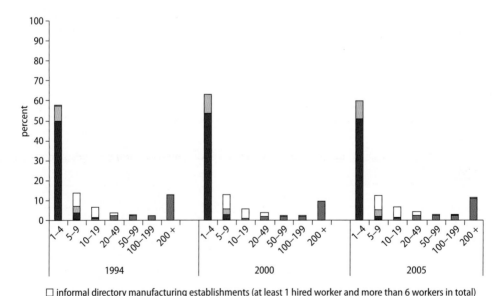

□ informal directory manufacturing establishments (at least 1 hired worker and more than 6 workers in total)
▨ informal nondirectory manufacturing establishments (at least 1 hired worker but fewer than 6 workers in total)
■ informal own-account manufacturing enterprises (no hired workers)
▨ formal

Sources: Authors, based on data on formal firms from the Annual Survey of Industries and data on informal firms from the National Sample Survey manufacturing surveys.
Note: The data show a small share (1 percent or less) of informal employment in the larger firms as well.

BOX 1.1   **Increasing productivity in agriculture**

The exit of workers from agriculture to industry and services, whether rural or urban based, is an important correlate of economic development. It is nevertheless critical to ensure that TFP in agriculture—the key driver of economic growth over the long haul—continues to grow. Increasing agricultural TFP is important for two reasons. First, it can provide better jobs for workers who remain in the sector. Second, it allows workers to transition more rapidly from agriculture to industry and services, where TFP growth is higher.

Notwithstanding South Asia's transformation from a food deficit to a food surplus region, the productivity of agriculture remains low. India and Pakistan have improved their agricultural productivity over the years; elsewhere in the region, improvements began only in the 1990s, after decades of relative stagnation. There is some room to expand area under cultivation in selected rain-fed parts of the region (in Afghanistan, Bhutan, Nepal, and eastern Sri Lanka). There are also some unexploited opportunities for expanding area through watershed development and irrigation (in Afghanistan, Bhutan, India, Nepal, and Pakistan). But the bulk of future growth will have to rely on boosting TFP growth, which has lagged international best practice.

The key to accelerating TFP growth lies in diversifying into cash crops (tea, sugarcane, cotton, spices, and rubber) and high-value activities. Cash crops have traditionally been important sources of agricultural growth and employment in many parts of South Asia. They are more labor intensive than food staples (mechanization options are limited) and well suited for small-scale production. Improved technology, together with a reduction of implicit taxation, could boost the yields of such crops.

Rising incomes, urbanization, and changing consumer preferences are creating strong demand for high-value commodities in most South Asian countries. The shift has increased incentives to diversify, to which farmers across the subcontinent are responding. Agricultural diversification has proceeded most rapidly for fruits and vegetables in Bangladesh, Bhutan, and Nepal; horticulture, fishing, and livestock in India; and livestock in Pakistan. These developments have occurred despite the disincentives created by policies that favor food security crops (rice and wheat), such as those in India, Pakistan, and Sri Lanka. A shift from cereal-based to high-value agriculture requires substantial farm-level investment, as well as greater exposure to risk. It is necessary to widen access to financial and insurance services for many smallholders in order to enable them to participate in the high-value supply chains.

Core public goods are particularly important in agriculture. Only the public sector can invest in much research and development, because private investors are not able to appropriate rents, except in a few cases, such as hybrid seeds. Public investment in agriculture has been an important driver of growth and poverty reduction in India and can provide high returns to investment in South Asia. The highest returns to public spending during the 1970s through the 1990s tended to be in research and development, roads, education, and irrigation (box table 1.1.1). Although marginal returns have diminished over

BOX TABLE 1.1.1   **Returns to agricultural growth from investments in public goods and subsidies in India, 1960s–90s**

(percent)

Public good	1960s	1970s	1980s	1990s
Agricultural research and development	3.12	5.90	6.95	6.93
Road investment	8.79	3.80	3.03	3.17
Educational investment	5.97	7.80	3.88	1.53
Irrigation investment	2.65	2.10	3.61	1.41
Credit subsidies	3.86	1.68	5.20	0.89
Power subsidies	1.18	0.95	1.66	0.58
Fertilizer subsidies	2.41	3.03	0.88	0.53
Irrigation subsidies	2.24	1.22	2.38	—

Sources: Fan, Gulati, and Thorat 2008; World Bank staff.
Note: — = Not available.

(continues next page)

time, they remain significant. In contrast, returns to input subsidies (fertilizer, power, and credit) are generally low.

Institutional weaknesses such as thin land markets, suboptimal water-use arrangements, and regulatory restrictions on marketing arrangements also constrain productivity growth in agriculture. There is thus a substantial agenda of institutional reform.

Sources: World Bank staff; Hazell et al. 2011.

FIGURE 1.15   **Ratio of working-age to nonworking-age population in South Asia, by country, 1960–2008**

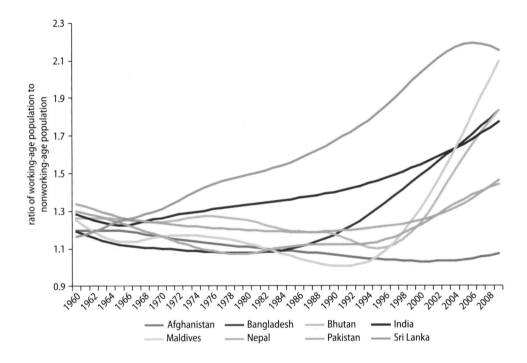

Source: Authors, based on data from World Bank 2011c.

Cashing the demographic dividend

South Asia's changing demographic profile can help it meet the enormous employment challenge it faces.[10] All South Asian countries are undergoing a process, known as the "demographic transition," by which high fertility and mortality rates are replaced by low ones. A key indicator of where a country is situated in the transition is the inverse dependency ratio, which is the ratio of the working-age population to the dependent population.

Typically, there is an initial decline in this ratio, reflecting a drop in the infant mortality rate that precedes a decline in the fertility rate. The ratio subsequently increases as the baby boom caused by the lagged decline in the fertility rate becomes part of the working-age population. The resulting rise in the share of the working-age to the nonworking-age population implies that there are fewer dependents to support (figure 1.15). The resources saved as a result—the "demographic dividend"—can be used for high-priority investments. Eventually, as the baby boom cohort ages, the demographic transition gives way to old age dependency.

Although the inverse dependency ratio has followed the same broad pattern in all of South Asia, there are country differences. Afghanistan's ratio started increasing only in 2005. Bangladesh's ratio rose sharply, catching up with India's in 2003 and exceeding it thereafter. The improvement reflected, among other things, a very rapid decline in fertility that was supported *inter alia* by the country's reproductive health program. Maldives saw the fastest increase in the ratio, thanks to its plunging fertility rate. Pakistan's ratio began a gentle climb in the 1980s and Nepal's in the 1990s.

In its medium-fertility scenario, the United Nations estimates that the inverse dependency ratio will peak for most South Asian countries around 2040. The exceptions are Sri Lanka, where it occurred around 2005, and Afghanistan, where it will still be rising in 2040. Bangladesh, Bhutan, India, and Maldives are already experiencing the demographic transition and therefore have the potential to benefit from it. Nepal and Pakistan, where the demographic transition started later, have yet to see a dividend.

The demographic dividend grows when the inverse dependency ratio rises more rapidly and peaks at a higher level. This will be the case if the fertility decline occurs soon after the decline in infant mortality and is rapid. Policies such as creating an effective reproductive health program and expanding female primary and secondary education, which reduces family size, can help bring this about.

The resources made available by the demographic dividend can be used for physical capital deepening (electricity, transport) and human capital formation (education, skills) if the business environment is conducive to making such investments. Policy also needs to help improve the quality of financial intermediation, so that the increased private savings of households find their way into the investments in physical and human capital that have the highest returns. Increased factor accumulation would then increase aggregate labor productivity, which would help absorb entrants into the labor market at rising wages and more remunerative self-employment.

Without policy reform, the demographic dividend cannot be increased or used to boost growth and living standards. In this event, entrants into the labor market will be absorbed at stagnant or slowly rising levels of productivity, and the potential of the demographic dividend will remain untapped. Policies to improve the environment for factor accumulation and raise the quality of physical and human capital formation are necessary to create better jobs whether or not there is a demographic dividend. But the fact that, for most of the region, the window of demographic opportunity will be open for only another three decades lends urgency to the need for policy reform.

Because of volatile economic growth, an uneven policy framework, and armed conflict in a number of countries, there is only a broad correspondence between per capita GDP growth and the demographic transition. The acceleration in India's economic growth started in the 1970s, when its inverse dependency ratio started its climb (see figures 1.9 and 1.15). Bangladesh's acceleration began in the 1980s; during the middle of the decade, its ratio began to increase as well. With the exception of a slowdown in the 1980s, Sri Lanka has seen an acceleration of economic growth over nearly five decades since the 1960s, when its inverse dependency ratio started rising rapidly. Pakistan, where economic growth has been volatile around a broadly declining trend across the decades, and Nepal, where growth has been low and stagnant, have yet to see a demographic dividend. With better policies, their growth performance could improve in the future as the demographic transition takes hold.

Except in Nepal and, to a lesser extent Bhutan, the female employment rate (the ratio of female employment to the female working-age population) in South Asia is among the lowest in the developing world—primarily a reflection of the region's low rates of female labor force participation. Participation rates are particularly low in the three largest countries: Pakistan, where almost four out of five women do not participate in the labor force, and Bangladesh and India, where slightly more than two out of every three do not participate. Nonparticipation does not imply inactivity: household duties were cited as the most important reason for nonparticipation. A rising proportion of working-age women in increasingly productive employment in the near future would provide a boost to growth in countries such as Bangladesh and India, which are going through the demographic transition. While the demographic transition is less advanced in Pakistan, the situation is no less urgent there since the female participation rate is the lowest in the region. (For a comprehensive discussion of options to improve economic opportunities for women, see World Bank 2012.)

The employment challenge in South Asia is one of improving job quality rather than quantity, as job growth over long periods tracks the growth of the working-age population. The challenge will be to find better jobs for a workforce whose size will increase 25–50 percent in the coming decades. In the presence of policy reform, the demographic transition can provide a favorable tailwind in support of economic growth and improving job quality. Policy will be needed, however, to address the main demand- and supply-side constraints to job creation, discussed in the next two sections respectively.

Improving an inconducive business environment

What constrains the demand for labor in South Asia? What types of policy reform would facilitate firm expansion and the demand for labor? How do the business environments of individual South Asian countries compare with the rest of the developing world?

Enterprise surveys ask firms to rate the severity of inadequacies in the various elements of the business environment for their ability to operate and expand their business. These elements, which are external to the firm and resemble public goods, include regulation, physical infrastructure, the availability of skilled labor, macroeconomic conditions, the quality of the judiciary, and crime and corruption. The question takes the form: "How much of an obstacle is X to the operation and growth of your business?" The firm's response regarding its severity—rated on a five-point scale, with 0 being no obstacle and 4 being a very severe obstacle—is a measure of the marginal reported cost imposed by the constraint on the operation and growth of its business. These data can be interpreted as the difference between the firm's profit in the hypothetical situation in which the business environment poses a negligible obstacle to its operations and the firm's actual profit, given the existing quality of the business environment.[11]

Power, payments, and politics

The three most common binding constraints for medium-size urban formal firms in South Asia are electricity, corruption, and political instability (table 1.1 and figure 1.16).[12] Although there are some variations, the top three constraints facing formal, urban firms are common to most countries. In every country except Bhutan and Maldives, electricity is one of the top two constraints; it is the top constraint in India and Sri Lanka. Except for Bhutan, political instability is among the top three constraints in all countries where it was included in the survey instrument. In five of the eight countries studied, corruption is among the four top constraints cited by urban formal sector firms.

TABLE 1.1   Top five constraints reported by South Asian benchmark firm in the urban formal sector, by country

	South Asia region	Afghanistan	Bangladesh	Bhutan	India	Maldives	Nepal	Pakistan	Sri Lanka
Electricity	2	2	1		1		2	2	1
Political instability	1	1	2		n.a.	n.a.	1	3	n.a.
Corruption	3	3	3		2	3	4		
Tax administration	4		5	5	3			1	
Labor regulations				3	4		5		5
Inadequately educated labor				2	5	2			
Access to land		4	4			1			
Transport				1			3		
Government policy uncertainty	5							4	2
Courts						4		5	
Crime, theft, and disorder		5				5			
Business licensing				4					
Macro instability									3
Competition									4

Source: Authors, based on Carlin and Schaffer 2011b (from World Bank enterprise surveys).
Note: A benchmark firm is a medium-size manufacturing firm with 30 employees that is domestically owned, does not export or import, is located in a large city, and did not expand employment in the preceding three years. n.a. = Not applicable (question was not asked). Analysis is based on pooled sample of enterprise surveys conducted between 2000 and 2010. Access to finance and tax rates constraints are excluded.

Table 1.1 and figure 1.16 show the severity and ranking of constraints for a benchmark firm in the urban formal sector. A benchmark firm is a medium-size manufacturing firm with 30 employees that is domestically owned, does not export or import, is located in a large city, and did not expand employment in the preceding three years. A comparison across countries and regions requires that these firm characteristics, which are distributed differently across countries, be controlled for. For instance, if a country has a dominance of skill-intensive firms, the answer to the question on labor skills ("How much of an obstacle are labor skills to the operation and growth of your business?") might be more important than it would be in countries that do not have firms requiring such skills. That said, although the severity of constraints differs between benchmark and nonbenchmark firms (for example, firms in the service sector), the ranking of the top constraints is very similar across types of firms within the urban formal sector across countries in South Asia.

Electricity
In most South Asian countries, the cost imposed on firms by the electricity constraint is among the highest in the world; in Afghanistan, Bangladesh, and Nepal, it is higher than in other countries at similar levels of per capita GDP (figure 1.17). Moreover, the severity of the constraint has increased over time in India, Nepal, and Pakistan. The downward slope in the figure implies that although firms in richer countries can be expected to make greater demands on the electricity grid, which would lead to rising severity of complaints, richer countries can more than offset those demands in the provision of electricity, resulting in lower levels of severity at higher incomes per capita.

The high frequency of power outages in South Asia is consistent with the reported severity of the electricity constraint. Indeed, Afghanistan, Bangladesh, and Nepal have

FIGURE 1.16   Severity of constraints reported by South Asian benchmark firm in the urban formal sector

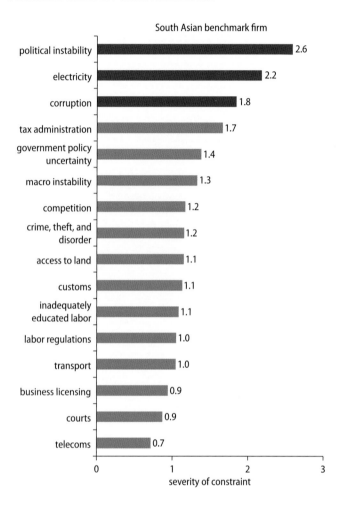

South Asian benchmark firm

Constraint	severity of constraint
political instability	2.6
electricity	2.2
corruption	1.8
tax administration	1.7
government policy uncertainty	1.4
macro instability	1.3
competition	1.2
crime, theft, and disorder	1.2
access to land	1.1
customs	1.1
inadequately educated labor	1.1
labor regulations	1.0
transport	1.0
business licensing	0.9
courts	0.9
telecoms	0.7

Source: Authors, based on Carlin and Schaffer 2011b (from World Bank enterprise surveys).
Note: A benchmark firm is a medium-size manufacturing firm with 30 employees that is domestically owned, does not export or import, is located in a large city, and did not expand employment in the preceding three years. Analysis is based on pooled sample of enterprise surveys conducted between 2000 and 2010. The severity of constraint is rated by firms on a 5-point scale, with 0 being no obstacle, 1 being a minor obstacle, 2 being a moderate obstacle, 3 being a major obstacle, and 4 being a very severe obstacle. Access to finance and tax rates constraints are excluded.

some of the highest reported outages in the world, with virtually 100 percent of firms experiencing them. Predictably, the use of generators to mitigate the effects of uncertain power supply is higher in South Asia than elsewhere, with 87 percent of firms in Afghanistan, 52 percent in Sri Lanka, and 49 percent in India having generators.

Corruption

Corruption is among the top five constraints in five South Asian countries (see table 1.1). Firms face high levels of corruption in a range of interactions with public officials, particularly for utilities and tax inspections (figure 1.18). Government interactions that have the highest frequency of bribes vary by country (with the proportion of firms reporting such payments in parentheses).

- Afghanistan: Government contracts (43 percent), electrical connections (38 percent)
- Bangladesh: Utilities (42–76 percent), tax meetings (54 percent), import licenses (51 percent)
- India: Construction permits (67 percent), tax meetings (52 percent), operating licenses (52 percent), electrical connections (40 percent)
- Pakistan: Electrical connections (71 percent), water connections (62 percent), tax meetings (59 percent).

The high frequency of bribes faced in connecting to power supply is another dimension of the issue of access to electricity and may be related to businesses having to compete to secure power (World Bank 2008a). More than half of firms in Bangladesh, India, and Pakistan are expected to pay bribes during tax inspections. The tax systems in these countries are complex and create not only high costs of compliance but also opportunities for corruption. (Chapter 4 compares the severity of corruption as an obstacle to doing business and the prevalence of bribes in individual South Asian countries and countries outside the region at similar levels of per capita GDP.)

Political instability

The reported costs of political instability are high in Afghanistan, Bangladesh, and Nepal; in all three countries, it is the most or second-most severe constraint (see chapter 4 for details). These three countries have some of the highest reported costs of political instability in the world. (Chapter 7 examines the costs imposed by armed conflict on firms and workers.)

FIGURE 1.17 **Cross-country comparisons of reported severity of electricity constraint and power outages for a benchmark firm**

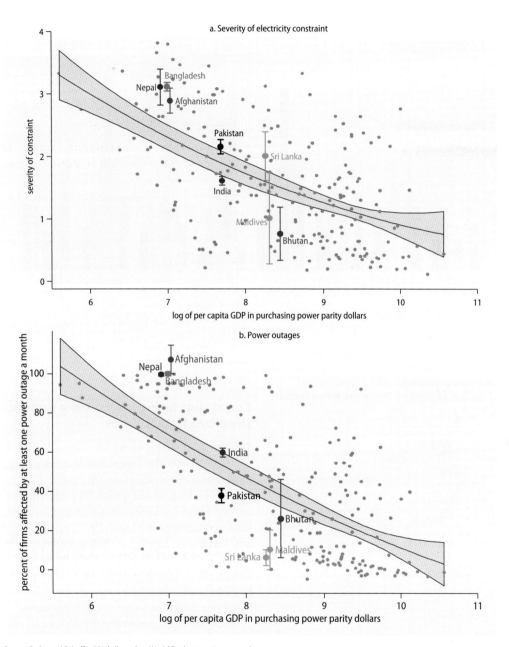

Source: Carlin and Schaffer 2011b (based on World Bank enterprise surveys).
Note: The cross-country regression line shows the relationship between the reported severity of the electricity constraint (panel a) and the percentage of firms experiencing more than one power outage per month (panel b) for a benchmark firm and the log of per capita GDP. The shaded area is the 95 percent confidence interval band around the regression line. Vertical bars show confidence intervals of 95 percent around the reported severity of the electricity constraint (panel a) and the percentage of firms experiencing more than one power outage per month (panel b) for countries in South Asia. Analysis is based on pooled sample of enterprise surveys conducted between 2000 and 2010. For further details, including why some observations in panel b are less than zero or are more than 100 percent, see notes to figures 4.2 and 4.3.

FIGURE 1.18   **Percentage of firms expected to give gifts to public officials, by type of interaction**

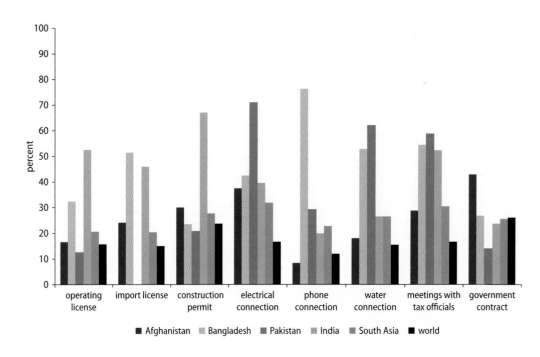

Source: Authors, based on data from World Bank enterprise surveys.
Note: Figures show percent of firms in South Asian countries citing corruption as one of their top three constraints.

FIGURE 1.19   **Severity of constraints identified by South Asian benchmark (nonexpanding) and expanding firm in the urban formal sector**

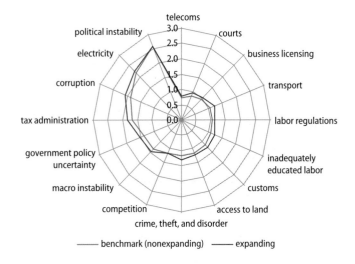

Source: Authors, based on Carlin and Schaffer 2011b (based on World Bank enterprise surveys).
Note: Analysis is based on pooled sample of enterprise surveys conducted between 2000 and 2010. A point farther away from the origin indicates that the business constraint is considered more severe. The severity of constraint is rated by firms on a 5-point scale, with 0 being no obstacle, 1 being a minor obstacle, 2 being a moderate obstacle, 3 being a major obstacle, and 4 being a very severe obstacle. Survey does not make clear what firms mean by "competition." Only statistically significant differences in severity between the benchmark (nonexpanding) and the expanding firms are shown.

Constraints facing job-creating firms in the urban formal sector

Job-creating firms, which are similar in all respects to the benchmark firm except that they expanded employment during the preceding three years, report significantly higher severity in 14 of the 16 business constraints (figure 1.19). The rankings are shown in Table 1.2. Job-creating firms also report higher levels of mitigation activities, such as using generators as a response to unreliable electricity supply and paying bribes to navigate a corrupt environment.

Job-creating firms in the urban formal sector perform well in other respects, too. They engage in research and development, introduce new processes and products, sell to multinational companies, offer in-firm training, and have better-educated managers. The increase in the cost of constraints for expanding firms versus the benchmark is highest in India and Pakistan. Job-creating firms report lower costs in Afghanistan and Bangladesh.

TABLE 1.2 Top five constraints reported by South Asian benchmark (nonexpanding) and expanding firm in the urban formal sector, by country

Constraint	South Asian region		Afghanistan		Bangladesh		Bhutan		India		Maldives		Nepal		Pakistan		Sri Lanka	
	Benchmark firm	Expanding firm	Benchmark firm	Expanding firm	Benchmark firm	Expanding firm	Benchmark firm	Expanding firm	Benchmark firm	Expanding firm	Benchmark firm	Expanding firm	Benchmark firm	Expanding firm	Benchmark firm	Expanding firm	Benchmark firm	Expanding firm
Electricity	2	2	2	2	1	1			1	2			2	2	2		1	1
Political instability	1	1	1	1	2	2			n.a.		n.a.		1	1	3	1	n.a.	n.a.
Corruption	3	3	3	4	3	3			2	1	3	4	4	4		1		
Tax administration	4	4			5	5	5	5	3	3					1	4		
Labor regulations							3	3	4	4			5	5			5	5
Inadequately educated labor							2	2	5	5	2	2						
Access to land			4	5	4	4					1	1						
Transport							1	1					3	3				
Government policy uncertainty	5	5													4	3	2	2
Courts											4	5			5			
Crime, theft, and disorder			5	3							5	3						
Business licensing							4	4										
Macro instability																5	3	3
Competition																	4	4

Source: Authors, based on Carlin and Schaffer 2011b (based on World Bank enterprise surveys).
Note: Analysis is based on pooled sample of enterprise surveys conducted between 2000 and 2010. n.a. = Not applicable (question was not asked). Access to finance and tax rates constraints are excluded.

Although the level of severity is different, job-creating firms rank constraints in much the same way that benchmark firms do, ranking electricity, corruption, and political stability as the top three constraints (see table 1.2).[13]

The severity of the electricity constraint facing urban formal firms—as well as urban informal firms and rural nonfarm enterprises—prompts a discussion of the problems facing the sector and the policies and other initiatives being undertaken to address them (box 1.2). The need to make substantial investment in electricity is an example of the point made earlier that a rapid reallocation of workers to more productive sectors will require accumulation of physical capital.

Constraints facing rural firms

Improving the business environment can spur development of the rural nonfarm economy, which accounts for an increasing share of rural employment in many South Asian countries and, therefore, the creation of better jobs within it. (See chapter 3 for a discussion of the rural nonfarm economy.) Doing so requires an understanding of the constraints firms in this sector face.

The severity of constraints reported by rural firms in Bangladesh, Pakistan, and

---

BOX 1.2   **Options for reforming the power sector in South Asia**

South Asia is characterized by low levels of access, low consumption per capita, and wide demand-supply gaps. Some 600 million people in the region lack access to electricity—more than 40 percent of the world total. Access rates range from 44 percent of the population in Nepal to 77 percent in Sri Lanka. The average annual per capita consumption for the region is 500 kilowatt hour, lower than anywhere else in the world except Africa.

Supply has not kept pace with demand, resulting in shortages at peak times ranging from 1 gigawatt (GW) in Bangladesh (13 percent) to 12 GW (10 percent) in India. The toll on the economy is enormous: in Pakistan, the cost of industrial load shedding is 400,000 lost jobs; in India, 17 percent of total capacity is based on expensive diesel generation.

Countries have responded through massive investment in expanding generation capacity. India added 50 GW of capacity between 2006 and 2011 and initiated a series of "ultra mega" (4 GW) generation projects based on competitive bidding by independent power producers. Bangladesh plans to develop 9.4 GW of new generation capacity by 2015. Bhutan has successfully established public-private partnerships for a large export-oriented hydropower project.

Significant institutional reforms have also taken place since the 1990s. Most countries have unbundled their power sectors or corporatized previously vertically integrated power utilities. The sector has been opened to private entry and greater competition in generation, transmission, and distribution, and new regulatory frameworks and independent regulatory bodies have been established. The degree of reform varies across countries and across states in India.

Sector financial losses across the region are large, resulting from the misalignment of tariffs, the high cost of power procurement, and high transmission and distribution losses. In India, the combined cash loss of state-owned distribution companies is more than $20 billion a year (total investment needs for 2010–15 are estimated at $300 billion). The sector deficit in Pakistan is estimated at about $2 billion a year (total investment needs for 2010–20 are estimated at $32 billion).

Several challenges need to be addressed to alleviate power shortages and improve service delivery. Each is addressed briefly below.

Improving the financial and commercial viability of the power sector

Policy makers can choose from a range of options to improve the financial and commercial viability of the power sector:

- Increase the level of tariffs to reflect the cost of supply, and rationalize tariffs to address cross-subsidization. Some countries have not revised tariffs in years. Others have made progress toward achieving cost-reflective tariffs, primarily to reduce fiscal pressure. All countries offer "lifeline" rates to residential consumers to enable the poor to access at least a minimum quantity of electricity as well as nominally priced electricity to agriculture consumers to support irrigation and food security. The burden of cross-subsidization falls on industrial and commercial consumers. Any tariff increase will need to ensure that adequate safety nets are in place to minimize the impact on the poor. Innovative initiatives such as the separate provision of heavy-duty agricultural feeders for agricultural needs and regular feeders for domestic and industrial purposes in the Indian state of Gujarat has allowed transparency of agricultural consumption and, by providing reliable supply to both farmers and rural domestic consumers, spurred the growth of rural productivity.
- Reduce losses by improving collection, curbing theft, and improving overall efficiency. India has initiated incentive schemes such as the Restructured Accelerated Power Development Reform Program (R-APDRP), which aims to limit losses to 15 percent.
- Improve the capacity and independence of regulatory agencies to ensure transparency and accountability in tariff setting, which continues to be driven by political exigencies. New initiatives in regulation have been put in place, such as the implementation of multiyear tariffs in India, which provide certainty regarding the costs for which utilities can be held accountable and reduce day-to-day regulatory interference.

Enhancing the business environment for private investment in power sector

The generation sector has attracted substantial private interest, but obstacles remain in the form of

(continues next page)

BOX 1.2   (continued)

procedural bottlenecks (for example, land acquisition, environmental and forest clearances, provision of water for thermal plants); limited technical and financial capacity to implement large projects; and the shortage of fuel (both domestic and imported) to ramp up capacity utilization. The region also needs to improve the operating environment to attract private players in transmission and distribution.

Exploiting the significant potential of intraregional energy trade

One of the most cost-effective options for alleviating shortages in the region is increasing intraregional energy trade. Such trade has increased in recent years, particularly in the form of hydro exports from

Bhutan to India and, to a limited extent, between Nepal and India.

Improving the governance of utilities and strengthening institutional capacity

Steps are being taken to develop strong boards and high-quality professional management. Doing so is necessary to transform an organizational culture of risk-averse top-down bureaucratic control to one more suited to commercialization. Some states in India (such as Andhra Pradesh and West Bengal) have adopted technology initiatives, particularly in metering, and accountability frameworks to improve sector performance.

Source: World Bank staff.

Sri Lanka is compared with the severity reported by urban (formal) firms in the same countries.[14] As rural firms typically employ far fewer than 30 employees, the comparison is with a micro benchmark firm—a benchmark firm with 5 employees. The results are as follows (table 1.3 and figure 1.20):

- Rural firms report less severe constraints to their operations than urban firms. This pattern is not unusual in developing countries, where larger urban firms are typically more productive and, during the course of their expansion, place more demands on publicly provided services than rural firms.
- Rural firms identify electricity as one of the most binding constraints to their operations. They report levels of power outages similar to those for urban firms and use generators more intensively than urban sector firms. In Bangladesh, 73 percent of nonmetropolitan nonfarm enterprises have an electricity connection, with 99 percent of them reporting power outages. In Sri Lanka, shortages and unreliability of power are severe in rural areas,

TABLE 1.3   **Top five constraints reported by micro benchmark firm in the urban and rural sectors of Bangladesh, Pakistan, and Sri Lanka**

Constraint	Bangladesh, Pakistan, Sri Lanka	
	Urban, formal	Rural
Electricity	1	2
Political instability	2	3
Corruption	3	
Macro instability	4	1
Access to land	5	
Transport		4

Source: Authors, based on Carlin and Schaffer 2011a (based on World Bank enterprise surveys).
Note: Analysis is based on a pooled sample of enterprise surveys conducted in Bangladesh, Pakistan, and Sri Lanka between 2000 and 2010. Access to finance and tax rates constraints are excluded. Crime, theft, and disorder as well as competition constraints were not asked in the rural surveys. Macro instability was asked only in Bangladesh and political instability was asked only in Bangladesh and Pakistan. Only the top four constraints are shown for rural firms, as the remaining constraints were not reported on average as obstacles.

where less than 70 percent of enterprises use electricity from the national grid.

- Unlike their urban counterparts, rural firms cite transport as one of their top four constraints. Firms in Bangladesh and Sri Lanka complain about the poor conditions and inaccessibility of rural roads. Poor transport limits access to larger,

FIGURE 1.20   Severity of constraints reported by micro benchmark firm in urban and rural sectors of Bangladesh, Pakistan, and Sri Lanka

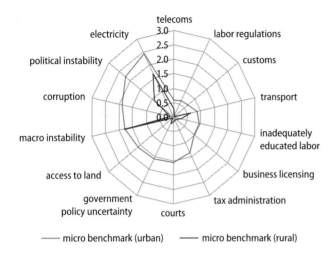

— micro benchmark (urban)   — micro benchmark (rural)

Source: Authors, based on Carlin and Schaffer 2011c (based on World Bank enterprise surveys).
Note: A point farther away from the origin indicates that the business constraint is considered more severe. The severity of constraint is rated by firms on a 5-point scale, with 0 being no obstacle, 1 being a minor obstacle, 2 being a moderate obstacle, 3 being a major obstacle, and 4 being a very severe obstacle. Only statistically significant differences in reported severity between the micro benchmark firms in urban and rural sectors are shown. For further details on the sample and constraints analyzed, see the note for table 1.3.

FIGURE 1.21   Severity of constraints reported by micro benchmark firm in India's urban formal and informal sectors

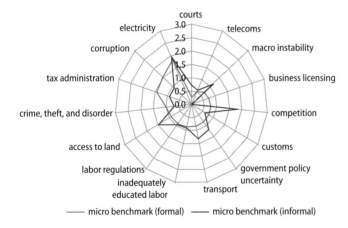

— micro benchmark (formal)   — micro benchmark (informal)

Source: Authors, based on Carlin and Schaffer 2011a (based on World Bank enterprise surveys).
Note: A point farther away from the origin indicates that the business constraint is considered more severe. The severity of constraint is rated by firms on a 5-point scale, with 0 being no obstacle, 1 being a minor obstacle, 2 being a moderate obstacle, 3 being a major obstacle, and 4 being a very severe obstacle. Only statistically significant differences in reported severity between the micro benchmark firms in urban formal and urban informal sectors are shown. For further details on the sample and constraints analyzed, see the note for table 1.4.

urban markets, forcing rural enterprises to sell predominantly to local customers, which limits the size of the market for their products and goods.[15] Rehabilitating and maintaining existing rural roads as well as building new roads would open up opportunities for rural firms.

Constraints facing informal urban firms

Enterprise surveys in the informal and formal urban sectors in India make it possible to compare the constraints encountered by informal firms with those facing formal firms. The comparison is between formal and informal urban benchmark firms. As the median firm in the informal urban sector has fewer than 30 employees, the benchmark firm size is 5 rather than 30.[16]

There are both similarities and differences between formal and informal firms in the ranking of business constraints (table 1.4 and figure 1.21). Both types of firms cite electricity as an important constraint. Informal firms are more likely to cite access to land and transport and less likely to cite corruption and tax administration.[17] Informal firms report access to finance as the most severe constraint to the operations of their businesses. However, this finding does not necessarily have implications

TABLE 1.4   Top five constraints reported by micro benchmark firm in India's urban formal and informal sectors

	India	
	Formal	Informal
Electricity	1	1
Corruption	2	
Tax administration	3	
Crime, theft, and disorder	4	
Access to land	5	3
Competition		2
Transport		4
Government policy uncertainty		5

Source: Authors, based on Carlin and Schaffer 2011a (based on World Bank enterprise surveys).
Note: Analysis is based on a pooled sample of enterprise surveys conducted in India between 2000 and 2010. Access to finance and tax rates constraints are excluded. Political instability was not asked in the India surveys.

for policy, as "access to finance" is a dimension of the business environment that, unlike the judiciary or tax administration, is not a public good. The firm's response regarding the inadequacy of finance could simply reflect the fact that some firms do not have bankable projects. Other indicators of access (for example, the proportion of firms using external finance) suggest that finance may indeed be an issue for micro and small firms in some countries.

The concern regarding access to land expressed by urban informal firms may reflect the impact of regulations that shape the operation of land markets in India. Density regulations in India, which limit the ratio of floor space to plot area, lead cities to expand outward instead of upward. Together with limited accessibility of public transport, such expansion can make it more difficult for informal manufacturing units to be located where they should be—close to buyers and suppliers. Relaxing density regulations, improving urban transport, and increasing the supply of property might help reduce the severity of the land constraint for informal urban firms (World Bank 2011a).

Improving workers' skills

Enterprise managers in the urban formal sectors in Bhutan, India, and Maldives report inadequate skills of the labor force among the top five constraints to the operation and growth of their firms (see table 1.1). In Bhutan and Maldives, inadequate skills of the labor force are among the top two constraints; in India they rank 5th. Firms in Afghanistan and Pakistan rate skills constraints among the least problematic.

Focused employer surveys in India and Sri Lanka highlight concerns with the skills of tertiary education graduates. Employers hiring fresh engineering graduates in India evaluated the degree of importance of a broad range of skills and their level of satisfaction with recent hires. They rated behavioral skills (teamwork, reliability, leadership, willingness to learn), creative thinking and problem-solving skills, and specific knowledge and

technical skills needed for the job. Two out of three employers reported that most of these skills are "very" important but that they were only somewhat satisfied (at best) with the graduates' skills (figure 1.22). (Similar concerns are echoed by Sri Lankan employers in a survey of the information technology workforce [Sri Lanka Information Communication Technology Association 2007].) The foundation for many of these skills is established well before graduates enter the world of work—in primary and secondary education and indeed even earlier.

The wage premium has been rising for higher levels of education in all countries, even as the supply of educated workers has increased. Figure 1.23 presents trends in wage premiums for different levels of education in three South Asian countries between about 2000 and 2008 and a longer period for India. The premiums reflect the differential between the average earnings of a worker with a particular level of educational attainment and the average earnings of a worker with the level of attainment just below (for details, see chapter 5). The pattern over time has been that the premium to lower levels of education has been falling while the premiums for upper-secondary and tertiary education have been increasing. These changes have been taking place in a context in which the educational attainment of the labor force has been rising. The pattern is thus consistent with a situation in which the supply of workers at lower levels of education is increasing faster than demand, whereas the demand for workers with secondary or tertiary education is outpacing the increased supply.

The heterogeneity of the region is reflected in variations across countries. India and Nepal have seen increases in premiums to both upper-secondary and tertiary education. Indeed, the wage premium for tertiary education more than doubled in India between 1999/2000 and 2009/10, despite a large increase in the share of the labor force with tertiary education. In Nepal, the largest relative increases in wage premiums were at the upper-secondary level, suggesting that demand increases at this level were greater

FIGURE 1.22   **Employers' perceptions of skills of recently graduated engineers in India**

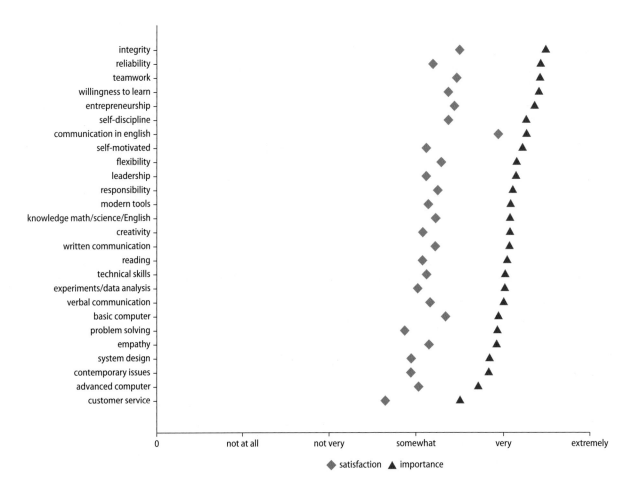

Source: Blom and Saeki 2011.

than the small increases in supply. In contrast, in Pakistan and Sri Lanka, the wage premium increased for upper-secondary education but decreased for tertiary education, particularly in Sri Lanka.

Despite significant progress in recent years, the contrast between increasing demand for higher levels of education and the educational attainment of the labor force remains stark. Educational attainment remains low, particularly in secondary and tertiary education, with well over a quarter of the labor force in all countries except Sri Lanka lacking any education at all (figure 1.24). The average years of education of people age 15–34 increased in all countries between the late 1990s and early 2000s, but it is still low in most countries, ranging from 2.5 years in Afghanistan to 7.1 years in India. (It is higher in Maldives [7.8 years] and Sri Lanka [10.2 years].) In many countries, the picture is considerably worse for women (see panel a of figure 1.24).

Success in school is affected by what happens to children before they enter school. In fact, the greatest payoffs to subsequent educational investments may well come from addressing poor nutrition and other factors in early childhood, before children enter formal schooling (box 1.3).

FIGURE 1.23   **Wage premiums in selected South Asian countries, by level of education**

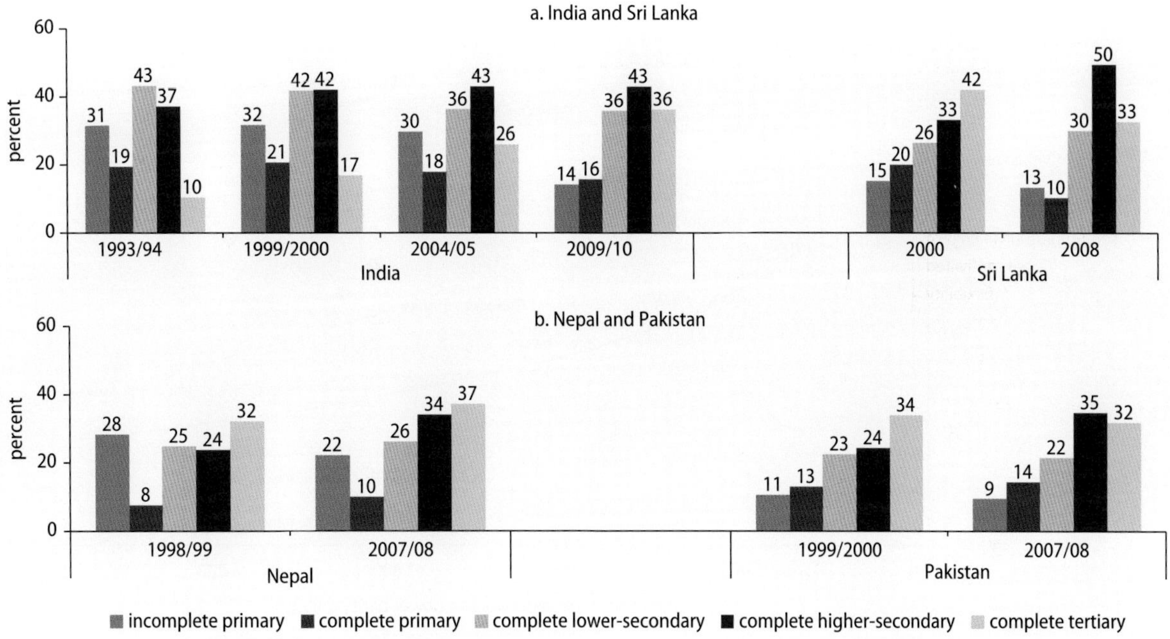

a. India and Sri Lanka

b. Nepal and Pakistan

■ incomplete primary   ■ complete primary   ■ complete lower-secondary   ■ complete higher-secondary   ■ complete tertiary

Source: Authors, based on data from national labor force and household surveys.
Note: The first bar for each country-year pair reflects the wage premium for even some primary education relative to no education; the last bar reflects the wage premium for completing tertiary relative to completing upper-secondary education.

The education challenge facing South Asia is broad. It includes improving nutrition and other factors in early childhood, increasing attainment from primary to secondary and higher levels, ensuring equal opportunity for all groups, and equipping graduates with the skills necessary to succeed in the world of work. Country priorities will vary. In Afghanistan and Pakistan, achieving universal primary education remains a priority, and these countries still have significant gender disparities in primary education. India, Maldives, and Sri Lanka are focusing on expanding upper-secondary school. All countries are expanding tertiary education. A key priority for all South Asian countries is to improve the quality of learning and skills of graduates at all levels.

Improving the quality of learning in primary and secondary schools requires strengthening incentives and capacity in the school system. To do so, governments could

consider the following actions in the school subsector:

• Address information gaps by developing national assessment systems that provide reliable feedback on learning.
• Improve capacity and accountability at the school level by devolving greater responsibility to schools while increasing their accountability to local stakeholders.
• Improve the quality and performance of teachers by engaging in transparent recruitment and development of career and pay systems that build capacity and provide incentives.

As more and more students enter higher levels of education, pressure to expand tertiary education will intensify. Priorities to ensure a focus on the quality and relevance of skills of graduates of both tertiary institutions and preemployment training systems include the following:

FIGURE 1.24   Share of South Asian labor force with no education, with international comparisons

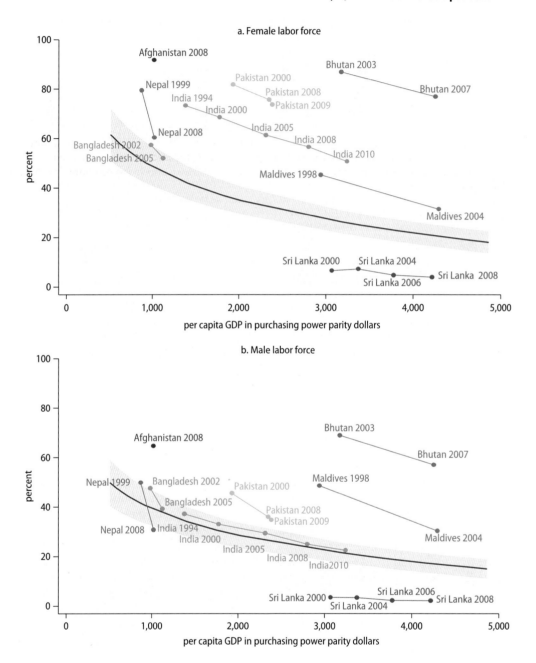

Sources: Authors, based on data from World Bank 2011c and national labor force and household surveys.
Note: The dark line shows the predicted values of the share of the labor force with no education by per capita GDP, based on a cross-country regression (excluding high-income countries). The shaded area is the 95 percent confidence interval band around the regression line. GDP = gross domestic product.

BOX 1.3   The critical role of nutrition in early childhood development

The first years of life— long before formal schooling begins—are a key period for building human capital. The benefits of health and nutrition early on can have effects that persist through life; damage from childhood disease and malnutrition in terms of lost opportunity for learning can be difficult to undo. Low levels of cognitive development in early childhood are often strongly correlated with low socioeconomic status and malnutrition. In addition to protein-energy malnutrition, micronutrient deficiencies, which often begin before birth, can impair cognitive and motor development and therefore school outcomes.

South Asia has some of the highest rates of malnutrition in the world, as well as high levels of anemia and iodine deficiency. As measured by stunting, underweight, and wasting, it has the world's highest prevalence of malnutrition in children under five (box figure 1.3.1).[a] Indeed, malnutrition rates are higher than in Sub-Saharan Africa. South Asia also has high levels of anemia and iodine deficiency.

In South Asia, as globally, rates of malnutrition, anemia, and iodine deficits improve with wealth, but only modestly. This means that high malnutrition and micronutrient deficiencies are likely important contributors to developmental delays in low-income groups in South Asia; they may also be important factors for overall cognitive development of the broader population. Income growth alone will not eliminate malnutrition and micronutrient deficiencies; focused attention is needed.

Most South Asian countries do not have integrated policy frameworks for early childhood development. Early childhood interventions—which include nutrition, hygiene, early cognitive stimulation, and preschool programs—are among the most cost-effective investments for improving the quality and efficiency of basic education, as well as labor market success.

India has the strongest enabling policy framework in South Asia, with a foundation deriving from the constitution, among other sources. National nutrition policies and programs in Bangladesh and some aspects of public health campaigns related to nutrition in Pakistan have contributed to improvements in nutrition in both countries, but neither

BOX FIGURE 1.3.1   Percentage of children under five with malnutrition, by region and country

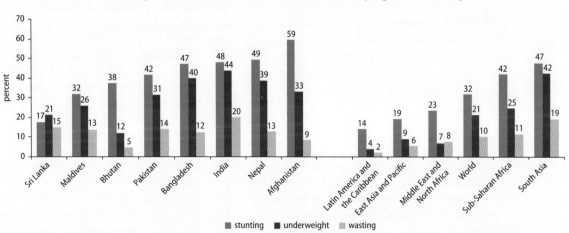

Source: Authors, based on World Bank 2011c.

(continues next page)

BOX 1.3   The critical role of nutrition in early childhood development (continued)

country has a national policy on early childhood development.

Very few programs at scale seek to integrate early childhood interventions. Several pilot projects can serve as a laboratory for designing cost-effective programs, but many lack careful plans for evaluation. Potentially promising efforts are under way, however. For example, pilots run by the International Center for Diarrheal Disease Research (ICDDR) in Dhaka have stronger evaluation designs and have proven the feasibility of promoting better parenting and

mother-child interactions through home visits. The Lady Health Workers Programme in Pakistan—a community-based government preventive care program—holds promise for promoting nutrition and child care through scaling up of carefully evaluated cost-effective pilot designs.

Source: Authors, based on Alderman 2011.
a. Wasting, stunting, and underweight indicators refer to the proportion of children under five whose weight for height, height for age, and weight for age respectively are more than two standard deviations below the medians of an international reference population recognized by the World Health Organization (WHO).

- Provide information on the quality of graduates of institutions and their employability, and strengthen quality assurance and accreditation.
- Increase the role of the private sector in provision and that of employers in the management of public institutions.
- Increase the autonomy of public higher education institutions and improve incentives for improved performance, such as those provided by moving from historically negotiated budgets to performance-based approaches.
- Increase contributions from students while protecting students less able to pay.

Reforming labor market institutions

Labor market policies in South Asia need to strike a balance between facilitating protection for the vast majority of workers, primarily in the informal sector, who are not covered by social protection instruments while enhancing their incentives for income generation. Efforts are needed on two fronts: (a) reforming statutory regulations and institutions to encourage job creation in the formal economy while protecting the fundamental rights of covered workers and (b) building on programs that can help informal workers adjust to labor market shocks and improve their productivity and future earnings potential.

Beyond protecting the basic rights of workers, labor market institutions have an important role to play in regulating the employment relationship, with potentially important implications for labor market efficiency and social protection. Employment protection legislation covers the kinds of contracts permitted and the conditions and procedures for termination. Restrictions on nonpermanent hiring and employer dismissal rights can increase employment security and provide protection to workers from arbitrary dismissal by employers. If excessively restrictive, however, they can discourage formal job creation, limit the efficient reallocation of labor, and fail to provide real protection, as employers find ways around the rules. The evidence suggests that, in some countries, notably India and Sri Lanka, the efficiency costs of employment protection legislation outweigh the benefits in terms of worker protection (see chapter 6).

Labor market policies in India, Nepal, and Sri Lanka are oriented toward protecting jobs. India, for example, has employment protection laws that are considerably tighter than laws in Western countries and most other major emerging economies (figure 1.25). India, Nepal, and Sri Lanka require not only notification but prior approval by the state to lay off or retrench workers, individually or collectively. In Sri Lanka, prior

FIGURE 1.25   Employment protection indicators in selected countries

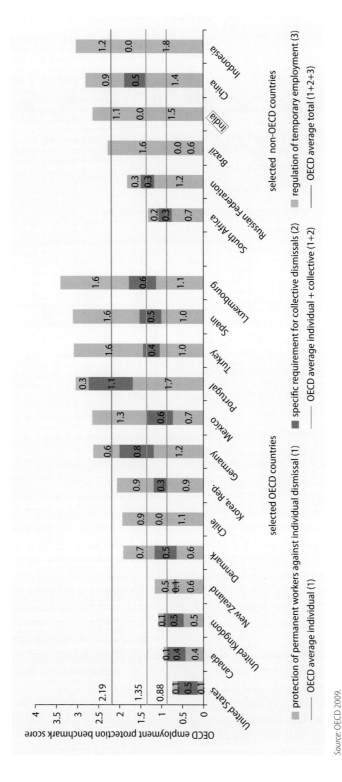

Source: OECD 2009.
Note: OECD = Organisation for Economic Co-operation and Development. The OECD employment protection indicators cover three aspects of employment protection: individual dismissal of permanent workers, regulation of temporary employment, and specific requirements for collective dismissal. Each subindicator ranges from 0 to 6, with 0 the least restrictive and 6 the most restrictive. The overall indicator—the sum of the three subindicators, weighted at 5/12, 5/12, and 2/12—also ranges from 0 to 6.

FIGURE 1.26   Weeks of wages required to be paid in severance in regions, country income groups, and selected South Asian countries, by length of service

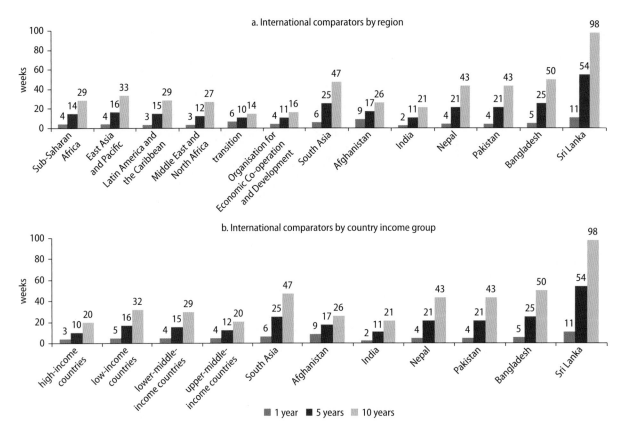

Source: Holzmann and others 2011.

approval is necessary only when the worker's written consent for layoff cannot be obtained. This is different from India, where large firms need prior approval from the government before they can dismiss an employee even if the worker consents to the dismissal. Severance pay, which typically requires minimum tenure in the establishment and increases with seniority, is also high in most South Asian countries, particularly in Sri Lanka but also in Bangladesh, Nepal, and Pakistan (figure 1.26).

Most countries have reasonably flexible contracting rules. Bangladesh, Nepal, and Pakistan place limits on the use of fixed-term contracts, however, and lack of clarity in India has led to widely varying interpretations, regulations, and practices across states.

Enterprise managers in India, Nepal, and Sri Lanka report labor regulations to be an important constraint to the operation and growth of their business. In contrast, formal sector firms in Afghanistan and Bangladesh rate labor regulations as among the least problematic. There is some evidence that labor regulations become more costly to firms as per capita GDP rises (figure 1.27). India, Nepal, and Sri Lanka report higher levels of severity of this constraint than other countries at their level of development, however. When asked which labor regulations most affected the operation of their businesses, nearly one in three firms in India for whom labor regulations were perceived as a moderate or severe constraint reported that restrictions on dismissal are a constraint to hiring. About one in four cited restrictions on casual work, and

FIGURE 1.27 **Cross-country comparison of reported severity of the labor regulation constraint**

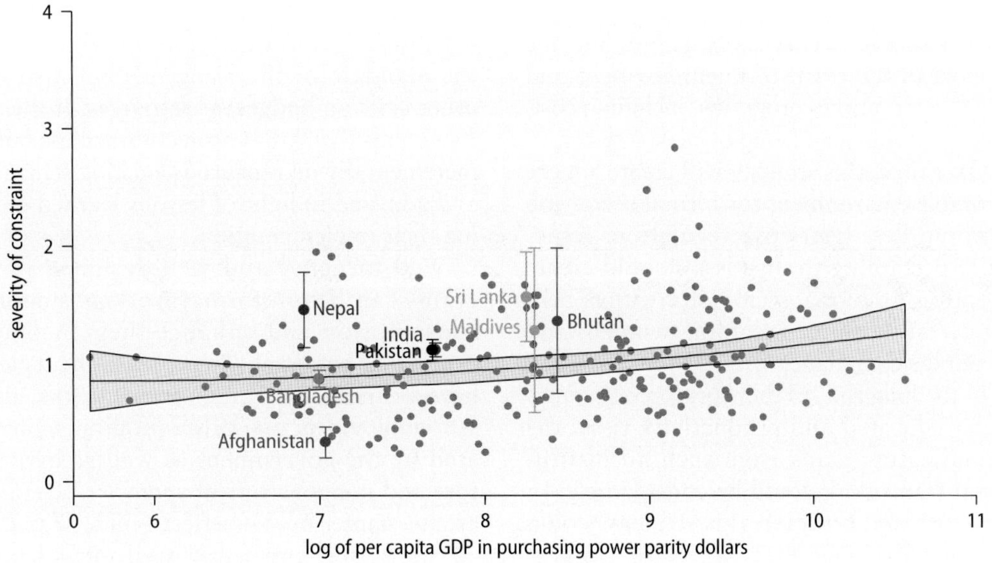

Source: Carlin and Schaffer 2011b (based on most recent World Bank enterprise surveys).
Note: The cross-country regression line shows the relationship between the reported severity of the constraint for a benchmark firm and the log of per capita GDP. The shaded area is the 95 percent confidence interval band around the regression line. Vertical bars show confidence intervals of 95 percent around the reported severity of the constraint for countries in South Asia. Analysis is based on a pooled sample of enterprise surveys conducted between 2000 and 2010.

one in five cited constraints on temporary work.

In addition to creating disincentives for expanding the formal sector, labor market rules in South Asia have failed to protect workers for two main reasons. First, these rules cover much less than 10 percent of the labor force in most countries and less than a third even in Sri Lanka, which has the most formalized labor market. Second, the impact of labor market rules is weakened by noncompliance. As regulations become more costly, firms increasingly employ strategies to circumvent them, reducing de facto protection from labor market regulations. In India, for example, medium-size and large firms in organized manufacturing adjust employment levels by hiring and terminating contract workers. In Sri Lanka, where statutory severance rights are generous, workers often fail to benefit from them because of nonpayment or partial payment, particularly during periods of economic distress. Limited options and lengthy and costly procedures for resolving disputes and grievances provide additional incentives for noncompliance.

South Asian countries would benefit from reorienting their labor market policies from "protecting jobs" to "protecting workers." As the region modernizes, an approach that moves away from protecting jobs through strong job security laws to encouraging more flexibility in the labor market, while providing workers with better tools to manage the fluctuations of the market, will lead to more job creation and offer more protection.

This approach requires two coordinated strategies. The first involves realigning labor market regulations and institutions to relax the procedures and costs associated with dismissals; extending the legality of nonpermanent contracts; improving protection of fundamental worker rights; improving the efficiency of dispute resolution and the enforcement of employment protection legislation; and streamlining and clarifying regulations.

The second involves strengthening the tools available to workers in both the formal and informal sectors to help them manage labor market shocks. These tools include income support in the event of unemployment and active labor market programs, including cost-effective training and employment services.

Over time, this strategy will create a more favorable environment for formal sector job creation. Less restrictive regulations, especially pertaining to dismissal, could create incentives for formal sector job creation; benefit certain groups, including women; and encourage compliance with the law.

In the long run, as the workforce becomes better educated and productivity rises, the formalization gains from such an institutional framework could be considerable. In the short run, however, this strategy would benefit only some informal sector workers who might be able to find formal sector jobs in a more favorable regulatory environment. The vast majority of workers would continue to lack social security benefits and disability and health coverage.

One way to close the gap between protected and unprotected workers would be to extend (statutory) social insurance to informal workers. India's Rashtriya Swasthya Bima Yojna (RSBY) is designed to provide hospitalization coverage to households below the poverty line. The new pension law in Maldives provides for matching pension contributions for informal sector workers such as fishers, in order to encourage informal sector participation in the pension scheme.

Any such plan needs to take account of financing, as well as the effect on the incidence of informality itself. Employers may be more likely to seek ways to opt out of formal contributory systems if they know employees can access social protection in other ways; workers themselves may prefer to remain informal, depending on how programs are financed. Thus the potential for social insurance to be extended into the informal sector will depend a great deal on financing and the scope to which individuals are able to contribute. Given the high prevalence of workers with very limited or no capacity to

contribute, coverage can be expanded only if governments are willing to allocate significant subsidies. The level of subsidies would need to be determined not only in light of the mandate of the programs but also by other calls on budgetary resources. It therefore seems likely that protection will be built incrementally on numerous existing schemes and adjusted in light of lessons learned during their implementation.

Well-targeted and well-designed programs can help informal workers smooth consumption and enhance their income-generating potential. Countries in the region have a variety of training, public works, and self-employment assistance programs, operated by the government as well as by private and nongovernment sponsors. (Details are in chapter 6.) The effectiveness of many of these programs is not well understood because of the lack of evaluation evidence. However, if well targeted and efficiently implemented, such programs can incorporate both a safety net perspective (helping workers manage income-related risks) and an activation perspective (helping them improve their capacity to generate income). A priority is to encourage evaluation and expand programs that meet standards of targeting and cost-effectiveness.

Creating jobs in conflict-affected areas

Measured by the proportion of country-years in conflict since 2000, South Asia is the most conflict-affected major region in the world (figure 1.28). Four of the top 10 countries in terms of direct deaths from armed conflict in 2008 were in South Asia (Afghanistan, Pakistan, India, and Sri Lanka). Ongoing conflicts affect all of Afghanistan and parts of Pakistan and, at a lower intensity, India. Nepal and Sri Lanka are in postconflict status.

Conflict affects the demand for and the supply of labor. On the demand side, it affects both the incentives and the ability of firms to invest in conflict-affected regions and create jobs. In addition to concerns about security,

FIGURE 1.28   **Proportion of country-years in armed conflict, by region, 2000–08**

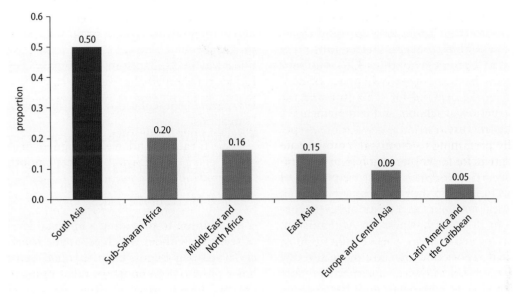

Source: UCDP/PRIO Armed Conflict Dataset version 4-2009 (http://www.prio.no/CSCW/Datasets/Armed-Conflict/UCDP-PRIO/Armed-Conflicts-Version-X-2009/).
Note: Armed conflict refers to internal armed conflicts between the government of a state and one or more internal opposition groups that result in at least 25 battle-related deaths a year.

disincentives to the operation of private firms may arise from inadequate infrastructure, confusing regulations and the poor quality of governance in areas affected by conflict. On the supply side, conflict affects the capacity of the population to supply labor—because of security concerns and, over time, disruptions to education, increased mortality and morbidity, and the loss of job-related skills and training. At the same time, economic need and the absence of key income earners could lead to an increase in labor supply, particularly among women.

Armed conflict in South Asia seems to be associated with an increase (or a smaller reduction) in the share of the working-age population that is economically active and employed. Between 1996 (preconflict) and 2004, for example, the proportion of the working-age population in Nepal that was employed increased about 2 percentage points in low-conflict areas and more than 4 percentage points in high-conflict areas. In India, employment rates in conflict-affected areas fell less than in peaceful areas.

In Afghanistan, 56 percent of the working-age population was employed in low-conflict and 68 percent in high-conflict provinces. These numbers usually reflect higher female labor force participation in conflict-affected areas.

Labor markets in conflict zones differ from labor markets in nonconflict areas in several other ways. First, except in Sri Lanka, jobs in high-conflict areas are more likely to remain rural and based on agriculture. The terrain in rural areas makes them more favorable to rebellion (Collier and Sambanis 2005). Furthermore, the conflict itself delays the structural transformation of the economy.

Second, there is a lower likelihood of moving to better jobs in conflict areas, as the workforce is more likely to remain engaged in unpaid family labor, partly because of the higher concentration of employment in agriculture and related activities. The workforce is also less likely to become regular wage or salaried employees because of the relative absence of employers.

Third, the workforce is less likely to be well educated—although conflict in Nepal seems to have been associated with an improvement in school access—and therefore less able to access better jobs were they to become available. This outcome reflects both the negative impact of conflict on the demand for schooling and the destruction of schools and complementary infrastructure.

Even when it is already over, armed conflict remains a serious obstacle to job creation in South Asia. Almost 60 percent of firms included in the enterprise surveys rank political instability as a major or severe constraint to doing business. In Afghanistan, firms located in areas where conflict is most violent report that they are more severely constrained than their counterparts in more peaceful areas with regard to infrastructure, the regulatory environment, security, and skills (figure 1.29).

Governments can improve security in conflict situations and help restore livelihoods by implementing disarmament, demobilization, and reintegration (DDR) programs. Such programs, which target excombatants, are underway in Afghanistan and Nepal. They include three broad phases:

- Disarmament (collecting and disposing of weapons)
- Demobilization (disbanding military structures)
- Reintegration (facilitating the return of former combatants to civilian life, the armed forces, or the police).

In addition to providing a minimal level of security, without which economic recovery is virtually impossible, the public sector has a potentially important role to play in creating jobs in the early stages of a post-conflict situation. In addition to employment through DDR programs, well-designed

FIGURE 1.29   **Severity of business environment constraints (average) reported by firms in low-conflict and high-conflict areas of Afghanistan, 2008**

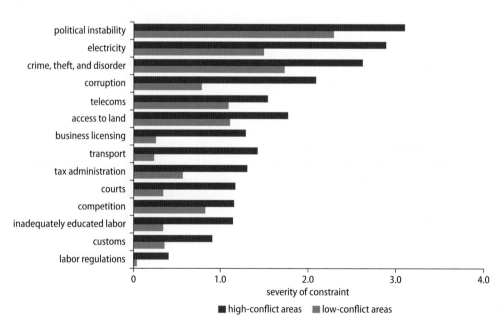

Source: Authors, based on data from the 2008 Afghanistan enterprise survey.
Note: High-conflict provinces are defined as provinces in which the number of deaths per 1,000 population caused by terrorist incidents in 2007 was greater than 0.1. By this definition, Baghlan, Ghazni, Farah, Helmand, Kandahar, Khost, Kunarha, Nimroz, Paktika, Paktya, Panjsher, Takhar, Urozgan, Wardak, and Zabul are high-conflict areas. Only differences that are statistically significant at at least the 5 percent in an ordinary least squares regression including firm size and industry fixed effects are shown.

and implemented public works programs that target rural areas and build or rehabilitate community infrastructure can play an important role. Training and self-employment assistance programs are also important.

Priority is often initially given to segments of the population that are particularly vulnerable and sectors that have the potential to absorb large numbers of workers. Initially, labor market programs and policies in conflict-affected areas need to target three types of populations with special needs:

- Excombatants, who need to be integrated into the workforce and given incentives to refrain from violence
- At-risk youth and war victims (families who lost members, people with physical or mental disabilities, and households that are extremely vulnerable as a result of the lack of a steady stream of income)
- People displaced by the conflict, who may wish to return to their homes but need to be able to find jobs and feel secure there.

Labor market programs are important, but fiscal and capacity constraints will limit the potential for direct job creation by the public sector in conflict environments. Both constraints are likely to be most severe for nationwide conflicts. Thus the government is in a better position to implement employment programs in Sri Lanka, where conflict was localized, than in Afghanistan or Nepal. International organizations and foreign governments have key roles to play in providing funding and building capacity, particularly in cases of nationwide conflict.

Given resource constraints and the risks of the politicization of extended public sector involvement, policy makers need to take early steps to gradually make the private sector a more significant creator of jobs once a minimum level of security is achieved. Improving the regulatory environment is important in this regard, but true institutional transformation could take a generation. Governments could begin by reducing

barriers to firm entry and tackling at least the most blatant pockets of corruption (World Bank 2011d). In addition, governments could facilitate private sector activities by creating "safe economic zones" that provide the needed security, services, and infrastructure in a focused manner and promoting "resource corridors" in areas rich in natural resources to better link them to the rest of the economy. Although much of the effort of job creation will initially be in agriculture and construction, the focus should shift over time from low-skilled agricultural jobs to higher-productivity nonfarm jobs and from targeted programs to broad-based job creation.

The peace dividend for job creation is potentially large. A striking example is the reduction in unemployment in the Northern and Eastern provinces of Sri Lanka during the 2002–04 ceasefire (figure 1.30). Unemployment fell from 13.0 percent to 9.2 percent in the Northern Province and from 15.9 percent to 10.5 percent in the Eastern Province, at a time when the national unemployment rate decreased from 8.8 percent to 8.3 percent.

FIGURE 1.30 **Unemployment rates in the Northern and Eastern provinces of Sri Lanka, 1997–2001 and 2002–04**

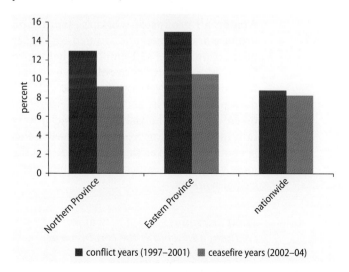

Source: Annual Reports of the Central Bank of Sri Lanka.

Conclusion

This overview began by posing three questions. This section summarizes the answers to those questions.

*Has South Asia been creating an
increasing number of jobs
and better jobs?*
South Asia has created jobs at a rate that broadly tracks the growth in the region's working-age population. Indeed, the ranking among five of the larger countries in the region, in descending order of growth of employment (Pakistan, Nepal, Bangladesh, India, and Sri Lanka), coincides with their ranking by growth of the working-age population.

But do workers have better jobs? This book uses two primary measures (increases in real wages for casual laborers and regular wage or salaried earners and decreases in poverty rates for the self-employed) and one secondary measure (mitigation of the risk of low and uncertain income arising from lack of work for the most vulnerable group of workers) to assess their well-being. Based on the primary criteria, South Asian workers are indeed better off than they were in the earliest period for which comparable data are available. Real wages have risen for wage workers, including both casual laborers and regular wage or salaried earners. Among all groups of workers—rural and urban workers, men and women—a higher proportion of the self-employed belong to households that are above the poverty line. In India—the only country in which the data permitted the secondary measure to be calculated—the risk of low and uncertain income arising from lack of work has been mitigated over the last decade for the most vulnerable segment of the labor force, casual workers.

*What determines the quality of job
creation, and what is the employment
challenge going forward?*
Strong economic growth in the region since the 1980s—second only to that of East

Asia—improved the well-being of workers in South Asia. Rising aggregate labor productivity has largely driven this growth. South Asia has seen the fastest growth in total factor productivity in the world over the last three decades. But not all countries in the region have enjoyed rapid growth. Some countries that had stagnant or slow growth experienced massive international out-migration, which opened up job opportunities for those who remained behind. Together with a substantial inflow of workers' remittances, the tighter labor market has contributed to rising real wages and declining poverty.

South Asia will have to accommodate 1.0–1.2 million new labor market entrants a month between 2010 and 2030—a 25–50 percent increase over the average number of new entrants in 1990–2010. Finding jobs of increasing quality for this massive number of new workers represents an enormous challenge. With TFP growth likely to return to more typical rates for the region as a whole, policy makers have to create incentives for physical capital deepening and human capital formation. The relative contribution of these factors to the growth of aggregate labor productivity will vary by country.

Faster reallocation of labor from agriculture to industry and services, where TFP growth is higher, can also raise aggregate TFP growth. Such a reallocation of workers will need physical capital accumulation (in, for example, electricity and transport) and investment in human capital. Reallocation across sectors needs to be complemented by moving labor out of low-productivity firms in manufacturing and services, where the bulk of workers in these sectors are employed.

*What bottlenecks need to be eased to
meet the employment challenge given
intensifying demographic pressure?*
Accommodating new entrants into the labor force at rising levels of productivity will require reforms to ease demand- and supply-side bottlenecks to expanding employment. Investing in electricity to ensure reliable power supply is the most important and pervasive reform. But the reform agenda is not

only about investment. Improvements in the regulatory framework and governance of the sector must go hand in hand. Urban formal sector firms consistently cite corruption in dealings with the state—in particular, utilities and tax administration—among the top constraints to their operations.

Improving the quality of education is a key supply-side priority. Efforts to do so should start with interventions in early childhood to improve nutritional status and prevent cognitive impairment before children get to school. Policies should focus on the quality of learning at all levels once children enter the school system. Ensuring that graduates are equipped not only with specific knowledge and technical skills but also with the behavioral, problem-solving, and creative thinking skills increasingly required in the world of work is critical. Moving labor market institutions away from protecting jobs for a minority of insiders toward protecting the vast majority of workers in the informal sector who lack protection is essential.

A challenging, but feasible agenda

The proposed reform agenda is challenging—but it is feasible, especially given the resources that will be freed up over the next three decades as a result of South Asia's demographic transition. Business as usual will accommodate new entrants to the labor force, but doing so at stagnant or barely rising levels of productivity will mean that the quality of employment will be poor. The vicious circle of poverty and low-productivity employment would then be drawn around another generation. This is the price of failure. It is a price that need not be paid.

Annex 1A   Summary statistics on South Asian countries

TABLE 1A.1   Summary economic statistics of South Asian countries

Statistic	Afghanistan	Bangladesh	Bhutan	India	Maldives	Nepal	Pakistan	Sri Lanka	South Asia
GDP per capita, 2009 (at 2005 purchasing power parity dollars)	879[a]	1,419	4,525	2,993	4,967	1,047	2,358	4,256	2,713
Gross capital formation (% of GDP)	25	24	54	36	53	30	19	25	33
Gross savings (% of GDP)	—	39	—	35	35	38	22	24	34
Total population (millions)	30	162	1	1,155	0.3	29	170	20	1,568
Sector share of GDP (%)									
1980									
Agriculture	—	32	44	36	—	62	30	28	35
Industry	—	21	15	25	—	12	25	30	24
Manufacturing	—	14	4	17	—	4	16	18	16
Services	—	48	42	40	—	26	46	43	41
2008									
Agriculture	32	19	19	18	6	34	20	13	18
Industry	26	29	46	29	18	17	27	29	29
Manufacturing	16	18	7	16	7	7	20	18	16
Services	42	53	35	54	76	50	53	57	54
Sector share of employment (%)									
Earliest year available in national labor force surveys	—	2002/03	2003	1983	1998	1998/99	1999/2000	2000	
Agriculture	—	51	80	63	25	77	47	37	60
Industry	—	14	3	16	25	10	19	25	16
Manufacturing	—	10	1	12	15	6	12	17	11
Services	—	35	18	21	49	13	34	38	24
Latest year available in national labor force surveys	2007/08	2005/06	2007	2007/08	2004	2007/08	2008/09	2008	
Agriculture	59	47	68	53	17	73	43	31	52
Industry	13	15	7	20	27	11	21	27	20
Manufacturing	5	11	4	12	20	7	13	19	12
Services	29	38	24	26	55	16	36	42	28

Sources: Authors, based on data from Aggarwal 2010; ILO KILM and LABORSTA databases 2010; World Bank 2011c; and national labor force surveys.
Note: Totals may sum to less than 100 percent because of employment in unknown or unclassifiable categories. Employment and GDP shares for 2008 are based on most recent year available. — = Not available.
a. GDP per capita 2008.

Annex 1B   Definition of key labor market terms

TABLE 1B.1   Definitions of key labor market terms used in this book

Term	Definition
Employed	Persons who worked during at least part of the reference period (typically the last seven days), regardless of whether employment was formal or informal, paid or unpaid. Reference period in Bangladesh, Bhutan, India, Nepal, Pakistan, and Sri Lanka was reference week (generally past seven days). Reference period in Afghanistan and Maldives was past month.
Unemployed	Persons who did not work in the reference period but actively sought work.
Inactive (nonparticipant in labor force)	Persons who were neither employed nor unemployed during the reference period. This category includes discouraged workers—people who left the labor force because they believed no jobs were available or did not know how to search.
Regular wage or salaried workers	Persons who receive regular wages or salary from a job in the public or private sector. These workers are usually on the payroll and usually earn leave and supplementary benefits. A significant proportion of these workers are in the public sector (ranging from 27 percent in India to 67 percent in Afghanistan).
Casual laborers	Persons who are paid on a casual, daily, irregular, or piece-rate basis. These workers typically do not have access to formal instruments of social protection. In rural areas, this category includes landless agricultural workers as well as workers in rural-based industry and services, such as construction.
Self-employed	Employers, own-account workers, and unpaid family enterprise workers. Except in Maldives and Sri Lanka, this is the largest group of workers in South Asia, where the majority of people work as own-account or family enterprise workers. In rural areas, this category comprises largely farmers working their own land, although many self-employed workers also work in the rural nonfarm sector.
High-end self-employed	Employers in all occupations and own-account workers and unpaid family workers working as managers, professionals, technicians, and clerks.
Low-end self-employed	Own-account workers and unpaid family workers working as service workers, skilled agricultural workers, craftspeople, machine operators, and workers in elementary occupations.

Source: Authors.

Annex 1C   What is a "better" job, and which jobs are "better"?

Two main criteria are used to assess job quality. The primary criterion is higher average earnings. For wage workers, earnings can be assessed using information on average wages. This information is not available on the self-employed, whose earnings are in the form of returns to both labor and capital. As these figures are not available, poverty rates (the percentage of workers living in households below the poverty line) are used as a proxy for job quality for this segment of the labor force. Better jobs are thus those associated with higher (average) wage rates and lower poverty rates.

The second criterion of job quality looks beyond average income to its variability. Lack of stable employment and the associated variation in income and consumption are of concern for casual wage workers, who are typically the poorest segment of the labor force. Data limitations in all countries except India precluded a consistent analysis of this secondary criterion. The primary criterion for better jobs thus guides most of this book.

Various additional dimensions of job quality are often cited, including access to nonwage benefits, access to public social protection mechanisms, the ability to upgrade skills and receive training on the job, and the presence of a safe working environment. These factors are strongly correlated with wages, poverty, and job security.

Based on the criteria of average wages or poverty rates and the risk of low and uncertain incomes, several observations can be made about where the "better" jobs are in South Asia (figures 1C.1 and 1C.2):

- Poverty rates are highest among casual wage workers and lowest among regular wage or salaried workers. Within the rural non-farm sector and in urban areas, regular wage workers earn 23–59 percent more than casual workers in the four countries— Bangladesh, India, Nepal, and Pakistan— where these comparisons can be made. In Bangladesh (with the exception of its rural non-farm sector), India, and Nepal, regular wage or salaried workers have poverty rates that are just a third or less than those of casual workers. The poverty rates for the self-employed are typically between those of casual and regular wage workers.

- In India and Nepal—the two countries for which data were available—casual labor is also associated with the least stability and regular wage work with the most stability. In India in 2009/10, for example, casual

workers reported being out of work for 0.9–1.4 months the previous year. In contrast, the self-employed reported 0.2–0.7 months out of work, and regular wage or salaried workers reported virtually no time out of work.

- Among the casual labor force, workers in the agricultural sector have the lowest average earnings and the highest poverty rates. Casual workers in rural-based industry and services (the rural nonfarm sector) earn 10–50 percent more than casual workers in agriculture, even though the skills profiles are broadly similar. Urban casual workers earn up to 20–30 percent more than casual agricultural workers in Nepal and Pakistan. In India, the risk of uncertain income arising from inability to find work is also highest for agricultural casual laborers, 49 percent of whom spent at least one month without work in the previous year, with an average of 1.4 months spent without work. In contrast, 40 percent of rural nonfarm casual labor reported being without work for at least 1 month the previous year, with an average of 1.1

FIGURE 1C.1   **Percentage of workers in households below the poverty line in Bangladesh, India, and Nepal, by employment status**

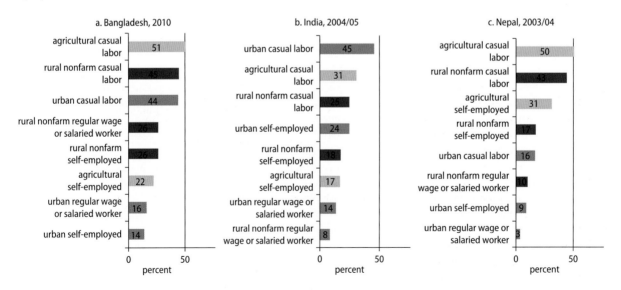

Source: Authors, based on data from national labor force and household surveys.
Note: Figures are for workers age 15–64. Poverty rates for India are based on official poverty lines prevailing until 2010. Using the new official poverty lines for 2004/05 (revised in 2011) would increase poverty rates in rural areas, making the poverty rates of rural workers higher than those of urban workers for the same employment type. The hierarchy in terms of employment type would remain the same.

FIGURE 1C.2 **Ratio of rural nonfarm and urban wages to agricultural wages in Bangladesh, India, and Nepal**

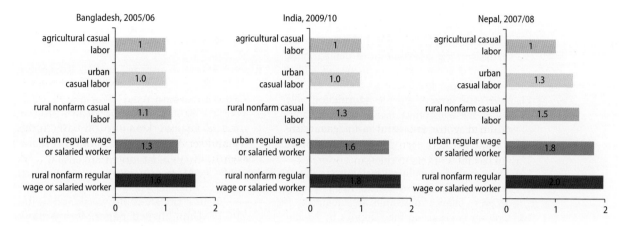

Source: Authors, based on data from national labor force and household surveys.
Note: Figures are median wages for latest year available.

months spent without work. This risk is lower still for urban casual workers, 31 percent of whom reported being without work for at least one month, with an average of 0.9 months spent without work.

- Wage differentials between sectors and employment types partly reflect educational attainment. Workers in industry and services are more educated than workers in agriculture. Regular wage or salaried workers are more educated than casual workers. Almost all have some education, and a significant proportion have secondary education or above. The self-employed are more educated than casual workers. Even after accounting for higher skills, however, the majority of industry and service jobs still pay more than casual jobs in the agricultural sector.

In summary, less desirable jobs are found in casual employment, with the most precarious and lowest-paying jobs held by agricultural casual workers. Self-employment is in the middle, with high-end self-employed workers having consumption profiles and poverty rates closer to regular wage workers and low-end self-employed having profiles and poverty rates that are closer to those of casual laborers. "Better jobs" are held by regular wage or salaried workers in industry and services.

Notes

1. See annex table 1A.1 for summary statistics on the eight South Asian countries
2. The absolute poor live on less than $1.25 a day in 2005 purchasing power parity dollars.
3. See annex table 1B.1 for a definition of key terms. Srinivasan (2010) provides a more detailed account.
4. It is not possible to rule out reasons other than improving job quality for falling poverty rates in these households. Such factors include the flow of workers' remittances in Nepal, which bring in close to a quarter of gross domestic product and are estimated to account for half of the decline in national poverty rates, or an increase in hours worked by household members in situations of low wage growth.
5. Young (1994, 1995) notes the dominance of physical and human capital accumulation compared with TFP growth in East Asia. Rodrik and Subramanian (2005) note the overwhelming importance of TFP growth in India during 1980–99.
6. These data update the point made in Easterly and others (1993).
7. Bosworth, Collins, and Virmani (2007) emphasize this point in the context of India.
8. Reallocation contributed only 5 percent to TFP growth in China between 1993 and 2004 because of an extraordinarily high rate of within-sector TFP growth (more than 6 percent a year in industry).

9. The discussion of India's manufacturing sector uses the terms *establishments* and *firms* interchangeably.
10. The discussion draws on Bloom, Canning, and Rosenberg (2011), which is based on an analysis of the contribution of demographic change to economic growth at the global level in Bloom and Canning (2008).
11. Enterprise surveys provide information only about the constraints facing existing enterprises; they are not useful in understanding constraints perceived by potential firms that did not enter in the first place.
12. The question on political instability was not asked in India and Sri Lanka. Tax rates and access to finance constraints are excluded.
13. Only in Pakistan do the rankings by benchmark and expanding firms differ: for expanding firms corruption and political instability are the top constraints.
14. The samples for the investment climate assessments of rural firms are pooled because of the limited sample size (500 firms) in each country.
15. The importance of urban-rural links for the nonfarm economy has been discussed in other studies. The World Bank's India poverty assessment (2011b) finds that that the expansion of the nonfarm sector is more closely linked to urban than to agricultural growth. This finding is also confirmed by a simple multivariate regression analysis using census data from Nepal.
16. To facilitate comparison, firms with more than 20 employees were dropped from the sample of formal firms.
17. Informal firms also cite "competition" as a severe constraint. The survey does not make clear what firms mean by competition.

References

Aggarwal, S. 2010. "Labor Input and Its Composition: An Industry-Level Perspective." Paper presented at the Worldklems conference, Cambridge, MA, August.

Alderman, H. 2011. "Early Childhood Development and the Role of Pre-school." Background paper prepared for Regional Quality of Education Study, South Asia Region, Human Development Unit, World Bank, Washington, DC.

Blom, A., and H. Saeki. 2011. "Employability and Skill Set of Newly Graduated Engineers in India." Policy Research Working Paper, World Bank, Washington, DC.

Bloom, D., and D. Canning. 2008. "Global Demographic Change: Dimensions and Economic Significance." *Population and Development Review* 33: 17–51.

Bloom, D., D. Canning, and L. Rosenberg. 2011. "Demographic Change and Economic Growth in South Asia." Working Paper 67, Harvard School of Public Health Program on the Global Demography of Aging, Cambridge, MA

Bosworth, B. 2005. *Economic Growth in Thailand: The Macroeconomic Context.* Washington, DC: Brookings Institution.

———. 2010. "Update of Bosworth and Collins 2003." Unpublished paper, World Bank, Washington, DC.

Bosworth, B., and S. Collins. 2003. "The Empirics of Growth: An update." *Brookings Papers on Economic Activity* 2: 113–206.

———. 2008. "Accounting for Growth: Comparing China and India." *Journal of Economic Perspectives* 22 (1): 45–66.

Bosworth, B., S. Collins, and A. Virmani. 2007. "Sources of Growth in the Indian Economy." NBER Working Paper W1290, National Bureau of Economic Research, Cambridge, MA. http://www.nber.org/papers/w12901.

Carlin, W., and M. Schaffer. 2011a. "A Comparison of Business Environment Constraints between Formal Sector Firms and Rural and Informal Sector Firms." Background study conducted for this book.

———. 2011b. "Which Elements of the Business Environment Matter Most for Firms and How Do They Vary across Countries?" Background study conducted for this book.

Central Bank of Sri Lanka. Various years. *Annual Reports.* Colombo.

Collier, P., and N. Sambanis. 2005. *Understanding Civil War: Evidence and Analysis.* Washington, DC: World Bank.

Easterly, W., M. Kremer, L. Pritchett, and L. Summers. 1993. "Good Policy or Good Luck? Country Growth Performance and Temporary Shocks." *Journal of Monetary Economics* 32 (3): 459–83.

Fan, S., A. Gulati, and S. Thorat. 2008. "Investment, Subsidies, and Pro-Poor Growth in Rural India." *Agricultural Economics* 39 (2): 163–70.

Gleditsch, N., P. Wallensteen, M. Eriksson, M. Sollenberg and H. Strand. 2002. "Armed Conflict 1946–2001: A New Dataset." *Journal of Peace Research* 39 (5): 615–37.

Harbom, L., and P. Wallensteen 2009. "Armed Conflict, 1946–2008." *Journal of Peace Research* 46 (4): 577–87.

Hazell, P., D. Headey, A. Pratt, and D. Byerlee. 2011. "Structural Imbalances and Farm Non-Farm Employment Prospects in Rural South Asia." Background study conducted for this book.

Holzmann, R., Y. Pouget, M, Vodopivec, and M. Weber. 2011. *Severance Pay Programs around the World: History, Rationale, Status, and Reforms*. Social Protection Discussion Paper 62726, World Bank, Washington, DC.

ILO (International Labour Organization). 2010. KILM and LABORSTA databases. Geneva.

OECD (Organisation for Economic Co-operation and Development). 2009. *Indicators of Employment Protection*. Paris: OECD.

Rodrik, D., and A. Subramanian. 2005. *From "Hindu Growth" to Productivity Surge: The Mystery of the Indian Growth Transition*. IMF Staff Papers 52 (2): 193–228.

Sri Lanka Information Communication Technology Association. 2007. *Rising Demand: The Increasing Demand for IT Workers Spells a Challenging Opportunity for the IT Industry*. Colombo.

Srinivasan, T. N. 2011. "The Utilization of Labor in South Asia." Background study conducted for this book.

UN (United Nations). 2010. *World Population Prospects: The 2010 Revision*. New York.

World Bank. 2008a. *Bangladesh Investment Climate Assessment*. Washington, DC.

———. 2008b. *The Growth Report: Strategies for Sustained Growth and Inclusive Development*. Report of the Commission on Growth and Development. Washington, DC.

———. 2010. *Large-Scale Migration and Remittances in Nepal: Issues, Challenges and Opportunities*. Washington, DC.

———. 2011a. *India Urbanization Review*. Washington, DC.

———. 2011b. *Perspectives on Poverty in India: Stylized Facts from Survey Data*. Washington, DC

———. 2011c. *World Development Indicators*. Washington, DC.

———. 2011d. *World Development Report 2011: Security and Development*. Washington, DC.

———. 2012. *World Development Report 2012: Gender Equality and Development*. Washington, DC.

Young, A. 1994. "Lessons from the East Asian NICs: A Contrarian View." *European Economic Review* 38 (3–4): 964–73.

———. 1995. "The Tyranny of Numbers: Confronting the Statistical Realities of the East Asian Growth Experience." *Quarterly Journal of Economics* 110 (3): 641–80.

Questions and Findings

Questions

- What is South Asia's recent track record with regard to the quantity and quality of job creation?
- What needs to be done to improve the quality of jobs in the face of intensifying demographic pressure?

Findings

- Rapid growth in aggregate output per worker in much of South Asia since 1980 has been associated with rising real wages for casual labor and regular wage or salaried workers and an increase in the proportion of the self-employed above the poverty line (a proxy for improved job quality). Larger shares of casual workers and regular wage or salaried earners now also belong to households above the poverty line.
- Rising real wages and declining poverty are the primary criteria used to assess job quality. By these measures, jobs improved for all three types of workers. A secondary criterion is the reduction in the risk of low and uncertain incomes for the most vulnerable workers. Data limitations allowed this criterion to be monitored only in India, where it is satisfied.
- Large-scale out-migration in countries, where growth has been slow, has exerted upward pressure on real wages, thus benefiting workers who remain.
- Employment growth has broadly tracked the growth of the working-age population, creating just under 800,000 new jobs a month between 2000 and 2010. A projected 1.0–1.2 million entrants will enter the labor force every month for the next two decades. The employment challenge is to absorb them at rapidly rising levels of productivity.
- Labor productivity growth since 1980 owes more to growth in total factor productivity than to accumulation of physical and human capital, reflecting the region's opening up to the world economy and deregulation. Going forward, creating an enabling framework for physical and human capital accumulation to occur will be important.
- Reallocation of workers across sectors has played a comparatively modest role in total factor productivity growth in South Asia. Labor will need to be reallocated more rapidly, not only from agriculture to industry and services but also from less productive to more productive units within industry and services. Doing so will require investment in physical and human capital.
- Much of South Asia is going through the demographic transition, where the number of workers is growing more rapidly than their dependents. The resources saved as a result of there being fewer dependents to support—the demographic dividend—can be channeled into high-priority investments, which can raise the productivity of the larger number of entrants into the labor force. But only if there is an enabling policy framework for doing so.
- Continuance of high growth is not assured: globally, correlations of country growth rates across decades are low. Structural reforms to ease demand- and supply-side bottlenecks to expanding employment are needed, irrespective of whether there is a dividend, in order to maintain and improve the pace of creation of better jobs even in lower-growth environments. But the prospect of reaping the demographic dividend, which will be available only for the next three decades, lends urgency to the need for reform.

Growth and Job Quality in South Asia | 2

This chapter looks at the growth context in South Asia in which labor market outcomes are embedded. The first section decomposes growth in aggregate gross domestic product (GDP) per worker (or aggregate labor productivity) during the past three decades into the contributions of physical and human capital accumulation and changes in total factor productivity (TFP). The second section explores how sources of growth may be different in the future. The third section examines South Asia's track record regarding the number and quality of jobs created. The last section argues for moving ahead quickly with reforms in order to absorb the rapidly growing number of new entrants to the labor market at rising levels of labor productivity even in situations of lower economic growth.

Economic growth in South Asia

Improving job quality for most segments of the labor force can usually occur only in a growing economy. South Asia has seen an acceleration of growth over the three decades since 1980 that is second only to that of East Asia (figure 2.1).[1] But growth experiences have varied within South Asia (figure 2.2).

Growth in per capita GDP has accelerated, particularly since the 1980s, in Bangladesh and India. Bhutan saw generally high growth starting in the 1980s, albeit with some fluctuations. Maldives also enjoyed high growth, although it experienced a deceleration between the 1990s and the first decade of the 21st century. Per capita growth has been marked by volatility around a broadly declining trend since the 1980s in Pakistan and has stagnated in Nepal. Sri Lanka has witnessed an acceleration of growth over the last five decades, except for a dip in the 1980s, avoiding the slowdown or stagnation of the 1970s that affected the rest of the region.

Aggregate labor productivity growth

Growth in aggregate output per worker, or aggregate labor productivity, may be decomposed into two factors:[2]

- "Extensive" growth, comprising growth in physical capital per worker (capital deepening) and growth of human capital per worker (education)
- "Intensive" growth, comprising growth in TFP—a combination of changes in the efficiency with which inputs are used and changes in technology.

FIGURE 2.1 **Annual growth in GDP per capita, by region, 1960s–2000s**

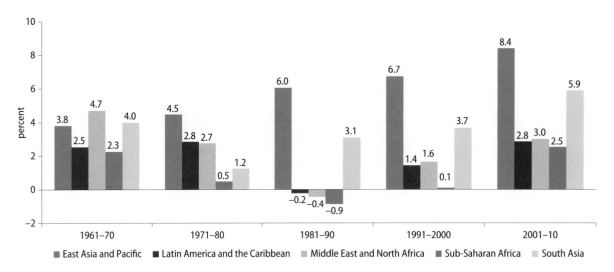

Source: Authors, based on data from World Bank 2011c.

FIGURE 2.2 **Annual growth in GDP per capita in South Asia, by country, 1960s–2000s**

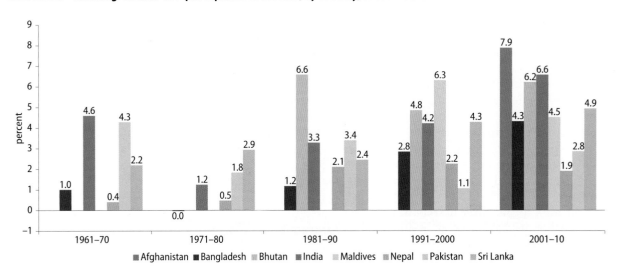

Source: Authors, based on data from World Bank 2011c.
Note: Growth in the earliest available decade for Afghanistan, Bhutan, and Maldives is not based on data for the entire decade because data for the entire decade were not available. Thus, Afghanistan 2001–10 is based on 2003–09, Bhutan 1981–90 is based on 1982–90, and Maldives 1991–2000 is based on 1996–2000.

Growth in aggregate labor productivity in South Asia between 1980 and 2008 benefited from rapid growth in TFP, in contrast to the 1960–80 period, when extensive growth accounted for the bulk of growth in aggregate labor productivity. Figure 2.3 presents the growth of aggregate output per worker in South Asia and its sources in relation to growth in other regions.[3] Figure 2.4 shows the sources of growth for Bangladesh, India, Pakistan, and Sri Lanka. Together they help illustrate the following points:

FIGURE 2.3   Sources of annual growth in labor productivity, by region, 1960–80 and 1980–2008

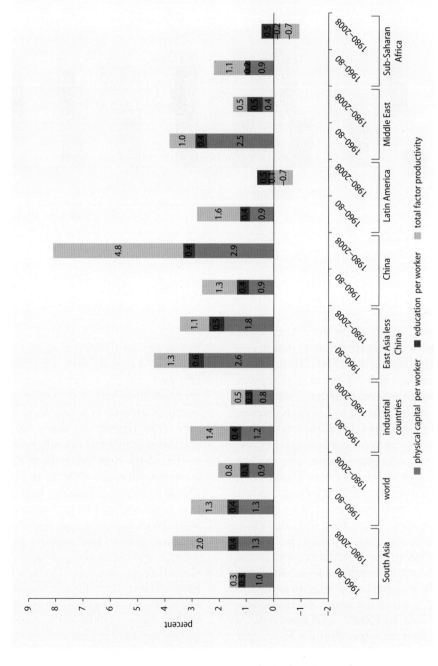

Source: Bosworth 2010.

FIGURE 2.4   **Sources of annual growth in labor productivity in selected countries in South Asia, by country, 1960–80 and 1980–2008**

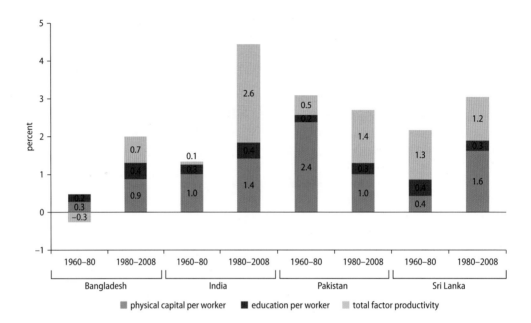

Source: Bosworth 2010.

- Growth in aggregate labor productivity in South Asia during 1980–2008, which averaged nearly 3.7 percent a year, was well above the world average and second only to that witnessed in China. However, excluding 1997 and 1998, the years when East Asia experienced a financial crisis, growth in aggregate output per worker in East Asia less China was higher than in South Asia during 1980–96 and lower during 1999–2008. Productivity growth varied within South Asia during 1980–2008, when it ranged from 2 percent in Bangladesh to nearly 4.5 percent in India.
- TFP growth in South Asia—which averaged about 2 percent a year over 1980–2008, 2.5 times the world average—was second only to China's and nearly twice that of East Asia less China.[4] This rapid growth represented a striking turnaround from the situation during 1960–80, when virtually all growth in aggregate output per worker in South Asia was the result of factor accumulation and TFP growth was the

lowest among all developing and industrial regions, including Sub-Saharan Africa. During 1980–2008, TFP growth accounted for more than half of aggregate labor productivity growth in South Asia. Its contribution ranged from just over a third in Bangladesh and Sri Lanka (a range comparable to that in the high-performing East Asian economies during 1960–96) to 50–60 percent in India and Pakistan. The transformation of the role of TFP growth is consistent with the picture of a region responding to improved policies that exposed it to greater internal and external competition.[5]
- Capital deepening was 2.5 times higher in East Asia less China than in South Asia during 1960–80; it was only about 40 percent higher during 1980–2008, when capital deepening accounted for about 35 percent of the growth in aggregate labor productivity. The contribution of capital deepening to labor productivity growth was about a third in India and Pakistan, more than 40 percent in Bangladesh, and more than

50 percent in Sri Lanka. The magnitude of capital deepening in South Asia was 1.5 times the world average during this period.

- The difference in the contribution of education in South Asia and in East Asia less China steadily narrowed between 1980 and 2008, falling from a factor of 2 during 1960–80 to a factor of 1.5 during 1980–90 and about 1.3 during 1990–2000 and 2000–08. The magnitude of growth in education in South Asia was comparable to the world average during 1980–2008. Within the region, education accounted for 10 percent of growth in aggregate labor productivity in South Asia during 1980–2008, ranging from the low double digits in India, Pakistan, and Sri Lanka to more than 20 percent in Bangladesh.

In summary, rising aggregate labor productivity in South Asia owed a great deal to accelerating TFP growth, which was second only to China. Although factor accumulation played a less prominent role than in the years of rapid investment-led growth of East Asia less China, both capital deepening and education were increasingly important sources of growth in India decade by decade over 1980–2008.

Demographic transition

Almost all South Asian countries are experiencing a demographic transition—the process by which high fertility and mortality rates are replaced by low ones.[6] A key indicator of where a country is situated in the transition is captured by the inverse dependency ratio, the ratio of the working-age (15–64) population to the dependent population (people under 15 and over 65) (figure 2.5). Initially, the inverse dependency

FIGURE 2.5 **Ratio of working-age to nonworking-age population in South Asia, by country, 1960–2008**

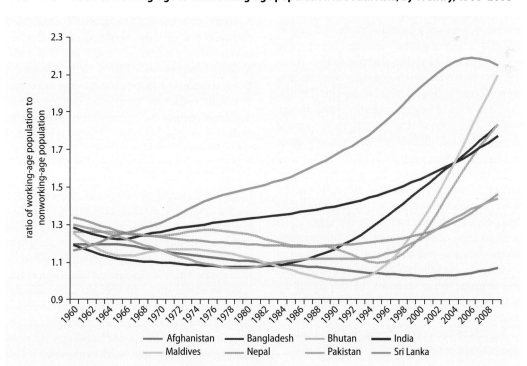

Source: Authors, based on data from UN 2008.

ratio decreases, because the infant mortality rate falls before the fertility rate. The ratio subsequently rises, as the baby boom caused by the lagged decline in the fertility rate becomes part of the working-age population. The resulting rise in the share of the working-age to the nonworking-age population means that there are fewer dependents to support. The resources saved as a result—the "demographic dividend"—can be used for high-priority investments. Eventually, as the baby boom cohort ages, the demographic transition gives way to old-age dependency.

Sri Lanka's inverse dependency ratio reached its peak around 2005. Since then it has been declining, making it the only aging country in the region. Bangladesh's ratio shows a sharp increase since the mid-1980s, catching up with India's in 2003 (the result, among other factors, of a very rapid decline in fertility, which was supported by a reproductive health program) and exceeding it thereafter. India's inverse dependency ratio began to increase in the 1970s. Maldives saw the fastest increase in the ratio, as a result of its plunging fertility rate. In Bhutan, the inverse dependency ratio fluctuated, rising in the mid-1970s and then falling through the mid-1990s before rising sharply again. Turning to countries with young populations, Nepal's ratio began to rise in the 1990s. Pakistan's ratio began a gentle climb in the 1980s. The inverse dependency ratio started increasing in Afghanistan, the region's most youthful country, only in 2005.

In the medium-fertility scenario in the United Nations' population projections, the ratio of the working-age to the nonworking-age population in South Asia is expected to peak around 2040, except in Afghanistan, where the ratio will still be increasing, and in Sri Lanka, where it has already peaked. Thus the demographic window of opportunity will close after 2040 for most South Asian countries.

Trends in each country suggest a classification into three groups:

• Young countries: Afghanistan, Nepal, and Pakistan

• Potential demographic dividend countries: Bangladesh, Bhutan, India, and Maldives[7]
• Aging country: Sri Lanka.

This classification (used later in the chapter to project the numbers of entrants into South Asia's labor markets in the coming decades) is chosen to reflect the following considerations. First, the demographic transition is over in Sri Lanka. Second, with improved policies, Bangladesh, Bhutan, India, and Maldives, which though growing rapidly, could benefit yet more from the demographic dividend. Third, Nepal, where growth has been stagnant, and Pakistan, where growth has been volatile around a broadly declining trend, have yet to see a demographic dividend, while the demographic transition has barely begun in Afghanistan.

The resources made available by a demographic dividend can be used to deepen physical capital (for example by investing in electricity or transport infrastructure) as well as human capital (by investment in education and skills training).

But the realization of the dividend requires a supportive policy framework, such as a financial sector that intermediates the additional savings effectively and a business environment that provides firms with the incentives to make high-priority investments. Without policy reform, the demographic dividend cannot be harnessed to productive ends.

Sources of future growth

Looking forward, productivity growth in the region will first need to rely more on factor accumulation (physical capital deepening and human capital accumulation) and less on the extraordinary growth of TFP seen in the last three decades. As the region has become more open to the global economy, it is importing better-quality capital goods and intermediate goods at world prices and using standard technology to produce goods that are sold domestically or exported in competitive world markets. Inasmuch as the technology used is widely used internationally, the increases in TFP arising from exports will be limited to what is routine in global best practice. For a country such as India, which has a large domestic market, domestic sales could lead to larger increases in TFP as less competitive producers exit the market. Even with acceleration in "second-generation" structural reforms, TFP growth, although still an important driver of long-run economic growth, is not likely to expand at the rates triggered by the reforms of the 1990s. Hence, a key task for policy makers is to create an improving enabling policy framework within which physical capital deepening and human capital formation can take place. Such a framework is needed to absorb the growing number of entrants into the labor force at rising productivity levels.

The transfer of underutilized labor from agriculture to the rest of the economy yields reallocation-driven gains in TFP. The share of agriculture in employment in South Asia has generally fallen more slowly than its share in GDP (figure 2.6). Indeed, shares of

employment by broad sector (agriculture, industry, and services) have changed more slowly than shares of value added in South Asia. In 2008, India was an outlier in having too large a share of workers in agriculture for its income level. Although the share of GDP provided by agriculture fell by almost half between 1983 and 2008, the proportion of employment fell by only 20 percent.

The comparison of the shares of employment and GDP relative to average development experience is captured more formally by comparing South Asian countries to a benchmark for market economies. The benchmark is derived by regressing the shares of employment and GDP in each sector against per capita GDP, its square, and a measure of country size, represented by its land area, for nearly 55 industrial countries and emerging economies in 2008. Figure 2.7 shows the market economy benchmarks for agriculture and services. The evolution of the benchmark is consistent with the stylized facts in the development literature—namely, that as per capita income rises, the share of employment in agriculture

FIGURE 2.6 **Sectoral shares of GDP and employment in selected countries in South Asia, 1980s–2008**

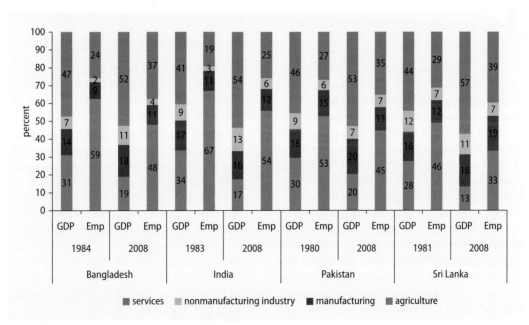

Sources: Authors, based on data from ILO 2010; World Bank 2011c; and India National Sample Survey.
Note: Emp = employment.

FIGURE 2.7   Shares of agriculture and services in employment and GDP in South Asian and comparator countries, 2008

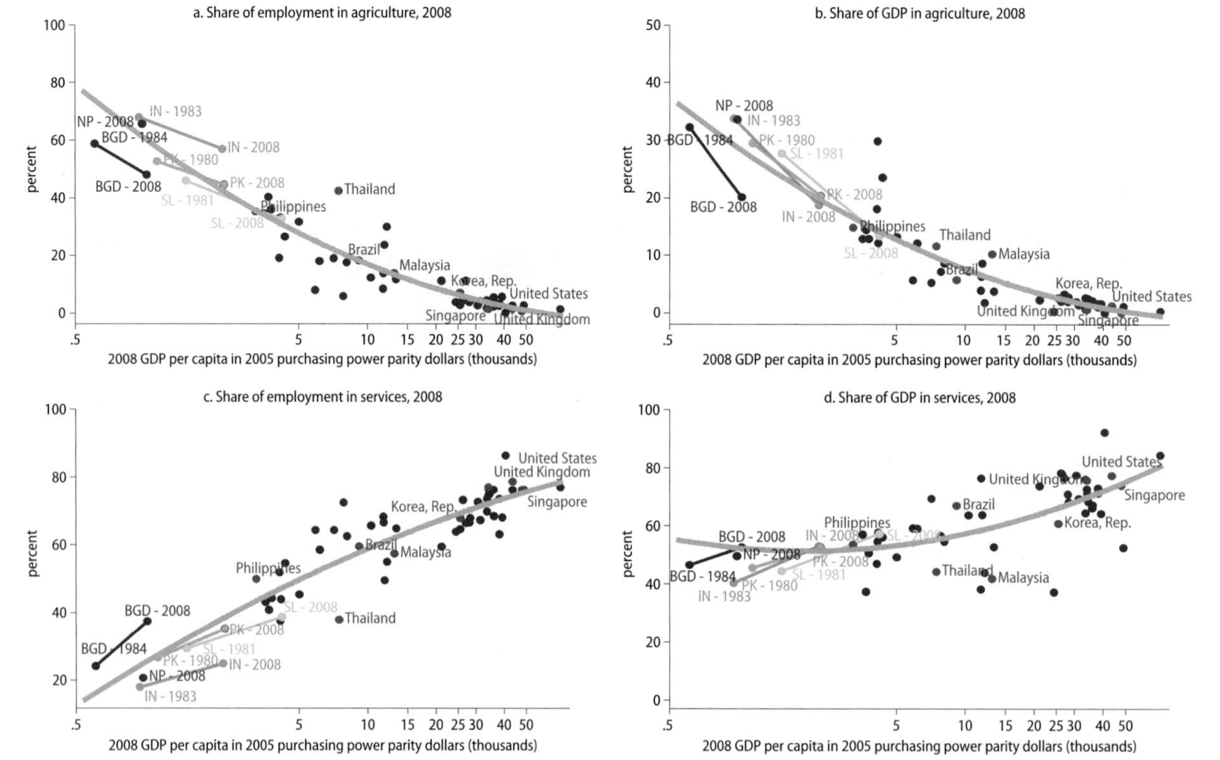

Sources: Authors, based on data from Aggarwal 2010; ILO 2010; World Bank 2011c; and India National Sample Survey.
Notes: The cross-country regression lines shown are shares of employment and GDP by sector regressed on the log of 2008 GDP per capita and the log of 2008 GDP per capita squared (in 2005 purchasing power parity dollars). Figure excludes the transition economies of Europe and Central Asia. The horizontal axis is on a log scale.

declines and the share of employment in services grows and that the share of employment in industry rises and subsequently declines (as workers move into services). The straight lines in figure 2.7 direct attention to the change in the share of employment and value added in South Asian countries from 1980 (or the first available year of employment data by sector subsequent to it) through 2008.

The regressions show that the share of agriculture in employment in India was 14 percentage points above the benchmark in 2008, reflecting among other things the limited absorption of labor in the nonagriculture economy compared with countries at India's level of per capita income (see column 1 in annex 2C, table 2C.1). The share of services in employment in India was 15 percentage points below the benchmark in 2008. The

share of services in employment was below the benchmark by nearly 10 percentage points in Sri Lanka, but, unlike in India, the share of GDP in services was significantly above the benchmark, indicating much higher output per worker in services. The share of employment in industry was significantly above the benchmark in Sri Lanka in 2008, but the share regressions for industry fit the data much less well than those for agriculture and services. The share of agriculture in GDP in Bangladesh—a predominantly agrarian economy at the time of its creation in 1971—was already below the benchmark by 14 percentage points in 2008 (see annex 2C for full regression results).

Reallocation across sectors has played a more limited role in boosting TFP in the two largest countries of South Asia than it did in some East Asian countries.[8] Figure 2.8 presents the results of a decomposition of TFP growth into within- and between-sector contributions over 1980–2008 for India and Pakistan, the two countries in South Asia for which data on capital stocks by broad sector allow growth accounting to be conducted for agriculture, industry, and services. On average, reallocation contributed 20 percent to aggregate TFP growth in India and 15 percent in Pakistan during the period. The share of employment in agriculture fell from 67 percent in 1983 to 54 percent in 2008 in India and from 53 percent in 1980 to 43 percent in 2008 in Pakistan.

Reallocation was considerably more important in East Asian countries such as China and Thailand (figure 2.9).[9] In China, the contribution of reallocation to the growth of total factor productivity was nearly 30 percent between 1978, when reforms started, and 1993. The share of agriculture in employment fell by more than a fifth, from 71 percent to 56 percent, over this period. (Reallocation contributed a mere 5 percent to TFP growth in China between 1993 and 2004, because of the extraordinarily high rate of within-sector TFP growth—averaging more than 6 percent a year—in industry.) The share of agriculture in employment fell by nearly a fifth, from 56 percent in 1993 to 47 percent in 2004. Reallocation amounted to two-thirds of aggregate TFP growth in Thailand between 1977 and 1996, a period during which the share of agriculture in employment fell by nearly a third, from 65 percent to 45 percent.

A comparison between China, India, and Pakistan reveals several patterns. Whereas the declining share of reallocation in China across the two subperiods studied reflects a steep rise in within-sector TFP growth in industry, the increasing share of reallocation in Pakistan since 1980 reflects an across-the-board decline in TFP growth. In India, the share of reallocation falls, but, in contrast to Pakistan, it does so as a result of increasing, rather than declining, within-sector TFP growth and, in contrast to China, in services rather than industry.

As a result of the slower evolution in the shares of employment than in changes

FIGURE 2.8 **Sources of annual growth in total factor productivity in India and Pakistan, by sector and reallocation effects, 1980–2008**

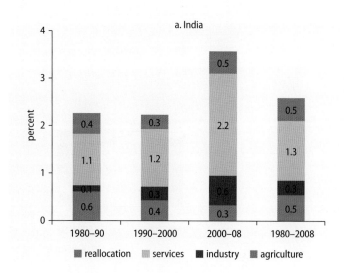

a. India

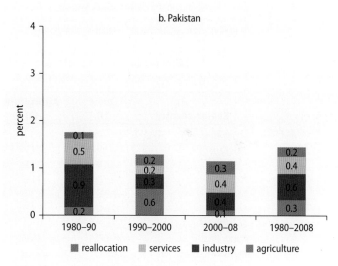

b. Pakistan

Source: Authors, based on data from Bosworth 2010.
Note: The contribution of reallocation during a decade is calculated as aggregate TFP growth minus the sum over the three sectors of TFP growth weighted by the share of the sector in GDP at the beginning of the decade.

in GDP in South Asia, output per worker in industry and services was three to eight times as large as in agriculture in 2008. This is evident from table 2.1, which shows large differences in output per worker across the three sectors, with agriculture the lowest and, except in Bangladesh, services the highest. The differences in sectoral output per worker are particularly marked in India.

FIGURE 2.9   **Sources of annual growth in total factor productivity in China, India, Pakistan, and Thailand, by sector and reallocation effects**

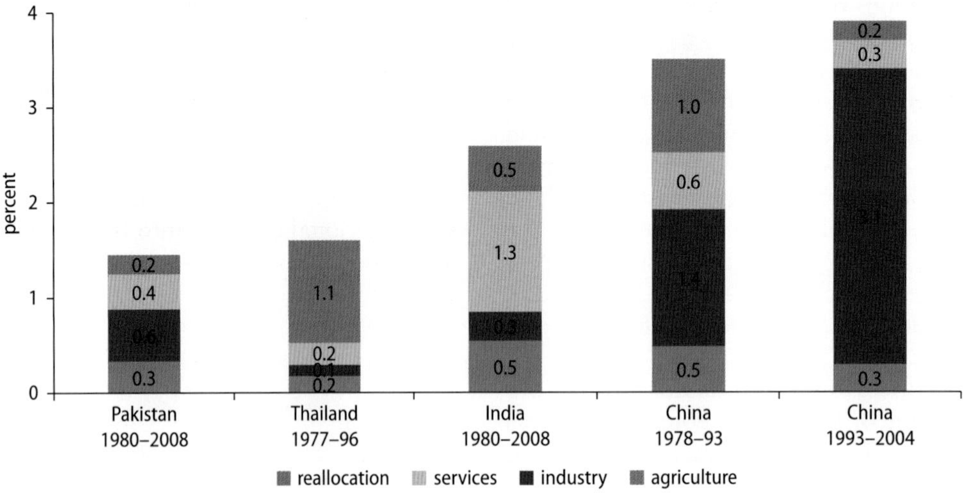

Sources: Authors, based on data from Bosworth 2005, 2010; Bosworth and Collins 2008.
Note: The contribution of reallocation during a decade is calculated as aggregate TFP growth minus the sum over the three sectors of TFP growth weighted by the share of the sector in GDP at the beginning of the decade.

TABLE 2.1   **Labor productivity in South Asia and East Asia, by sector, 2008**
(per worker, in 2005 purchasing power parity dollars)

Region/country	Total (1)	Agriculture (2)	Industry (3)	Services (4)	Ratio (3)/(2)	Ratio (4)/(2)
South Asia						
Bangladesh	4,116	1,754	6,876	5,635	3.9	3.2
India	7,049	2,202	10,368	14,939	4.7	6.8
Nepal	2,577	1,125	3,861	8,691	3.4	7.7
Pakistan	8,287	3,778	11,097	12,430	2.9	3.3
Sri Lanka	12,842	5,257	14,334	17,928	2.7	3.4
East Asia						
Korea, Rep. of	49,677	17,625	73,013	44,305	4.1	2.5
Malaysia[a]	36,156	26,439	60,590	27,335	2.3	1.0
Thailand	14,744	4,324	30,747	15,906	7.1	3.7

Source: Bosworth 2010.
a. The utilities industry in Malaysia is included in services rather than industry.

Gaps in output per worker between agriculture and the rest of the economy remain in East Asia as well, with larger gaps for industry than services.

Hence an acceleration in the movement of resources from agriculture (where TFP growth has been slowest) into industry and services (where growth has been brisker) has the potential to increase aggregate TFP growth. Reallocation of workers is also necessary to accelerate the movement of resources from low-productivity to high-productivity activities within the three broad sectors. However, the limited educational attainment of the labor force in South Asia, analyzed in chapter 5, implies that realizing higher TFP growth through the intersectoral and intrasectoral reallocation of labor will require substantial investment in human capital. Deficiencies in infrastructure, analyzed in chapter 4, imply that reallocation will require investment in physical capital as well. Creating an enabling environment for accelerated physical and human capital formation and reallocation of labor to higher-productivity areas must go hand in hand. Doing so represents the most pressing growth challenge facing South Asia.

The track record on employment

This section examines South Asia's record on the quantity of jobs created, the quality of jobs created, and the degree to which workers move across job categories.

Job quantity

In all South Asian countries, the number of jobs created has grown broadly in line with the working-age population, for two reasons (figure 2.10). First, rates of labor force participation—the proportion of the working-age population that is in the labor force—have moved slowly in South Asia, implying that the growth of the labor force has tracked that of the working-age population. Second, in countries where the lack of social safety nets does not allow the luxury of open unemployment, the proportion of the labor force that is unemployed is low and does not change very much. At the margin, additional entrants into the labor force are absorbed into low-productivity occupations. Hence the growth of employment moves broadly in line with that of the labor force.

Taken together, these observations imply that employment growth can be expected to broadly track growth in the working-age population.[10] Total employment in South Asia (excluding Afghanistan and Bhutan) rose from 473 million in 2000 to 568 million in 2010, an average annual rate of growth of 1.8 percent, ranging from just over 1 percent a year in Sri Lanka to nearly 4 percent a year in Pakistan.[11, 12]

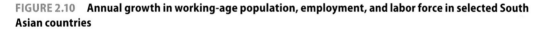

FIGURE 2.10 **Annual growth in working-age population, employment, and labor force in selected South Asian countries**

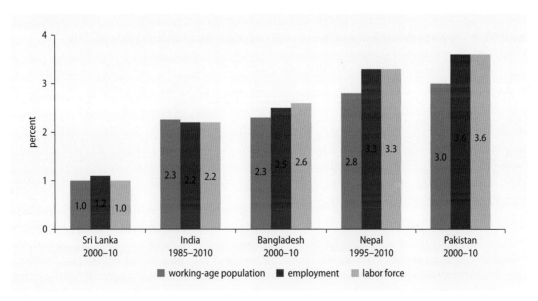

Sources: Authors, based on data on working-age population from UN 2010 and data on employment and labor force from national labor force surveys.

Job quality

Two criteria are used to assess job quality. The primary criterion is higher average earnings. For wage or salaried workers, it can be assessed using information on average earnings. Survey data do not contain information on earnings of the self-employed, the largest segment of the labor force in South Asia (except Maldives). Changes in poverty rates (the percentage of workers living in households below the poverty line) are used as a proxy for job quality for this segment of the labor force. Based on these primary criteria, better jobs are those associated with higher (average) wage rates for wage workers and lower poverty rates for the self-employed.

A secondary criterion of job quality looks beyond average income to its variability. Variation in income and consumption arising from the lack of stable employment exposes workers to the risk of low and uncertain income. These risks can be major for casual wage workers. Because data limitations in all countries in the region except India preclude a consistent application of this secondary criterion, the primary criterion for better jobs guides most of this book.[13]

The creation of better jobs is reflected in rising real wages for both casual workers and regular wage or salaried workers and falling poverty rates for the self-employed. Real wages in much of South Asia grew 0.1–2.9 percent a year during various subperiods between 1983 to 2010 for which comparisons can be made (figure 2.11). A higher proportion of the self-employed belong to households that are above the national poverty line in Bangladesh, India, Nepal, Pakistan, and Sri Lanka (figure 2.12). This proportion is used as a proxy for improving job quality for the self-employed, although falling poverty rates in households of the self-employed could also be a result of an increase in other sources of income, such as workers' remittances (which are very important in Nepal and somewhat important in Bangladesh) or increased hours worked by household members.[14]

Higher proportions of casual workers and regular wage or salaried workers in Bangladesh, India, and Nepal and all wage workers in Pakistan and Sri Lanka also belong to households above the poverty line (figure 2.12).[15] This trend is consistent with the evidence of improving job quality provided by rising real wages and, in Nepal, the poverty-reducing impact of workers' remittances.

Poverty rates for all types of workers during all time periods also show a decline when the data are disaggregated by location (rural

FIGURE 2.11 **Average annual increases in mean real wages in selected countries in South Asia**

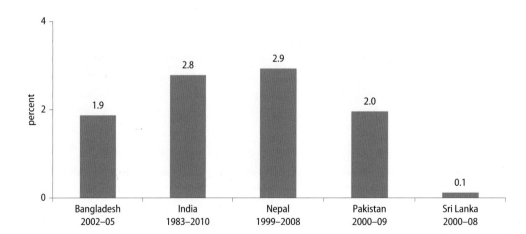

Source: Authors, based on data from national labor force and household surveys.

FIGURE 2.12   Percentage of workers in households below the poverty line in selected South Asian countries, by employment status

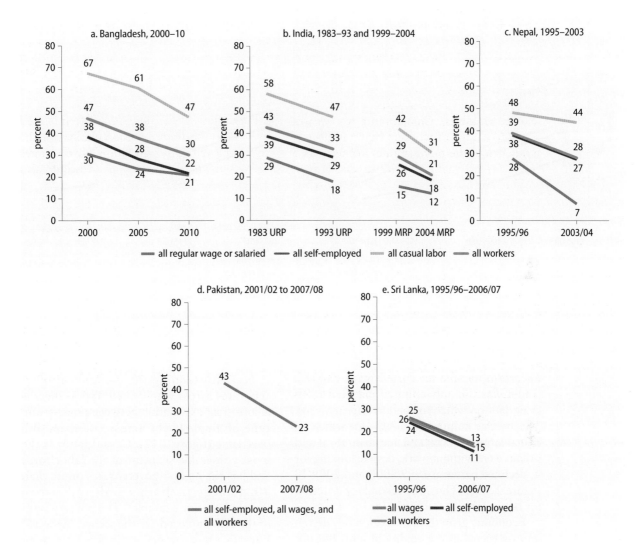

Source: Authors, based on data from national labor force and household surveys.
Note: URP = uniform recall period (the period in which respondents were asked to recall all consumption items over the same recall period [for example, 7 days]). MRP = mixed recall period (the period need not be the same for all items, [for example, 7 days for some and 365 days for others]). Figures are for workers age 15–64.

or urban) or gender, although details vary by country. Whereas urban poverty fell somewhat faster than rural poverty in Bangladesh and Sri Lanka and considerably faster in Nepal, the opposite was true in India between 1983 and 1993 and between 1999 and 2004.[16] In Pakistan, urban and rural worker poverty rates fell equally rapidly between 2001/02 and 2007/08. Poverty rates for both male and female workers declined in all five

countries, but poverty rates for female workers remained higher than for male workers in urban Bangladesh, India, and Pakistan (figure 2.13 shows data on India). In sum, using the primary criteria of higher wages for wage workers and lower poverty rates for the self-employed, South Asia has created better jobs.

There has also been an improvement in job quality in India based on the secondary criterion, namely, a reduced risk of low and

FIGURE 2.13   **Percentage of workers in households below the poverty line in India, by employment status and gender**

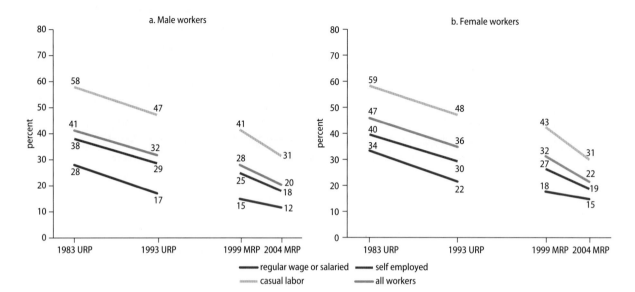

Source: Authors, based on data from national labor force and household surveys.
Note: URP = uniform recall period (the period in which respondents were asked to recall all consumption items over the same recall period [for example, 7 days]).
MRP = mixed recall period (the period need not be the same for all items, [for example, 7 days for some and 365 days for others]). Figures are for workers age 15–64.

uncertain income for casual wage workers (India was the only country that had sufficient data on which to conduct this analysis). The average number of months for which all casual laborers (farm and nonfarm, rural and urban) were without work, despite looking for it, declined between 1999/2000 and 2009/10 (figure 2.14).[17] Thus, the secondary criterion for better jobs is established for India.

Economic growth in the region has driven improvements in the quality of jobs. But not all countries have enjoyed high or accelerating growth. Per capita GDP was virtually stagnant in Nepal in the 1960s and 1970s and has grown at 2 percent or less a year since the 1980s (figure 2.2). Despite sluggish growth, real wages have risen nearly 3 percent a year since the 1980s, and poverty among workers fell between the mid-1990s and the 2000s. These improvements reflect massive out-migration of workers in response to limited job opportunities, which has improved labor market outcomes for those who stay behind. A large inflow of remittances has contributed to declining poverty (box 2.1).

Notwithstanding the variation in poverty rates across employment types, there is a consistent association between poverty and type of employment across countries and over time (figure 2.12). Casual labor is the most vulnerable segment of the labor force and has the highest poverty rates (more than 40 percent in both rural and urban Bangladesh, for example). The poverty rates of the self-employed are the second highest.[18] Poverty rates are generally lowest among regular wage or salaried workers; on average, they are one-third or less of those for casual labor. This pattern of association is evident in the consumption distribution by type of employment (figure 2.15). It is also consistent with observed wage differentials between regular wage or salaried workers and casual labor (see chapter 3). These patterns have endured over time. Hence, better jobs could be created either through improvement within an employment type or through the reallocation of workers from job types with higher poverty rates and lower wages to those with lower poverty rates and higher wages.

FIGURE 2.14   **Average number of months without work in the past year, casual laborers in India, by sector, 1999–2010**

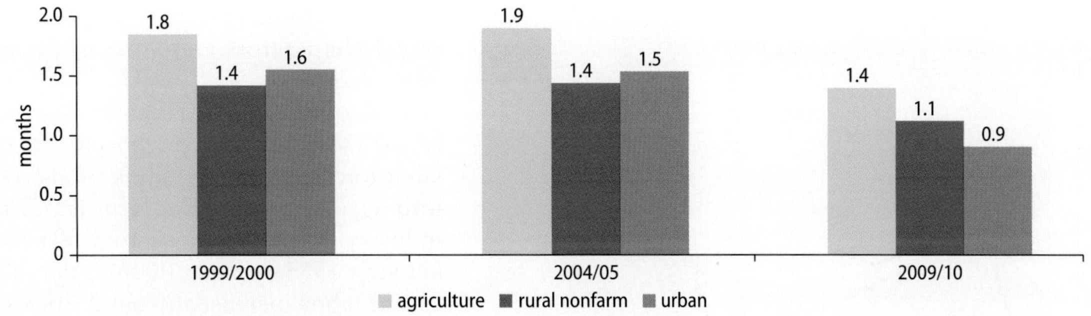

Source: Authors, based on data from Indian labor force and household surveys.
Note: Figures are for workers age 15–64 who were available for work during at least part of the month.

BOX 2.1   International migration in Nepal and its effects on poverty

Despite slow economic growth, Nepal has enjoyed higher wages and a significant decline in poverty rates among workers—thanks in large part to massive out-migration and inflow of workers' remittances. Labor migration has been a feature of life in Nepal for 200 years. The primary destination for migrants was traditionally India, although since the 1990s migrants have increasingly headed to the Middle East and Malaysia. The Maoist insurgency from 1996 to 2006 accelerated the pace of migration, especially after fighting intensified in 2001, as many people fled rural communities affected by the hostilities.

The total number of migrants is estimated at about 4.2 million, equivalent to 13 percent of Nepal's population. Migration is widespread, occurring in households of all income groups and from all parts of the country. Almost half of all households have had at least one migrant abroad at some time. The vast majority of migrants (93–94 percent) are men, most of them 20–40 years old. At least one-third of working-age men in Nepal are migrants.

Why is migration so prevalent in Nepal? The phenomenon is viewed as a response to limited domestic job opportunities in a stagnant economic environment with a poor business climate and political instability. The majority of migrants worked in agriculture in Nepal but moved into manufacturing, construction, and services (such as hotels and catering) after migration. More than 87 percent of migrants are literate compared with 62 percent of nonmigrants. Before migration, migrants earned about Nr 4,000 a month; after migration their average

earnings were Nr 16,000. Despite higher living costs overseas, migrants are able to save, with a typical migrant saving about Nr 8,000 a month—twice the amount earned in Nepal.

Nepal has the largest remittances as a share of GDP of any country in the world with more than 10 million people. Official remittances totaled $2.7 billion in 2009, equivalent to 22 percent of GDP; including informal flows and remittances from India, total inflows are estimated to have exceeded 25 percent of GDP.

Remittances have increased household income significantly. An estimated 39 percent of all households and 84 percent of households with recent migration experience received remittances in 2009. Income from remittances accounted for 24 percent of the annual income of all households and two-thirds of the income of remittance-receiving households. The additional income is spent largely on consumption, education, and childcare. More than half the decline in Nepal's poverty rate between 1996 and 2004 (from 42 percent to 31 percent) is estimated to have been the result of remittances.

Migration has also had a significant impact on the labor force. The male labor supply has fallen, especially in rural areas. Remittances have caused recipient households to increase their consumption of leisure and reduce labor supply as well. The decline in the male labor supply has reduced domestic unemployment and underemployment and led to rising real wages.

Source: World Bank 2011a.

FIGURE 2.15 **Distribution of per capita household expenditure in India and Nepal, by employment status**

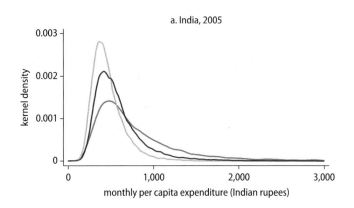

a. India, 2005

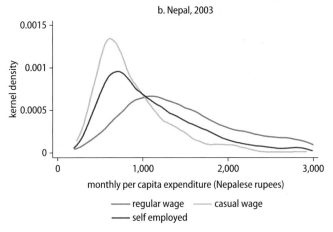

b. Nepal, 2003

— regular wage — casual wage
— self employed

Source: Authors, based on data from national labor force and household surveys.

The proportion of workers in the three employment types has remained broadly unchanged over time, in both rural and urban areas (figure 2.16). In India, which has the longest time series, the decline in self-employment and increase in casual labor observed between 1983/84 and 1999/2000 was reversed by 2004/05 but observed again between 2004/05 and 2009/10.[19] Given the hierarchy of poverty rates (which are highest among casual workers and lowest among regular wage and salary earners), this implies that no significant change in poverty status

occurred over time as a result of transitions across the three groups. Workers in South Asia have better jobs than they previously did mainly as a result of increasing quality within rather than across employment categories (table 2.2).

Disaggregating further by sector can reveal more across-type movements in the labor force. Separating India's rural economy into agriculture and nonfarm (rural-based industry and services) sectors reveals that between 1983/84 and 2004/05, the share of casual labor increased (from 25 percent to 28 percent) and the share of regular wage or salaried jobs decreased (from 27 percent to 25 percent) (figure 2.17). The share of casual labor in the rural nonfarm sector increased to 38 percent by 2009/10, because most rural nonfarm employment was casual work.[20]

The World Bank's poverty assessment of India (World Bank 2011b) notes the increasingly bimodal nature of consumption by rural nonfarm regular wage or salaried workers, among whom a minority earns wages that are much higher than average. These trends in the nonfarm economy notwithstanding, median wages of casual and regular wage or salaried workers in the rural nonfarm economy increased and poverty rates fell during this period. In addition, the number of months in which rural nonfarm casual laborers were available for work but unemployed declined between 2004/05 and 2009/10 (see figure 2.14). Thus, both the primary and the secondary criteria for improved job quality were met in the rural nonfarm economy.

The effect of a growing labor force, declining poverty rates, and changes in the proportion of workers by different employment types has generally led to a decline in the number of working poor (for details, see annex 2E). In Bangladesh, the number of working poor decreased 18 percent between 2000 and 2010, with declines in most types of employment except rural nonfarm casual labor, urban casual labor, and urban regular wage or salaried workers. In India, the number of working poor increased 2 percent between 1985 and 1995 for all types of

FIGURE 2.16   **Distribution of rural and urban workers in selected South Asian countries, by employment type**

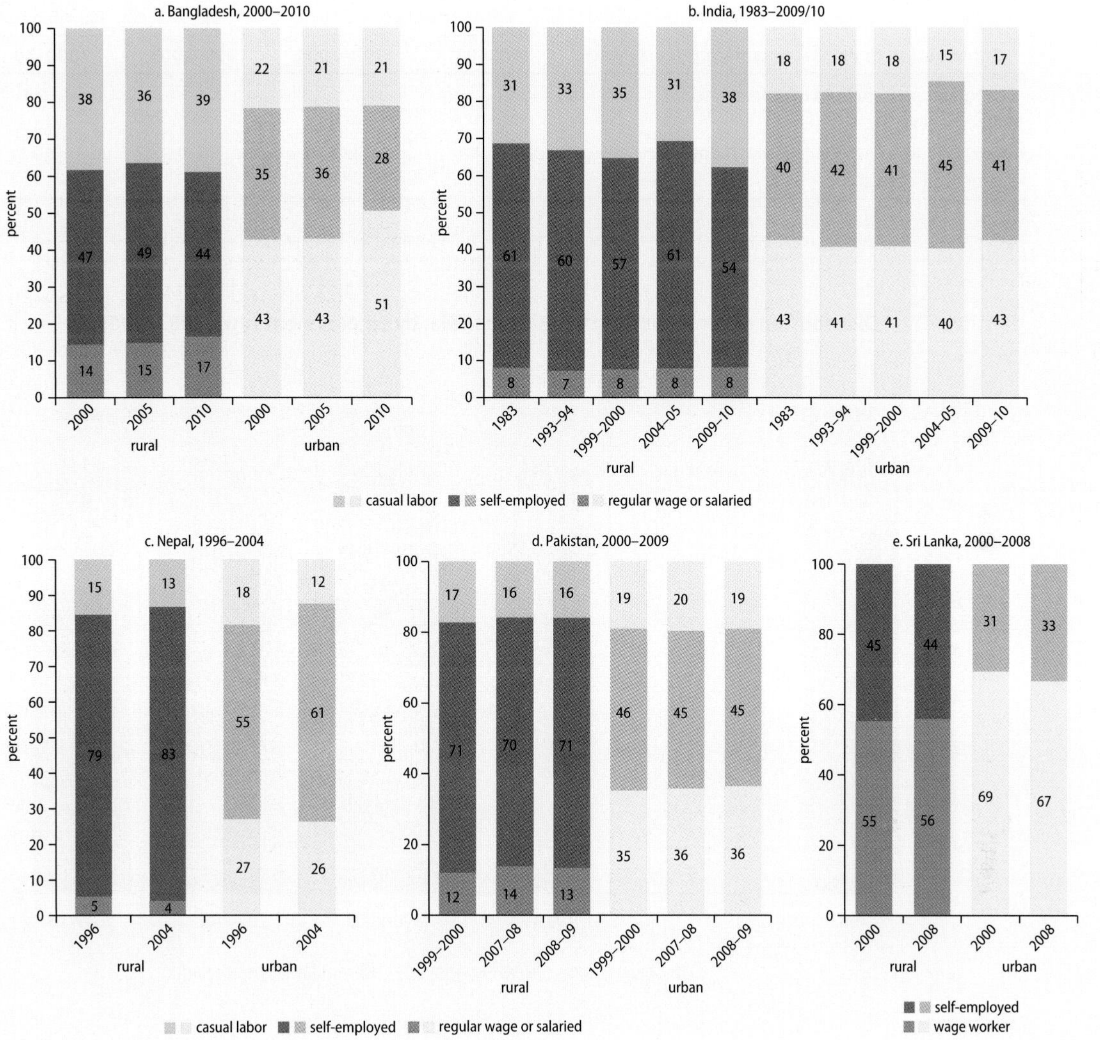

a. Bangladesh, 2000–2010

b. India, 1983–2009/10

casual labor ■ self-employed ■ regular wage or salaried

c. Nepal, 1996–2004

d. Pakistan, 2000–2009

e. Sri Lanka, 2000–2008

casual labor ■ self-employed ■ regular wage or salaried

■ self-employed
■ wage worker

Source: Authors, based on data from national labor force and household surveys.
a. Data from the Bangladesh Household Income and Expenditure Surveys (HIES) were used to calculate worker poverty rates. The share of workers by employment type in the HIES differs from the share in the Bangladesh labor force surveys. The difference is likely to be partly driven by how female employment is captured, with female participation rates in the HIES less than half those reported in the labor force survey. Therefore, the changes in the share of workers by type in Bangladesh from the HIES should be interpreted carefully. For example, between 2005 and 2010 the significant increase in the share of regular wage or salaried work in urban areas was driven largely by changes in the female urban workforce reported in the HIES 2005 and HIES 2010.
b. Although there is variation in the shares of casual labor and self-employment in rural areas in India, there is no persistent increase or decline in the shares throughout the whole period (for example, the increase in casual labor between 2004/05 and 2009/10 mostly reversed the decline between 1999/2000 and 2004/05); the share of regular wage or salaried workers remained constant throughout the 25-year period.

casual labor—agricultural, rural nonfarm, and urban—and for the urban self-employed. In contrast, the number of working poor fell 18 percent between 2000 and 2005 and in most employment types.[21] In Nepal, the

number of working poor decreased 2 percent between 1995 and 2005, falling among rural nonfarm regular wage or salaried workers, rural nonfarm self-employed and urban casual labor.

TABLE 2.2 **Decomposition of decline in worker poverty rates**
(percent)

	India		Nepal	Bangladesh
Contribution to decline in worker poverty rates	1983–93	1999–2004	1995–2003	2000–10
Changes in poverty rates of different employment types	101.0	90.7	78.6	93.3
Changes in distribution of employment type	−1.9	12.9	20.0	10.0
Interaction/residual	0.9	−3.6	1.5	−3.4

Sources: Authors, based on national labor force and household surveys.
Note: Changes in poverty rates holds distribution of employment status constant; changes in distribution of employment status holds poverty rates constant. The interaction term equals 100 percent − (A + B).

FIGURE 2.17 **Distribution of rural nonfarm workers in India, by employment type, 1983–2009/10**

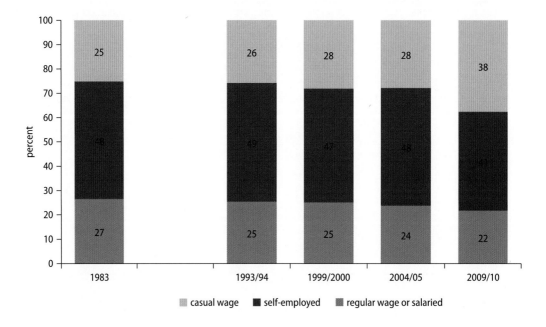

Source: Authors, based on data from national labor force and household surveys.

Labor mobility

The broad constancy in the share of workers across employment types does not necessarily imply a lack of mobility at the level of individual workers across employment types. As an illustration, the analysis focuses on labor transition for rural workers from agricultural work (less desirable jobs on average) to rural nonfarm work (more desirable jobs on average) and vice versa (figure 2.18). Lower- and upper-bound estimates of the shares of rural workers falling

into each of the four possible states (the combinations of the two possible employment types in each of the two time periods shown in the figure) are generated by adapting a technique developed by Lanjouw, Luoto, and Mckenzie (2011) to study poverty transitions.[22]

A sizable share of rural workers in the three countries is moving in both directions between agriculture and the rural nonfarm sector (figure 2.19). The share of rural workers moving from agriculture to rural nonfarm work was 5–17 percent in Bangladesh

FIGURE 2.18   **Labor transitions in rural areas**

		Second period	
		Agriculture	**Rural nonfarm**
First period	**Agriculture**	No transition: agriculture both periods	**More desirable transition: agriculture to rural nonfarm**
	Rural nonfarm	**Less desirable transition: rural nonfarm to agriculture**	No transition: rural nonfarm both periods

Source: Authors.

between 2002 and 2005, 10–20 percent in India between 1999 and 2004 and 3–13 percent between 2004 and 2007, and 4–11 percent in Nepal between 1996 and 2004. The movement from the rural nonfarm sector back to agriculture was 5–17 percent in Bangladesh between 2002 and 2005, 2–12 percent in India between 1999 and 2004 and 8–18 percent between 2004 and 2007, and 3–10 percent in Nepal between 1996 and 2004. The data do not allow a conclusion to be drawn as to which transition was larger, as the bounds for both the more desirable (agriculture to rural nonfarm labor) and less desirable (rural nonfarm labor to agriculture)

FIGURE 2.19   **Probability of moving into or out of better jobs in rural Bangladesh, India, and Nepal**

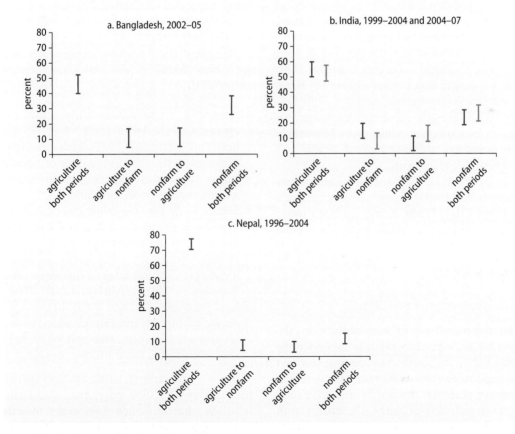

Source: Authors, based on national labor force and household surveys.
Note: The upper -and lower-bound estimates shown by the bars indicate the share of rural workers in the states of labor transitions described in figure 2.19. In panels a and c, the red bar represents the given years. In panel b, the red bar represents 1999–2004 and the blue bar represents 2004–07.

transitions overlap. In fact, the similarity of both sets of transition bounds, especially in Bangladesh and Nepal, suggests that the proportion of workers could be similar in both types of transitions. These results are consistent with the observed constancy of the share of the rural workforce engaged in rural nonfarm activities noted later in chapter 3. Although the bounds still overlap by a small amount in India between 1999 and 2004, the size of the more desirable transition is noticeably larger than that of the less desirable one. This finding is consistent with the large increase in the share of the rural workforce in rural nonfarm activities—from 25 percent in 2000 to 30 percent in 2004—noted in chapter 3. The bounds of the more desirable and less desirable transitions overlap much more between 2004 and 2007, when the share of the rural nonfarm workforce in India was virtually flat.

The less desirable transition suggests that the nature of the rural nonfarm work itself might be transient and temporary in nature. In fact, the variance of the wage distributions for casual nonfarm workers is higher than that for casual agricultural workers in India in all labor force surveys except 2004/05. Chapter 5 takes the labor transition analysis farther by looking at which types of workers are more likely to make more desirable and less desirable transitions.

In summary, the labor transition analysis suggests that there is labor mobility in South Asia and that labor moves to both more desirable and less desirable jobs. These two-way transitions are masked when looking at cross-sectional data at the aggregate level.

The urgency of reform

The continuation of economic growth, which has been associated with improved job quality in South Asia during the last three decades, cannot be taken for granted. Growth rates are famously unstable over time: across five decades, the correlation of growth rates of GDP per capita for 94 countries for which data are available in the *World Development Indicators* is just

0.1–0.4. The correlation between growth rates in 1971–80 and growth rates thereafter is 0.37 for 1981–90, 0.28 for 1991–2000, and negligible thereafter (table 2.3). Easterly and others (1993) attribute this finding to exogenous shocks, such as adverse movements in the terms of trade and armed conflict, both of which are prevalent in South Asia. The presence of such shocks is an important reason for undertaking reforms of the business environment (chapter 4) and education systems (chapter 5) to ensure that the creation of better jobs is not overly dependent on continued high economic growth.

Demographic pressures lend further urgency to the need for reform. Most countries in the region have a demographic window of opportunity during which an enabling policy framework can help them reap a demographic dividend. But the opportunity is time bound and will close for most of South Asia around 2040. Population projections and the age structure of the population are used to develop two scenarios (details of the projections are in annex 2D):

- Scenario 1: South Asia adds 1 million entrants to the labor force every month between 2010 and 2030. This scenario assumes no increase in the rates of female labor force participation, which are among the lowest in the world.
- Scenario 2: Female labor participation rates in Bangladesh, India, and Pakistan increase 10 percentage points by 2030, in line with observed behavior in labor force participation rates in Indonesia, the Republic of Korea, Malaysia, and Thailand between 1960 and 2000. In this scenario, 1.2 million entrants are added to the labor force between 2010 and 2030, further intensifying labor market pressure.

By way of comparison, an average of just under 800,000 entrants joined the labor market in South Asia every month between 1990 and 2010. The two scenarios thus represent increases of 25–50 percent above the average for this period.

TABLE 2.3   **Correlations of country growth rates of per capita GDP across decades**

	1961–70	1971–80	1981–90	1991–2000	2001–10
1961–70	1	0.34***	0.37***	0.22**	−0.18*
1971–80		1	0.37***	0.28***	0.14
1981–90			1	0.43***	0.07
1991–2000				1	0.18*
2001–10					1

Source: Authors' calculations, based on data from World Bank 2011c.
Note: Findings are based on 94 countries. *** Significant at the 1% level; ** significant at the 5% level; * significant at the 10% level.

The critical question is whether increases of this magnitude will be absorbed at rising or low levels of productivity. The two scenarios, together with the possibility that high economic growth may not continue, highlight the importance of proceeding quickly with reform in order to meet the employment challenge.

Annex 2A   Methodology for decomposing growth

A country's output in any given year depends on its factor inputs—labor and (human and physical) capital—as well as the efficiency with which factors are used in production.[23] Define Y as real GDP, K as the physical capital stock, A as the level of technology, and L as labor (measured as "bodies of economically active persons"), which is assumed to be "augmented" by H, an index of the average level of labor quality, measured by average years of schooling. Assume that a country's output can be expressed as a function of these inputs, using the specific functional form shown in equation (2A.1), and that returns to scale are constant.

$$Y = AK^{\alpha}(HL)^{(1-\alpha)} \qquad (2A.1)$$

The results are reported in a form that decomposes growth in output per worker into the contributions from the growth of physical capital per worker, education per worker, and total factor productivity, as shown in equation (2A.2) (lower-case letters denote a variable's average annual growth rate).

$$y/l = \alpha(k/l) + (1-\alpha)h + a \qquad (2A.2)$$

Given an estimate for α and measures of Y, L, K, and H, it is straightforward to solve for A (or a) and construct the decomposition. It is assumed that capital's share $\alpha = 0.35$. An analysis that used actual income shares in each period would allow for the consideration of a much wider range of underlying production functions. However, few countries are able to allocate the incomes of the self-employed between capital and labor, a particular problem in South Asia, where the self-employed make up the bulk of the labor force.

L is employment for industrial countries plus Bangladesh, India, Pakistan, and Sri Lanka and labor force for all other countries. The capital stock measure is constructed from investment data using the perpetual inventory method, with annual depreciation rate of 0.05 percent. The construction of H assumes that human capital is directly related to average years of schooling (S) and that there is a 7 percent return to each additional year of schooling:

$$H = (1.07)^{S} \qquad (2A.3)$$

Annex 2B   Sources of average annual growth in output per worker

TABLE 2B.1   Sources of average annual growth in output per worker, by region, 1960–2008
(percent)

Region/period	Change in		Contribution of		
	Output	Output per worker	Physical capital per worker	Education per worker	Total factor productivity
World (83 countries)					
1960–80	4.91	3.12	1.29	0.41	1.34
1980–90	3.81	1.96	0.81	0.38	0.60
1990–2000	4.03	2.41	0.97	0.38	0.85
2000–08	4.30	2.73	0.93	0.24	0.99
1980–08	4.03	2.34	0.90	0.34	0.80
Industrial countries (22 countries)					
1960–80	4.45	3.21	1.20	0.42	1.45
1980–90	3.08	1.91	0.73	0.31	0.78
1990–2000	2.43	1.61	0.84	0.33	0.57
2000–08	1.83	1.08	0.76	0.14	0.13
1980–2008	2.49	1.56	0.77	0.27	0.52
Sub-Saharan Africa (19 countries)					
1960–80	4.53	2.16	0.87	0.18	1.15
1980–90	1.62	(1.47)	(0.11)	0.47	(1.78)
1990–2000	1.92	(1.60)	(0.76)	0.48	(1.38)
2000–08	4.72	2.24	0.25	0.41	1.58
1980–2008	2.61	(0.47)	(0.24)	0.45	(0.69)
China					
1960–80	4.89	2.65	0.91	0.44	1.27
1980–90	9.29	6.62	2.09	0.39	4.03
1990–2000	10.42	9.11	3.28	0.50	5.12
2000–08	10.18	9.25	3.45	0.39	5.20
1980–2008	9.95	8.25	2.90	0.43	4.75
East Asia less China (7 countries)					
1960–80	7.84	4.46	2.58	0.56	1.27
1980–90	7.42	4.26	2.15	0.64	1.18
1990–2000	6.13	3.98	2.35	0.50	0.78
2000–08	4.46	2.53	0.78	0.49	1.30
1980–2008	6.11	3.66	1.83	0.55	1.07
1980–96	7.57	4.68	1.50	0.59	2.31
1999–2008	4.81	2.76	1.50	0.49	0.78
Latin America and the Caribbean (21 countries)					
1960–80	6.06	2.84	0.87	0.36	1.58
1980–90	1.49	(1.65)	0.11	0.52	(2.32)
1990–2000	3.15	0.47	0.08	0.48	(0.14)
2000–08	3.52	1.28	0.24	0.39	0.69
1980–2008	2.66	(0.06)	0.14	0.47	(0.69)
Middle East (9 countries)					
1960–80	5.68	3.40	2.45	0.43	0.95
1980–90	3.78	1.26	0.44	0.60	0.36
1990–2000	3.80	1.11	0.15	0.57	(0.02)
2000–08	4.84	2.74	0.73	0.46	1.39
1980–2008	4.09	1.63	0.42	0.55	0.52

(continues next page)

TABLE 2B.1 Sources of average annual growth in output per worker, by region, 1960–2008 (continued)

Region/period	Change in		Contribution of		
	Output	Output per worker	Physical capital per worker	Education per worker	Total factor productivity
South Asia (4 countries)					
1960–80	3.93	1.63	1.04	0.27	0.31
1980–90	5.24	3.18	1.11	0.42	1.46
1990–2000	5.37	3.47	1.21	0.37	1.92
2000–08	7.05	4.94	1.67	0.34	2.90
1980–2008	5.80	3.78	1.30	0.38	2.04

Source: Bosworth 2010.
Note: Average annual growth in output per worker is the sum of the physical capital, human capital, and TFP contributions to growth in productivity. Totals may not add up to total growth in output per worker because of interaction terms. Table is based on aggregated growth accounts, except for Bangladesh, India, Pakistan, and Sri Lanka data from 1980 onward, which are based on disaggregated growth accounts. For South Asia, growth accounts use employment data from national labor force surveys (latest available in August 2010). Aggregated growth accounts for regions other than South Asia use labor force estimates from World Bank 2011c (taken from the International Labour Organization [ILO]), which include the unemployed population. ILO data include extrapolated data.

TABLE 2B.2 Sources of average annual growth in output per worker in South Asia, by country, 1960–2008
(percent)

Country/period	Change in		Contribution of		
	Output	Output per worker	Physical capital per worker	Education per worker	Total factor productivity
Bangladesh					
1960–80	2.39	0.21	0.27	0.21	−0.26
1980–2008	4.66	2.01	0.87	0.44	0.69
India					
1960–80	4.67	1.34	1.00	0.25	0.08
1980–2008	6.2	4.39	1.41	0.42	2.60
Pakistan					
1960–80	5.94	3.1	2.38	0.19	0.53
1980–2008	5.28	2.67	1.00	0.30	1.40
Sri Lanka					
1960–80	4.49	2.18	0.43	0.43	1.31
1980–2008	4.91	3.08	1.62	0.27	1.16

Source: Bosworth 2010.
Note: Average annual growth in output per worker is the sum of the physical capital, human capital, and TFP contributions to growth in productivity. Totals may not add up to total growth in output per worker because of interaction terms. The growth accounts use employment data from national labor force surveys (latest available in August 2010).

Annex 2C   Shares of agriculture, industry, and services in employment and GDP

TABLE 2C.1   **Regressions of shares of agriculture, industry, and services in employment and GDP, 2008**

Variable	Employment			GDP		
	Agriculture (1)	Industry (2)	Services (3)	Agriculture (4)	Industry (5)	Services (6)
ln (per capita GDP, 2008 in 2005 constant purchasing power parity dollars)	−64.77** (25.82)	28.92 (18.30)	29.87 (26.93)	−44.96*** (14.13)	69.57 (56.68)	−24.61 (54.82)
ln (per capita GDP, 2008 in 2005 constant purchasing power parity dollars, squared)	2.783** (1.365)	−1.505 (0.954)	-0.988 (1.425)	2.040*** (0.724)	−3.780 (2.990)	1.740 (2.899)
ln (land area, square kilometers)	0.316 (0.216)	−0.210 (0.348)	0.0783 (0.470)	−0.226 (0.378)	1.245 (0.887)	−1.019 (0.826)
Bangladesh dummy	−12.28 (7.444)	1.169 (5.946)	9.185 (7.745)	−13.90** (5.659)	11.22 (15.89)	2.679 (14.92)
India dummy	13.96*** (3.497)	1.102 (2.895)	−15.26*** (3.661)	−3.045 (2.693)	−2.457 (8.026)	5.502 (7.433)
Nepal dummy	4.107 (7.754)	0.396 (6.180)	−6.753 (8.069)	−1.170 (5.842)	1.490 (16.61)	−0.320 (15.61)
Pakistan dummy	2.393 (3.380)	1.812 (2.748)	−5.220 (3.462)	−1.613 (2.776)	−2.101 (7.036)	3.714 (6.454)
Sri Lanka dummy	2.905 (1.900)	4.758*** (1.462)	−9.682*** (2.079)	−2.062 (1.954)	−1.629 (2.232)	3.691** (1.828)
Constant	373.0*** (121.0)	−112.7 (86.40)	−133.0 (125.7)	251.1*** (69.45)	−300.2 (260.1)	149.1 (250.8)
N	55	55	55	53	53	53
Adjusted R-squared	0.860	0.095	0.799	0.827	0.080	0.376

Sources: Authors, based on data from ILO 2010; World Bank 2011c; and India National Sample Survey.
Note: Standard errors in parentheses. Sample restricted to countries for which employment data were available from both 1980 (or the earliest year in the subsequent five-year period) and 2008 (or the latest year in the preceding five-year period). Data exclude transition economies in Europe and Central Asia. *** Significant at the 1% level; ** significant at the 5% level; * significant at the 10% level.

Annex 2D   Methodology and data sources for labor force projections

This annex describes the assumptions used to generate the labor force projections for 2030. The scenarios are developed at the country level and aggregated for the region.

Historical period (1990–2010)

Trends in the region's labor force cover the period 1990–2010. The source of the labor force in 1990 for each country is the LABORSTA database of the International Labour Organization (ILO). The labor force in 2010 is obtained by applying the (five-year) age/gender labor force participation rates obtained from the latest available

household surveys (mostly 2008) to the 2010 age-gender populations from the United Nations (UN 2008).[24]

Scenario 1 (demographic case)

Labor force projections in 2030 under scenario 1 are based purely on demographic projections, using UN (2008). In this and the next scenario, the labor force in 2010 for each country is calculated using the same method described in the historical description. Similarly, the 2030 labor force projections are obtained by multiplying the 2030 (five-year) age/gender populations by the same current age/gender–specific labor force participation rate, calculated from the latest household surveys.

Scenario 2 (behavioral case)

Scenario 1 assumes no change in labor force participation rates over the projection period for specific age/gender groups. Scenario 2 assumes that participation by women in Bangladesh, India, and Pakistan will increase between 2010 and 2030. These three countries are selected for this scenario because each has very low female participation rates by international standards. Together with the fact that they dominate South Asia's overall population (accounting for 95 percent of the working-age population), this implies that any increases in female participation in these three large countries could have an important effect on the region's labor force. Under scenario 2, participation rates are assumed to remain at current levels for men in all countries and women in the other five countries in the region (scenarios 1 and 2 are identical for Afghanistan, Bhutan, Maldives, Nepal, and Sri Lanka).

The experience of four Asian countries (Indonesia, the Republic of Korea, Malaysia, and Thailand) was used to develop this scenario. These countries represent an interesting example for South Asia, for a variety of reasons. First, as neighbors they share some social and cultural characteristics. Second, they developed earlier than the large South Asian countries and can therefore provide insights as benchmark countries. Third, at the beginning of their "take-offs," Indonesia, Korea, and Malaysia (though not Thailand) had female participation rates comparable to those of Bangladesh and India and a bit higher than Pakistan. In the past 50 years, to different degrees, these countries experienced strong economic growth and modernization; in the process, all of them except Thailand experienced increases in female participation rates (box 2D.1). Tracking these historical development indicators and roughly matching them with projected trends (for example, per capita GDP) for the South Asian countries to 2030 suggest that an increase in the female labor force participation rate of 10 percentage points would approximate a convergence with the historical experience of these benchmark countries.

BOX 2D.1   Trends in female labor force participation in southeast and East Asian comparator countries

Table 2D.1.1 summarizes what happened to female labor force participation in Indonesia, Korea, Malaysia, and Thailand during the periods when per capita GDP increased through the range projected for Bangladesh, India, and Pakistan to 2030. In Indonesia, Korea, and Malaysia, female participation rates increased consistently, in some cases, substantially, with per capita GDP (in 2005 purchasing power parity dollars) rising from the mid-$2,000s to almost $10,000. When per capita GDP was at the lower end of this range, female participation rates in Indonesia, Korea, and Malaysia were in the low to mid-30s—not too different from rates in India and Bangladesh today, though about 10 points higher than in Pakistan. The case of Thailand demonstrates that increasing participation is not inevitable as per capita GDP increases. Although female rates in Thailand did rise as per capita GDP grew to about $5,000, they subsequently stalled and then started to decline.

BOX TABLE 2D.1.1   Female labor force participation in Bangladesh, India, and Pakistan and Asian comparator countries

Country	Projected per capita GDP 2007–30 (in 2005 purchasing power parity dollars)	Southeast and East Asian comparators	Projected changes in female labor force participation rate (percentage points)
Bangladesh	Mid-$2,000s to high $3,000s	Indonesia 1980–90s	Almost +10
		Malaysia 1960–70s	More than +5
		Thailand 1970–80s	About +5
		Republic of Korea 1960–70s	About +10
India	High $3,000s to low $9,000s	Malaysia 1970s–90s	Almost +10
		Thailand 1980s onward	About −10
		Republic of Korea 1970s–90s	About +10
Pakistan	Mid $3000s to Low $6000s	Indonesia 1990 onward	About +5
		Malaysia 1970–80	About +3
		Thailand 1980–90	No change
		Republic of Korea 1970–80	About +2

Sources: Authors, based on GDP trends from Penn World Tables 6.3 and female labor force participation rates from ILO LABORSTA.
Note: Projections of per capita GDP assume that the 1990–2007 annual growth rates will continue through 2030. The per capita GDP data used are 2005 purchasing power parity estimates from the Penn World Tables 6.3.

Annex 2E Poverty rates and the number of working poor in South Asia

TABLE 2E.1 **Percentage of workers in households below the poverty line in Bangladesh, by employment type, 2000–10**

Type of employment	2000			2005			2010		
	Poverty rate	Lower bound	Upper bound	Poverty rate	Lower bound	Upper bound	Poverty rate	Lower bound	Upper bound
Rural agricultural regular wage or salaried	39.6	29.5	49.7	58.8	48.8	68.8	54.1	42.5	65.7
Rural agricultural self-employed	39.5	37.4	41.6	29.7	28.0	31.4	22.0	20.3	23.6
Rural agricultural casual labor	72.1	69.9	74.3	66.2	63.9	68.5	51.0	48.7	53.3
Rural nonagricultural regular wage or salaried	33.8	30.7	37.0	25.7	23.2	28.2	26.2	23.9	28.5
Rural nonagricultural self-employed	41.1	38.2	44.0	32.9	30.3	35.5	26.1	24.0	28.2
Rural nonagricultural casual labor	60.9	57.6	64.1	55.7	53.0	58.4	44.8	42.4	47.1
Urban regular wage or salaried	25.7	23.4	28.0	19.2	17.3	21.1	15.6	14.1	17.1
Urban self-employed	29.3	26.8	31.9	18.6	16.9	20.4	13.6	12.1	15.2
Urban casual labor	62.2	58.8	65.6	55.5	52.8	58.2	44.1	41.6	46.6
Regular wage or salaried	30.5	28.6	32.3	23.6	22.1	25.2	20.9	19.6	22.2
All self-employed	38.3	36.9	39.7	28.2	27.0	29.3	21.6	20.5	22.6
All casual labor	67.4	65.8	69.0	60.6	59.1	62.0	47.3	45.9	48.7
All rural	50.0	48.8	51.2	41.7	40.6	42.7	33.8	32.8	34.8
All urban	34.9	33.3	36.5	26.8	25.6	28.0	21.0	20.0	22.1
All workers	46.8	45.8	47.7	37.7	36.9	38.5	30.0	29.3	30.8

Source: Authors, based on data from labor force and household surveys.

Note: Lower and upper bounds in the table refer to the 95 percent confidence intervals of the poverty rate estimate by employment type.

TABLE 2E.2 Number of working poor in Bangladesh, by employment type, 2000–10

| Type of employment | Number of working poor (thousands) | | | Percentage change in number of working poor | | | |
| | 2000 | 2005 | 2010 | 2000–05 | | 2005–10 | |
				Total	Annual	Total	Annual
Rural agricultural regular wage or salaried	186	244	162	31	6	−50	−8
Rural agricultural self-employed	4,025	3,555	2,177	−12	−2	−63	−9
Rural agricultural casual labor	6,036	4,938	4,018	−18	−4	−23	−4
Rural nonagricultural regular wage or salaried	1,478	1,284	1,601	−13	−3	20	5
Rural nonagricultural self-employed	2,293	1,851	1,881	−19	−4	2	0
Rural nonagricultural casual labor	2,687	3,205	3,181	19	4	−1	0
Urban regular wage or salaried	1,017	1,092	1,267	7	1	14	3
Urban self-employed	962	877	617	−9	−2	−42	−7
Urban casual labor	1,249	1,564	1,484	25	5	−5	−1
Regular wage or salaried	2,681	2,620	3,030	−2	0	14	3
Self-employed	7,280	6,282	4,675	−14	−3	−34	−6
Casual labor	9,972	9,707	8,683	−3	−1	−12	−2
All rural	16,704	15,076	13,020	−10	−2	−16	−3
All urban	3,228	3,534	3,369	9	2	−5	−1
All workers	19,932	18,609	16,389	−7	−1	−14	−3

Source: Authors, based on data from labor force and household surveys
Note: The number of working poor for each employment type is calculated by multiplying the estimated total employment (estimated in five yearly intervals) by the share of employment and poverty rate by employment type from the closest year of the household survey. For example, for the number of working poor in India in 1985, the share of employment and poverty rate by employment type used was estimated from the 1983 labor force survey.

TABLE 2E.3 Percentage of workers in households below the poverty line in India, by employment type, 1983–2004/05

Type of employment	1983			1993/94			1999/2000			2004/05		
	Poverty rate	Lower bound	Upper bound	Poverty rate	Lower bound	Upper bound	Poverty rate	Lower bound	Upper bound	Poverty rate	Lower bound	Upper bound
Rural agricultural regular wage or salaried	52.7	51.0	54.5	43.3	40.5	46.1	37.0	34.8	39.2	26.6	24.1	29.2
Rural agricultural self-employed	37.1	36.7	37.4	28.6	28.3	29.0	24.6	24.3	24.9	17.0	16.7	17.3
Rural agricultural casual labor	60.6	60.0	61.1	47.8	47.2	48.4	43.2	42.6	43.8	30.8	30.1	31.4
Rural nonagricultural regular wage or salaried	25.2	24.2	26.1	13.6	12.9	14.2	11.0	10.4	11.6	8.4	8.0	8.8
Rural nonagricultural self-employed	41.2	40.4	42.0	27.2	26.4	27.9	26.3	25.7	27.0	17.6	17.1	18.0
Rural nonagricultural casual labor	47.0	45.9	48.1	38.0	36.9	39.1	30.2	29.2	31.2	24.7	23.9	25.5
Urban regular wage or salaried	26.2	25.6	26.7	17.8	17.3	18.2	15.6	15.1	16.0	13.7	13.3	14.1
Urban self-employed	42.8	42.2	43.4	32.3	31.8	32.9	28.2	27.7	28.7	24.3	23.8	24.8
Urban casual labor	59.9	58.9	60.9	57.1	56.1	58.0	51.5	50.6	52.4	45.5	44.5	46.4
Regular wage or salaried	28.8	28.3	29.2	17.8	17.4	18.2	15.5	15.1	15.8	12.3	12.0	12.6
Self-employed	38.6	38.3	38.9	29.0	28.8	29.3	25.5	25.3	25.8	18.5	18.3	18.7
Casual labor	58.2	57.8	58.7	47.4	46.9	47.9	42.0	41.6	42.4	31.2	30.7	31.6
All rural	43.7	43.5	44.0	33.4	33.2	33.7	29.8	29.5	30.0	20.3	20.1	20.5
All urban	38.8	38.4	39.2	30.7	30.4	31.1	27.2	26.9	27.5	23.1	22.8	23.4
All workers	42.6	42.4	42.9	32.8	32.6	33.1	29.2	29.0	29.4	20.9	20.8	21.1

Source: Authors, based on data from labor force and household surveys.
Note: Lower and upper bounds in the table refer to the 95 percent confidence intervals of the poverty rate estimate by employment type.

TABLE 2E.4   Number of working poor in India, by employment type, 1985–2005

| Type of employment | Number of working poor (thousands) | | | | Percentage change in number of working poor | | | |
| | 1985 | 1995 | 2000 | 2005 | 1985–95 | | 2000–05 | |
					Total	Annual	Total	Annual
Rural agricultural regular wage or salaried	2,290	1,177	1,320	639	−49	−6	−52	−13
Rural agricultural self-employed	36,916	36,007	31,661	25,639	−2	0	−19	−4
Rural agricultural casual labor	30,943	33,898	34,635	22,177	10	1	−36	−9
Rural nonagricultural regular wage or salaried	2,974	2,209	1,965	1,943	−26	−3	−1	0
Rural nonagricultural self-employed	9,156	8,553	8,807	8,302	−7	−1	−6	−1
Rural nonagricultural casual labor	5,641	6,336	6,079	6,701	12	1	10	2
Urban regular wage or salaried	6,210	5,484	5,355	5,438	−12	−1	2	0
Urban self-employed	9,453	10,192	9,772	10,806	8	1	11	2
Urban casual labor	5,988	7,597	7,757	6,514	27	2	−16	−3
Regular wage or salaried	11,474	8,870	8,641	8,021	−23	−3	−7	−1
Self-employed	55,525	54,751	50,240	44,746	−1	0	−11	−2
Casual labor	42,571	47,831	48,470	35,392	12	1	−27	−6
All rural	87,919	88,181	84,467	65,401	0	0	−23	−5
All urban	21,651	23,272	22,884	22,758	7	1	−1	0
All workers	109,570	111,453	107,351	88,159	2	0	−18	−4

Source: Authors, based on data from labor force and household surveys.
Note: The number of working poor for each employment type is calculated by multiplying the estimated total employment (estimated in five yearly intervals) by the share of employment and poverty rate by employment type from the closest year of the household survey. For example, for the number of working poor in India in 1985, the share of employment and poverty rate by employment type used was estimated from the 1983 labor force survey.

TABLE 2E.5   Percentage of workers in households below the poverty line in Nepal, by employment type, 1995/96 and 2003/04

| Type of employment | 1995/96 | | | 2003/04 | | |
	Poverty rate	Lower bound	Upper bound	Poverty rate	Lower bound	Upper bound
Rural agricultural regular wage or salaried	50.9	41.8	59.9	30.1	4.9	55.3
Rural agricultural self-employed	39.7	38.2	41.1	30.7	29.4	32.0
Rural agricultural casual labor	50.2	46.3	54.2	50.0	45.7	54.3
Rural nonagricultural regular wage or salaried	21.2	15.4	27.0	10.0	6.3	13.7
Rural nonagricultural self-employed	30.4	25.9	34.8	16.7	13.3	20.0
Rural nonagricultural casual labor	44.8	39.5	50.0	43.4	37.8	49.1
Urban regular wage or salaried	9.7	6.6	12.8	3.3	1.9	4.8
Urban self-employed	18.4	15.6	21.2	8.9	7.4	10.4
Urban casual labor	45.2	38.2	52.1	16.1	11.7	20.6
Regular wage or salaried	27.6	24.2	31.0	7.4	5.6	9.1
Self-employed	38.1	36.8	39.3	27.3	26.2	28.3
Casual labor	48.1	45.2	51.0	43.7	40.8	46.7
All rural	40.0	38.8	41.2	31.1	29.9	32.2
All urban	21.0	18.7	23.2	8.3	7.2	9.5
All workers	39.0	37.9	40.1	28.0	27.1	29.0

Source: Authors, based on data from labor force and household surveys.
Note: Lower and upper bounds in the table refer to the 95 percent confidence intervals of the poverty rate estimate by employment type.

TABLE 2E.6   **Number of working poor in Nepal, by employment type, 1995–2005**

Type of employment	Number of working poor (thousands)		Percentage change in number of working poor 1995–2005	
	1995	2005	Total	Annual
Rural agricultural regular wage or salaried	92	9	−91	−21
Rural agricultural self-employed	2,456	2,464	0	0
Rural agricultural casual labor	432	463	7	1
Rural nonagricultural regular wage or salaried	60	41	−31	−4
Rural nonagricultural self-employed	181	136	−25	−3
Rural nonagricultural casual labor	207	215	4	0
Urban regular wage or salaried	13	14	11	1
Urban self-employed	50	89	79	6
Urban casual labor	41	33	−20	−2
Regular wage or salaried	165	65	−61	−9
Self-employed	2,687	2,689	0	0
Casual labor	680	711	5	0
All rural	3,427	3,328	−3	0
All urban	104	137	31	3
All workers	3,531	3,465	−2	0

Source: Authors, based on data from labor force and household surveys
Note: The number of working poor for each employment type is calculated by multiplying the estimated total employment (estimated in five yearly intervals) by the share of employment and poverty rate by employment type from the closest year of the household survey. For example, for the number of working poor in India in 1985, the share of employment and poverty rate by employment type used was estimated from the 1983 labor force survey.

Annex 2F   Analysis of poverty and unemployment in India

A more complete analysis of the links between poverty and unemployment is possible in India, where time series data for a longer period are available. Some data comparability issues merit attention, however.

Data used

Data from the employment and unemployment surveys by the India National Sample Survey—which are equivalent to labor force surveys—were used for 1983, 1993/04, 1999/2000, and 2004/05. The old official state level poverty lines for the same time periods were used for the analysis, because they are available for all survey years. Employment and unemployment surveys were used instead of consumption expenditure surveys because they contain both consumption expenditure and labor force variables, which allow the estimation of poverty rates by employment types—something the consumption expenditure survey does not.

In 1983 and 1993/94, the same households were sampled for the employment and unemployment surveys and the consumption expenditure survey. The household consumption expenditure aggregate in the employment and unemployment surveys is the unabridged uniform recall period measure from the consumption expenditure survey. These two datasets are comparable.

In 1999/2000 and 2004/05, the employment and unemployment surveys and consumption expenditure survey sampled different households. The consumption expenditure survey used unabridged uniform recall period and mixed recall period consumption measures. The consumption module in the employment and unemployment surveys used an abridged (fewer questions) mixed recall period to measure the household consumption expenditure aggregate.

The estimates of poverty rates using abridged mixed recall period in these two employment and unemployment surveys are comparable with each other but not comparable with the 1983 and 1993/94 unabridged uniform recall period measures. The abridged mixed recall period measures should not be interpreted as accurate estimates of poverty rates, because mixed recall period measures tend to generate lower poverty rates than uniform recall period measures and abridgement creates differences in the estimates using unabridged measures. Therefore, the poverty estimates from the 1999/2000 and 2004/05 employment and unemployment surveys should only be used to look at trends by employment type.

Given the changes in the consumption measure, the estimated worker poverty rates of 1993/94 and 1999/2000 cannot be compared to determine whether poverty declined. However, official poverty measures using unabridged uniform recall period from the consumption expenditure survey in 1993/94

and 2004/05 show a significant decline in poverty rates for the whole population, from 36.0 percent to 27.5 percent. It is highly unlikely that poverty increased between 1993/94 and 1999/2000, as this would imply an even higher percentage decline between 1999/2000 and 2004/05. It is also unlikely that during a period in which poverty rates declined significantly for the whole population, worker poverty rates would not also have fallen.

Categories of Employment

Nine categories of employment are considered, based on the main activity of each working member of a household. They include regular wage or salaried, self–employed, and casual labor in the rural agricultural, rural nonagricultural, and urban sectors.

TABLE 2F.1   **Official and authors' estimated poverty rates for urban, rural, and all workers in India, 1983–2004/05**

Year/estimate	Urban workers	Rural workers	All workers
1983			
Official estimates (based on unabridged uniform recall period from consumption expenditure survey)	40.8	45.7	44.5
Authors' estimates (based on unabridged uniform recall period from employment and unemployment survey/consumption expenditure survey)	38.8	43.7	42.6
1993/94			
Official estimates (based on unabridged uniform recall period from consumption expenditure survey)	32.4	37.3	36.0
Authors' estimates (based on unabridged uniform recall period from employment and unemployment survey/consumption expenditure survey)	30.7	33.4	32.8
1999/2000			
Official estimates (based on unabridged mixed recall period from consumption expenditure survey)	23.6	27.1	26.1
Authors' estimates (based on abridged mixed recall period from employment and unemployment survey)	27.2	29.8	29.2
2004/05			
Official estimates (based on unabridged uniform recall period from consumption expenditure survey)	25.7	28.3	27.5
Official estimates (based on unabridged mixed recall period from consumption expenditure survey)	21.7	21.8	21.8
Authors' estimates (based on abridged mixed recall period from employment and unemployment survey)	23.1	20.3	20.9

Source: Authors, based on data from national labor force and household surveys.
Note: Official estimates include the entire population living in households below the poverty line; authors' estimates include only people age 15–64. The unabridged mixed recall period measures from the consumption expenditure surveys conducted in 1999/2000 and 2004/05 are roughly but not strictly comparable, because of differences in design.

Sample

The sample includes 209,223 employed individuals in 1993/94, 213,986 in 1999/2000, and 228,244 in 2004/05, about 30 percent of whom are women. Rural agricultural regular wage or salaried workers represent just 1.7 percent of the sample in 1983 and 0.6 percent in 2003/04. Given this small sample size, estimated poverty rates for this type of worker should not be treated as reliable.

In 1983 and 1993/94, the headcount poverty rates from the employment and unemployment surveys were comparable to official poverty rates, as the consumption expenditure survey sampled the same households (table 2F.1). The differences reflect the fact that the estimates are for workers and not the whole population.

Between 1999/2000 and 2004/05, official estimates using the unabridged mixed recall period measure from the consumption expenditure survey also show a decline in poverty. The differences between the official poverty estimates and the authors' estimates reflect the fact that (a) the authors' estimates refer to workers and not the whole population and (b) the mixed recall period measure is unabridged in the consumption expenditure survey and abridged in the employment and unemployment surveys. The comparison of the mixed recall period and uniform recall period measures from the consumption expenditure survey in 2004/05 also shows that the mixed recall period measures estimate lower poverty rates than the uniform recall period. Hence, it is not possible to compare the results from the 1983 and 1993/94 employment and unemployment surveys with the 1999/2000 and 2004/05 employment and unemployment surveys.

Notes

1. Europe and Central Asia, (not shown in the figure) grew faster than South Asia during the 2000s, but this reflected, in part, recovery from a transition recession following the exit from the command economy.
2. The decomposition is formally presented in annex 2A. Data constraints allowed growth accounting to be conducted only for Bangladesh, India, Pakistan, and Sri Lanka.
3. The figures for South Asia are GDP at purchasing power parity–weighted averages of the figures for Bangladesh, India, Pakistan, and Sri Lanka and are therefore weighted most heavily by India. For further details, see annex 2B, which contains sources of growth by region per decade between 1960 and 2008.
4. Young (1994, 1995) highlights the relatively limited role of TFP growth in East Asia less China during its years of rapid investment-led growth.
5. Bosworth, Collins, and Virmani (2007) develop this point in the context of India.
6. This discussion draws on Bloom, Canning, and Rosenberg (2011).
7. "Potential" is used because without enabling policies, a rising ratio of the working-age population to the nonworking-age population will not necessarily boost economic growth.
8. Reallocation during a period is calculated as a residual by subtracting the weighted sum of TFP growth in each sector (agriculture, industry, services) from aggregate TFP growth during that period, where the weights are the share of each sector in GDP at the beginning of the period.
9. The choice of countries is dictated by the availability of sectorally disaggregated growth accounts. The Thailand numbers are from Bosworth (2005); data from China were adapted by the authors from Bosworth and Collins (2008).
10. The ratio of employment to the working-age population can be written as follows: (employment/labor force) × (labor force/working-age population). The first term is (1 − the unemployment rate); the second is the labor force participation rate.
11. Afghanistan and Bhutan are excluded, because 2000 data are not available. Including them in 2010 would bring total employment to 577 million in 2010.
12. The employment status of workers is defined here on the basis of questions on current weekly status (generally the past seven days) in the labor force surveys of Bangladesh, Bhutan, India, Nepal, Pakistan, and Sri Lanka and on the basis of employment status in the last month in the labor force surveys of Afghanistan and Maldives (where weekly status questions were not included).
13. Various additional dimensions of job quality are often cited, such as access to nonwage

benefits and public social protection mechanisms, the ability to upgrade skills and receive training on the job, and a safe working environment. There is typically a strong correlation between better jobs as defined by the criteria used in this book and many of these additional dimensions.

14. The use of this proxy for the self-employed was proposed in the Indian context by Sundaram (2004).

15. The household survey data for Pakistan and Sri Lanka used for the poverty-employment analysis do not distinguish between casual workers and regular wage and salaried workers.

16. This trend prompted an investigation into the cost of living in urban India and a recent revision of the official poverty lines.

17. This question was based not on a reference week but on a reference year. A worker's usual principal activity is determined by the activity the worker spent most of his or her time doing in the year preceding the survey. Any activity other than the principal status constitutes a worker's subsidiary status. "Usual'" status workers include principal status workers (who spent most of their time employed or looking for jobs) and subsidiary workers (who spent part of their time working or looking for jobs in the year preceding the survey).

18. An exception is Nepal, where the poverty rate for urban casual workers is significantly lower than the rate for the rural self-employed, which is driven by the subsegment of urban casual labor employed in short-term contract work. This group is more educated than daily wage workers and has poverty rates that are closer to those of urban regular wage or salaried workers.

19. The number of self-employed workers declined between 2004/05 and 2009/10. Casual labor accounted for nearly 80 percent of net additional employment in those sectors that expanded employment between 2004/05 and 2009/10 (the remaining net additional employment was in regular wage or salaried jobs).

20. This trend toward casualization of the rural nonfarm labor force was highlighted in the World Bank's India poverty assessment for 1983–2004/05 (World Bank 2011b).

21. The number of working poor in India is likely to have declined between 1985 and 2005. Annex 2F explains why poverty rates for the first and second subperiods cannot be directly compared.

22. The details of the methodology are described in appendix B.

23. This annex is based on Collins (2007).

24. The household survey–based participation rates are used to maintain consistency with the methodology used for the projections. ILO estimates of the labor force in 2010 are slightly different from the estimates developed here. The ILO estimate of the total labor force in South Asia in 2010 is about 27 million higher, with an annual growth rate between 1990 and 2010 of 2.3 percent, compared with the 2.1 percent posited in this book.

References

Aggarwal, S. 2010. "Labor Input and Its Composition: An Industry–Level Perspective." Paper presented at the Worldklems conference, Cambridge, MA, August.

Bloom, D., D. Canning, and L. Rosenberg. 2011. "Demographic Change and Economic Growth." In *Reshaping Tomorrow*, ed. E. Ghani. New Delhi: Oxford University Press.

Bosworth, B. 2005. *Economic Growth in Thailand: The Macroeconomic Context*. Brookings Institution, Washington, DC.

———. 2010. "Update of Bosworth and Collins, 2003." Unpublished paper, World Bank, Washington, D.C.

Bosworth, B., and S. Collins, 2003. "The Empirics of Growth: An Update." *Brookings Papers on Economic Activity* (2): 113–206.

———. 2008. "Accounting for Growth: Comparing China and India." *Journal of Economic Perspectives* 22 (1): 45–66.

———. 2010. "Update of Bosworth and Collins 2003." Unpublished notes for this book.

Bosworth, B., S. Collins, and A. Virmani 2007. "Sources of Growth in the Indian Economy." NBER Working Paper 12901, National Bureau of Economic Research, Cambridge, MA.

Collins, S. 2007. "Economic Growth in South Asia: A Growth Accounting Perspective." In *Growth and Regional Integration in South Asia*, ed. S. Ahmed and E. Ghani, 45–60. Delhi: Macmillan India Ltd.

Easterly, W., M. Kremer, L. Pritchett, and L. Summers. 1993. "Good Policy or Good Luck? Country Growth Performance and Temporary Shocks." *Journal of Monetary Economics* 32 (3): 459–83.

ILO (International Labour Office). 2010. KILM and LABORSTA databases. Geneva.

Lanjouw, P., J. Luoto, and D. Mckenzie. 2011. "Using Repeated Cross–Sections to Explore Movements in and out of Poverty." Policy Research Working Paper 5550, World Bank, Washington, DC.

Sundaram, K. 2004. "Growth of Work Opportunities in India: 1983 to 1999–2000." Paper presented at a conference in honor of K. N. Raj on Planning, Institutions, Markets and Development, Thrissur, Kerala, India, October.

UN (United Nations). 2008. *World Population Prospects: The 2008 Revision*. New York: United Nations.

———. 2010. *World Population Prospects: The 2010 Revision*. New York: United Nations.

World Bank. 1993. *The East Asian Miracle*. Washington, DC.

———. 2011a. *Large-Scale Migration and Remittances in Nepal: Issues, Challenges and Opportunities*. Washington, DC.

———. 2011b. *Perspectives on Poverty in India: Stylized Facts from Survey Data*. Washington, DC.

———. 2011c. *World Development Indicators*. Washington, DC.

Young, A. 1994. "Lessons from the East Asian NICs: A Contrarian View." *European Economic Review* 38: 964–73.

———. 1995. "The Tyranny of Numbers: Confronting the Statistical Realities of the East Asian Growth Experience." *Quarterly Journal of Economics* 110 (August): 641–80.

Questions and Findings

Questions

- What are they key features of labor markets in South Asia?
- Where are the better jobs, and who holds them?
- What are the implications for the region's employment challenges?

Findings

- Although employment in South Asia has been expanding, employment rates have remained steady and are below those in other regions, as a result of persistently low female employment and participation rates.
- The majority of workers in the region are still engaged in agriculture. Self-employment is the predominant type of employment, and a high share of wage employment is casual labor. Thus, the vast majority of work in South Asia—86–95 percent of total employment and 71–81 percent of nonagricultural employment in most countries—is informal in nature. This picture is unlikely to change significantly in the short to medium term.
- Jobs that pay higher wages and are associated with lower poverty rates are found outside of agriculture. Faster intersectoral reallocation of employment into industry and services will require the development of not just the urban industrial and services sectors but also the rural nonfarm sector.
- Within industry and services, better jobs are with large formal firms. The majority of workers, however, work in informal micro firms, where value added per worker is lower and which pay lower wages. Creation of better jobs will require faster intrasectoral reallocation of labor from lower-productivity—typically micro and small informal—firms to higher-productivity—typically medium and large formal—firms within manufacturing and services.
- The educated are more likely to work outside agriculture and be employed in regular wage or salaried work. Female workers are less likely to be in better jobs than men, except at the highest levels of education; they also earn less, even after controlling for differences in educational attainment. Members of ethnic minorities are less likely to hold better jobs; they also earn less, although much of this differential can be explained by differences in educational attainment.

A Profile of South Asia at Work | 3

This chapter profiles employment in South Asia. Relying on household survey data from the region's eight countries, it describes the patterns of participation, employment, unemployment, and earnings in the region.

Describing the labor market in South Asia is a formidable task. The region's eight countries vary widely in size, ranging from less than 1 million people each in Bhutan and Maldives to 1.2 billion people—about three-quarters of South Asia's population—in India. There is diversity in the stages of development, economic structures, social and cultural characteristics, and conflict. Even within countries there is significant diversity.

The profile of South Asia at work presented is based primarily on microlevel data collected by national statistical agencies. The analysis relies on labor force surveys in some countries and on living standards surveys in others (depending on survey availability and data quality). The latest surveys were conducted between 2004 and 2009/10 (see appendix table A.1).

Two caveats should be noted regarding analysis across countries. First, there are limits to the standardization that is possible, especially between labor force and living standards surveys. In countries that

conduct labor force surveys (Bangladesh, India, Nepal, Pakistan, and Sri Lanka), measurement of labor market indicators such as labor force participation, employment, and unemployment is common and generally consistent with international standards. In countries in which other household surveys are used (Afghanistan, Bhutan, and Maldives), definitions of these (and other) indicators can differ from international norms. As a result, measurement differences explain some of the variation across countries presented in this chapter (Srinivasan 2010 discusses in further detail how labor market concepts are measured in different surveys). (Annex table 3A.1 provides more detail on the measurement of employment and unemployment from the national surveys as used in this book.) Second, as South Asian economies are still heavily rural, agricultural, and informal, the productive activities of many individuals may not be fully captured by standard labor market indicators.

This chapter is organized as follows. The first section provides an overview of the main labor market trends, including employment, unemployment, and labor force participation, for the eight countries in South Asia, with a focus on the employment and participation patterns of women. The second section takes a closer look at the nature of employment in the region, including location, sector, employment status, and informality. The third section examines where the better jobs are. The last section analyses how gender, caste/ethnicity, and education are correlated with access to better jobs.

Overview of employment and labor force participation in South Asia

This section first examines employment in the region. It then addresses labor force participation and unemployment.

Employment

Total employment in South Asia is estimated at 574 million in 2010, with India accounting for 75 percent, Bangladesh 10 percent, and Pakistan 9 percent of employment in the region (figure 3.1). In the region as a whole, 55 percent of the 1.04 billion working-age population is employed.

Employment rates are low by international standards in all countries except Bhutan and Nepal. Employment growth looks favorable because of the region's growing working-age population, as discussed in chapter 2. The picture is less positive in terms of employment rates. Employment rates among people age 15–64 range from 48 percent in Maldives (2004) to 80 percent in Nepal (2008) (the other countries in the region have employment rates of 50–65 percent). Analysis within countries shows moderate differences in regional employment rates within countries (see annex 3B). Internationally, the average employment rate is 60–70 percent for low- and lower-middle-income countries (figure 3.2). The employment rate in the three largest countries in South Asia (India, Bangladesh, and Pakistan) is significantly below the average rate for countries at similar levels of development.

These relatively low employment rates in South Asia reflect persistently low female employment rates in all countries except Bhutan and Nepal (figure 3.3). Employment rates among men are not low by international standards. The (unweighted) national average for male employment in South Asia is 77 percent, which is almost identical to the male average for comparator countries (Bolivia, Cambodia, China, Ghana, Guatemala, Indonesia, Lao People's Democratic Republic, Nigeria, and the Philippines). In contrast, the average employment rate for women in South Asia is 21 percentage points lower than in comparator countries. The male-female employment rate ratio is 2.2 in the region and just 1.3 in comparator countries.

There is no consistent evidence of an upward trend in employment rates in South Asian countries (figure 3.4). Total employment

FIGURE 3.1 **Total employment in South Asia, by country, 2010**

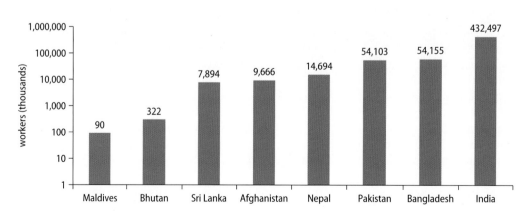

Sources: Authors, based on working-age population figures from UN 2010 and employment rate data from national labor force surveys.

FIGURE 3.2   **Employment rates in lower- and lower-middle-income countries**

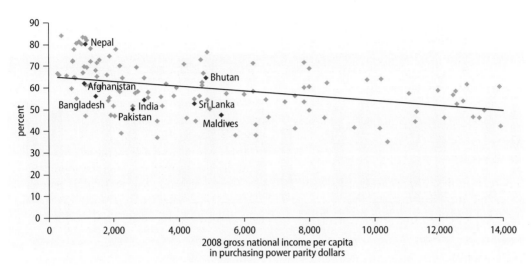

Source: Authors, based on data from World Bank 2011b and national labor force and household surveys.
Note: Employment rates are for population age 15 years and above. For all countries, gross national income per capita in 2008 is adjusted for purchasing power parity. Employment rates for countries in South Asia are for latest survey year; employment rates for other countries are for 2008.

FIGURE 3.3   **Male and female employment rates in South Asia, by country**

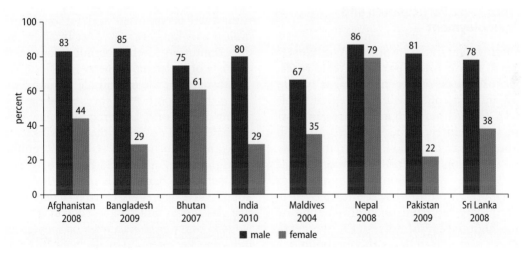

Source: Authors, based on data from national labor force and household surveys.

rates increased in Maldives and Pakistan, declined moderately in India and Nepal and significantly in Bhutan, and remained fairly constant in Bangladesh and Sri Lanka.[1] These trends mirrored those of female employment rates, which increased in Maldives and

Pakistan, declined in Bhutan and India, and changed little in the other countries.

These employment figures are for the working-age population (15–64). Child labor, which this book does not address, remains an important aspect of the overall employment

FIGURE 3.4 **Trends in employment rates in South Asia, by country**

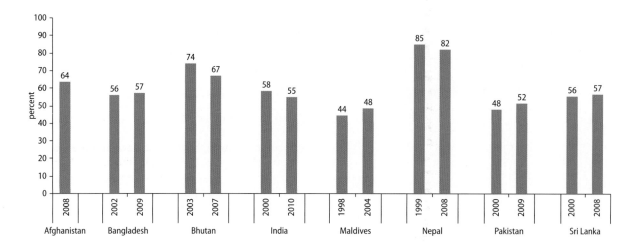

Source: Authors, based on data from national labor force and household surveys.
Note: Trend analysis does not take into account cyclical factors. Although the analysis attempted to use standard, consistent definitions of employment over time, differences may reflect differences in the questions used to define employment in different survey rounds (see annex table 3A.1 for details).

picture in South Asia, as it is in many parts of the developing world (box 3.1).

Labor Force Participation and Unemployment

Employment rates in South Asia closely track labor force participation rates, because measured unemployment is very low in most countries in the region (table 3.1). Open unemployment rates in low-income countries tend to be low, even if labor market conditions are unattractive. For the region as a whole, 3.2 percent of the labor force—19 million people in a labor force of 593 million—was unemployed in 2010. The reported unemployment rate was high only in Maldives (15.3 percent), where it mainly reflects the methodology used to calculate unemployment.[2] Unemployment in other countries ranged from 1.1 percent in Pakistan to 5.6 percent in Sri Lanka. In Bangladesh, Sri Lanka, and especially Maldives, women have higher unemployment rates than men. In the rest of the region, there is little gender difference.

Although open unemployment is low in South Asia, underemployment—the under-utilization of labor—may be prevalent.

Underemployment is conventionally defined as working fewer hours than desired in mature labor markets. This may not be an appropriate definition in developing countries, where people often work for long hours even if earnings are very low. In addition, data limitations do not permit a consistent estimate of underemployment.

Estimates of the magnitude of underemployment in South Asia vary, based on different definitions. Underemployment was estimated at 48 percent of the total workforce in Afghanistan in 2008 (Islamic Republic of Afghanistan and World Bank 2010) and 24.5 percent in Bangladesh in 2006 (Rahman 2008). These figures are based on a definition that classifies as underemployed workers who work 35 or fewer hours a week on average. In India one measure used by the National Sample Survey organization (which defines underemployment as the proportion of the usually employed according to the usual status criteria not employed the previous week) estimates underemployment at 9–17 percent for women and 2–4 percent for men in 2004/05 (Government of India 2006). One problem with these measures is that they may overestimate underemployment, because they do not take into account individuals who did not wish to

BOX 3.1   Child labor in South Asia

According to the International Labour Organization (ILO 2010), 215 million children between the ages of 5 and 14 were working in South Asia in 2008, with 115 million engaged in hazardous work. These figures indicate that 13 percent of all working children in the world live in South Asia; among these children, 7 percent are engaged in hazardous work. According to these figures, the incidence of child labor in Asia is the second highest of all regions, behind Africa. (The ILO statistics do not separate South Asia from the rest of the continent).

Child labor has long played an important role in many traditional and agriculturally based societies. It can also be a product of poverty and inequality, poor education, and conflict. In South Asia, as in some other regions, concerns about child labor are heightened by the presence of practices such as child trafficking and bonded child labor (ILO 2010).

How prevalent is child labor in South Asia? Many of the surveys used for this book include questions that provide data on the incidence of child labor. The employment rates for children can be computed in the same way they have been calculated for the working-age population. However, surveys differ in their age coverage: in some countries, employment rates can be computed for the 5- to 14-year age group; in others, surveys do not cover children under 10.

Survey evidence suggests that the incidence of child labor varies across the region (box table 3.1.1). Nepal has the highest incidence, with about 3 in

10 children between the ages of 5 and 14 working. Significant numbers of children are also working in Afghanistan, Bhutan, and Pakistan. Bangladesh, India, and Sri Lanka report lower incidences.

Additional dimensions of the statistical picture of child labor in South Asia include the following:

- In most countries, boys are somewhat more likely than girls to work. However, in Bhutan and Nepal, two countries with high child labor rates, employment is higher among girls.
- Child labor is much more prevalent in rural areas than in cities. The vast majority of working children are engaged in agriculture and fishing. Other sectors with some child labor are commerce (retail trade) and manufacturing.
- Although some children are employed as wage workers (in Bangladesh and, to a lesser extent, in India), most are household enterprise workers. In Nepal, for example, 96 percent of working children work in household enterprises.
- The incidence of child labor continues to decline gradually in Bangladesh, India, and Sri Lanka. In Nepal and Pakistan, where the incidence of child labor is higher, there is no clear evidence of decreases in child labor over time.

The nefarious effects of child labor can be mitigated when working children continue their studies. In Nepal, for example, the country with the highest child

BOX TABLE 3.1.1   Incidence of child labor in South Asia, by age group and country
(percentage of age group)

Country	Year	Age group		
		5–9	10–14	5–14
Afghanistan	2008	8.5	23.2	16.1
Bangladesh	2005	0.7	7.1	4.1
Bhutan	2003	—	19.7	—
India	2008	0.2	3.4	1.8
Nepal	2008	10.9	47.0	29.7
Pakistan	2009	—	11.8	—
Sri Lanka	2008	—	1.1	—

Source: Authors, based on data from national labor force and household surveys.
Note: — = Not available. No data on child labor are available for Maldives.

(continues next page)

BOX 3.1   Child labor in South Asia (continued)

labor rates in the region, almost 90 percent of children who are working also attend school. In contrast, although a smaller percentage of children in Afghanistan, Bangladesh, Bhutan, India, and Pakistan work, most are not in school (box figure 3.1.1).

The international community has passed a number of conventions designed to protect the rights of children in the labor market, through both minimum working ages and protection from hazardous and other harmful forms of employment. The three most important conventions are the UN Convention on the Rights of the Child and ILO Conventions 138 (minimum age of employment) and 182 (Elimination of the Worst Forms of Child Labor). All eight countries in South Asia have ratified the UN Convention on the Rights of the Child; only Afghanistan, Nepal, Pakistan, and Sri Lanka have ratified the two ILO conventions (see chapter 6).

BOX FIGURE 3.1.1   Percentage of child workers attending school in South Asia, by age group and country

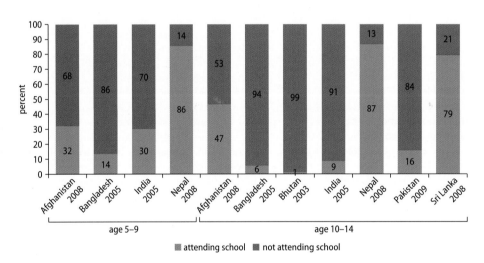

Source: Authors, based on data from national labor force and household surveys.
Note: Data on 5- to 9-year-olds are not available for Bhutan, Pakistan, and Sri Lanka.

TABLE 3.1   Male and female labor force participation, employment, and unemployment rates in South Asia, by country

Country	Year	Participation rate			Employment rate			Unemployment rate		
		All	Male	Female	All	Male	Female	All	Male	Female
Afghanistan	2008	65	85	45	64	83	44	2	3	2
Bangladesh	2009	60	89	31	57	85	29	5	4	8
Bhutan	2007	69	76	62	67	75	61	2	2	2
India	2010	57	82	30	55	80	29	3	3	4
Maldives	2004	57	72	46	48	67	35	15	8	24
Nepal	2008	84	88	80	82	86	79	2	2	1
Pakistan	2009	52	82	22	52	81	22	1	1	1
Sri Lanka	2008	60	81	41	57	78	38	6	4	8

Source: Authors, based on data from national labor force and household surveys.
Note: See annex table 3A.1 for definition of employment and unemployment used in each country. The term *participation* refers to the formal definition of labor force participation according to international norms. Application of these norms can be problematic in South Asia, because they do not take into account nonmarket activities of women.

work additional hours. In India, defining the underemployed as people who worked at least three days during the week and spent at least a half day searching for work, results in an estimated underemployment rate of 5 percent.[3]

Low female employment rate is primarily a result of low levels of labor force participation among women. The lowest female labor force participation rates are in the three large South Asian countries: Pakistan, where almost four out of every five women do not participate in the labor force, and Bangladesh and India, where slightly more than two out of every three women do not participate.[4]

Because female participation is such an important factor in defining the region's employment picture and its evolution over time, this issue merits a more detailed look. Before proceeding, a caveat about labor force statistics and the concept of participation is needed. All of the surveys collect data that make it possible to measure labor force participation according to international norms, but the application of these norms to low-income, traditional societies can be problematic. For this reason, it seems unlikely that the actual participation of women, especially in the region's large countries, is as low as the rates of participation in the surveys indicate. In what follows, the term *participation* needs to be understood as referring to the formal definition of labor force participation; it does not take into account other activities of South Asian women, including reproduction and household labor.

Except in Bhutan and Nepal, South Asian countries generally have low female participation rates across age groups (figure 3.5). This is especially true in Pakistan and, to a lesser degree, Bangladesh, where even in the prime-age groups, the large majority of women are not in the labor force.

In all three countries in which data on caste/ethnicity are collected (India, Nepal, and Sri Lanka), there is considerable variation in female labor force participation along this dimension; differences in male labor force participation are small. The finding on caste/ethnicity is not surprising, as cultural factors

can be important determinants of whether women participate in the labor market. In India, for example, where the overall female participation rate was 30 percent in 2010, the rate among women from scheduled tribes (46 percent) was 16 points higher and the rate among Muslim women (18 percent) almost 12 points lower. In Sri Lanka, where aggregate female participation was 41 percent in 2008, the rate for Indian Tamil women was 62 percent and the rate for Sri Lankan Moors just 17 percent.

Female participation is especially low in urban areas. Overall labor force participation is generally lower in cities than it is in rural areas, where labor-intensive, family-oriented agricultural production still dominates, but this gap is especially striking for women. Female rural participation rates are higher than urban participation rates in all countries except Bangladesh (where female participation is low everywhere); in Afghanistan and Pakistan, the participation rate

FIGURE 3.5 **Female labor force participation rates in South Asia, by age group and country**

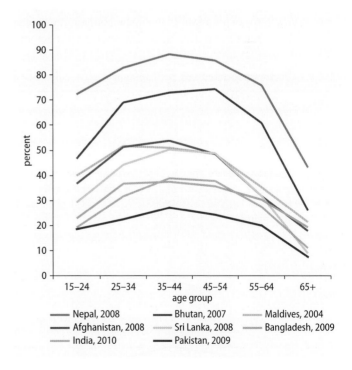

Source: Authors, based on data from national labor force and household surveys.

for rural women is nearly three times that for urban women. The most recent female urban participation rates are just 10 percent in Pakistan, 18 percent in Afghanistan, and 19 percent in India. Moreover, there is little evidence of any significant change, with the (unweighted) average female urban participation in the region increasing from 30 percent to 33 percent over the periods studied.

What factors are associated with female labor force participation? The labor force participation status of working-age women was regressed on individual and family characteristics, using separate logit models for rural and urban women in each country. Table 3.2 summarizes the key determinants of participation in urban areas.

The negative relationship between education and the labor force participation of women has been noted by others studying the region's labor market (World Bank 2010). Various explanations have been put forward to explain this relationship. One hypothesis is that better-educated women may opt out of the labor market because of the scarcity of good jobs that are available to them and that an income effect may be at play, with relatively high family incomes reducing the incentives for well-educated women to participate

in the labor force. Sociocultural explanations have also been put forward, based on the possible stigma attached to educated women who choose to work.

In all countries except India, the surveys ask women not participating in the labor force why they were not employed or searching for work. In all countries, household duties were the number one reason cited for nonparticipation (table 3.3). This is especially true of countries with very low rates of female labor force participation (Afghanistan, Bangladesh, and Pakistan). This finding is consistent with the fact that women in South Asia, like women across the world, bear a disproportionate share of household and care responsibilities and therefore face high opportunity costs when they work in the marketplace. Social norms also affect these tradeoffs.

Education was the second-most frequently cited reason, but there are large cross-country differences. Substantial numbers of young women in Bhutan, Nepal, and Maldives report being in school instead of the labor force. In contrast, in Afghanistan, Bangladesh, Pakistan, and Sri Lanka, fewer than 2 in 10 urban women not participating in the labor force cite education as the main reason.

TABLE 3.2   Factors associated with participation of women in urban areas

Factor	Effect
Age	• Age increases probability of female participation in all countries. Effect weakens later in age distribution.
Education	• More years of schooling decreases the probability of female participation in all countries except Bhutan. Participation rates tend to be lowest for women who complete secondary or lower-secondary school; they rise only at higher-secondary levels and tertiary levels.
Household characteristics	• Living in a larger household reduces the probability of female participation in all countries except Afghanistan, Nepal, and Maldives (where there is no effect). • The number of children under the age of six reduces the probability of female participation in all countries except Afghanistan and Bhutan. • Ethnic minority or lower caste status increases the probability of female participation in countries for which data are available (India, Nepal, and Sri Lanka).
Marital status	• Being married reduces the probability of female participation in all countries except Bangladesh (one of two surveys) and Nepal.
Characteristics of other adults in the household	• More years of schooling of the best-educated male in the household reduces the probability of female participation in all countries, presumably because it signals an income effect. • Having males in the household who are employed increases the probability of female participation in all countries. • Having a migrant away from the household increases the probability of female participation in India and Nepal but not Maldives (no data on other countries).

Source: Authors, based on data from national labor force and household surveys.

TABLE 3.3 Reasons why urban women in South Asia do not participate in the labor force, by country
(percent)

Country/year	Old age	Illness	Household duties	Education	Discouraged	Other
Afghanistan, 2008	0.2	0.6	81.0	12.9	2.2	3.2
Bangladesh, 2005	0.3	2.2	81.1	15.0	0.2	1.0
Bhutan, 2007	3.6	2.7	60.4	26.9	2.6	3.8
Maldives, 2004	—	11.1	46.7	22.8	—	19.5
Nepal, 2008	7.0	0.7	51.6	29.6	4.7	6.3
Pakistan, 2009	1.3	1.0	81.1	16.2	0.1	0.4
Sri Lanka, 2008	5.3	1.8	75.5	15.8	0.4	1.3

Source: Authors, based on data from national labor force and household surveys.
Note: — = Not available.

Improving economic opportunities for and educational attainment of women could contribute to improved utilization and allocation of South Asia's female labor force. Women's decision to participate in market work is not independent of the occupational and earnings opportunities available to women in the labor market as these impact incentives to participate. Consistent with global evidence on employment segregation by gender (World Bank 2012), women in South Asia are less likely to access the better jobs (see last section of this chapter). They also earn significantly less for the same type of job, even after controlling for differences in education. Improving opportunities requires interventions that relax time constraints, increase access to productive inputs, and correct institutional and market failures that contribute to employment segregation. (For a comprehensive discussion of options to improve economic opportunities for women, see World Bank 2012.)

The nature of employment

This section begins by describing employment patterns by location and sector in South Asia. It then looks at employment status and informality.

Employment patterns by location and sector

Most South Asians work in rural areas (table 3.4). The concentration in rural areas reflects the fact that more than 70 percent of the region's working-age population lives in rural areas and rural employment rates are higher than urban rates in all countries except Maldives.

In Afghanistan, Bhutan, India, and Nepal, at least half of all employment remains in agriculture. Only in Maldives is this sector a relatively minor source of employment. Services are important in most countries, representing more than 40 percent of total employment in Bangladesh, Maldives, and Sri Lanka. The industrial sector, including manufacturing, utilities, and construction, is relatively small, despite the great importance attached to industrialization since independence (Srinivasan 2010). In Bangladesh, India, Maldives, Pakistan, and Sri Lanka, 20–27 percent of the employed workforce works in industry, with most of them in manufacturing. As expected, these sectoral patterns differ substantially between rural and urban areas. Agriculture is the largest sector of employment in rural areas in all countries except Maldives and Sri Lanka. In urban areas, most workers are in the service sector. Manufacturing accounts for about a quarter of urban workers in Bangladesh, India, Pakistan, and Sri Lanka.

Sectoral employment patterns are changing. The share of agriculture employment in total employment has been declining by about 0.5 percentage points a year in recent decades in countries where statistics are available over time. In the five largest countries in the region, employment growth in agriculture was slower than other sectors in the first decade of this century (figure 3.6).

TABLE 3.4   **Distribution of employment in South Asian countries, by location and sector**

(percent)

Country/ year	Total			Total		Rural			Urban		
	Agriculture	Industry	Services	Rural	Urban	Agriculture	Industry	Services	Agriculture	Industry	Services
Afghanistan, 2007	59	13	29	85	15	68	12	21	9	19	72
Bangladesh, 2009	39	21	40	76	24	47	18	35	12	30	57
Bhutan, 2007	68	7	24	78	22	85	4	11	9	19	72
India, 2010	50	23	27	74	26	65	19	16	7	34	59
Maldives, 2004	17	27	55	66	34	24	33	43	5	16	79
Nepal, 2008	73	11	16	87	13	80	9	11	31	21	48
Pakistan, 2009	43	21	36	69	31	60	16	24	6	32	62
Sri Lanka, 2008	31	27	42	90	10	34	26	39	2	31	68

Source: Authors, based on national labor force and household surveys.
Note: These data pertain to the area in which the worker's main employment is located. The classification of the area is based on each country's classification of rural and urban. Sri Lanka's classification of rural areas includes the tea estate sector, where a large number of workers are employed. Differences in classification may account for some of the variations across countries.

FIGURE 3.6   **Annual percentage increases in number of employed workers in South Asia, by sector and country**

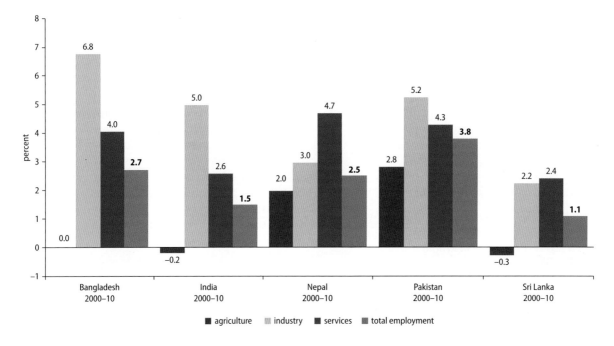

Sources: Authors, based on data from ILO 2011and national labor force and household surveys.

Total agricultural employment increased significantly in Nepal and Pakistan during this period; it remained constant in Bangladesh and declined in Sri Lanka and India.

The major contributors to job creation everywhere have been industry and services. Industrial employment has grown very rapidly in Bangladesh (at almost 7 percent a year), Pakistan (just over 5 percent a year), and India (just over 4 percent a year). Services employment growth has been strongest in Bangladesh, Nepal, and Pakistan, at 4–5 percent a year.

The gradual decline in the shares of agricultural employment reflects not just rural-urban migration but also the growth of the rural nonfarm sector across the region. The rural nonfarm sector employs 12–59 percent of the total workforce (15–65 percent of the rural workforce) in South Asia (figure 3.7). Countries that are still primarily rural and agricultural (Bhutan, Nepal) have the smallest rural nonfarm sectors.

The pace of development of the rural nonfarm sector varies widely across countries and time (figure 3.8). In Nepal, the nonfarm sector share of the rural workforce increased

by only 1 percentage point over nine years. In contrast, in Bhutan, Maldives, Pakistan, and Sri Lanka, it increased 5–11 percentage points over six to nine years.

In India, employment in the nonfarm sector increased steadily for 25 years, rising from 20 percent of the rural workforce in 1983 to 35 percent in 2009/10. The pace of diversification away from agriculture increased over time. During 1983–1993/94, the average annual growth in nonfarm jobs was just over 2 percent. During 1993/94–1998/99, it increased to 3 percent; between 1999 and 2004/05, it increased to 4 percent. In the 1980s, of the nearly 40 million additional rural jobs generated in India, 6 out of 10 were in the farm sector. In contrast, of the 56 million new rural jobs created between 1993 and 2004, 6 out of 10 were in the nonfarm sector (World Bank 2011a). This trend has continued in recent years: between 2004/05 and 2009/10, the nonfarm sector increased from 30 percent to 35 percent of the rural workforce.

According to data from the 2000 and 2008 China National Rural Surveys, transformation of the rural labor market has been one of the most salient trends in China's

FIGURE 3.7   **Distribution of employment in South Asia, by sector and country**

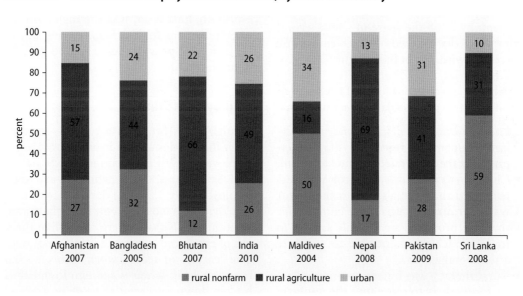

Source: Authors, based on data from national labor force and household surveys.

FIGURE 3.8   **Percentage of rural workers in the nonfarm sector in South Asia, by country**

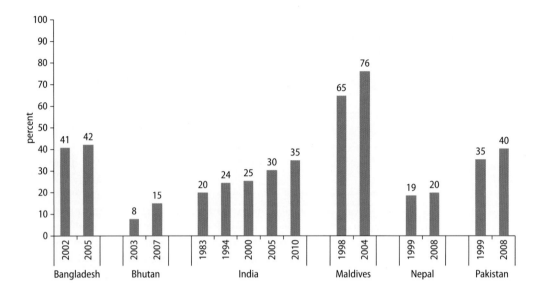

Source: Authors, based on data from national labor force and household surveys.

development since the 1980s. India's overall pace of transition has been slower than China's. The share of rural labor force off the farm in China was lower than in India in the early 1980s (a few years after the start of the major rural reforms adopted in 1978 that abolished the commune system and introduced the household responsibility system). However, by 2000 the share had become significantly greater than India's, at 43.5 percent; by 2008 the share of China's rural labor force that worked off the farm was 62 percent—twice that of India (figure 3.9).

Mukherjee and Zhang (2007) offer a number of explanations for the faster pace of rural nonfarm sector development in China:

- Local governments in China were incentivized to support the town and village enterprises, as they generated revenue for them.
- China's rural nonfarm sector was less protected than India's. When the sector was liberalized, it was more competitive than the protected small-scale sectors in India, which were not able to compete after liberalization.
- Rural literacy was higher, making it easier for workers to move into the nonfarm sector.

- Local public rural infrastructure provision was superior (as a result of higher levels of decentralization in China).

Unlike in East Asia, most nonfarm jobs in South Asia are in the service sector, with commerce the largest subsector, employing 12–33 percent of nonfarm rural workers (figure 3.10). The manufacturing sector—which in other developing countries, especially East Asia, was the major source of employment for workers moving out of agriculture—provides less than 30 percent of nonfarm jobs.

Employment Status

South Asia is far from a typical, modern labor market dominated by wage or salaried employees. In all countries except Maldives and Sri Lanka, most workers are self-employed (box 3.2). The dominance of self-employment is most extreme in Afghanistan, Bhutan, and Nepal, where more than three out of every four workers are self-employed. The scarcity of secure work forms is even more striking when wage employment is broken down into regular wage or salaried workers and casual workers. In Afghanistan,

FIGURE 3.9   **Percentage of rural workers in the nonfarm sector in China and India, 1983–2008**

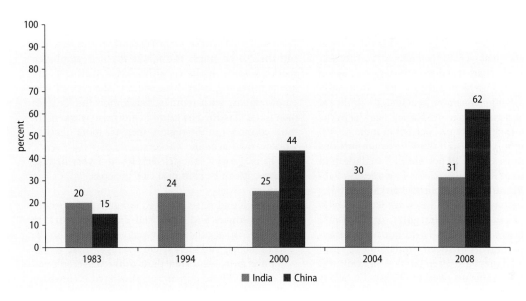

Source: Wang, Huang, and Zhang 2011.
Note: Data for China are not available for 1994 and 2004.

FIGURE 3.10   **Rural nonfarm sector employment in South Asia, by economic activity and country**

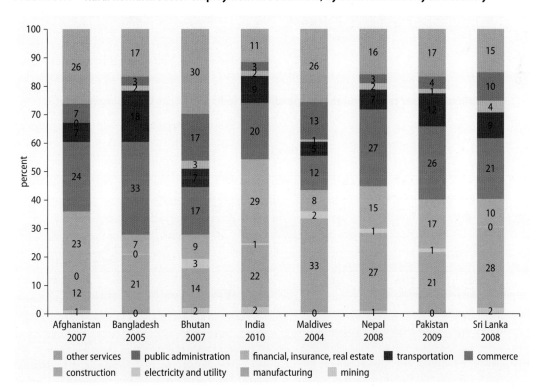

Source: Authors, based on data from national labor force and household surveys.

BOX 3.2   Composition of the labor force by employment status

Regular wage or salaried workers are defined as regularly paid wage employees in the public or private sectors. These workers are usually on the regular payroll of the enterprises for which they work and usually earn leave and supplementary benefits. A significant proportion of regular wage or salaried work is in the public sector, ranging from 27 percent in India (2010) to 66 percent in Afghanistan (2007) (the proportions in other countries were 29 percent in Bangladesh in 2005; 42 percent in Nepal in 2008; 40 percent in Pakistan in 2009; and 52 percent in Sri Lanka in 2008).

Casual laborers are defined as wage workers who are paid on a casual, daily, irregular, or piece-rate basis. These workers typically do not have access to formal instruments of social protection. In rural areas, casual laborers are often landless agricultural help, though a significant number of casual workers work in the rural nonfarm sector (in, for example, construction).

Self-employed workers consist of employers, own-account workers, and unpaid family enterprise workers. They represent the largest group of workers in most South Asian countries, ranging from 43 percent in Sri Lanka to 82 percent in Nepal. The majority of the self-employed are own-account workers or family enterprise workers. In rural areas,

self-employed workers are typically farmers working their own land, though many self-employed workers work in the rural nonfarm sector. There are significant gender differences in the type of self-employment, with women much more likely than men to be classified as family enterprise workers. In most countries in the region, men are more likely to work as own-account workers.

The category of the self-employed is very heterogeneous. It can be split into two groups:.

• The high-end self-employed subgroup consists of all employers and other self-employed workers who work as officials, managers, professionals, technicians, and clerks. On average, these workers are more educated than other self-employed workers. Their consumption distribution profile is more similar to regular wage or salaried workers.

• The low-end self-employed subgroup consists of own account and unpaid family workers who work as service workers, skilled agricultural workers, craftspeople, machine operators, and workers in elementary occupations. Their consumption profiles are similar to those of casual laborers (box figure 3.2.1).

BOX FIGURE 3.2.1   **Distribution of per capita household expenditure in India and Nepal, by employment status**

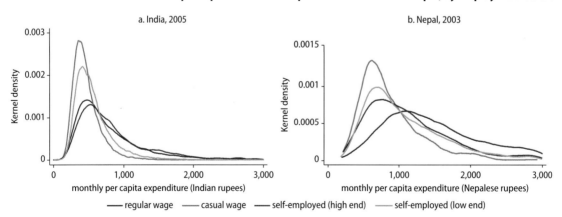

Source: Authors, based on data from national labor force and household surveys.

Bangladesh, India, and Nepal, more than half of wage earners are casual workers. Only in Bhutan is wage employment dominated by regular wage or salaried workers.

The pattern of employment differs by location. A larger share of rural workers than urban workers is self-employed. The majority of rural wage earners are casual laborers, whereas the majority of urban wage earners are regular wage or salaried workers.

The distribution of workers by employment status changed very little, if at all, in the past decade (table 3.5). Only in Bhutan and Maldives did employment shift markedly toward wage work, and it is not known if the increase there was in regular wage or salaried work, casual labor, or both. In the other countries, self-employment continues to dominate, with the share of wage employment growing very little in the past decade. Within wage employment, there was a slight shift toward regular wage work in Nepal and Pakistan. In contrast, within the rural nonfarm sectors in Bangladesh (2002–05) and India (1983–2010), there was an increase in the share of casual labor, both as a share of total rural nonfarm employment and as a share of rural nonfarm wage employment.

Informality

The issue of informality is a prominent one in South Asia. Since the term *informal sector* was coined, about 40 years ago, considerable efforts have been made to define and measure informality. (For a comprehensive discussion of measurement and statistics, see ILO 2002. For a definition of informal employment in India, see the National Commission for Enterprises in the Unorganised Sector 2009.)

TABLE 3.5   Distribution of employment in South Asian countries, by type of employment
(percent)

Country/year	Wage employment		Self-employment		
	Regular wage or salaried	Casual labor	Employer	Own account	Family enterprise
Latest year					
Afghanistan, 2008	9	14	0.5	44	33
Bangladesh, 2005	14	22	0.3	41	22
Bhutan, 2007	21	4	0.2	25	50
India, 2010	17	32	1	33	17
Maldives, 2004	55		4	31	10
Nepal, 2008	8	10	1	35	46
Pakistan, 2009	21	17	1	34	28
Sri Lanka, 2008	57		3	29	11
Earlier year					
Bangladesh, 2002	14	22	0.4	44	19
Bhutan, 2003	14		0.2	18	68
India, 2000	15	31	1	31	21
Maldives, 1998	48		6	37	9
Nepal, 1999	6	10	1	39	44
Pakistan, 2000	19	18	1	41	21
Sri Lanka, 2000	57		2	28	13

Source: Authors, based on data from national labor force and household surveys.
Note: Labor force surveys in Bhutan, 2003; Maldives; and Sri Lanka do not allow the separation of wage employment into regular wage workers and casual laborers. Afghanistan has only one survey.

Information on employment status and sector, firm characteristics, and worker education from national labor force surveys is used to compare levels of informal employment across the region. Informal workers include all workers in the informal sector as well as workers in the formal sector performing informal jobs: all workers in agriculture; wage workers in informal enterprises; and casual laborers, family enterprise workers, and self-employed workers with less than senior-secondary education in the nonagricultural sectors. (Annex table 3A.2 shows country details.) Based on this definition, an estimated 86–95 percent of employment is informal in all countries except Maldives and Sri Lanka, and 71–81 percent of nonagricultural employment is informal in all countries except Bhutan, Maldives, and Sri Lanka (figure 3.11).

The estimated rates are consistent with other studies showing that the vast majority of employment in South Asia is informal.[5] Using lack of pension coverage as a proxy, Loayza and Wada (2011) estimate that 91 percent of the labor force in South Asia is informal (figure 3.12). Informality rates based on pension coverage in all South Asian countries except Sri Lanka are higher than in other countries with similar levels of gross domestic product (GDP). Together with Africa, South Asia has the highest rate of informal employment in the world (figure 3.12).

Although informal employment has traditionally been seen as a labor market problem—because informal workers tend to have low earnings and little access to formal social protection systems—recent research, especially in Latin America, suggests that in some situations, individuals may choose to work informally. Analysis in South Asia has emphasized the vulnerability and involuntary nature of informality in the region (Chen and Doane 2008; National Commission for Enterprises in the Unorganised Sector 2009). The next section of this chapter shows that informal workers in South Asia are less skilled, earn less, and have higher poverty rates than formal workers and that informal manufacturing and services firms have lower labor productivity and pay lower wages than

FIGURE 3.11   Percentage of employment in South Asia classified as informal, by country

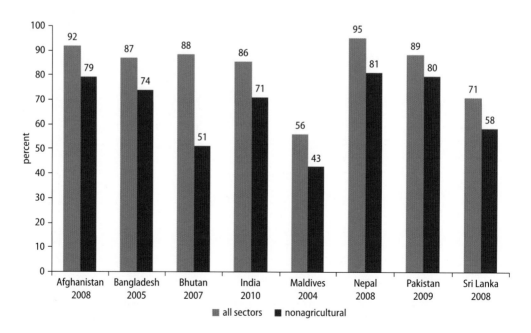

Source: Authors, based on data from national labor force surveys.

formal firms in the same size class. Loayza and Wada (2011) also point out that labor informality is higher than predicted by the level of production informality, suggesting that the productivity of informal workers in South Asia is relatively low compared with that of informal workers in other countries.

The pervasiveness of informality in South Asia is likely to remain a core feature for a long time. Informality is a complex, multi-faceted phenomenon that is shaped by both the modes of socioeconomic organization and the relationship the state establishes with private agents through regulation and moni-toring. Loayza and Wada (2011) show that the actual rates of labor informality in South Asia are similar to predicted levels based on the determinants of informality: the legal and regulatory framework, educational achieve-ment, the share of youth or rural popula-tion, and the sectoral production structure (box 3.3). Most of these determinants are

FIGURE 3.12 **Percentage of labor force not covered by pension schemes, by region**

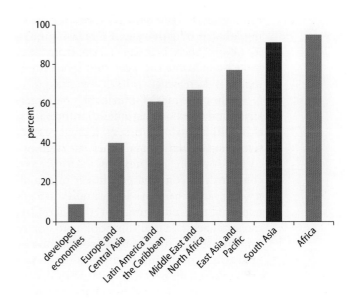

Source: Loayza and Wada 2011.

BOX 3.3 **Determinants of informality**

Using two labor informality measures (self-employment and lack of pension coverage), Loayza and Wada (2011) show that in cross-country regres-sions, labor informality is negatively and significantly related to the strength of law and order, business freedom from regulations, and average years of sec-ondary schooling and positively and significantly associated with sociodemographic transformation factors (the share of agriculture, youth population, and rural population). All correlation coefficients are highly statistically significant (*p*-values of less than 1 percent) and of large magnitude (0.68–0.83). The predicted levels of informality for South Asian coun-tries are similar to actual levels.

These results have several implications. First, informality is more prevalent when the regulatory framework is burdensome, the quality of government services to formal firms is low, and the state's moni-toring and enforcement power is weak. Second, the structural characteristics of underdevelopment play an important role in explaining informality. Other things equal, a higher level of education is likely to reduce informality by increasing productivity, potentially increasing returns to formalization. A production

structure tilted toward agriculture favors informality by making legal protection and contract enforcement less relevant and valuable. Third, larger shares of youth or rural populations are likely to increase infor-mality, make monitoring more difficult and expensive, place greater demands on resources for training and the acquisition of abilities, create bottlenecks in the initial school-to-work transition, and make it more difficult to expand formal public services.

Bangladesh, India, Pakistan, and Sri Lanka have larger predicted informality levels than the grow-ing East Asian countries (the Republic of Korea, Malaysia, and Singapore). Sociodemographic factors, in particular the region's high ratio of rural popula-tion, are the largest contributors to the differences in predicted informality levels between South Asian and East Asian comparator countries. Lower busi-ness regulatory freedom (for all countries) and low levels of education (for all countries except Pakistan) play a moderate but consistent role in explaining dif-ferences in informality. Law and order does not play a major role in explaining the differences.

Source: Loayza and Wada 2011.

structural and take time to change. For this reason, large informal sectors continue to exist even after economies have experienced rapid growth.[6] In South Asia, despite growing labor productivity and increasing quality of jobs, there is little evidence from labor force or industrial surveys that labor informality is decreasing.[7]

As the correlates of informality are largely structural, the book assumes that formalization will be a slow process. Easing restrictive labor legislation and other interventions to improve the business regulatory environment can contribute to lower informality, but large increases in formality are not expected to occur immediately. Therefore, the approach taken in this book is to aim to improve the quality of all types of jobs by addressing constraints to the productivity of all workers and firms, formal or informal. Such an approach is likely to have a positive effect on reducing informality, as increasing productivity may increase the returns to formalization. As the majority of workers will remain informal at least in the near term, efforts should be made to increase their access to programs that help manage labor market shocks (see chapter 6).

Where are the better jobs?

This book defines "better jobs" as jobs associated with higher wages (for wage workers), lower poverty, and a lower risk of low and uncertain income. This section examines which sectors, types of employment, and types of firms are associated with better job quality.

By sector

Employment in industry and services—in urban areas or the rural nonfarm sector—yields higher wages and is associated with lower poverty rates than agricultural casual labor. Chapter 2 showed that labor productivity (measured as output per worker) is much higher in industry and services than in agriculture. The higher productivity in these sectors is manifested in higher earnings.

Among South Asian countries in which headcount poverty rates by employment sector and status of household members can be analyzed, agricultural casual workers have the highest poverty rates in Bangladesh and Nepal and the second highest in India (after urban casual labor) (figure 3.13).[8] Agricultural self-employment provides a relatively good source of income (as proxied by poverty rates) in Bangladesh and India but not in Nepal. The jobs associated with the lowest poverty rates in all countries are regular wage work outside of agriculture in the urban or rural nonfarm sectors. Urban self-employment in Bangladesh and Nepal is also associated with lower poverty rates.

The wage data tell a consistent story: workers in industry and service sectors are better paid than workers in agriculture (figure 3.14). Rural nonfarm employment (regular wage and casual labor) and urban regular wage employment offer higher wages than agricultural casual labor in Bangladesh, India, Nepal, and Pakistan (the countries for which wage employment can be split into regular wage or salaried and casual labor in all time periods observed):

- Rural nonfarm and urban regular wages are 30–100 percent higher than wages for agricultural labor.
- Wages for rural nonfarm casual labor are 10–50 percent higher than wages for agricultural labor. Even with the consistent increase in the share of rural nonfarm jobs, nonfarm casual labor wages in India have remained about 30–50 percent higher than agricultural wages since 1983.
- Wages for urban casual labor are higher than wages for agricultural casual labor in Nepal and Pakistan (20–30 percent) but the same in Bangladesh and India. This evidence is consistent with the high poverty rates observed among urban casual labor in Bangladesh and India.

Wage differentials between services and agriculture are especially large (figure 3.15). In India, average hourly wages in services were 135 percent higher than in agriculture in 2010. In Nepal, Pakistan, and Sri Lanka, the

FIGURE 3.13 **Percentage of workers in households below the poverty line in Bangladesh, India, and Nepal, by employment status**

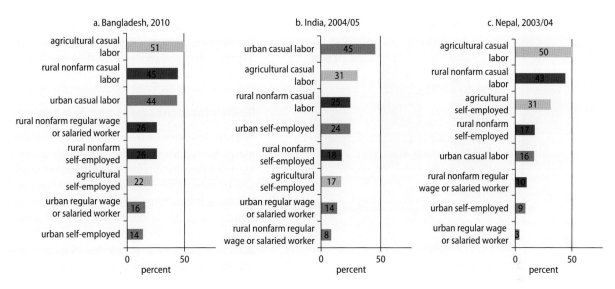

Source: Authors, based on data from national labor force and household surveys.

Note: Figures are for workers age 15–64. Poverty rates for India are based on official poverty lines prevailing until 2010. Using the new official poverty lines for 2004/05 (revised in 2011) would increase poverty rates in rural areas, making the poverty rates of rural workers higher than those of urban workers for the same employment type. The hierarchy in terms of employment type would remain the same.

FIGURE 3.14 **Ratio of median rural nonfarm and urban wages to agricultural wages in selected South Asian countries**

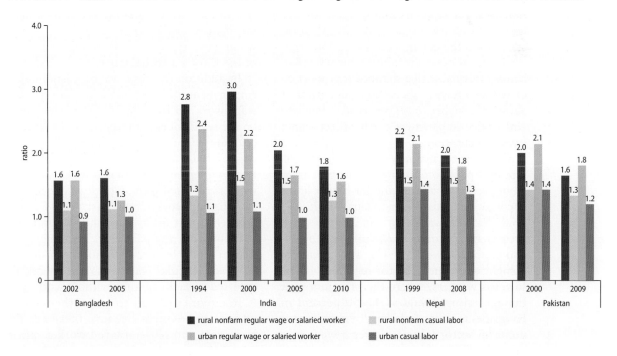

Source: Authors, based on data from national labor force and household surveys.

Note: A ratio of 1 means the median wage was equivalent to the median wage of agricultural casual labor.

FIGURE 3.15 Ratio of median industry and service sector wages to agricultural wages in selected South Asian countries

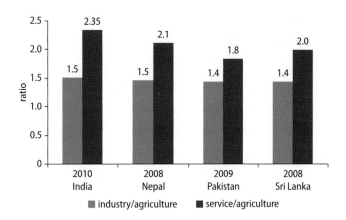

■ industry/agriculture   ■ service/agriculture

Source: Authors, based on data from national labor force and household surveys.
Note: A ratio of 1 means the median wage was equivalent to the median wage in agriculture.

ratio of wages in services to wages agriculture was also very high (112 percent higher in Nepal, 84 percent higher in Pakistan, and 99 percent higher in Sri Lanka).

Industry and service jobs are better paid partly because they are higher-skilled jobs. Nonagricultural workers have higher average levels of education than agricultural workers. Within the nonagricultural sector, regular wage workers are more educated than casual workers, with a significant proportion of workers having secondary education or above. The higher wages observed in industry and service employment partly reflect higher levels of education.

However, the majority of industry and service jobs pay more than agricultural casual labor even after accounting for higher levels of education (and other individual and household characteristics that can affect wages, such as age, gender, caste/ethnicity, religion, and household wealth).[9] The wage premium is highest for public sector regular wage or salaried workers, where the premium over the agricultural wage is 41–50 percent in Bangladesh, India, and Nepal. Private sector nonfarm sector jobs also offer a wage premium. In India, for example, the wage differential between nonfarm casual labor and

agricultural casual labor without controlling for other factors was 40 percent in 2000 and 50 percent in 2008; after controlling for other factors, including educational attainment of the workers, it was 24 percent in both years. There is thus a reallocation gain even without additional investment in education.

By employment status and firm type

Within industry and services wage employment, better jobs can be defined from two main angles: by worker's employment status and by type of firm. Regular wage or salaried workers have considerably higher average hourly wages than casual laborers (see figure 3.14). The two types of wage employment correspond roughly to formal and informal employment in the wage sector.[10] In Bangladesh, India, Nepal, and Pakistan, regular wage workers earn 20–48 percent more than casual workers in the rural nonfarm sector and 14–74 percent more than casual workers in the urban sector. These wage differentials partly reflect differences in education levels between regular wage workers and casual laborers. Casual labor has the highest poverty rates; poverty rates are generally lowest for regular wage or salaried workers, among whom poverty rates are on average one third or less those for casual labor.

In addition to lower wages, casual labor employment offers less stability than regular wage work. In India in 2009/10 (depending on the sector of employment), 31–49 percent of casual laborers, 8–23 percent of the self-employed (own- account and family helper), and 4–7 percent of regular wage or salaried workers reported spending at least one month looking for work in the past year. Casual laborers spent an average 0.9–1.4 months without work the past year. Self-employed workers reported 0.2–0.7 months of unemployment; regular wage or salaried workers reported virtually no time without work.[11]

It is more difficult to assess the quality of self-employment because there are no wage data and self-employed workers are a very heterogeneous group. The small proportion of workers classified as "high-end" self-employed have poverty rates that are similar to those of regular wage or salaried workers. Most self-employed workers—who are typically involved in small-scale enterprises (enterprises with no more than five workers) as own-account workers or family enterprise workers—have lower poverty rates than casual workers but higher rates than regular wage workers in India and Nepal. The India poverty assessment (World Bank 2011a) reports that only about half of nonfarm self-employed workers regard their earnings from self-employment as remunerative.

Analyzing the question from the point of view of the firm is more challenging because of the lack of nationally representative firm-level industrial data. Only India conducts national surveys that cover all firms in the manufacturing and services sectors, informal and formal, rural and urban. Based on the estimated level of informality and self-employment (especially own-account and family enterprise work) indicated in national labor force surveys, there is reason to believe that the statistics presented below for India are typical of other South Asian countries.[12]

Among Indian manufacturing and services, workers in larger formal firms earn higher wages, which reflect higher value added per worker. However, the majority of manufacturing and services employment is in micro/small informal firms, which have lower value added per worker and, hence, pay lower wages.

India's manufacturing sector

In 2005, 99 percent of the 17.1 million manufacturing firms in India were informal (the term used in India is *unorganized*); nearly all firms were micro/small enterprises (1–49 workers) (table 3.6). Even in the formal sector (referred to in India as the *organized sector*), 74 percent of firms were micro/small.[13] Seventy-one percent of all firms were rural.

Average productivity (value added per worker) and average wages are lower in smaller firms than in larger firms and much lower in informal firms than in formal firms the same size. Value added and wages per worker in formal firms with one to four employees are on average one-quarter the

TABLE 3.6   Distribution of formal and informal manufacturing firms in India, by location and size, 2005
(percent)

Firm characteristic	Formal sector	Informal sector	Total
Percentage of all firms	0.7	99.3	100.0
Location			
Urban	60.2	29.0	29.2
Rural	39.8	71.0	70.9
Firm size			
1–49	74.4	100.0	99.8
50–99	11.9	0.0	0.1
100+	13.7	0.0	0.1

Sources: Authors, based on data on formal firms from the Annual Survey of Industries and data on informal firms from the National Sample Survey manufacturing surveys.

levels of firms employing more than 200 workers (figure 3.16). Informal firms with one to four employees have 25 percent of the value added per worker and less than 50 percent of the wages per worker of formal firms the same size. Although productivity is lower in rural firms than in urban firms of the same size class and type, especially in the informal sector, real wages (adjusted using consumption-based household deflators rather than industry deflators) in rural and urban firms of the same size and type are similar.[14]

Although the firm size productivity/wage differential exists in other regions, it is particularly high in India. In East Asia (China; Indonesia; Korea; Malaysia; the Philippines; Taiwan, China; and Thailand), the productivity of small enterprises (enterprises with 5–49 workers) is about 20–40 percent that of enterprises with more than 200 workers (ADB 2009). In India, small firms have 12 percent of the productivity and pay 19 percent of the wages of large firms.

A number of factors may accounts for the firm size productivity/wage differentials observed everywhere: [15]

- Smaller and informal firms are less capital intensive. In India, for example, informal firms have less than a quarter of the capital per worker of formal firms in the same size class.

FIGURE 3.16   Average wage, value added, and capital per manufacturing worker in India, by firm size and type, 2005
(percentage of average wages/value added/capital per worker in formal firms with 200 or more employees)

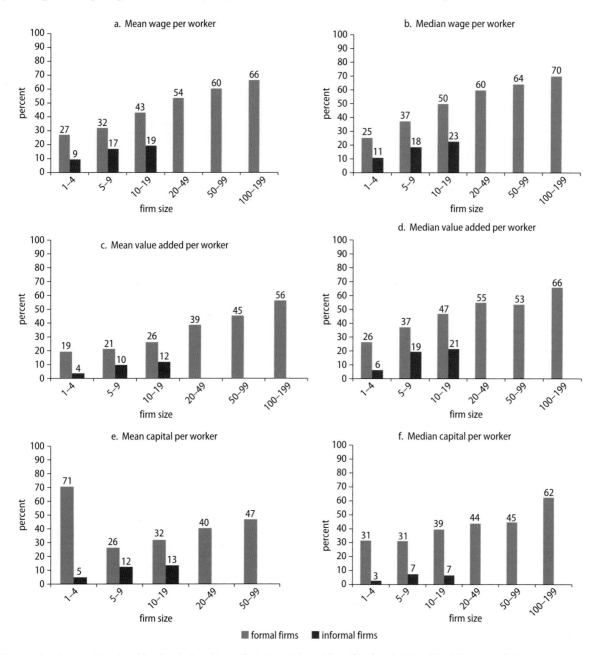

Sources: Authors, based on data on formal firms from the Annual Survey of Industries and data on informal firms from the National Sample Survey manufacturing surveys.
Note: Formal firms with 200 or more employees = 100 percent.

- Workers in larger formal enterprises are more skilled.
- Large formal enterprises are more productive with the labor and capital they have (their total factor productivity is higher),

perhaps as a result of economies of scale, and they may pay "efficiency wages" (higher than market-clearing wages paid to encourage higher output, raise worker morale, and discourage absenteeism and shirking).

Eighty-one percent of workers in India work in informal firms, and 83 percent of workers are in micro or small firms, with most working in own-account manufacturing enterprises with fewer than five workers. Combined with the large productivity and wage differentials observed, these figures translate into low-productivity and low-wage jobs for the majority of the 45.1 million manufacturing workers in India in 2005.

The distribution of employment across firm size groups has not shifted over time: the share of employment in micro/small firms and the informal sector in 2005 is almost the same as it was in 1994 (figure 3.17). Between 1994 and 2000, employment in the informal sector increased 4 percent a year, from 28.8 to 37.0 million, whereas employment in the formal sector remained stagnant at 7.7 million (employment in the largest firms actually fell 1 percent a year). Between 2000 and 2005, employment in the formal sector became more dynamic, growing at 3 percent a year to 8.7 million. At the same time, employment in the informal sector declined by 0.3 percent a year. The opposing dynamics of the two periods resulted in very similar share of employment in the informal sector and in micro/small firms in 1994 and 2005.

The share of employment in micro and small firms is much larger in India than it is in East Asia (figure 3.18). A number of factors can affect the enterprise size distribution, including industrial composition, infrastructure, product market segmentation, coordination failures, credit constraints for small firms, regulations that differ according to enterprise size, and industrial policy (ADB 2009). Lower-income countries tend to produce less complex goods, which are better suited to small-scale production.

Part but not all of India's concentration of employment in small firms can be explained

FIGURE 3.17   Share of manufacturing employment in India, by firm size and type, 1994–2005

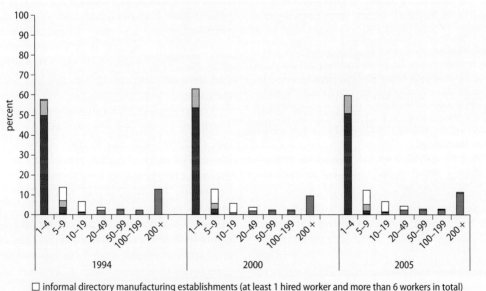

☐ informal directory manufacturing establishments (at least 1 hired worker and more than 6 workers in total)
▨ informal nondirectory manufacturing establishments (at least 1 hired worker but fewer than 6 workers in total)
■ informal own-account manufacturing enterprises (no hired workers)
▦ formal

Sources: Authors, based on data on formal firms from the Annual Survey of Industries and data on informal firms from the National Sample Survey manufacturing surveys.
Note: The data show a small share (1 percent or less) of informal employment in the larger firms as well.

FIGURE 3.18   Share of manufacturing employment by firm size in India and selected East Asian economies

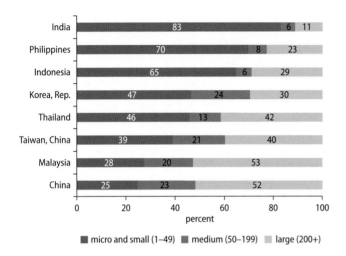

Sources: Authors, based on data from ADB 2009, India Annual Survey of Industries, and National Sample Survey manufacturing surveys.
Note: Data for India are for 2005. Data for East Asia data are for latest year available between 2004 and 2007.

by its level of income and industrial composition. For example, India's apparel industry is dominated by small firms, whereas China's industry is dominated by medium-size and large firms (ADB 2009). It is possible that past industrial policies in India, particularly the policy of reserving production of certain products for small-scale industries, which started in the late 1960s, has had significant effects on firm size distribution that are still being felt today.

Data from the Annual Survey of Industries since 2005 show continued dynamism in the growth of employment in the formal sector, suggesting that a *J*-curve effect may be at work: reforms in the 1990s led to an initial decline of employment in the formal sector in medium-size and large firms before increasing from 2000 onward (box 3.4). (National Sample Survey data on the informal sector are not available after 2005, making it impossible to analyze the growth of the informal manufacturing employment and determine how the overall distribution of manufacturing employment has evolved since then.)

India's service sector

India had 16.5 million services firms in 2006, 15 percent of which were establishments and 85 percent were own-account enterprises.[16] Ninety-eight percent of own-account enterprises and 73 percent of establishments have one to four workers, and nearly all firms are micro or small (table 3.7). In contrast to the manufacturing sector, India's service sector has very few establishments with 50 or more workers. Sixty percent of all services firms are rural.

Average productivity (value added per worker) and average wages are lower in smaller firms than in larger firms (figure 3.19). For example, mean wages at firms with fewer than 19 employees are 20–47 percent those of firms with 20–49 workers. Although the average wage monotonically increases with firm size, average productivity and capital per worker do not always increase among firms with 5–9 and firms with 10–19 employees.

Productivity and wages are also much lower in own-account enterprises firms than in establishments of the same size class. Own-account enterprises with one to four employees (the vast majority of such enterprises) have less than half the value added per worker and less than 15 percent of the mean wage per worker of establishments the same size. One reason for this differential is that own-account enterprises are less capital intensive.

An estimated 27.5 million workers were employed in the service sectors covered in India's 2006 National Sample Survey. Sixty percent of service workers worked in own-account enterprises and 40 percent in establishments. The majority of workers worked in lower-productivity and lower-wage micro firms (own-account enterprises and establishments with fewer than five workers). The concentration of employment in micro and small enterprises (enterprises with 1–49 workers) is even higher in the service sector (96 percent of workers) than in manufacturing (83 percent).

The employment pattern in services has not changed significantly over time, with the share of employment in micro/small and own-account enterprises remaining fairly stable between 2001 and 2006 (figure 3.20).

BOX 3.4   Trends in India's formal manufacturing sector, 1998–2007

Total employment in India's formal manufacturing sector follows a *U*-shaped path, declining from 1998, reaching a trough between 2001 and 2003, and growing rapidly thereafter. This path was driven by employment in large firms; employment in small and medium-size firms (enterprises employing fewer than 100 workers) was fairly stable through 2003 and grew thereafter.

The *U*-shaped pattern in employment can be explained by the large compositional change over the decade, with employment in nonprivate/state sector firms (mostly large firms) declining steadily and significantly as the public sector downsized. Initially, this pattern led to a decline in overall employment, as private sector employment remained stable through 2003. Beginning in 2003, private sector employment rapidly increased, more than offsetting the continuing decline in the state sector.

BOX FIGURE 3.4.1   Employment in India's formal manufacturing sector, by firm size, type, and location, 1998–2007

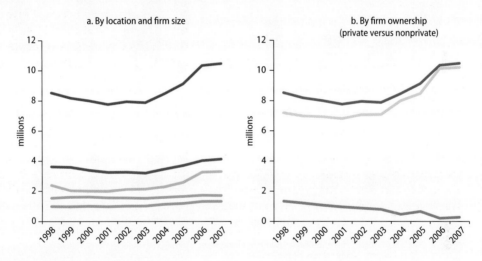

Source: Authors, based on data from Annual Survey of Industries.
Note: Annual data on the formal manufacturing sector are available for 1998–2007. The year refers to the reference period in the survey. For example, the reference period in the 2000/01 survey is the accounting year ending March 31, 2001. As three-quarters of the reference period fell in 2000, the survey is labeled 2000. SME = small to medium enterprise.

Employment in establishments increased 1.2 percent a year, from 10.7 million in 2001 to 11.4 million in 2006; employment in own-account enterprises increased 0.4 percent a year, from 15.9 to 16.2 million. Data after 2006 are not available.

Although industrial surveys with the same coverage of the manufacturing and service sectors are not available for other South Asian countries, other enterprise and firm surveys suggest a similar picture elsewhere. Rural nonfarm enterprise surveys conducted in Bangladesh, Pakistan, and Sri Lanka show large numbers of rural

TABLE 3.7   Distribution of service firms in India, by location and size, 2006
(percent)

Firm characteristic	Establishments	Own-account enterprises	Total
Percentage of all firms	14.7	85.3	100.0
Location			
Urban	63.0	36.1	40.0
Rural	37.0	63.9	60.0
Number of employees			
1–49	99.7	100.0	99.96
50–99	0.17	0.00	0.03
100 +	0.04	0.00	0.02

Source: Authors, based on data from National Sample Survey service sector surveys.

FIGURE 3.19   **Average wage, value added, and capital per service sector worker in India, by firm size and type, 2006**

(percentage of average wages/value added/ capital per workers in establishments with 20–49 employees)

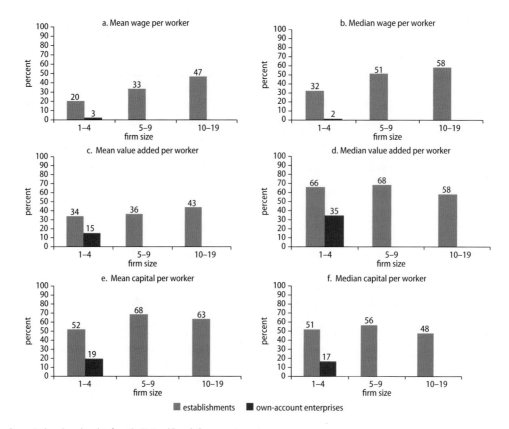

Source: Authors, based on data from the National Sample Survey service sector surveys.
Note: Establishments with 20–49 employees = 100 percent.

FIGURE 3.20   **Share of service sector employment in India, by firm size and type, 2001 and 2006**

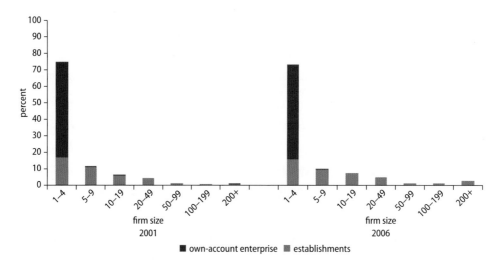

Source: Authors, based on data from the National Sample Survey service sector survey.
Note: Employment in 2006 excludes the financial intermediation sector, because the sector was not covered in 2001.

nonfarm enterprises and large numbers of workers employed in the sector. The majority of rural nonfarm enterprises are micro family enterprises with few hired workers, low use of capital, and lower productivity than urban formal firms.

Who holds better jobs?

This section examines the factors that affect access to better jobs in South Asia. These factors include education, gender, and caste and ethnicity.

Education

Education is an important determinant of access to better jobs. It is strongly correlated with the sector of employment in South Asian labor markets. Industry and services rely on workers who are considerably more educated than workers in agriculture (table 3.8). The average educational attainment is particularly high in service sector industries such as utilities, finance, and public administration. Although manufacturing and construction jobs do not usually require as much education as these service industries, their workforces have much more education than workers in agriculture.

Within industry and services, education is correlated with better jobs. Regular wage or salaried workers are more educated than self-employed or casual workers. Almost all have some education, and a significant proportion have secondary education or above. The self-employed are better educated than casual workers. The relative educational levels of employment types are found in both the urban and rural nonfarm sectors and across all South Asian countries (figure 3.21). These data suggest that education is an important determinant of access to better jobs and that lack of education is likely to be a barrier to mobility to moving into better jobs. (For an analysis of the effect of education on workers' ability to access and move into better jobs, see chapter 5.)

Gender

Labor force participation rates for women are low in South Asia, particularly in urban areas. Among women who do participate in the labor force, the majority live in rural areas, where 70 percent of South Asians of working age live. Most rural female workers are employed in traditional agricultural activities. The more modern and better-paid rural nonfarm sector employs mostly men. In all countries except Maldives, a higher percentage of male rural workers are in the nonfarm sector. Although more female rural workers are entering the

TABLE 3.8 **Average years of education in South Asian countries, by sector of employment**

Country/year	Agriculture	Mining	Manufacturing	Utilities	Construction	Commerce	Transport	Financial	Public administration	Other services
Afghanistan, 2008	0.9	1.9	1.4	—	2.0	3.5	3.5	—	9.8	4.2
Bhutan, 2007	0.9	3.8	3.5	8.2	4.2	4.2	4.3	9.9	5.7	7.2
India, 2010	4.1	6.1	6.4	10.1	4.4	7.7	6.9	12.9	11.2	9.7
Maldives, 2004	3.5	4.4	3.5	6.8	4.7	7.2	7.8	9.2	7.8	8.2
Nepal, 2008	3.1	2.9	4.5	6.3	3.5	6.2	5.4	9.6	9.8	9.6
Pakistan, 2008	2.7	5.5	5.7	10.4	4.0	6.8	5.6	11.7	9.9	9.9
Sri Lanka, 2008	7.1	7.6	9.4	10.9	8.6	9.3	9.9	12.2	11.6	10.9
South Asia unweighted mean	3.2	4.6	4.9	8.8	4.5	6.4	6.2	10.9	9.4	8.5

Source: Authors, based on data from national labor force and household surveys.
Note: Bangladesh is not included, because its surveys do not permit comparable calculations. — = Not available.

FIGURE 3.21   **Percentage of workers with some education and percentage of workers with secondary education or above in South Asia, by employment type and country**

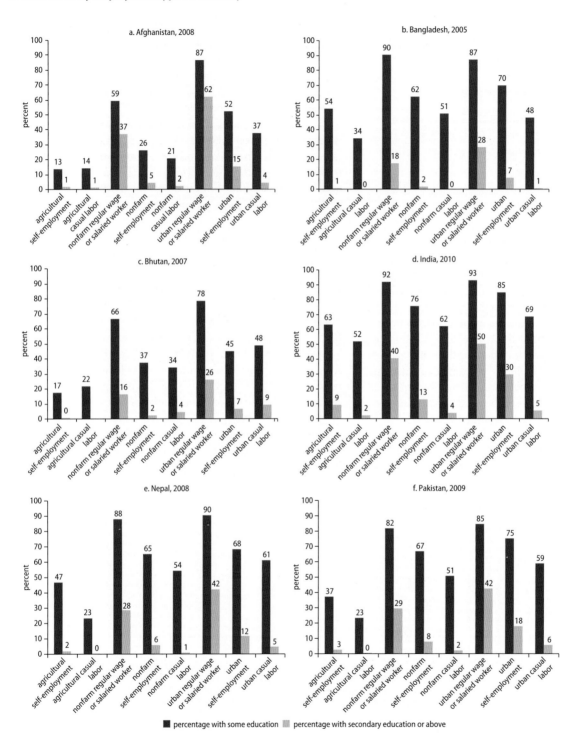

Source: Authors, based on data from national labor force and household surveys.

sector, the gender gap has widened over time, increasing from 10 percentage points in 1983 to 16 percentage points in 2010 in India, for example (figure 3.22).

A cohort analysis for India, Nepal, and Pakistan provides further evidence that women are generally stuck in agriculture across all countries in the region (figure 3.23). This analysis tracks participation in the rural nonfarm sector for the same age groups of male and female workers for 8–10 years beginning in 1999/2000.

Several findings emerge. First, for every age cohort, women were less likely than men to work in the rural nonfarm sector. Second, younger men were more likely than older men to leave agriculture for the nonfarm sector and stay there. In all countries, the cohort of men that was 15–24 in 1999/2000 had the largest share of nonfarm labor by 2009/10 (40–55 percent), followed by the 25–34 cohort. Among men in cohorts other than 15–24, and in some cases 25–34, the share of workers in the nonfarm sector by the end of the period declined or remained the same. Third, younger women were more likely than older women to exit agriculture in India

and Nepal, but less than 30 percent of rural women in India and less than 20 percent in Nepal worked in the nonfarm sector at the end of the period.

A multinomial logit analysis that looks at the determinants of labor participation and occupational choice shows that among workers with less than upper-secondary education, men are more likely than women to hold regular wage jobs within the rural nonfarm and urban sectors. In contrast, female workers with upper-secondary education are more likely than male workers to hold regular wage jobs (see chapter 5). Given the small percentage of women who participate in the labor force, the share of working-age women in better jobs is still much lower than the share of working-age men in better jobs, even at the highest levels of education.

The lower level of educational attainment among women is one reason why they are less likely than men to be in better jobs. More than half of the female workforce in five of the eight countries in the region has no education. Occupational segregation and lower pay for the same jobs and qualifications are other likely factors.

FIGURE 3.22   **Percentage of rural workers in the rural nonfarm sector in South Asia, by gender and country**

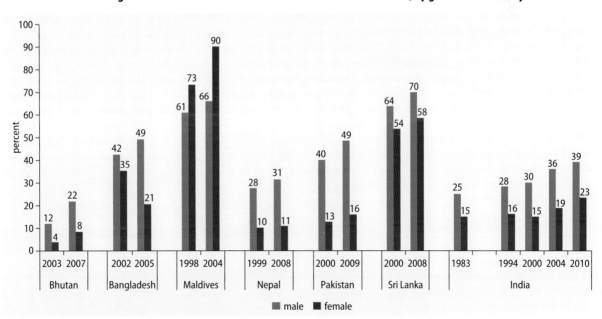

Source: Authors, based on data from national labor force and household surveys.

FIGURE 3.23 **Percentage of rural workers in the rural nonfarm sector in India, Nepal, and Pakistan, by gender and age cohort, 1999–2009/10**

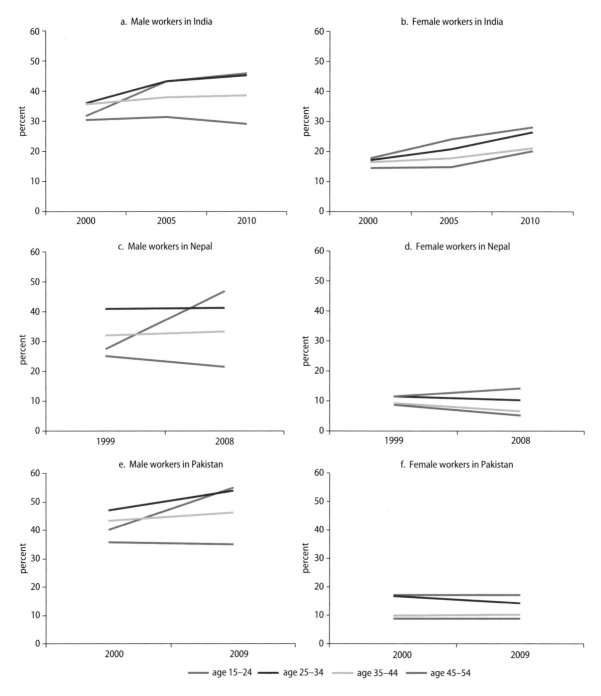

Source: Authors, based on data from national labor force and household surveys.
Note: The age cohort refers to the age of the cohort in the earliest period, that is, the line of the cohort of age 15–24 in India refers to the same cohort group: the cohort that was 15–24 years old in 2000.

Women earn wages that are 20–40 percent lower than those of men, even after controlling for education levels, type of employment, and other individual and household characteristics associated with productivity. This result holds true for all countries and almost all types of wage employment. The lower wages could be a result of unobserved or unmeasured characteristics in the wage regressions; they are also consistent with some other type of discrimination in the market that is not associated with productivity differentials. If discrimination in the labor market is a major factor behind the observed wage gap, a policy focus on increasing the skill levels of women will not be sufficient.

It is important to determine how much of the observed wage gap is a result of productive characteristics, such as education. The technique proposed by Blinder and Oaxaca (1973) has been used to decompose the wage gap into the part explained by differences in levels of observable characteristics (including education) and the part not explained by these differences. The unexplained portion reflects in part differences in returns to skills.[17] Figure 3.24 plots the decomposition for rural and urban workers for all survey years. It indicates that part of the wage gap is the result of differences in observable productive characteristics but that most of the wage gap is unexplained.

FIGURE 3.24 **Decomposition of wage gap between male and female workers in South Asia, by country**

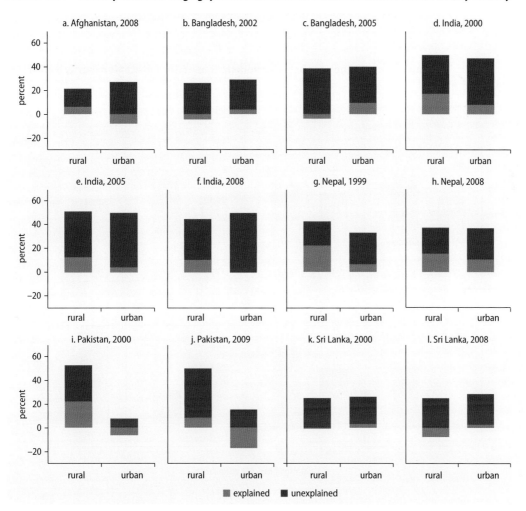

Source: Authors, based on data from national labor force and household surveys.

Caste and ethnicity

Caste and ethnicity have long been important factors shaping employment in South Asia. Female labor force participation and employment rates in India, Nepal, and Sri Lanka vary by ethnic/caste groups.

The multinomial logit analysis shows that workers from ethnic minority groups, particularly women, are less likely to be in better jobs even after controlling for education and other factors. Among men in rural areas, members of ethnic minority groups are more likely to be involved in agriculture. In urban areas, men from ethnic minority groups are more likely to be involved in casual work and self-employment.

Similar trends appear for women, and the differences appear larger in magnitude.

Women are more likely to work, particularly in rural areas, if they belong to an ethnic minority. Among women who work, women from ethnic minority groups are more likely to be in casual or self-employment in urban areas and agriculture in rural areas.

Ethnic minority groups earn lower wages than other groups, after controlling for education levels and employment type. The difference, though smaller in size than gender differentials, appears significant in India but not in Nepal.[18]

The results of the decomposition of the wage differential show that in India and Nepal, much of the wage gap is explained by differences in observable characteristics, including education (figure 3.25). In contrast, in Sri Lanka most of the wage differential is unexplained.

FIGURE 3.25   **Decomposition of wage gaps between nonethnic minority and ethnic minority workers in India, Nepal, and Sri Lanka**

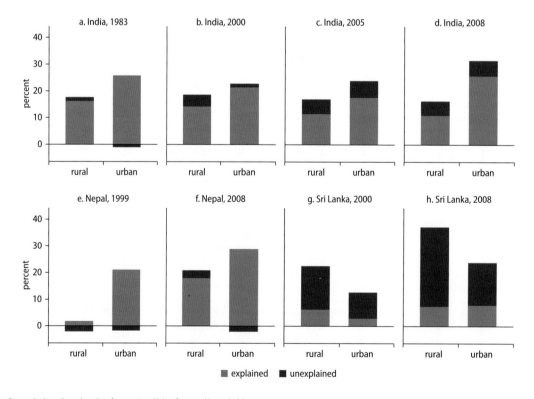

Source: Authors, based on data from national labor force and household surveys.

Annex 3A   Definitions and criteria used in profile of South Asia at work

Definitions of employment and unemployment

Table 3A.1 provides the specific definitions for employment and unemployment used for each country based on the national surveys.

Criteria used to define formal and informal workers

Table 3A.2 provides information on how the national surveys are used to estimate informal employment for each country.

TABLE 3A.1   **Definition of employment and unemployment used based on national surveys**

Country	Year	Definition of employment	Definition of unemployment (for people who are not employed)
Afghanistan	2007/08	In past 30 days, did any one of the following: • Worked for any organization or any individual • Performed any agricultural work, even without pay, on land owned, rented, or used by household • Performed any nonagricultural work, on own account, in a business enterprise • Performed occasional paid work, such as helping someone in his or her business • Has a permanent or long-term job from which he or she will be temporarily absent	In past 30 days, did any of the following: • Attempted to find a job or start a business • Found a job that has not yet started • Awaited recall from an employer
Bangladesh	2002/03	In past seven days, did either of the following: • Worked for at least one hour on any day for pay or profit, family gain, or final use or consumption • Even if did not work in past seven days, has a job, business, enterprise, or attachment to a job such as a business, farm, or shop	• Was available for work in past seven days and tried to find a job during past two months
	2005/06	Same as Bangladesh 2002	In past seven days, did any of the following: • Was prepared for and tried to find a job • Was waiting for reappointment • Was waiting to start work after appointment
	2009	In past seven days, did either of the following: • Engaged in any economic activity for at least one hour as paid worker, for family gain or profit, or own use or consumption • Was temporarily absent from work	• In past seven days, looked for job
Bhutan	2003	In past seven days, did any of the following: • Any farming, fishing, hunting, or gathering of fruits • Worked for money or have profitable business • Performed unpaid work on enterprise or farm of friends or relatives	In past seven days, did any of the following: • Actively looked for a job or tried to start a new business • Was waiting for a job to start • Was waiting for employer's reply
	2007	Same as 2003	In past seven days, did any of the following: • Actively looked for a job or tried to start a new business • Did not actively look for a job because was waiting for employer's reply • Did not actively look for a job because was waiting for employers recall

(continues next page)

TABLE 3A.1   Definition of employment and unemployment used based on national surveys (continued)

Country	Year	Definition of employment	Definition of unemployment (for people who are not employed)
India	1999/2000, 2004/05, 2007/08, and 2009/10	In past seven days, did any of the following: • Worked or helped in household enterprise • Worked as regular or casual wage labor • Was involved in public or other works	• In past seven days, sought work and/or was available for work
Maldives	1998 and 2004	In past 30 days, did either of the following: • Was involved in economic activity most of the time • Engaged in any activity that generated income	• Not currently working because unable to find a suitable job, but if hired, would be available to work
Nepal	1998/99 and 2007/08	In past 7 days, did either of the following: • Was involved at least one week in any economic activities • Did not work but have a permanent job he or she will return to	In past 7 days, did either of the following: • Was available and looked for work in past 30 days • Awaited reply on earlier inquiries or start of prearranged job or business
Pakistan	1999/2000 and 2008/09	In past 7 days, did any of the following: • Performed any work for pay, profit, or family gain during for one hour on any day • Did not work but has a job or enterprise to return to • Worked/helped in family business or family farm for family gain	In past 7 days, did any of the following: • Looked for job • Did not work but will take a job within a month • Was temporarily laid off and awaiting recall
Sri Lanka	2000	In past 7 days, did either of the following: • Engaged in economic activity during past 7 days • Did not engage in economic activity but had an economic activity to return to	In past 7 days, was available or looking for work.
	2008	In past 7 days, did either of the following: • Engaged in economic activity • Had an economic activity to return to	• Already obtained a job or made arrangements to start self-employment activity OR • Took some steps to find a job or start self-employment activity within the last four weeks OR • Awaited results of interview for work

Source: Authors' compilation.

TABLE 3A.2   Definition of formal and informal workers used based on national surveys

Country	Year	Informal workers	Formal workers
Afghanistan	2007/08	• Daily laborers	• Workers in public sector • Workers who receive pensions
Bangladesh	2002/03	• Casual workers and day laborers • Domestic workers • Workers in private informal sector	• Workers in public sector • Workers in private or nongovernmental formal sector
	2005/06	• Domestic workers and apprentices • Workers working in personal households • Casual workers and day laborers	• Workers in public sector • Workers in private formal sector
Bhutan	2003	a	• Workers in public sector
	2007	• Casual paid employees	• Workers in public sector
India	1999/2000	• Workers in firms that do not keep written accounts • Workers in firms with fewer than 10 employees	• Workers in public and semipublic sector • Workers covered under a provident fund • Workers in firms that keep written accounts • Workers in firms with more than 10 employees

(continues next page)

TABLE 3A.2   **Definition of formal and informal workers used based on national surveys** (continued)

Country	Year	Informal workers	Formal workers
	2004/05 and 2009/10	• Casual workers • Workers without written contracts • Workers working in firms with fewer than 10 employees • Workers not receiving any social security benefits	• Workers in public sector • Workers receiving social security benefits • Workers with written job contracts • Workers in firms with more than 10 employees
Maldives	2004	a	• Workers in public sector
Nepal	1998/99	• Workers in unregistered organizations • Workers in firms with fewer than 10 employees	• Workers in public sector • Workers in firms with 10 or more employees
	2007/08	• Workers who are not eligible for paid leave and do not receive social security contributions • Workers in establishments with fewer than 10 employees	• Workers in public sector • Workers for whom employers pay social security contributions • Workers who are eligible for paid leave • Workers working in establishments with 10 or more employees
Pakistan	1999/2000 and 2008/09	• Casual and day laborers • Workers in enterprises that do not keep written accounts • Workers in establishments with fewer than 10 employees	• Workers in public sector • Workers in enterprises that keep written accounts • Workers in establishments with 10 or more employees
Sri Lanka	2000	• Daily laborers	• Workers in public sector
	2008	• Casual workers • Workers whose employers do not contribute to pension scheme or provident fund and do not provide paid annual leave • Workers in unregistered enterprise • Workers in enterprise that does not maintain formal written accounts • Workers in firms with fewer than 10 employees	• Workers in public sector • Workers for whom employer contributes to pension scheme or provident fund or provides paid leave • Workers in registered enterprise • Workers in enterprise that maintains formal written accounts • Workers in firms with 10 or more employees

Source: Authors' compilation.
Note: All family enterprise workers are in the informal sector. All self-employed workers with less than senior-secondary education are considered informal, and all self-employed individuals with higher education are considered formal. All workers involved in agriculture are informal. Some workers could not be identified as formal or informal. In all countries except Maldives, the unclassified portion was 10 percent or less. In Maldives 32 percent could not be classified. For the subsample of workers that could not be identified as formal or informal in each country, their status was allocated according to the formal/informal split for the employment that could be classified. The assumption that the distribution of formality/informality is the same for classified and unclassified workers may lead to some overestimation of informality, as the classified portion includes some block assignments, such as agriculture to the informal sector. Because the unidentified portion is small in most countries, this should not be a major issue, except perhaps in Maldives. a = No additional criteria specific to the survey.

Annex 3B   Regional employment patterns

Figure 3B.1 shows how employment rates vary within each of the South Asian countries. The overall picture is one of relatively moderate differences in regional rates. Unweighted coefficients of variations are 5–10 percent for all countries except Afghanistan, where regional differences are much larger. For all countries except Afghanistan, the range is fairly narrow: in most cases, the difference in employment rates between the regions with the highest and lowest rates is only about 10 percentage points. Although the disparities in employment rates may not be large, there are major differences in the nature and quality of employment across regions (for example, the share of employment that is in the formal wage-earning sector).

FIGURE 3B.1   Regional variations in employment rate in South Asia, by country

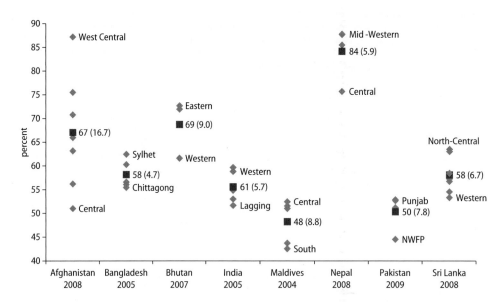

Source: Authors, based on data from national labor force and household surveys.
Note: Each diamond represents the employment rate in a region. The regions with the highest and lowest employment rates are named. Each box represents the average employment rate of all regions in the country; figures in parentheses are coefficients of variation, calculated as the standard deviation of the regional employment rates normalized by the mean of these rates.

Notes

1. The labor force participation rate and the employment rate in India in 2009/10 were 56.6 percent and 54.8 percent, respectively. There is a sharp decline from 2004/05, leading to only a very small increase (in absolute terms) in the labor force and total employment between 2004/05 and 2009/10. The decline has been driven by a sharp fall in female labor force participation and employment rates (male rates have also declined, but far less sharply), which led to a significant decrease in rural female labor force and employment in absolute terms. The decline in female participation was observed in all age groups including school age cohorts (15–19 years old and 20–24 years old) but also older cohorts. Rural female employment declined particularly in agriculture. Self-employment declined both in number and as a share of total employment, while casual wage labor accounted for nearly 80 percent of net additional employment in those sectors that expanded employment between 2004/05 and 2009/10. Usual subsidiary employment rates

(identified as activity pursued by the individual for a relatively minor time, but not less than 30 days during the past year) fell sharply compared to previous years. Usual principal employment status (defined on the basis of the activity pursued for the longest—major—time during the reference year) only experienced a modest decline. The reasons for the decline in labor force participation and employment rates remain to be analyzed fully, but possible reasons include (a) younger workers, especially women, staying longer in education; (b) rising family incomes reducing the need for women to work; and (c) shocks in the agriculture sector. It is important to note that over the longer period between 1983 and 2010 labor force participation and employment rates have increased and decreased without a consistent trend, although the employment and participation rates in 2010 are lower than in any previous period. Using current weekly status, the labor force participation rate was 59.7 percent, 62.0 percent, 60.4 percent, 62.2 percent, and 56.6 percent in 1983, 1994, 2000, 2005, and 2010, respectively, and the employment rate was 57.5 percent,

60.1 percent, 58.2 percent, 59.8 percent, and 54.8 percent in 1983, 1994, 2000, 2005, and 2010, respectively. It may thus be premature to see the past five years as necessarily being evidence of a longer-term trend.

2. In the absence of better questions in the survey in Maldives, the criterion "available for work, conditional on getting a job" was use to define unemployment. This criterion, which is much broader than that used in other countries, yielded a much higher unemployment rate.

3. This measure, based on current weekly status questions, is an adjusted version of the definition of underemployment used by the National Commission for Enterprises in the Unorganised Sector (2009).

4. Using household survey data, Srinivasan (2010) reviews labor market indicators over the longer term for Bangladesh (from 1983/84), India (from 1972/73), and Pakistan (from 1990). He finds that female participation rates in Bangladesh rose from 8 percent to 30 percent between 1983/84 and 2005/06, female participation rates in India were positive in rural but not urban areas, and female participation in Pakistan has been essentially stagnant since 1990.

5. The informality shares in figure 3.11 are similar to those in Chen and Doane (2008).

6. For example, more than a third of total employment in the Republic of Korea is informal (OECD 2007).

7. Based on the definition of informality used in this book, there is no clear pattern of increasing or decreasing informality. In Bangladesh (2002–05), India (2000–05), and Pakistan (2000–09), there have been no significant changes. In Maldives (1998–2004) and Sri Lanka (2000–08), informal employment declined significantly. In Bhutan (2003–07) and Nepal (1998–2008), it increased significantly. However, because the concepts used to measure informality changed from the earlier to the later year in the countries in which changes were observed, it is not clear how much of the observed increase or decrease was real. In Bangladesh and Pakistan, where there was no change in the way of measuring informality, no change in the degree of informality was observed. Other studies, using alternative definitions, have found increasing informality in India (NCEUS 2009).

8. Poverty rates for India are based on the official poverty lines prevailing until 2010. Using the new official poverty lines for 2004/05 (revised in 2011) would increase the poverty rates in rural areas, causing rural poverty rates to exceed urban workers for the same employment type. The hierarchy in terms of employment type would remain the same, however: agricultural casual labor would have the highest poverty rate, followed by rural nonfarm casual labor and urban casual labor. Agricultural and rural nonfarm self-employment would have higher poverty rates than urban self-employment. The lowest poverty rates would be among urban regular wage or salaried workers.

9. Results are based on regressions for each country-survey year. Log hourly wages were regressed on individual and household characteristics, including educational attainment and sector and type of employment.

10. All casual labor is classified as informal in this book. Some regular wage work is also classified as informal (see annex table 3A.2 for details of definition used in each country's labor force survey).

11. The India poverty assessment (World Bank 2011a, p. 133) also highlights the transient nature of rural nonfarm casual labor work: "Casual workers tend not to have year-round employment and make ends meet by working at several jobs, often combining agricultural and nonfarm activities. In 2004/05, more than half (55 percent) of casual nonfarm workers report that they are without work for one or more months in the year compared to 8 percent of salaried workers or 12 percent of self-employed. Fourteen percent of casual nonfarm workers report that they were seeking or available for additional employment even when working."

12. Estimates from labor force surveys of informality in the nonagricultural sector indicate that Afghanistan, Pakistan, and Nepal have a higher proportion of informal nonagricultural employment (about 80 percent) than Bangladesh (74 percent), India (72 percent), and Sri Lanka (68 percent).

13. "Organized" (formal) manufacturing firms are registered firms, typically with more than 10 workers. The most commonly used definition of the unorganized (informal) sector flows from the Indian Factories Act (1948), which

requires that an enterprise register with the state government if it employs 10 or more workers and uses power or employs 20 or more workers and does not use power. Units that do not come under the purview of this law constitute the unorganized sector. Businesses that are organized are required to comply with health, safety, and welfare requirements. Firms are required to contribute toward insurance against sickness, disability, and maternity and to deposit linked provident funds or pension schemes. The state monitors compliance through a system of inspections. Unorganized firms largely fall outside this system. The unorganized manufacturing sector comprises own-account manufacturing enterprises, directory manufacturing enterprises, and nondirectory manufacturing enterprises subcategories. Own-account manufacturing enterprises are informal firms that operate without any hired worker employed on a regular basis. Nondirectory manufacturing establishments are informal firms that employ fewer than six workers (with at least one hired worker); directory manufacturing establishments employ six or more workers (with at least one hired worker). Ninety-nine percent of unorganized manufacturing firms have fewer than 10 workers.

14. Among firms in the formal sector, real wages are slightly higher in rural firms than urban firms of the same size class. Among firms with one to nine employees in the informal sector (the vast majority of the unorganized sector), wages in urban and rural unorganized firms are very similar.

15. Assessing the contribution of each factor is challenging, given the difficulty in matching information across workers and firms. For example, the industrial surveys for India, which provide firm productivity and wage data, do not survey the education and skills levels of workers. See ADB (2009) for a discussion of firm-size wage differentials.

16. The National Sample Survey service sector survey classifies firms as either establishments or own-account enterprises. Own-account enterprises do not employ hired workers on a regular basis; establishments do. Own-account enterprises belong to the informal sector; establishments are a mix of informal and formal sector firms. As services firms are not required to register under the Factories Act unless they are engaged in manufacturing, most private sector service enterprises, whether small or large, are officially in the informal sector. The service sector survey covers service firms in rural and urban locations for a large number of service sectors but excludes trade. Dehejia and Panagariya (2010) estimate that the survey covers about half of output and employment in the service sector.

17. This interpretation becomes problematic if the observable characteristics are improperly measured or omitted or unobservable characteristics, such as motivation, could be influencing wages. Such characteristics will bias the results if the errors and omissions are systematically different for men and women.

18. Ethnic minorities are scheduled caste and tribes in India and Dalits and Janajatis in Nepal.

References

ADB (Asian Development Bank). 2009. *Enterprises in Asia: Fostering Dynamism in SMEs.* Manila.

Chen, M., and D. Doane. 2008. "Informality in South Asia: A Review." Background working paper for the Swedish International Development Cooperation Agency (Sida), Sweden.

Dehejia, R., and A. Panagariya. 2010. "Services Growth in India: A Look inside the Black Box." Working Paper 2010-4, Columbia University, Program on Indian Economic Policies, New York.

Government of India. 2006. *Employment and Unemployment Situation in India 2004–05 National Sample Survey 61st Round.* Ministry of Statistics and Programme Implementation, National Sample Survey Office, New Delhi.

ILO (International Labour Office). 2002. *Women and Men in the Informal Economy: A Statistical Picture.* Geneva: International Labour Office.

———. 2010. *Accelerating Action against Child Labour: Global Report under the Follow-Up to the ILO Declaration on Fundamental Principles and Rights at Work.* Geneva: International Labor Office.

———. 2011. *Key Indicators of the Labour Market.* Geneva: International Labour Office.

Islamic Republic of Afghanistan, and World Bank. 2010. *Poverty Status in Afghanistan: A Profile Based on the National Risk and Vulnerability Assessment (NRVA) 2007/08.* Ministry of Economy, Kabul, and Economic Policy and Poverty Sector, Washington, DC.

Loayza, M., and T. Wada. 2011. "Informality in South Asia." Background study conducted for this book.

Mukherjee, A., and X. Zhang. 2007. "Rural Industrialisation in China and India: Role of Policies and Institutions." *World Development* 35 (10): 1621–34.

National Commission for Enterprises in the Unorganised Sectors. 2009. *The Challenge of Employment in India: An Informal Economy Perspective*. New Delhi.

OECD (Organisation for Economic Co-operation and Development). 2007. "Labour Markets in Brazil, China, India and Russia and Recent Labour Market Developments and Prospects in OECD Countries." *OECD Employment Outlook*. Paris.

Rahman, R. I. 2008. "A Review of Open Unemployment and Underemployment Concepts: Measurement, Methods, and Application" (in Bengali with title "Unmukto Bekaratta O Angshik Bekaratta Dharanar Porjalochana, Parimap Paddhati O Proiog"). Bangladesh Unnayan Shamikkha, Golden Jubilee Number.

Volume 26. Bangladesh Institute of Development Studies, Dhaka.

Srinivasan, T. N. 2010. "The Utilization of Labor in South Asia." Background study conducted for this book.

UN (United Nations). 2010. *World Population Prospects: The 2010 Revision*. New York: United Nations.

Wang, X., J., Huang, and L. Zhang, 2011. "Creating the Entrepreneur Farmers Needed Yesterday, Today and Tomorrow." Paper presented at the International Fund for Agricultural Development (IFAD) conference on new directions for smallholder agriculture, Rome.

World Bank. 2010. *India's Employment Challenge: Creating Jobs, Helping Workers*. India: Oxford University Press.

———. 2011a. *Perspectives on Poverty in India: Stylized Facts from Survey Data*. Washington, DC: World Bank.

———. 2011b. *World Development Indicators*. Washington, DC: World Bank.

———. 2012. *World Development Report: Gender Equality and Development*. Washington, DC: World Bank.

Questions and Findings

Questions

- What are the business environment constraints affecting firms in South Asia?
- Do these constraints vary by sector and firm characteristics?
- What are the main policy priorities for overcoming the identified business constraints?

Findings

The chapter identifies constraints facing firms and four areas of policy focus.

Constraints

- The most binding constraints facing all types of urban formal firms (where the highest-productivity and highest-paid jobs are) are electricity, corruption, and political instability. Job-creating firms are more severely affected than other firms by virtually the entire range of constraints. Labor regulations rank high in India, Nepal, and Sri Lanka.
- The rural nonfarm sector is an important route out of low-paid agricultural work. For firms in this sector, electricity and political instability also rank high on the list of constraints. Transport (poor road quality and inaccessibility) ranks much higher as a constraint for rural firms, as it affects access to larger markets.
- Increasing the productivity of informal firms is fundamental, as they employ the majority of workers. Electricity is the top constraint for informal urban firms in India. Relative to formal urban firms, they are less concerned about corruption, taxes, and labor regulations and more concerned about access to land.
- Firms cite inadequate access to finance as one of the top five constraints in every sector; this constraint is particularly severe for informal firms. However, without information on whether inadequate finance reflects the lack of bankable projects, one cannot infer directly that access to finance is a binding constraint. Other evidence suggests that access to finance may be an issue for micro and small firms in some countries.

Policy focus areas

- The severity of the electricity constraint for all types of firms reflects the large gap in the region between demand for and supply of power. Closing the gap requires a substantial increase in investment, which in turn requires that power sector reforms be sustained and deepened.
- South Asian firms face high levels of corruption in a range of interactions with public officials, particularly for utilities and tax inspections. Simplifying processes in, for example, tax administration and reducing unnecessary interaction with local officials could be an effective way of tackling corruption, as it has the additional benefit of reducing the cost of red tape on firms.
- Key policy options for improving access to finance for micro and small firms include strengthening the institutional environment (secured transactions registry, credit information); creating a conducive environment for downscaling commercial banks and upscaling microfinance institutions; and providing financial literacy and training to micro and small firms.
- Easing business registration could benefit potential firm entrants. Significant improvements in the registration process would help entrepreneurs who were previously in wage employment or out of the labor force start new activities and create new employment.

What Is Preventing Firms from Creating More and Better Jobs? | 4

This chapter looks at the constraints faced by South Asian firms in the manufacturing and service sectors where, as shown in chapter 3, jobs are more productive and better paid. Addressing constraints to the operations of firms in these sectors is therefore important for creating more and better jobs.

The chapter is organized as follows. The first section describes the methodological framework. The second section looks at constraints facing firms in the urban formal sector. The third section extends the analysis to the rural nonfarm and urban informal sectors. The fourth section suggests policy options for overcoming the most binding constraints. The last section examines the regulatory constraints faced by potential firm entrants.

Methodological framework

This chapter is based on findings from three background studies by Carlin and Schaffer (2011a, 2011b, 2011c), who draw on 30 country enterprise surveys, covering more than 26,000 firms, conducted in South Asia between 2000 and 2010.[1] The methodological approach taken to identify binding business environment constraints uses the reported severity of constraints and reported mitigation behaviors by firms in the enterprise surveys. The business environment is considered external to the firm; its components resemble public goods and are considered common to all firms in the economy.

All enterprise surveys include a standard question that asks firms to rate the severity of different business environment constraints.[2] The question takes the form: "How much of an obstacle is X to the operation and growth of your business?" The firm's response regarding its severity, rated on a five-point scale, with 0 being no obstacle and 4 being a very severe obstacle, is a measure of the marginal cost imposed by the constraint on the operation and growth of its business. The cost can be interpreted as the difference between the firm's profit in the hypothetical situation in which the business environment poses no obstacle to the firm's operations and the firm's actual profit given the existing quality of the business environment.

Differences in firms' perceptions of the severity of constraints and mitigation behaviors reflect the different costs of the constraint to firms, which may reflect differences in the quality of the business environment faced by firms or differences in the firms' characteristics. Differences in firm characteristics are more likely if the business environment is shared. For example, almost all firms in

Afghanistan, Bangladesh, and Nepal report at least one power cut per month, but the valuations of the electricity constraint vary across firms. A higher-productivity firm should report higher severity of a constraint than a lower-productivity firm, because the marginal cost/forgone profits are higher. The data confirm this prediction.

In addition to subjective perceptions of the severity of constraints, this chapter examines objective measures, such as the frequency of power outages and mitigation behaviors, including the use of generators and payment of bribes. Mitigation behaviors are a firm's reaction to the poor quality of the business environment. According to Carlin and Schaffer's methodological framework (2011c), expenditures on mitigation behavior are decreasing in the quality of the external business environment (the better the environment, the less mitigation is needed) and increasing in the productivity of the firm (more productive firms undertake more mitigation actions, because their marginal costs/forgone profits are higher). The findings from these objective measures are largely consistent with those from the analysis of subjective constraints: countries in which firms report higher severity of the electricity constraint also report higher frequency of power outages.

The average reported severity of constraints and the average reported level of mitigation activities are measured for a "benchmark firm" in each country individually and for the region as a whole (by pooling the country sample data), in order to account for differences in the composition of firms in the enterprise surveys and facilitate cross-country comparisons. A benchmark firm is a medium-size manufacturing firm with 30 employees that is domestically owned, does not export or import, is located in a large city, and did not expand employment in the preceding three years. The reported severity of each element of the business environment was regressed on the firm's characteristics. Hence, the average reported severity of a constraint for a benchmark firm is a conditional mean for the period covered by the surveys available for each country (2000–10). The country surveys were pooled across time to generate

sufficiently large samples to analyze. The sample size of individual surveys generally did not allow analysis of how the reported severity of constraints changed over time.

The ranking of constraints for individual countries as well as the region as a whole guides the prioritization of constraints to tackle. Some countries, notably India, report lower absolute levels of severity of constraints across the board. It is unlikely that there are no significant business environment constraints in India. Therefore, it is important to look at the ranking of constraints, not just the reported absolute severity level.

The average severity of constraints reported by a benchmark firm in the urban formal sector is compared across countries at similar levels of per capita gross domestic product (GDP).[3] These data indicate whether the severity reported by South Asian firms is greater than expected given their country's level of development.

The framework reveals how the reported level of severity (and ranking) of constraints and mitigation activities varies for nonbenchmark firms (for example, how the reported severity of constraints changes with firm size, sector, location, formality, history of job creation, and so forth). This book is particularly interested in firms that expanded employment in the past three years (job-creating firms), because identifying and addressing constraints to their operations and growth is likely to lead to the creation of more and better jobs.

Application of methodology to rural nonfarm and informal firms

One of the main drawbacks of standard enterprise surveys is that their sampling frames are generally limited to the formal urban sector. This bias is problematic in South Asia, given the high levels of informality. Enterprise surveys also omit the rural nonfarm sector, an important source of better jobs in South Asia. The constraints analysis is conducted here for four South Asian countries that conducted enterprise surveys of the rural nonfarm and informal sectors.

For the rural nonfarm sector, the analysis examines the severity of constraints reported by a benchmark firm in Bangladesh, Pakistan, and Sri Lanka, where rural enterprise surveys have been conducted.[4] These results are then compared with those of an urban benchmark firm in these countries.

For the urban informal sector, the severity of constraints reported by benchmark firms is compared with that of the urban formal sector. (The informal survey in India was the only one with a large enough sample size to facilitate this comparison. The comparison is therefore limited to India's formal and informal urban manufacturing sector.[5])

Rural nonfarm and informal sector firms are typically microenterprises: in the surveys, the median employment in rural nonfarm sector firms in Bangladesh, Pakistan, and Sri Lanka is 1.5 (compared with a median of 35 employees in the urban formal sector in these countries); in India, the median employment in the informal (urban) survey is 4 (compared with 20 for all firms in the urban formal sector). As the median size of firms in the rural and informal sectors is much smaller, the benchmark firm in the rural nonfarm and informal sector analyses is defined as having five employees.[6]

In the analysis of the rural nonfarm and informal sectors, the focus is on the constraints to the benchmark firm, which is a nonexpanding firm. The average rural and informal sector firm reported very little employment growth:

- In the Bangladesh rural survey, 81 percent of firms experienced no growth in employment between 2005 and 2007 (World Bank 2008c).
- In the survey of informal firms conducted in India in 2005, 40 percent of firms had not grown since they started operations (Ferrari and Dhingra 2009).
- In the Sri Lanka rural survey, 90 percent of firms had not increased employment the previous year (World Bank 2005).

For this reason, it was not possible to analyze the constraints facing an expanding firm in these sectors.

Even if addressing the constraints reported for a benchmark firm in the rural nonfarm and informal sectors does not lead to substantial creation of new jobs, it is still important for increasing the productivity and job quality of a large proportion of existing workers in manufacturing and services.

Limitations of the methodology

The methodology allows the costs of different business environment constraints to be assessed and compared. Two constraints that many firms in South Asia frequently report as severe—access to finance and tax rates—cannot be analyzed in the same framework as the others, as neither has the character of a public good. Even when the finance system is working well, one would expect that access to finance would be a constraint to potential borrowers with low-quality projects. Indeed, less productive firms report more severe problems with access to finance. A high reported severity does not necessarily mean that access to finance is a problem or that increasing access to finance would necessarily boost output and productivity.

With respect to taxes, managers do not take into account the social benefits of taxation. In virtually all countries, irrespective of their level of development, managers consider high tax rates a constraint, but cutting taxation is not a priority everywhere. As the reported severity cannot be used to assess whether access to finance and tax rates are binding constraints, other indicators of the financial sector and tax system are examined.

A second limitation with the methodology is that it identifies binding constraints to existing firms. It does not identify constraints facing potential entrants. Regulatory constraints faced by potential entrants are examined later in this chapter.

Constraints in the urban formal sector

This section examines constraints facing urban formal sector firms. It compares benchmark firms across countries and identifies the constraints facing both expanding/job-creating firms and other types of nonbenchmark firms.

Constraints facing benchmark firms

The three most common binding constraints facing urban formal firms in South Asia are electricity, corruption, and political instability (figure 4.1 and table 4.1). Although the ranking of these constraints varies across countries, most countries identify the same top three constraints. In every country except Bhutan and Maldives, electricity is one of the top two constraints. It is the

FIGURE 4.1 **Severity of constraints reported by South Asian benchmark firm in the urban formal sector**

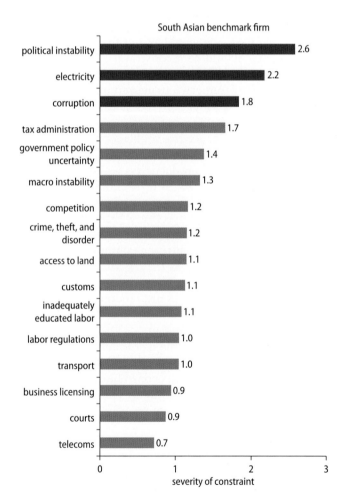

South Asian benchmark firm

Constraint	Severity
political instability	2.6
electricity	2.2
corruption	1.8
tax administration	1.7
government policy uncertainty	1.4
macro instability	1.3
competition	1.2
crime, theft, and disorder	1.2
access to land	1.1
customs	1.1
inadequately educated labor	1.1
labor regulations	1.0
transport	1.0
business licensing	0.9
courts	0.9
telecoms	0.7

severity of constraint

Source: Authors, based on Carlin and Schaffer 2011b (from World Bank enterprise surveys).
Note: A benchmark firm is a medium-size manufacturing firm with 30 employees that is domestically owned, does not export or import, is located in a large city, and did not expand employment in the preceding three years. Analysis is based on pooled sample of enterprise surveys conducted between 2000 and 2010. The severity of constraint is rated by firms on a 5-point scale, with 0 being no obstacle, 1 being a minor obstacle, 2 being a moderate obstacle, 3 being a major obstacle, and 4 being a very severe obstacle. Access to finance and tax rates constraints are excluded.

highest-ranked constraint in India and Sri Lanka. Political instability is among the top three constraints in all five countries where it was included in the survey except Bhutan. This finding is not surprising given that South Asia contains some of the most conflict-affected areas in the world. In five of the eight countries, corruption is among the top four constraints.

Though not as binding as electricity, corruption, and political instability, tax administration is a severe concern in some countries, especially India and Pakistan. Labor regulations are important in Bhutan, India, Sri Lanka, and Nepal. (Chapter 6 analyzes labor regulations and other labor market institutions in more detail). Firms in most countries report tax rates and access to finance as one of the top five most severe constraints. However, because of endogeneity issues described in the methodology, their reported severity cannot be interpreted in the same way as the other constraints or ranked alongside them.

Given the heterogeneous nature of India, separate analyses of firm constraints were conducted for higher- and lower-income states (see annex 4A).[7] The top three constraints (corruption, electricity, and tax administration) are the same for low- and high-income states. Firms in low-income states complain more about inadequate physical infrastructure (electricity, transport, access to land) and crime; firms in high-income states complain more about policy uncertainty and labor regulation. These results parallel cross-country results that show that firms in poor countries tend to complain more about physical infrastructure and firms in rich countries complain more about labor regulation (Carlin and Schaffer 2011b).

Electricity

Most South Asian countries rank electricity as one of the top constraints. The reported severity of the constraint in Afghanistan, Bangladesh, and Nepal is higher than in other countries at similar GDP levels and among the highest in the world. The downward slope in figure 4.2 implies that although

TABLE 4.1   **Top five constraints reported by South Asian benchmark firm in the urban formal sector, by country**

	South Asia region	Afghanistan	Bangladesh	Bhutan	India	Maldives	Nepal	Pakistan	Sri Lanka
Electricity	2	2	1		1		2	2	1
Political instability	1	1	2		n.a.	n.a.	1	3	n.a.
Corruption	3	3	3		2	3	4		
Tax administration	4		5	5	3			1	
Labor regulations				3	4		5		5
Inadequately educated labor				2	5	2			
Access to land		4	4			1			
Transport				1			3		
Government policy uncertainty	5							4	2
Courts						4		5	
Crime, theft, and disorder		5				5			
Business licensing				4					
Macro instability									3
Competition									4

Source: Authors, based on Carlin and Schaffer 2011b (from World Bank enterprise surveys).
Note: A benchmark firm is a medium-size manufacturing firm with 30 employees that is domestically owned, does not export or import, is located in a large city, and did not expand employment in the preceding three years. n.a. = Not applicable (question was not asked). Analysis is based on pooled sample of enterprise surveys conducted between 2000 and 2010. Access to finance and tax rates constraints are excluded.

FIGURE 4.2   **Cross-country comparisons of reported severity of the electricity constraint**

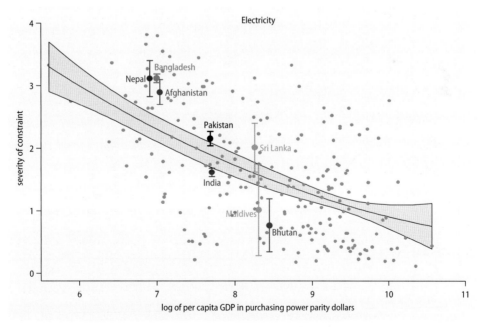

Source: Carlin and Schaffer 2011b (based on World Bank enterprise surveys).
Note: The cross-country regression line shows the relationship between the reported severity of the constraint for a benchmark firm and the log of per capita GDP. The shaded area is the 95 percent confidence interval band around the regression line. Vertical bars show confidence intervals of 95 percent around the reported severity of the constraint for countries in South Asia. The lack of overlap between the South Asian country confidence interval and the regression line confidence interval is a conservative test of the statistically significant difference between the reported severity of a constraint for the South Asian country and the average reported severity of constraint for countries at the same level of per capita GDP. The reported severity could still be significantly different even when there is an overlap. Analysis is based on pooled sample of enterprise surveys conducted between 2000 and 2010. The severity of constraint is rated by firms on a 5-point scale, with 0 being no obstacle, 1 being a minor obstacle, 2 being a moderate obstacle, 3 being a major obstacle, and 4 being a very severe obstacle.

firms in richer countries can be expected to make more demands on the electricity grid, which would lead to rising severity of complaints, those countries are better able to meet increased demand, resulting in lower levels of reported severity at higher incomes per capita. The severity of the constraint increased over time in India (between 2005 and 2010), Nepal (between 2000 and 2009), and Pakistan (between 2002 and 2007 and between 2007 and 2010).

This analysis covers only the urban formal sector. Electricity is also one of the top binding constraints in the rural nonfarm and informal sectors, as discussed later in this chapter.

Reported frequency of power outages—a direct firm-level estimate of the shared business environment—is consistent with the reported severity of the constraint. Indeed, in Afghanistan, Bangladesh, and Nepal, virtually 100 percent of firms experience outages (figure 4.3). In Bangladesh, urban firms face an average of 98.5 power outages a month—more than three a day (World Bank 2008c). Predictably, the use of generators to mitigate the effects of uncertain power supply is higher in South Asia than elsewhere, with 87 percent of firms in Afghanistan, 52 percent in Sri Lanka, and 49 percent in India having generators.

The high reported severity of the electricity constraint and level of power outages reflect the significant demand-supply gap in electricity across the region caused by the failure of electricity supply to expand rapidly enough to keep up with robust economic and population growth (box 4.1).

The unreliability of power supply and the frequency of power outages causes firms to

FIGURE 4.3   **Cross-country comparisons of power outages**

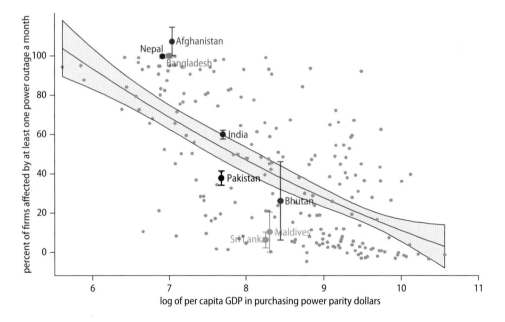

Source: Carlin and Schaffer 2011b (based on World Bank enterprise surveys).
Note: The cross-country regression line shows the relationship between the percentage of firms experiencing more than one power outage per month and the log of per capita GDP. The percentage of firms is a conditional mean for benchmark firms in each country. As the conditional means are calculated by holding constant the effects of the firm controls (firm characteristics) using a simple linear procedure, the effect of this can be, for unconditional country values that are at or close to 0 percent or 100 percent, to push the conditional mean under 0 percent or over 100 percent. The shaded area is the 95 percent confidence interval band around the regression line. Vertical bars show confidence intervals of 95 percent around the percentage of firms experiencing power outages for countries in South Asia. The lack of overlap between a South Asian country confidence interval and the regression line confidence interval is a conservative test of the statistically significant difference between the share of firms experiencing power outages in the South Asian country and the average share of firms experiencing power outages in countries at the same level of per capita GDP. The share of firms could still be significantly different even when there is an overlap. Analysis is based on pooled sample of enterprise surveys conducted between 2000 and 2010.

lose production and incur high costs of self-generation. Firms in South Asia lose a larger share of their output to power losses than firms in other regions—10.7 percent of sales for the region as a whole, up to 27 percent for Nepal—and spend more on generators

(table 4.2). In addition to using generators, there is growing evidence that to cope with unreliable supply, firms adopt second-best production technologies, which imply large efficiency gaps (Alby, Dethier, and Straub 2010). The persistent shortage of electricity

---

BOX 4.1   Electricity challenges facing South Asia

Access to and consumption of electricity are low in South Asia, where some 600 million people—more than 40 percent of the worldwide total—lack access to electricity. Access rates range from 44 percent of the population in Nepal to 77 percent in Sri Lanka (box table 4.1.1). Annual per capita electricity consumption is highest in Bhutan (1,174 kilowatts [KWh]) and lowest in Nepal (KWh 89). India consumes 566 KWh, Pakistan 436 KWh, and Sri Lanka 409 KWh. The average annual per capita consumption for the region is 500 KWh—lower than in Africa (513 KWh) and China (2,500 KWh) and just 3.8 percent of consumption in the United States (13,000 KWh) (World Bank 2011e).

Robust economic and population growth over the past two decades have led to rapidly rising energy demand. Although the 2008 global financial crisis slowed economic activity, regional growth prospects remain strong, with annual growth forecast to average 6 percent until 2015 (IMF 2010). Electricity consumption is likely to increase at an annual rate of about 6.0 percent in Bangladesh, 7.0 percent in India, and 8.8 percent in Pakistan, the region's largest power markets (by comparison, annual growth in Organisation for Economic Co-operation and Development countries is projected at 0.7 percent).

The demand-supply gap is particularly wide in some countries. In addition, industrial consumers typically pay high tariffs and cross-subsidize other consumer categories. In Bangladesh, the gap is estimated to be 1,000 megawatts (MW). About 90 percent of generation is fired by gas, which itself is in short supply. Power outages are estimated to cost Bangladesh about $1 billion a year, reducing GDP growth by about 0.5 percent (USAID 2007). In India, the gap between peak demand and supply is about 10 percent (World Bank 2010a). Industrial consumers in India pay 30–60 percent above the

average level of tariffs, subsidizing agricultural and domestic consumers (KPMG 2009). Nepal's grid-connected installed generation capacity stands at 698 MW, but available capacity falls to nearly one-third of installed capacity during the dry season. Peak demand stands at 885 MW, and consumers face 16 hours of load shedding in dry winter months. In Pakistan, installed capacity is about 22 gigawatts (GW), but technical problems, including lack of fuel and inadequate maintenance of public sector thermal generation companies over prolonged periods, reduced actual available capacity to 18 GW in 2010. Electricity demand exceeds supply by about 2–4 GW, and rolling blackouts can stretch up to 8–10 hours a day. The Ministry of Finance estimates the cumulative effect of the energy crisis on the economy at more than 2 percent of GDP (Government of Pakistan 2010). An independent study conducted in 2008 estimated the cost of industrial load shedding to the economy at PRs. 210 billion, resulting in the loss of 400,000 jobs and $1 billion worth of exports (IIP 2009). Industrial consumers typically pay high tariffs, subsidizing other consumers. The share of industrial consumption is about 26 percent, but industries contributed 30 percent to revenue, indicating the extent of cross-subsidy. In Sri Lanka, the average customer paid $0.12/KWh in 2009, considerably more than the average tariff in Bangladesh, India, Pakistan, or Thailand of $0.05–$0.09/KWh (World Bank 2010b).

Sector financial losses across the region are high, largely as a result of the misalignment of tariffs with the cost of supply and high transmission and distribution losses, which arise from theft, faulty metering, and poor technology in transmitting power. The total sector deficit in Bangladesh amounts to almost $300 million a year. In India, the combined

(continues next page)

BOX 4.1   Electricity challenges facing South Asia (continued)

cash loss of state-owned distribution companies rose by nearly $22 billion a year, $9 billion attributable to transmission and distribution losses and the rest attributable to tariffs that did not cover the cost of generation (Mint 2011). The annual sector deficit in Pakistan resulting from noncollection by distribution companies and below-cost recovery tariff is estimated at about $2 billion. These deficits are met through subsidy payments by the government, short-term borrowing by companies, and the accumulation of receivables and payables on balance sheets.

BOX TABLE 4.1.1   Selected energy indicators in South Asia, by country

| Country | Per capita electricity consumption (KWh per capita) | Percentage of population with access to electricity | Installed capacity (MW) | Estimated deficit or surplus | | Estimated investment required in the medium term (billions of dollars) |
				MW	Percent	
Bangladesh	208	49	6,727	−1,000	−13	15.0 (2015)
Bhutan	1,174	56	1,498	+1,300	+15	3.1 (2020)
India	566	66	159,000	−15,700	−13	280.0 (2015)
Nepal	89	44	698	−200	−30	—
Pakistan	436	62	22,000	−4,500	−20	32.5 (2020)
Sri Lanka	409	77	2,684	+800	+30	10.0 (2020)

Sources: Data on access to electricity and per capita electricity consumption data are from International Energy Agency database 2010. Data on estimated supply gaps and investment requirements are from the following sources: Bangladesh, India, and Pakistan: World Bank 2010a; Bhutan: Bhutan Electricity Authority (http://www.bea.gov.bt); Nepal: Banerjee, Singh, and Samad 2011; Pakistan: Trimble, Yoshida, and Saqib 2011; Sri Lanka: Ceylon Electricity Board 2009; World Bank, 2011d.
Note: Data are for most recent year available. — = Not available.

TABLE 4.2   Electricity constraints faced by firms, by developing region

Region/country	Percentage of firms citing electricity as major or severe constraint	Average total time of power outages per month	Value lost due to power outages (percent of sales)	Percentage of firms owning generators
Africa	49.7	69.5	6.2	42.2
East Asia and Pacific	24.1	14.4	3.1	29.6
Eastern Europe and Central Asia	35.1	23.3	3.8	16.9
Latin America and the Caribbean	39.0	8.7	4.2	19.5
Middle East and North Africa	42.9	45.9	5.6	36.3
South Asia	53.4	139.4	10.7	42.8
Afghanistan	66.2	280.3	6.4	71.1
Bangladesh	78.4	113.2	10.6	52.3
Bhutan	5.8	8.5	4.3	17.8
India	32.0	—	6.6	41.4
Nepal	75.6	226.2	27.0	15.7
Pakistan	74.5	69.0	9.2	26.3
Sri Lanka	41.3	—	—	75.1

Source: World Bank Enterprise Surveys.
Note: Regional averages are unweighted. Country averages are unconditional (that is, not for the benchmark firm). — = Not available.

for industrial and commercial activities is likely to be a major factor limiting the competitiveness of firms and dampening employment growth.[8]

Corruption

Corruption is the abuse of power, usually for personal gain or the benefit of a group to which allegiance is owed. Corruption in government is defined as the abuse or misuse of public office or authority for private gain and benefit that occurs at the interface of the public and private sectors.

Corruption poses serious challenges to development: it undermines democracy and good governance by subverting formal processes, reduces accountability and representation in policymaking, and erodes the institutional capacity of government as procedures are disregarded (Dininio, Kpundeh, and Leiken 1988). It may also create distortions and inefficiencies by diverting public investment away from priorities and into sectors and projects where kickbacks are more likely. Corruption also shields firms with access to influence from competition and may prevent small companies from growing.

Measuring the impact of corruption on firms is challenging because of the difficulty of causal attribution and the fact that corruption data are subject to measurement error. Some observers claim that corruption reduces costs by cutting through red tape. In fact, corruption may increase red tape, in order to allow public officials to obtain more bribes. A survey of the literature on econometric studies that analyze the economic costs of corruption suggests that corruption is bad for economic growth and bad for a number of factors that tend to be correlated with economic growth: domestic investment, the quantity and composition of foreign direct investment, government expenditures on health and education, the quantity and quality of government investment in infrastructure, and the returns to business and trade. Whatever the econometric and data problems of measuring the impact of corruption on final outcomes such as growth, corruption affects the perceptions of businesses, which in turn leads them to be more cautious regarding decisions to invest, expand, and hire.

The importance of corruption as a constraint for firms is reflected in both the high reported severity of the corruption constraint and the high prevalence of bribes. The relationship between the reported severity of the corruption constraint and per capita GDP is characterized by low levels and low variation in rich countries and higher levels and more variation in low- and middle-income countries (figures 4.4 and 4.5). Bhutan and Sri Lanka have lower levels of reported severity of the corruption constraint than is typical at their level of per capita GDP. Of the five countries in which corruption was among the top five constraints (Afghanistan, Bangladesh, India, Maldives, and Nepal), only Bangladesh has higher levels of reported severity than typical for countries at the same level of per capita GDP.

The data on the prevalence of bribes are consistent with those on corruption. Firms in Bangladesh report a very high prevalence of bribe payments in absolute and relative terms. Pakistan also has a higher prevalence of bribes than is typical at its level of per capita GDP.

The high reported severity and prevalence of bribes is fairly consistent with the Corruption Perceptions Index 2010 reported by Transparency International (2010), which ranks (out of 178 countries) Afghanistan at 176, Bangladesh at 134, and Pakistan at 143 (India is 87). Box 4.2 describes in more detail the nature of corruption in South Asia.

South Asian firms report significant costs associated with corruption, including direct costs (for example, the value of bribes paid) and indirect costs (for example, management time spent dealing with officials). Enterprises in Afghanistan pay more than 2 percent of their sales as bribes (World Bank 2008a). Firms in India report spending an average of 2.2 percent of sales on informal payments and an average 8.1 percent of managers' time dealing with government (Ferrari and Dhingra 2009).

Corruption also distorts the economy by creating an unlevel playing field. The

FIGURE 4.4   **Cross-country comparison of reported severity of corruption constraint**

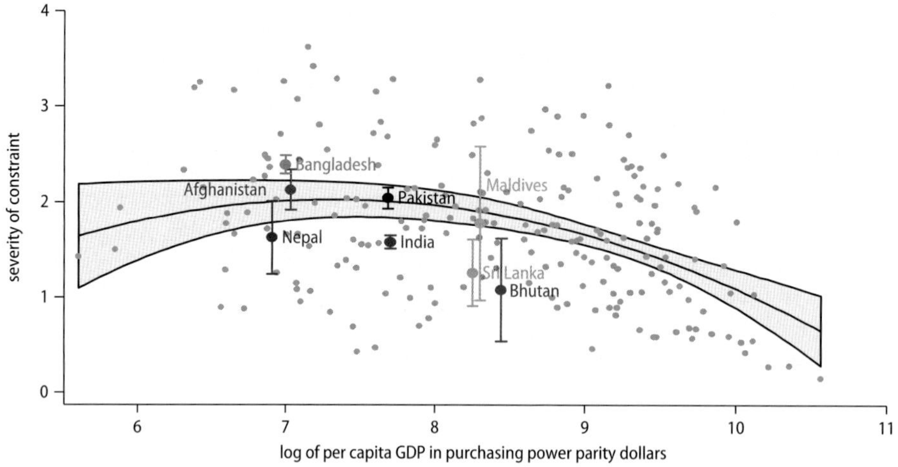

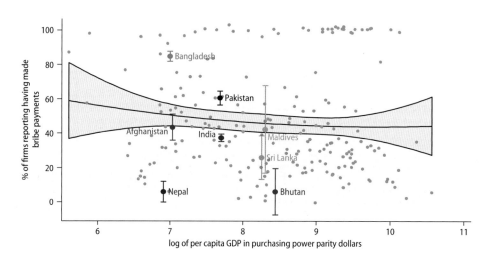

Source: Carlin and Schaffer 2011b (based on World Bank enterprise surveys).
Note: The cross-country regression line shows the relationship between the reported severity of the constraint for a benchmark firm and the log of per capita GDP. The shaded area is the 95 percent confidence interval band around the regression line. Vertical bars show confidence intervals of 95 percent around the reported severity of the constraint for countries in South Asia. The lack of overlap between the South Asian country confidence interval and the regression line confidence interval is a conservative test of the statistically significant difference between the reported severity of a constraint for the South Asian country and the average reported severity of constraint for countries at the same level of per capita GDP. The reported severity could still be significantly different even when there is an overlap. Analysis is based on pooled sample of enterprise surveys conducted between 2000 and 2010. The severity of constraint is rated by firms on a 5-point scale, with 0 being no obstacle, 1 being a minor obstacle, 2 being a moderate obstacle, 3 being a major obstacle, and 4 being a very severe obstacle.

FIGURE 4.5   **Cross-country comparison of bribe payments**

Source: Carlin and Schaffer 2011b (based on World Bank enterprise surveys).
Note: The cross-country regression line shows the relationship between the percentage of firms reporting having made bribe payments and the log of per capita GDP. The percentage of firms is a conditional mean for benchmark firms in each country. As the conditional means are calculated by holding constant the effects of the firm controls (firm characteristics) using a simple linear procedure, the effect of this can be, for unconditional country values that are at or close to 0 percent or 100 percent, to push the conditional mean under 0 percent or over 100 percent. The shaded area is the 95 percent confidence interval band around the regression line. Vertical bars show confidence intervals of 95 percent around the percentage of firms reporting having made bribe payments for countries in South Asia. The lack of overlap between a South Asian country confidence interval and the regression line confidence interval is a conservative test of the statistically significant difference between the share of firms reporting having made bribe payments in the South Asian country and the average share of firms reporting having made bribe payments in countries at the same level of per capita GDP. The share of firms could still be significantly different even when there is an overlap. Analysis is based on a pooled sample of enterprise surveys conducted between 2000 and 2010.

BOX 4.2   **Corruption in South Asia**

Enterprise surveys, which asks firms if they have encountered bribes by different types of interactions with public officials, suggest that firms in South Asia face a high level of corruption in a range of interactions with public officials, particularly for utilities and tax inspections.

The government interactions that have the highest frequency of bribes vary by country (box figure 4.2.1). The highest frequency occurs in the following situations:

- Afghanistan: Government contracts (43 percent) and electrical connection (38 percent)
- Bangladesh: Utilities (42–76 percent), tax meetings (54 percent), and import licenses (51 percent)
- India: Construction permits (67 percent), tax meetings (52 percent), operating licenses (52 percent), electrical connections (40 percent)

- Pakistan: Electricity (71 percent), water connections (62 percent), and tax meetings (59 percent)

The high frequency of bribes faced in connecting to power supply is another dimension of the issue of access to electricity. It may be related to businesses having to compete to secure much needed power (World Bank 2008c).

More than half of firms in Bangladesh, India, and Pakistan are expected to pay bribes during tax inspections. These countries also report very high severity of tax administration (among their top five constraints). The tax systems in these countries are complex, creating not only high costs of compliance but also opportunities for corruption.

BOX FIGURE 4.2.1   Percentage of firms expected to give gifts to public officials, by type of interaction

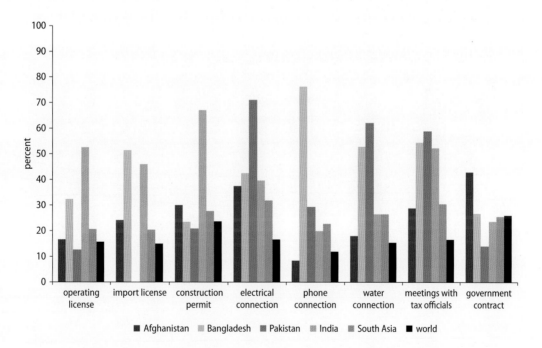

Source: Authors, based on data from World Bank enterprise surveys.
Note: Figures show percent of firms in South Asian countries citing corruption as one of their top three constraints.

constraints analysis finds that expanding/job-creating firms, manufacturing firms, importing and exporting firms, and firms in larger cities are more constrained by corruption than other firms. The greater severity probably reflects the greater use of public services, such as electricity for manufacturing firms; higher levels of interactions with public officials (to, for example, obtain import licenses); and the fact that larger cities have higher concentrations of economic resources. These firms are also the most productive, making the opportunity cost of corruption—goods and services not produced because of resources and time dedicated to overcoming corruption activities—even higher. The India investment climate assessment (Ferrari and Dhingra 2009) indicates that manufacturing firms on average pay a higher percentage of sales in bribes and spend more time

on average dealing with government officials than do service firms (manufacturing firms reportedly pay 4.9 percent of sales in and devote 12.6 percent of managers' time to bribes). In Pakistan, manufacturing firms are also more likely than service firms to pay bribes across a range of interactions with public officials.

Political instability
In the five countries in which surveys asked about the political instability constraint (Afghanistan, Bangladesh, Bhutan, India, Nepal, and Pakistan), all except Bhutan reported it as one of the top three constraints. The reported costs of political instability are higher in Afghanistan, Bangladesh, and Nepal than in other countries at similar levels of per capita GDP (figure 4.6). These three countries have some of the highest reported

FIGURE 4.6   **Cross-country comparison of reported severity of political instability constraint**

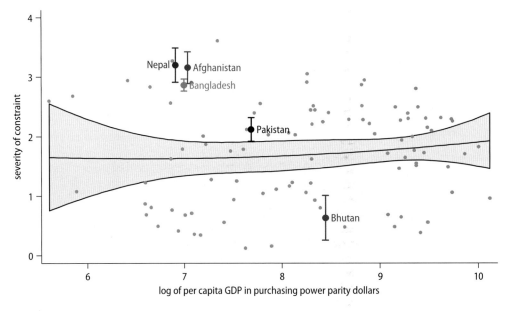

Source: Carlin and Schaffer 2011b (based on World Bank enterprise surveys).
Note: The cross-country regression line shows the relationship between the reported severity of the constraint for a benchmark firm and the log of per capita GDP. The shaded area is the 95 percent confidence interval band around the regression line. Vertical bars show confidence intervals of 95 percent around the reported severity of the constraint for countries in South Asia. The lack of overlap between the South Asian country confidence interval and the regression line confidence interval is a conservative test of the statistically significant difference between the reported severity of a constraint for the South Asian country and the average reported severity of constraint for countries at the same level of per capita GDP. The reported severity could still be significantly different even when there is an overlap. Analysis is based on a pooled sample of enterprise surveys conducted between 2000 and 2010. The severity of constraint is rated by firms on a 5-point scale, with 0 being no obstacle, 1 being a minor obstacle, 2 being a moderate obstacle, 3 being a major obstacle, and 4 being a very severe obstacle. Enterprise surveys in India, Maldives, and Sri Lanka did not ask firms about political instability.

costs of political instability in the world. (Chapter 7 examines the effect of armed conflict, which is one key aspect of political instability, on firms and workers.)

Tax administration

Tax administration is a major issue in some countries in South Asia (table 4.1). It is the top-ranked constraint in Pakistan, where the reported severity is above the average for countries at similar levels of per capita GDP (figure 4.7). As annex 4B shows, many tax systems in South Asia are complex, making tax compliance very costly for firms.

Tax rates

Taxes matter to business and individuals. Businesses and people talk about them, complain about them, and often try to avoid paying them when they can. Taxation also affects the ways in which businesses organize their activities and produce goods and services, which in turn affects the structure of taxation (Bird and Zolt 2007).

Firms in India and Pakistan report tax rates as their top constraint in terms of severity; Sri Lankan firms report tax rates to be the third-most severe constraint. However, as explained in the methodology, one cannot directly infer the real cost of the constraint from the reported severity. Other measures have been used to assess whether tax rates are indeed a binding constraint (see annex 4B).

It seems likely that it is the complexity and lack of uniformity of tax systems rather than the tax rates themselves that impose significant costs on firms. These tax systems create distortions in the economy and make it difficult to raise adequate revenues. Simplifying the tax regimes (by reducing the number of taxes and exemptions) and widening the tax base is likely to benefit firms and remove

FIGURE 4.7   Cross-country comparison of reported severity of tax administration constraint

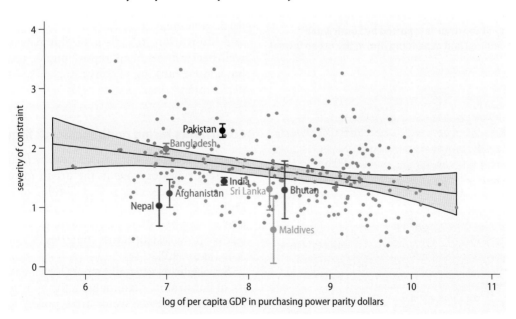

Source: Carlin and Schaffer 2011b (based on World Bank enterprise surveys).
Note: The cross-country regression line shows the relationship between the reported severity of the constraint for a benchmark firm and the log of per capita GDP. The shaded area is the 95 percent confidence interval band around the regression line. Vertical bars show confidence intervals of 95 percent around the reported severity of the constraint for countries in South Asia. The lack of overlap between the South Asian country confidence interval and the regression line confidence interval is a conservative test of the statistically significant difference between the reported severity of a constraint for the South Asian country and the average reported severity of constraint for countries at the same level of per capita GDP. The reported severity could still be significantly different even when there is an overlap. Analysis is based on a pooled sample of enterprise surveys conducted between 2000 and 2010. The severity of constraint is rated by firms on a 5-point scale, with 0 being no obstacle, 1 being a minor obstacle, 2 being a moderate obstacle, 3 being a major obstacle, and 4 being a very severe obstacle.

distortions in the economy. By increasing compliance, governments can maintain tax revenues while reducing statutory rates.

Constraints facing expanding/job-creating firms

The benchmark firm is useful for comparing the costs of constraints to firms across South Asia and the rest of the world. However, the main interest here is in understanding how these constraints affect employment creation. This section therefore examines the reported cost of constraints facing expanding/job-creating firms, because relaxing constraints on these firms is likely to produce the largest increases in employment. Job-creating firms also perform well: employment growth is positively and significantly correlated with research and development, introduction of new processes and products, sales to multinational companies, the education level of the manager, and in-house training.[9] Therefore, relaxing constraints on job-creating

firms is likely to produce large increases in output as well.

Job-creating firms—which are similar in all respects to the benchmark firm except that they expanded employment during the preceding three years—report higher levels of severity than the benchmark firm for 14 of the 16 constraints (figure 4.8). They also report higher levels of mitigation activities (paying bribes and using generators). This pattern holds strongly in India and Pakistan, where the difference between the cost of constraints facing expanding firms and the benchmark firm is largest.[10]

Although the level of severity changes, job-creating and benchmark firms in most countries rank constraints in a similar order: electricity, corruption, and political stability are the top three constraints among both types of firms, and the rankings of other constraints are similar (table 4.3). Only in Pakistan do the rankings by the benchmark and job-creating firms differ: corruption becomes the joint top constraint for expanding firms. Using alternative performance measures, such as productivity and innovation, reveals a similar pattern: well-performing firms report higher costs but similar ranking of constraints as poorly performing firms.

Constraints facing nonbenchmark firms

In general, the ranking of constraints facing different types of firms in the urban formal manufacturing sector is very similar to the ranking by the benchmark firm, although the level of severity differs. The patterns described below are consistent across countries in South Asia (figure 4.9).

Service firms generally report lower severity of constraints than manufacturing firms. Firms in the service sector are typically less capital intensive, more dependent on communications, and less engaged in trade than manufacturing firms. Indeed, service firms in South Asia report lower constraints for electricity, labor regulations, and custom administration (but higher cost for telecommunications). The difference between manufacturing and service

FIGURE 4.8 **Severity of constraints reported by South Asian benchmark (nonexpanding) and expanding firm in the urban formal sector**

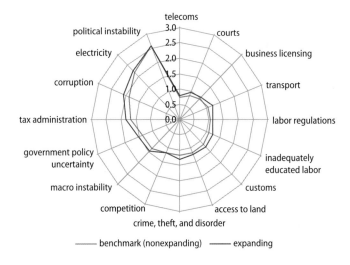

Source: Authors, based on Carlin and Schaffer 2011b (based on World Bank enterprise surveys).
Note: Analysis is based on a pooled sample of enterprise surveys conducted between 2000 and 2010. A point farther away from the origin indicates that the business constraint is considered more severe. The severity of constraint is rated by firms on a 5-point scale, with 0 being no obstacle, 1 being a minor obstacle, 2 being a moderate obstacle, 3 being a major obstacle, and 4 being a very severe obstacle. Only statistically significant differences in reported severity between benchmark and nonbenchmark firms are shown. Access to finance and tax rates constraints are excluded.

TABLE 4.3 Top five constraints reported by South Asian benchmark (nonexpanding) and expanding firm in the urban formal sector, by country

Constraint	South Asian region		Afghanistan		Bangladesh		Bhutan		India		Maldives		Nepal		Pakistan		Sri Lanka	
	Benchmark firm	Expanding firm	Benchmark firm	Expanding firm	Benchmark firm	Expanding firm	Benchmark firm	Expanding firm	Benchmark firm	Expanding firm	Benchmark firm	Expanding firm	Benchmark firm	Expanding firm	Benchmark firm	Expanding firm	Benchmark firm	Expanding firm
Electricity	2	2	2	2	1	1			1	2			2	2	2		1	1
Political instability	1	1	1	1	2	2			n.a.		n.a.		1	1	3	1	n.a.	n.a.
Corruption	3	3	3	4	3	3			2	1	3	4	4	4	1			
Tax administration	4	4			5	5	5	5	3	3					1	4		
Labor regulations							3	3	4	4			5	5			5	5
Inadequately educated labor							2	2	5	5	2	2						
Access to land			4	5	4	4					1	1						
Transport							1	1					3	3				
Government policy uncertainty	5	5													4	3	2	2
Courts											4	5			5			
Crime, theft, and disorder			5	3							5	3						
Business licensing							4	4										
Macro instability																5	3	3
Competition																	4	4

Source: Authors, based on Carlin and Schaffer 2011b (based on World Bank enterprise surveys).
Note: Analysis is based on pooled sample of enterprise surveys conducted between 2000 and 2010. n.a. = Not applicable (question was not asked). Access to finance and tax rates constraints are excluded.

firms is particularly marked in India, where service firms report far less severe constraints than manufacturing firms in electricity, labor regulations, customs, tax rates and administration, and access to finance.[11]

Relative to smaller firms, larger formal firms which, on average produce higher output per worker (see chapter 3), report more severe constraints and a larger number of mitigation activities, including management time spent on regulations and use of generators.[12] They are also subject to more inspections. The difference between the benchmark firm with 30 employees and a firm with the same characteristics but with 60 employees is small in India and larger in Nepal, Pakistan, and Sri Lanka. In Nepal, and to a lesser extent Sri Lanka, the cost of labor regulations increases significantly with firm size (see annex 4C).

Exporters and importers in South Asia report more severe constraints, except in Bangladesh. Importers are more constrained by customs administration and anticompetitive behavior. Macroeconomic instability is more problematic for both types of firms, which is likely to reflect sensitivity to exchange rate movements and uncertainty. Exporters in Bangladesh report lower costs of constraints relative to nonexporters for electricity and most aspects of institutional

FIGURE 4.9   **Severity of constraints reported by South Asian benchmark (manufacturing) and service firm in the urban formal sector**

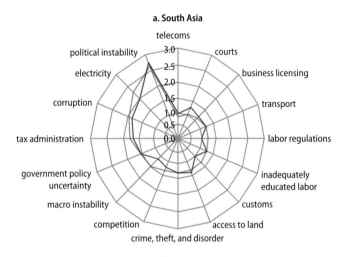

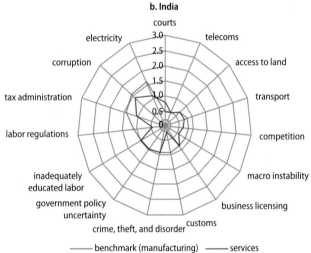

Source: Authors, based on Carlin and Schaffer 2011b (based on World Bank enterprise surveys).
Note: Analysis is based on a pooled sample of enterprise surveys conducted between 2000 and 2010. A point farther away from the origin indicates that the business constraint is considered more severe. The severity of constraint is rated by firms on a 5-point scale, with 0 being no obstacle, 1 being a minor obstacle, 2 being a moderate obstacle, 3 being a major obstacle, and 4 being a very severe obstacle. Only statistically significant differences in reported severity between benchmark and nonbenchmark firms are shown. Access to finance and tax rates constraints are excluded.

infrastructure pattern (see annex 4C). This pattern may be explained by the large number of export processing zones in Bangladesh, which offer better infrastructure and regulatory environments.

In conclusion, addressing the top constraints of electricity, political stability, and corruption would benefit all types of firms. But larger job-creating firms in the manufacturing sector would benefit most, as the costs of the constraints are higher for them.

Constraints in the rural nonfarm and informal sectors

This section looks at the severity of constraints on firm operations reported by micro benchmark firms (firms with no more than five employees) in the rural nonfarm sector and informal (urban) sector and compares them with those reported by micro benchmark firms in the urban formal sector. The rural nonfarm sector has been shown to offer higher-paid jobs to rural workers than the agricultural sector, with wages on par with or even higher than similar categories of employment in the urban sector. The growth of rural nonfarm enterprises will play an important role in the creation of better jobs. Although informal firms are smaller and less productive than formal firms, they employ the most workers. Addressing their constraints is therefore important in creating better jobs.

Rural nonfarm sector

In general, rural firms face fewer and less severe constraints than urban firms (figure 4.10 and table 4.4). This pattern is not unusual in developing countries, where urban firms are typically more productive and place more demands on public services than their rural counterparts. Electricity, macroeconomic instability, and political instability remain important constraints for rural firms. Transport is a greater concern for rural firms than it is for urban firms. Rural firms are less concerned about corruption, taxes, and labor regulations than their urban counterparts.

Like urban firms, rural firms rank electricity as one of their top constraints and report similar levels of power outages. In Bangladesh, 73 percent of nonmetropolitan nonfarm enterprises have an electricity connection. Of firms without electricity: 32 percent complain about high connection costs, 32 percent report not needing electricity, and 25 percent report no supply in their location. Among firms with connections, 99 percent report outages. In Pakistan, the median number of outages per month is 20 days in villages and 15 days in small towns. In Sri Lanka, the shortage and unreliability of power is exacerbated in rural areas where less than 70 percent of enterprises use electricity from the national grid. The propensity for rural households to start up a nonfarm enterprise is 14 percent lower in areas where electricity is found to be a major constraint.[13]

Rural firms also rank macroeconomic and political instability as important constraints. One should be cautious in interpreting these results, however, as the macroeconomic instability question was asked only in Bangladesh and refers to inflationary concerns and the political instability question was asked only in Bangladesh and Pakistan.

Rural firms (especially microenterprises) report access to finance as one of the top constraints. In Pakistan, more than 30 percent of small towns and rural firms report access to finance, cost of finance, and loan procedures (separately) as a major or severe constraint. In contrast, none of the other constraints was ranked as major or severe by more than 16 percent of firms. These results cannot be interpreted directly as evidence that access to finance is a constraint to operations, though the finding is consistent with other evidence that suggests that access to finance may be an issue for micro and small firms (including rural nonfarm enterprises) (see annex 4D).

In Bangladesh, India, and Pakistan, rural firms perceive low demand for their products as one of the top five constraints, reflecting low access to larger markets.[14] Rural firms sell predominantly to local customers, limiting the size of the market for their products and services. In Bangladesh, the majority of nonmetropolitan enterprises sell their goods and services directly to customers located within the same union or ward; less than 1 percent of nonmetropolitan enterprises have subcontracting arrangements with metropolitan firms.[15] Infrastructure bottlenecks, limited contacts and business

FIGURE 4.10 Severity of constraints reported by micro benchmark firm in urban and rural sectors of Bangladesh, Pakistan, and Sri Lanka

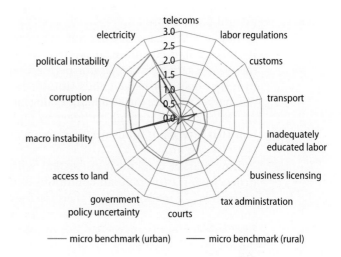

Source: Authors, based on Carlin and Schaffer 2011a (based on World Bank enterprise surveys).
Note: Analysis is based on a pooled sample of enterprise surveys conducted in Bangladesh, Pakistan, and Sri Lanka between 2000 and 2010. A point farther away from the origin indicates that the business constraint is considered more severe. The severity of constraint is rated by firms on a 5-point scale, with 0 being no obstacle, 1 being a minor obstacle, 2 being a moderate obstacle, 3 being a major obstacle, and 4 being a very severe obstacle. Only statistically significant differences in reported severity between the micro benchmark firms in urban and rural sectors are shown. Access to finance and tax rates constraints are excluded. The low demand constraint is excluded because it was asked only in the rural surveys and is susceptible to endogeneity issues. Crime, theft, and disorder as well as competition constraints were not asked in the rural surveys. Macro instability was asked only in Bangladesh, and political instability was asked only in Bangladesh and Pakistan.

TABLE 4.4 Top five constraints reported by micro benchmark firm in the urban and rural sectors of Bangladesh, Pakistan, and Sri Lanka

Constraint	Bangladesh, Pakistan, Sri Lanka	
	Urban, formal	Rural
Electricity	1	2
Political instability	2	3
Corruption	3	
Macro instability	4	1
Access to land	5	
Transport		4

Source: Authors, based on Carlin and Schaffer 2011a (based on World Bank enterprise surveys).
Note: Analysis is based on a pooled sample of enterprise surveys conducted in Bangladesh, Pakistan, and Sri Lanka between 2000 and 2010. Access to finance and tax rates constraints are excluded. The low demand constraint is excluded because it was asked only in the rural surveys and is susceptible to endogeneity issues. Crime, theft, and disorder as well as competition constraints were not asked in the rural surveys. Macro instability was asked only in Bangladesh and political instability was asked only in Bangladesh and Pakistan. Only the top four constraints are shown for rural firms, as the remaining constraints were not reported on average as obstacles.

networks, poor contract enforcement, and low quality of production are the main factors behind limited access to larger markets and subcontracting. Concerns over quality lead to vertical integration of metropolitan firms. A quarter of the firms that did not subcontract cited difficulties in ensuring quality control; another quarter cited lack of predictability and reliability of supply (World Bank 2008c).

Low market demand does not necessarily reflect market failure. It is affected by the firms' characteristics (a poor-performing firm that does not make goods suitable for the market will face low demand). Endogeneity issues make it difficult to interpret high reported severity as a business environment constraint to firms.

Low market demand is consistent with firms citing transport (road conditions and accessibility of roads) as one of their top four constraints. Nonmetropolitan enterprises in Bangladesh identify inaccessibility of roads during certain seasons as a major or severe constraint. Regression analysis shows that the greater the distance to the nearest medium-size city (a city with a population of 100,000 or more), the greater the likelihood that a nonmetropolitan manufacturer will identify low demand as a major or severe constraint. In Pakistan, 16 percent of rural enterprises surveyed (far more than small town enterprises) cite road quality and 14 percent cite availability of transport as a major or severe constraint. In Sri Lanka, nearly a third of rural enterprises (versus 20 percent of urban enterprises) cite transport as a major or severe obstacle to operation or growth of business. Among firms that describe transport as an obstacle, 35 percent cite road quality, 33 percent cite lack of access to roads, and 32 percent cite lack of available transport as the underlying issue. These results are not surprising, as poor transport limits access to larger, urban markets.

Good-quality transport infrastructure is critical for facilitating urban-rural nonfarm sector linkages. The India poverty assessment (World Bank 2011b) uses the variation in the nonfarm sector across India to explore the determinants of rural nonfarm growth. It finds that the expansion of employment in the nonfarm sector is more closely linked to urban than agricultural growth. A simple multivariate regression

analysis using Nepal census data also shows that rural nonfarm employment has a statistical and practical positive association with income growth in nearby urban centers.[16] A one percentage point decline in urban poverty is associated with a 0.1–0.2 percentage point increase in the rural nonfarm employment rate. Urban growth can increase the demand for goods and services produced by the rural nonfarm sector, which otherwise might be limited by the small size of their local markets. The rural nonfarm sector can produce goods to be directly consumed by urban consumers or by urban firms through backward contracting arrangements. Linkages to urban markets are hindered by weak transport infrastructure connecting rural areas to urban areas (as well as lack of market information and the inability of rural nonfarm firms to produce goods demanded in the urban areas). Assessments of rural transport in South Asia would help policy makers develop specific options.

Rural firms are much less concerned than urban firms with corruption, taxes, and labor regulations. This finding is consistent with the fact that rural firms report less engagement with officials than urban firms (inspections and management time) and that about half of rural firms are informal (just 40 percent of rural firms in Bangladesh and 53 percent in Sri Lanka were registered).

Informal urban sector

Figure 4.11 and table 4.5 contrast the ranking and severity of constraints reported by micro benchmark firms in the formal and informal sectors of urban areas of India.

Like formal firms, informal firms rank electricity as one of their top constraints and report similar levels of power outages. Formal firms in India cite power as their greatest constraint; informal firms cite it as their second-greatest constraint (after access to finance). Power outages and loss of sales as a result of outages are very high for informal firms (11.3 percent of annual sales lost to power outages).

Informal firms cite lack of access to finance as the top constraint they face: in 2005, more than a third of informal firms viewed it as the single greatest obstacle. In contrast, formal firms cite access to finance as the fifth-greatest obstacle. This finding does not necessarily mean that access to finance is a binding constraint for informal firms (see the earlier discussion of the endogeneity problem), nor does it necessarily mean that access to finance is a greater constraint to informal firms than formal firms. However, given the overwhelming response by informal firms, this issue merits the analysis reported in the next section.

Informal firms are more concerned about access to land and transport than formal firms and (like rural firms) less concerned about corruption, taxes, and labor regulations. This finding is consistent with the fact that informal firms report less management time spent with officials than formal firms.

The concern regarding access to land expressed by urban informal firms in India may reflect the impact of regulations that shape the operation of land markets. Density regulations, which limit the ratio of floor space to plot area, lead cities to expand outward instead of upward. Together with limited accessibility of public transport, such expansion can make it more difficult for informal manufacturing units to locate where they should—close to buyers and suppliers. Relaxing density regulations, improving urban transport, and increasing the supply of property might help reduce the severity of the land constraint for informal urban firms (World Bank 2011a).

Access to finance

A growing body of empirical research has established a positive association between financial sector and economic development (countries with higher levels of credit to the private sector relative to GDP experienced higher real per capita GDP growth rates between 1980 and 2007) and between access to external finance and firm productivity (see, for example, Banerjee and Duflo 2008;

FIGURE 4.11   Severity of constraints reported by micro benchmark firm in India's urban formal and informal sectors

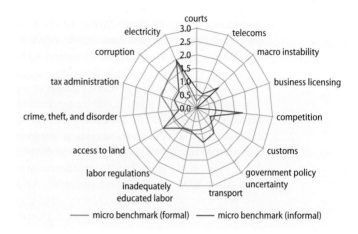

— micro benchmark (formal)   — micro benchmark (informal)

Source: Authors, based on Carlin and Schaffer 2011a (based on World Bank enterprise surveys).
Note: Analysis is based on a pooled sample of enterprise surveys conducted in India between 2000 and 2010. A point farther away from the origin indicates that the business constraint is considered more severe. The severity of constraint is rated by firms on a 5-point scale, with 0 being no obstacle, 1 being a minor obstacle, 2 being a moderate obstacle, 3 being a major obstacle, and 4 being a very severe obstacle. Only statistically significant differences in reported severity between the micro benchmark firms in formal and informal sectors are shown. Access to finance and tax rates constraints are excluded. The low demand constraint is excluded because it was asked only in the informal surveys and is susceptible to endogeneity issues. Political instability was not asked in the India surveys.

TABLE 4.5   Top five constraints reported by micro benchmark firm in India's urban formal and informal sectors

	India	
	Formal	**Informal**
Electricity	1	1
Corruption	2	
Tax administration	3	
Crime, theft, and disorder	4	
Access to land	5	3
Competition		2
Transport		4
Government policy uncertainty		5

Source: Authors, based on Carlin and Schaffer 2011a (based on World Bank enterprise surveys).
Note: Analysis is based on a pooled sample of enterprise surveys conducted in India between 2000 and 2010. Access to finance and tax rates constraints are excluded. The low demand constraint is excluded because it was asked only in the informal surveys and is susceptible to endogeneity issues. Political instability was not asked in the India surveys.

Beck, Demirgüç-Kunt, and Maksimovic 2005). Though in general it is very difficult to control for endogeniety in these types of analyses, the studies suggest that if finance is indeed a binding constraint, it could have a significant adverse effect on productivity and growth.

Firms in all South Asian countries report access to finance as one of their top five constraints. The reported severity is higher for informal, rural, and small firms. To circumvent endogeniety issues, this book looks at alternative indicators, including financial depth and outreach/access indicators, to see whether there is other evidence suggesting that access to finance is a severe constraint to firms (see annex 4D). It does not find strong evidence that access to finance is a binding constraint for all types of firms in South Asia. Firm-level data from enterprise surveys show that smaller firms in South Asia use less external finance (this evidence is consistent with evidence from other regions). Small firms in Afghanistan and Pakistan use less external finance than small firms in other regions. Microenterprises in the informal and rural sector report even lower use of external finance than small firms in the formal sector, reflecting less access to banking services in general and the large number of firms that are unable to apply for credit because they cannot meet the loan requirements, especially with regard to collateral. The evidence suggests that addressing access to finance issues for micro, small, and medium-size enterprises may be important in some countries.[17]

After studying the evidence on whether small and medium-size enterprises in Asia are credit constrained, the Asian Development Bank (2009) concluded that studies are subject to numerous endogeniety issues. It noted that although the evidence may be inconclusive, policy makers believe lack of credit is an important issue and have already introduced many active interventions. The next section assesses which of these interventions is technically appropriate and economically justified.

Demand-side policy options

This section suggests policy options to overcome some of the binding constraints faced by firms in South Asia. Policy options are based on experiences from countries inside and outside the region. The relevance of each option for an individual country will depend on country-specific issues and contexts.

Electricity policy options

Alleviating the demand gap across all segments in the value chain requires at least $300 billion by 2020 ($280 billion for India only) (see box 4.1). The private sector is projected to continue to be the leading financier. Since 1990, it has invested $121 billion in the sector, 85 percent since 2000 (table 4.6). India has attracted about 90 percent of the regional investment in the power sector with private participation (World Bank 2011c). The private sector's contribution to total power sector investments in India rose from 21 percent under the 10th Plan to 36 percent under the 11th Plan; it is expected to reach about 50 percent in the 12th Plan, beginning in 2012 (Economic Times 2011; Government of India 2009).

If these improvements in closing the electricity gap are to be sustained or increased, countries will need to continue to create enabling environments to improve sector performance and foster additional investment. Key actions include deepening market and institutional reforms and improving the commercial and financial viability of the sector.

Deepening market and institutional reforms
Beginning in the mid- to late 1990s, countries put in place overarching policy and legal frameworks and restructured power utilities to make investments more attractive and commercialize utilities to enhance service delivery. Most countries established regulatory bodies; separated segments (generation, transmission, and distribution); and implemented a host of measures to attract the private sector, particularly in generation. (See table 4.7 for a summary of market reforms in the power sector in South Asia.) Bangladesh and Pakistan also unbundled their power markets to some extent, with the prevailing market model the single buyer with independent power

producers or rental power plants selling their power at regulated prices. The unbundling of the Water and Power Development Authority in Pakistan into a number of generation companies was formalized in 2001 and 2002. Bhutan unbundled only the power generation segment by establishing a power company responsible for domestic power (Bhutan Power Corporation) and another company responsible for operating the export-oriented hydropower projects (Druk Green Power Company). In India, the generation, transmission, distribution segments include a number of players (both

TABLE 4.6   Private investment in electricity in South Asia, by country, 1999–2000 and 2001–10
(millions of dollars)

Country	1999–2000	2001–10	Total
Afghanistan	0	2	2
Bangladesh	573	823	1,397
Bhutan	0	201	201
India	11,039	97,683	108,722
Nepal	239	34	273
Pakistan	5,937	4,496	10,433
Sri Lanka	177	271	488
Total	17,966	103,510	121,475

Source: World Bank PPI database (http://www.ppi.worldbank.org).
Note: Data on Maldives are not available.

TABLE 4.7   Market reforms in the power sector in selected countries in South Asia

Country	Market structure	Regulator	Role of public sector	Role of private sector	Role of competition
Bangladesh	Unbundled	Bangladesh Electricity Regulatory Commission	Companies created after unbundling continue to be state owned.	Government launched program in 2010 to attract independent power producers and boost private investment in generation. Because of gas shortages, most independent power producers and rental plants are small and oil fired.	Competition limited and confined to generation sector
India	Unbundled	Electricity regulatory commissions in most states	Public sector owns large shares of the transmission and distribution segments.	Private sector assets and financing are concentrated in generation; limited private presence in transmission and negligible presence in distribution.	Long-term agreements by independent power producers, public-private partnerships in transmission, distribution franchisees. Policy framework shifting from guaranteed return on assets to tariffs based on competitive bidding
Nepal	Horizontally integrated	None	Public sector owns large shares of the transmission and distribution segments.	Significant participation of independent power producers in generation.	Competition introduced in generation.
Pakistan	Unbundled	National electric power regulatory authority	Companies created after unbundling continue to be state owned.	Independent power producers own one-third of generation capacity.	Further strengthening of the regulatory framework envisaged to enable competition and market-oriented systems for power pricing, trading, and exchange.
Sri Lanka	Horizontally integrated	Multisector public utilities regulatory	Public sector owns large shares of the transmission and distribution segments.	Limitation of private investment above 25 MW unless there is shareholding by the government. Independent power producers supply oil-dependent power to the grid.	Limited

Source: Authors' compilation, based on Besant-Jones 2006.

public and private) as well as electricity traders, who participate in a competitive electricity wholesale market. Nepal and Sri Lanka retain their vertically integrated state-owned company.

Countries also have to strengthen institutions in order to efficiently expand capacity. The region has pursued ambitious plans to meet power shortages. In India alone, power sector investments have to increase from about $7 billion a year to about $30–$40 billion a year by 2012, under the 11th Plan, which calls for total investment of $150 billion. Total investment is expected to double to $300 billion under the 12th Plan (2012–17) (Banerji and Mishra 2010). India added 50 GW between 2006 and 2011 and implemented a series of "ultra mega" (4,000 MW) generation projects based on competitive bidding by independent power producers. It also set up a functioning trading market for contracts of less than a year. In 2010/11, the short-term power market constituted 10 percent of the total power procured in India (Central Electricity Regulatory Commission 2011).

Bangladesh plans to develop 9,426 MW of new generation capacity by 2015, at an estimated cost of about $15 billion, including associated transmission and distribution investments and fuel development and supply facilities. Bhutan has established public-private partnerships and secured financing on commercial terms for a large export-oriented hydropower project (Dagachhu HPP). Between 2008 and 2010, Pakistan added more than 2,000 MW of capacity. It expects to commission 300 MW of hydropower by 2012.

Further improvements in the operating environment are needed to increase investments in generation. Generation shortages are caused primarily by procedural bottlenecks (land acquisition, environmental and forest clearances, and provision of water for thermal plants); limited technical and financial capacity to implement large projects; the lack of fuel and the inability to import it; and difficulty in accessing domestic resources (such as coal in India, which lies under forests or in tribal areas, or hydropower in Nepal, the

development of which has been limited by political instability).

There is more scope for private players in the transmission and distribution sectors, where investments have been considerably lower than in generation, reflecting the natural monopoly nature of transmission and difficulties in tackling longstanding underpricing and theft in distribution. In India, several public-private partnership contracts have been competitively awarded on a Build, Own, Operate, and Maintain or a Design, Build, Finance, Operate, and Transfer basis. India and Pakistan have also pursued private participation in power distribution as a means of improving the commercial orientation and service delivery. In India, power distribution has been privatized in Delhi and the state of Orissa, and some states, such as Maharashtra, are developing "franchise" models akin to lease contracts to bring in the private sector. Pakistan privatized distribution in the Karachi Electricity Supply Corporation. The results of these initiatives have been mixed, reflecting the difficulties in moving to and sustaining cost-covering tariffs and reducing nonpayment and theft.

Skill mapping and skill development need to appear on top of the business agenda among sector players, as the lack of skilled manpower is emerging as a constraint hindering massive investment. The active participation of private players in the sector has resulted in higher attrition rates from the public sector and steep competition for talent. In India, demand for manpower is expected to increase through 2013/14, when the sector will require an estimated 85,000 additional workers (CRISIL 2011).

Exploiting the significant potential of intraregional energy trade

Countries need to build on the unexploited potential of interregional trade and improve the efficiency of existing investments, two of the most cost-effective options for alleviating shortages in the region. Interregional trade, particularly hydro exports from Bhutan to India, has increased in recent years. Initiatives continue, with the government of Bangladesh signing a memorandum of understanding with India in 2010 for cross-border power trade that will facilitate the import of 500 MW of electricity and a new Nepal-India electricity and trade project that will facilitate the trading of up to 1,000 MW of electricity. As a result of transmission bottlenecks, electricity exchange between Nepal and India was limited to about 70 MW in 2010. The potential for more efficiently deploying existing generation capacity through rehabilitation, maintenance, and technical optimization is also important.

Improving the commercial and financial viability of the sector
Governments in the region have been proactive in curbing losses in the power sector. India's power development reform program (R-APDRP), launched under the 11th Plan, which aims to limit losses to 15 percent, focuses on demonstrable and measurable performance in reducing distribution losses. Pakistan has conducted technical and operational audits of distribution and generation companies, which provide a menu of actions for the government and utilities to implement (for instance, investments to reduce losses and improve efficiency, administrative and commercial steps to enhance accountability, and upgrading of information systems and management practices).

Many states in India have undertaken rural feeder segregation programs to reduce losses in rural distribution lines and provide uninterrupted power to rural nonagricultural consumers. These mechanisms have had a transformative effect on rural livelihoods in Gujarat, the state where the scheme has functioned the longest and been subject to many evaluations (box 4.3).

Tariff rationalization—that aligns tariffs with costs and better targets implicit subsidies—is critical. In Bangladesh, policy makers envisage addressing the sector's financial deficit through a combination of tariff increases, cost reduction, and demand-side management. Retail tariffs were raised by 5 percent in February 2011, but additional tariff increases are required. In Bhutan, the government adopted a more cost-reflective tariff structure after the corporatization of the electricity utility in 2002. During 2004–09, the average electricity tariff increased by 66 percent. Even after the increase, however, tariffs need to rise 73 percent for residential customers and 28 percent for industrial consumers to cover the cost of production (ADB 2010). In Pakistan, consumer tariffs were not increased at all between 2003 and 2007, despite substantial increases in the international prices of fuel oil and gas. Changes in the tariff level and structure carried out in March 2008 were implemented to reduce the

---

BOX 4.3   Bringing light to rural consumers in Gujarat, India

Although most villages in the Indian state of Gujarat were electrified by 2003, the power supply remained erratic and unreliable, because the feeders to rural areas were joined and utilities had no incentive to supply 24-hour power to a group of mostly unmetered consumers paying below cost-recovery tariff. The Jyotigram Yojana (JGY) aimed to segregate agriculture from rural domestic and industrial power supply. Feeders were laid to provide 24/7 uninterrupted supply, and farmers were rationed an uninterrupted, pre-announced 8-hour supply. The scheme was launched in 2003 on a pilot basis and then scaled up to include the whole state. The scale-up created 1,888 feeders at

a cost of $285 million in a record 1,000 days from initiation to implementation. The scheme was expected to provide better quality power supply to nonagriculture consumers, charge farmers for power use, and ration the power supply to agriculture consumers.

The impact of the scheme has been significant: both the quantity and quality of power and enterprise operations improved. As a result, families can now work at night. The Gujarat Electricity Board also experienced increases in revenue collection and made profits in 2010.

Sources: Devaiah 2010; Mishra 2010.

fiscal burden of tariff subsidies and improve the benefit incidence of such subsidies. Tariffs have since increased by 75 percent, which has helped cut the gap between the cost of supply and notified tariffs in half (from 35 percent to 17 percent). The Public Utilities Commission of Sri Lanka announced a new set of electricity tariffs for 2011–15 in late 2010. The tariffs are expected to be gradually restructured to reflect cost-effectiveness by 2015.

More remains to be done, particularly in rationalizing industrial tariffs by reducing the cross-subsidy and improving targeting. Doing so would help industries go back to the grid (instead of depending on captive generators) and use open access options (IDFC 2010).

Regulators with adequate capacity can ensure transparency and accountability in tariff setting, a process that continues to be driven by factors such as political exigencies. In Pakistan, the regulator (NEPRA) has exclusive responsibility for determining tariffs after public hearings, but tariffs become legally binding only once they have been notified by the government in the official gazette. In India, there are instances of tariffs not being filed annually and subsidies not paid to utilities in time. New initiatives have been implemented, however, particularly the multiyear tariff, which provides certainty on the costs for which utilities can be held accountable, and the stepping back from regulatory

interference in day-to-day utility matters. At least eight states in India have passed multiyear tariff orders. Regulators have also made attempts to improve the consumer interface by enabling consumers to have input into regulatory decision making.

Governance and the institutional capacity of utilities need to be strengthened. Most countries have unbundled their power sectors, corporatized previously vertically integrated power utilities, or both. However, many newly formed utilities are still not empowered to act autonomously and suffer from severe institutional capacity constraints. Their accountability, efficiency, and customer service are well below industry benchmarks. The freedom to make important decisions—such as setting up performance-based remuneration systems and providing market-linked remuneration to new employees—is limited. Robust and effective corporate governance is widely accepted as the essential foundation for performance improvement. Without the support of a strong board and high-quality senior management, the complete transformation in organizational culture needed to commercialize in the face of a long tradition of risk-averse top-down bureaucratic control will not be achieved. Some states in India (such as Andhra Pradesh and West Bengal) have adopted technology initiatives and accountability frameworks to improve sector performance (box 4.4).

BOX 4.4   Improving performance of state-owned power suppliers in Andhra Pradesh

In 1999, the government of Andhra Pradesh undertook a comprehensive reform program to control theft of electricity from state-owned power companies and improve its revenue collection. The campaign focused on four measures: enacting a new law to address electricity theft, strengthening enforcement mechanisms, reorganizing the anticorruption function in the utilities, and reengineering businesses processes to improve management control and customer service.

The distribution companies installed modern bulk metering, data-logging equipment, and mil-

lions of digital meters; they automated meter reading and reduced billing cycles. They also consulted extensively with customers and communicated with the general public about their reforms—a major change from previous practice. Under this campaign, the distribution companies regularized large numbers of consumers and prosecuted extreme cases of theft of electricity. As a result, they reduced losses from 38 percent in 1999 to 26 percent in 2003 and increased the collection rate to 98 percent.

Source: Bhatia and Gulati 2004.

Corruption policy options

Two broad strategies are discussed for addressing corruption based on experiences from countries in South Asia and other regions. The first strategy focuses on cutting red tape and simplifying administrative procedures to reduce unnecessary interaction with public officials and reduce opportunities for discretionary abuse by officials. In addition to reducing corruption, these policies should benefit firms by reducing the administrative burden on firms. Box 4.5

provides examples of red tape reforms that have had an impact on corruption.

The second broad strategy involves legislative and administrative interventions, such as establishing anticorruption laws and setting up anticorruption institutions, such as an independent anticorruption commission. Direct interventions have had a mixed record, with success depending on the governance structure of these institutions, their independence, and their resources and authority. Box 4.6 provides successful examples of direct legislative and administrative intervention.

BOX 4.5   Cutting red tape to reduce corruption

Investment climate assessments conducted by the World Bank identify several reforms that have reduced corruption by cutting red tape.

Bangladesh port and customs

The port of Chittagong, which handles 85 percent of Bangladesh's trade, was highly inefficient, with, for example, ship turnaround times of five to six days compared with one day at more efficient ports. Main problems included long and complex procedures, labor shortages, and lack of accountability of officers and employees of customs and port, leading to rent-seeking behavior and irregularities.

Following the handover of the Chittagong Container Terminal to a private operator, there have been noticeable improvements in handling operations. A one-stop service incorporating shipping agents, freight forwarders, customs, clearing and forwarding agents, and banks has ensured document clearance within 20 minutes. The turnaround time of ships has decreased to three to four days. Port efficiency has increased 30 percent, and the cost of doing business in the port has decreased 40 percent.

India land registration

Uncertainty surrounding property titles drives up the cost of land acquisition by limiting the supply of reliable investments. In many states, land records and registration of deeds have not been computer-

ized. Manual transcriptions are more prone to errors and misplacement.

Although recent reforms in some states have improved the registration process, it takes on average 87 days to register a property in India. Because of the lengthy and complex land transfer process, informal payments are considerable.

Recent reforms include computerization of land records in Gujarat, Karnataka, Madhya Pradesh, Maharashtra, and Tamil Nadu and computerization of the registration of deeds in Andhra Pradesh, Karnataka, Maharashtra, Rajasthan, and Tamil Nadu.

These reforms have led to substantial improvements. In cities where reforms have taken place, it takes a little more than one month to register land, rather than the more than five months in cities with no reforms. The reform has also had an impact on corruption: computerization of land records in Karnataka reduced informal payments by Rs 800 million and saved Rs 66 million in waiting time (Ferrari and Dhingra 2009).

Pakistan tax reform

The recent literature on tax reforms stresses the importance of tax administration and the effect it has on compliance costs. Recent reforms have focused on improving the management and organization of revenue administration; updating information technology and systems to efficiently process massive information flows from taxpayers; strengthening

(continues next page)

Cutting red tape to reduce corruption (continued)

investigation, so that authorities can develop risk analysis to closely follow cases that violate tax laws; and credibly conducting audits to improve enforcement. Such reforms signal credibility in the tax regime, a critical part of improving the system that can in turn increase voluntary compliance.

Reforms that simplify tax procedures and reduce interactions between tax officials and taxpayers, such as the reforms adopted in Chile, Colombia, and Latvia (Gill 2003), also reduce opportunities for corruption. Other anticorruption measures enabled by automation include restricting access of employees to scanned copies of original records to prevent tampering and creating audit trails of administrative decisions and changes to taxpayer current accounts.

In an attempt to decrease corruption by reducing the interaction between tax officials and private agents, the government of Pakistan raised the threshold for general sales tax registration from Rs 0.5 million to Rs 5 million, freeing 42,000 previously registered taxpayers from corruption-related

problems. However, this solution came at the cost of decreased tax revenue.

A less costly, and arguably more effective, effort was made by the Federal Bureau of Revenue to improve the integrity and accountability of its inspectors. It implemented a task force's recommendations to allow only minimal contact between taxpayers and tax officials; establish end-to-end automation of tax filing and refunds; improve recruitment policies, to weed out potentially corrupt officials; simplify tax structures; and reduce the discretion of tax officials in determining tax liabilities.

These attempts to decrease corruption should have an important side benefit in reducing tax administration costs, which firms in Pakistan cite as their second-highest constraint (after tax rates). Cross-country data on time to prepare and pay taxes show firms in Pakistan spending 560 hours versus an average of 314 hours for South Asia (World Bank 2011e).

Sources: Ferrari and Dhingra 2009; World Bank 2008c, 2009.

Legislative and administrative interventions to reduce corruption in East Asia

The annual Transparency International Corruption Perceptions Index ranks countries in terms of the degree to which corruption is perceived to exist among public officials and politicians.[a] Singapore has consistently ranked among the least corrupt countries in the index, ranking third in 2010 (after Denmark and New Zealand).

Singapore has a long tradition of fighting corruption. It implemented a comprehensive anticorruption system aimed at reducing the incentives and opportunities for corruption. This system includes legislation against corruption, called the Prevention Corruption Act; an independent authority called the Corrupt Practices Investigation Bureau, with strong powers to implement the law, including functions of investigation, prevention, and training in cases

related to corruption; and public information campaigns that promote whistleblowing and the fight against corruption.

Several countries in East Asia have tried to follow Singapore's recipe, with varying degrees of success. The Republic of Korea introduced the Anticorruption Act (2001), the Money Laundering Prevention Act (2001), and the Code of Conduct for Maintaining the Integrity of Public Officials (2003). It also created the Korea Independent Commission against Corruption (later called the National Integrity Commission). Korea's ranking in the Corruption Perceptions Index declined from 48 in 2001 to 39 in 2010. However, other East Asian countries that introduced similar reforms saw their rankings deteriorate (Malaysia ranked 44th in 2006 and 56th in 2010).

(continues next page)

BOX 4.6 (continued)

Analysis of the factors that may have led to success in Singapore suggests that there must be strong political will to fight corruption. This political will is partially reflected in the issuance of legislation and the creation of an independent implementation authority, but the authority must also have full powers, there must be strong political support for its actions at the highest level, and it must have the budget and personnel to carry out its functions. The anticorruption agency must be independent from the police and political control and incorruptible itself;

any corruption within the agency must be subject to harsh penalties. Major causes of corruption (including low civil service salaries and excessive red tape) must be tackled and corrupt offenders punished (Quah 2007).

a. The Transparency International Corruption Perceptions Index is a composite index drawing on corruption related data from expert and business surveys carried out by a variety of independent institutions. The index ranks more than 175 countries in terms of perceived levels of corruption as determined by expert assessment and opinion surveys (see http://www.transparency.org/policy_research/surveys_indices/cpi/2010/results).

Access to finance policy options

Access to finance is an issue for many micro, small, and medium enterprises in some South Asian countries. Policies to increase access to finance for such firms address the various demand- and supply-side constraints and the underlying institutional and regulatory environment that affects credit. Commercial banks face higher costs in lending to small, often geographically dispersed businesses, because identifying potential borrowers, conducting due diligence, and maintaining contact after a loan is made are all more difficult. For their part, small businesses often do not know what is needed to qualify for bank financing and lack market information. Governments should focus on developing an enabling environment that makes small business lending safer, cheaper, and faster rather than on prescriptive measures such as directed lending programs, which have created distortions and inefficiencies in financial intermediation in many South Asian countries.

Good practices from countries that have been able to expand access to finance for micro, small, and medium-size enterprises include the following:

- Establishing efficient secured transactions registries for available movable assets, in order to address micro, small,

and medium-size enterprises' lack of conventional collateral
- Strengthening credit bureaus, in order to help overcome adverse selection and moral hazard related to asymmetric information in credit markets
- Supporting financial intermediation by facilitating downscaling of commercial banks (for instance, through simplification of documentation and collateral requirements, reducing the number of days to approve a loan, and so forth) and upscaling microfinance institutions
- Providing technical assistance and financial literacy training to micro, small, and medium-size enterprises.

Annex 4E expands on these policy options.

The "how" of tackling constraints: public-private collaboration

This chapter so far has identified binding constraints to firms and suggests reforms that may be needed to facilitate the expansion of employment. The next question is how to design and implement successful reforms to address these constraints.

Reforms can be designed and implemented through coordinated public and private sector efforts. International experiences of successful industrial development indicate that such collaboration can play an important role in identifying binding constraints and designing, championing and implementing reform/actions in a coordinated and integrated manner, leading to increased competitiveness and growth. Efforts often focus on a particular sector, because many binding constraints and market failures are sector specific and private sector players find it easier to coalesce around a particular sector. Box 4.7 looks at the role of public-private collaboration to implement reforms in the export garment industry in Cambodia.

The World Bank's Financial and Private Development Network developed the Competitiveness Partnership Initiative (CPI), which is being piloted in several countries, including India, Jordan, and Kenya. CPI is a collaborative process between the public and private sectors around a sector or sectors with high growth potential. In Kenya, for instance, the selected sectors are tourism and business process outsourcing.

The CPI is developed around three broad steps:

- *Identify sector opportunities.* The first step is to use agreed upon selection criteria and demand-side/market signals (such as factor endowments, which identify where a country's latent comparative advantage lies) to identify existing sectors that have the potential to compete in regional and global markets, attract investment, and create jobs.
- *Conduct sector analyses.* The second step is to conduct evidence-based technical analyses of the opportunities and constraints of the selected sector—by, for example, performing value-chain diagnostics to identify constraints at each stage of the chain.
- *Develop action and implementation plans.* The last step is to create country-level task forces and joint public-private working groups that develop action plans to remove constraints and lead their implementation. Types of public, private, and public-private collaborative actions that could come out of this process include both hard and soft infrastructure delivery.

This targeted sector approach has several potential drawbacks. First, sectors could be

---

BOX 4.7   Public-private collaboration to implement reforms in the Cambodian garment industry

Cambodia's garment industry—the country's top export earner and top employer—consists of about 270 export-orientated factories. Total garment export revenue increased from $1.2 billion in 2001 to $2.9 billion in 2010, representing 78 percent of exports and 15 percent of GDP. The industry employs 290,000 workers, 92 percent of them women, representing 70 percent of formal manufacturing employment.

In 1999, the Government-Private Sector Forum (G-PSF) was established. Chaired by the prime minister, the G-PSF comprises eight working groups, each made up of government officials and private sector representatives. The export processing working group is co-chaired by the Ministry of Commerce and the Garment Manufacturers Association.

The International Finance Corporation (which funded G-PSF from 2000 to 2010) ranked it as one of the top most effective public-private dialogue mechanisms in the world. By reducing business costs, the 11 reforms the forum has implemented have saved the private sector an estimated $100 million.

A wide range of reforms has been implemented to improve the competitiveness of the garment and other export sectors. These reforms include the following:

- Simplifying import/export procedures, such as customs clearance at point of import
- Reducing export management fees
- Reducing contributions to the National Social Security Fund
- Developing the Trade Union Law
- Establishing joint trade missions between the private sector and the government
- Conducting government negotiations to obtain trade preferences and free trade agreements.

Source: Van 2011.

chosen arbitrarily or on the basis of noneconomic reasons rather than on latent comparative advantage or potential economic benefits. To prevent scarce resources from being unproductively invested, it is important to agree on objective selection criteria, use demand-side/market signals to identify sectors with comparative advantage, gauge trade potential and interest by private investors, and ensure that a wide set of private sector representatives from different sectors is consulted during the process of identifying priority sectors.

Second, the approach could create an uneven playing field between firms in different sectors and between firms within a sector if the reforms benefit disproportionately certain firms. To reduce the risks of being captured by vested interests of rent-seeking firms with privileged access to political and governance structures, it is important to ensure broad representation of private sector players—and not just the largest firms—in the public-private dialogue process; use objective, evidence-based analyses to identify constraints and assess costs and benefits of proposed actions; and establish processes that elicit structured and transparent dialogue, analysis, and decision making.

Cameroon provides an example of a competitiveness partnership initially diverted into rent-seeking activity. Most of the private sector members of the competitiveness committee, created in 1998, were members of a single business lobbying association. In 2007, the World Bank and the International Finance Corporation helped restructure a new collaboration platform, which was more inclusive and included a process for selecting proposals that followed good practice. The focus of the proposals was also narrowed to enable better scrutiny of the details (large reform proposals tend to provide opportunities to hide details). The results have been broader participation and wider acceptance of the reforms.

Constraints facing potential firm entrants: Business entry regulations

One of the limitations of the analysis of firm constraints is that it does not necessarily identify the constraints facing potential entrants. Doing so is important because new firms create jobs. The ease of business entry regulations has been identified as an important determinant of new firm entry, with studies showing that large reductions in business entry regulations—by, for example, introducing a one-stop shop of business registration centers or reducing registration fees—can spur the establishment of new formal firms by individuals who were previously wage workers or out of the labor force. Box 4.8 summarizes the evidence.

BOX 4.8   Effects of easing business entry regulations on firm entry, employment, and formalization

Large reductions in the ease of opening a business are positively and strongly associated with higher levels of business registration and new firm entry. A cross-country study by Klapper and Love (2010) finds that large reforms—reforms that achieve more than a 40 percent reduction in costs, days, or procedures of business registration—lead to an increase in rates of new firm entrance. Multiple and simultaneous reforms have a larger impact on business registration. A country's initial conditions matter: countries that start out with high registration costs need larger reforms to induce a significant number of new registrations.

In Mexico, a reform that reduced the average number of days needed to start a business from 30 to 1.4 led to a 5.0 percent increase in the number of new businesses and a 2.2 percent increase in wage employment (Bruhn 2008). The increase in registration and employment came from new activities from

(continues next page)

BOX 4.8   **Effects of easing business entry regulations on firm entry, employment, and formalization** (continued)

former wage earners. Former unregistered business owners were not more likely to register their business after the reform.

A field experiment in Sri Lanka by De Mel, McKenzie, and Woodruff (2011) aimed to estimate the demand for formality among informal firms with 1–14 workers. The experiment took 500 firms and divided them into 5 groups, each with 100 firms. The first group was the control group. The second group was given information on how to register with the district secretariat and obtain a business registration certificate and offered reimbursement of the cost of doing so. The remaining groups were also given this information. In addition, they were offered payments of Rs 10,000 (about $88, just under half a month's profits for the median firm); Rs 20,000; or Rs 40,000 if they registered within a set timeframe.

The study found that providing information and reducing the cost of registering to zero was not enough to induce firms to register. In contrast, the Rs 10,000 and Rs 20,000 payments were enough to induce about one-fifth of eligible informal firms to register, and the Rs 40,000 payment was enough to induce almost half of eligible informal firms to do so. The finding that additional monetary incentives were required supports the "exit" hypothesis, which posits that the net benefits to formalization may be very low (if not negative) and that firms are therefore rational in choosing to remain informal, rather than the "exclusion" hypothesis, which posits that there are high net positive benefits to formalization and that it is the upfront costs or complexity of registration that keeps firms informal. Firm owners asked about the possible costs of registering most often cited paying taxes (corporate and employee) and being subject to tax and labor

inspections. In terms of benefits, most mentioned being able to obtain a bank account, apply for bank loans, operate on a larger and more visible scale, and get contracts.

Does formalization of existing informal firms result in increased productivity and employment? The Sri Lanka study reinterviewed the same firms 12–18 months after formalizing, to see whether there was any evidence that formality had benefitted them. Over this time frame it found little evidence of any of the main channels through which formality is argued to benefit firms: the newly formalized firms had not received more credit or obtained more government contracts, they had not become more visible, and they had not hired more workers. There was also no significant impact on sales or profits (although the study could not rule out large negative or positive impacts given how noisy the data were). These findings suggest that informal enterprise owners acted rationally by formalizing only when provided with monetary incentives to do so.

Simplification of entry regulations alone is unlikely to be enough to get informal firms to formalize, although the results show that it does not take too much of a change in net benefits of formalizing to induce formalization (half the firms were ready to formalize for an amount equal to 1.5–2.0 months' profits). Moreover, formalization is not sufficient for increasing productivity. Therefore, rather than focusing on inducing existing informal firms to register their businesses, it may be more effective to focus on directly easing constraints to their productivity. Increasing their productivity is likely to have a second-round effect on reducing informality, as increasing productivity can increase returns to formalization.

The 2010 World Bank Doing Business indicator for starting a business indicates that the average number of procedures, time, and cost of starting a business in South Asia are on a par with or lower than in Africa, East Asia, or Latin America and the Caribbean.

India has the largest number of procedures (12) and costs in the region and is ranked lowest (165th in the world) for this indicator.[18] Nepal ranks 96th, Pakistan 85th, Bhutan 84th, Bangladesh 79th, Maldives 50th, Afghanistan 25th, and Sri Lanka 24th.

Annex 4A Business environment constraints in high- and low-income states in India

The division into high-income and low-income states in India is based on their net state domestic product per capita over the period 1999/2000 to 2009/10. The high income group comprises Andhra Pradesh, Goa, Gujarat, Haryana, Himachal Pradesh, Karnataka, Kerala, Maharashtra, Punjab, Tamil Nadu, Andaman and Nicobar Islands, Chandigarh, Delhi, and Puducherry.

The low income group comprises Arunachal Pradesh, Assam, Bihar, Chattisgarh, Jammu and Kashmir, Jharkand, Madhya Pradesh, Manipur, Meghalaya, Mizoram, Nagaland, Orissa, Rajasthan, Sikkim, Tripura, Uttar Pradesh, Uttarakhand, and West Bengal.

TABLE 4A.1 Top five constraints reported by benchmark firm in the urban formal sector in high- and low-income states in India

Constraint	Low-income states	High-income states
Electricity	1	3
Corruption	2	1
Tax administration	3	2
Transport	4	
Crime, theft, and disorder	5	
Labor regulations		4
Government policy uncertainty		5

Source: Authors, based on Carlin and Schaffer 2011b (based on World Bank enterprise surveys).
Note: A benchmark firm is a medium-size manufacturing firm with 30 employees that is domestically owned, does not export or import, is located in a large city, and did not expand employment in the preceding three years. Analysis is based on a pooled sample of enterprise surveys conducted in India between 2000 and 2010. Access to finance and tax rates constraints are excluded. Political instability was not asked in the India surveys.

FIGURE 4A.1 Severity of constraints reported by benchmark firm in urban formal sector in high- and low-income states in India

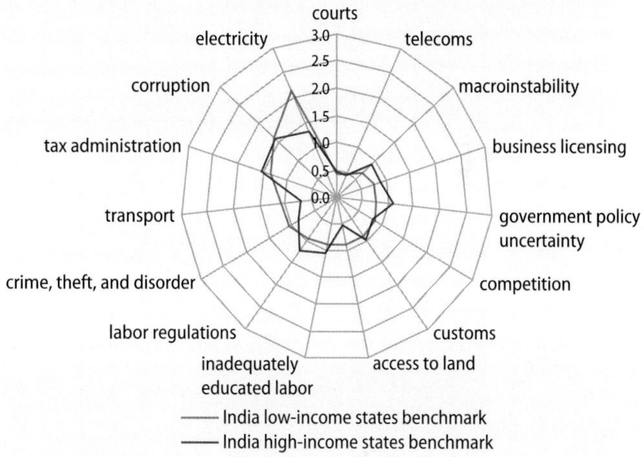

Source: Authors, based on Carlin and Schaffer 2011b (based on World Bank enterprise surveys).
Note: A benchmark firm is a medium-size manufacturing firm with 30 employees that is domestically owned, does not export or import, is located in a large city, and did not expand employment in the preceding three years. Analysis is based on a pooled sample of enterprise surveys conducted in India between 2000 and 2010. A point farther away from the origin indicates that the business constraint is considered more severe. The severity of constraint is rated by firms on a 5-point scale, with 0 being no obstacle, 1 being a minor obstacle, 2 being a moderate obstacle, 3 being a major obstacle, and 4 being a very severe obstacle. Access to finance and tax rates constraints are excluded. Political instability was not asked in the India surveys.

Annex 4B Tax rates as a constraint to firms

The reported severity of the tax rate constraint cannot be interpreted directly as evidence that tax rates are binding constraints in South Asia. This annex looks at alternative indicators.

Cross-country comparison of reported severity

Although comparing the level of severity reported for the tax rate constraint with other elements of the business environment is problematic, cross-country comparisons can be used to show whether the severity reported in South Asia is atypical. Figure 4B.1 shows the reported severity of the tax rate constraint for a benchmark firm in different countries. It shows that independent of the level of income of the country, firms complain significantly about tax rates. Only Pakistan reports higher severity than is typical of countries at its level of development;

FIGURE 4B.1 **Cross-country comparison of reported severity of tax rate constraint**

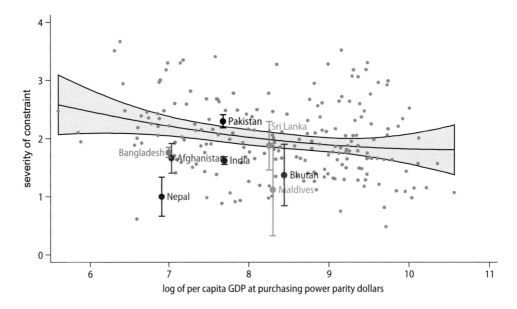

Source: Carlin and Schaffer 2011b (based on World Bank enterprise surveys).
Note: The cross-country regression line shows the relationship between the reported severity of the constraint for a benchmark firm and the log of per capita GDP. The shaded area is the 95 percent confidence interval band around the regression line. Vertical bars show confidence intervals of 95 percent around the reported severity of the constraint for countries in South Asia. The lack of overlap between the South Asian country confidence interval and the regression line confidence interval is a conservative test of the statistically significant difference between the reported severity of a constraint for the South Asian country and the average reported severity of constraint for countries at the same level of per capita GDP. The reported severity could still be significantly different even when there is an overlap. Analysis is based on a pooled sample of enterprise surveys conducted between 2000 and 2010. The severity of constraint is rated by firms on a 5-point scale, with 0 being no obstacle, 1 being a minor obstacle, 2 being a moderate obstacle, 3 being a major obstacle, and 4 being a very severe obstacle.

elsewhere in the region, firms consider tax rates less of an obstacle than do firms in other countries at the same income levels.

Total tax revenues to GDP ratio

The ratio of total tax revenues to GDP is low in many countries in the region—just 9 percent in Bangladesh, for example, and 10 percent in Pakistan (figure 4B.2). These ratios do not necessarily reflect low taxes, however. Rather, they represent a lower level of development and very narrow tax bases. In Pakistan, the tax base is very small, and firms that are in the tax base bear a heavy tax burden. The same is true for Bangladesh, where only 1.4 million of the country's 145 million people are registered in the tax base. In 2004,

only 0.85 million out of a registered tax base of 1.25 million are actually taxpayers.

Statutory and effective tax rates

Although tax rates in India, Pakistan, and Sri Lanka are lower than they were in the 1990s, these countries still have the highest marginal corporate tax rates in the region. Rates are higher than comparator countries such as Brazil, China, Ghana, Indonesia, the Philippines, and Thailand (figure 4B.3).

Because of poor compliance, however, and system of exemptions and loopholes, there is a significant divergence between statutory and actual average effective tax rates in South Asia. There is also a wide variance in effective tax rates across activities and sectors, which

FIGURE 4B.2   **Tax revenue as a percentage of GDP in South Asia**

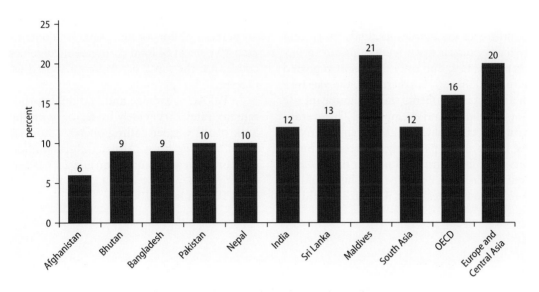

Source: World Bank 2011e.
Note: OECD = Organisation for Economic Co-operation and Development.

FIGURE 4B.3   **Highest marginal corporate tax rate in South Asian countries and selected comparator countries**

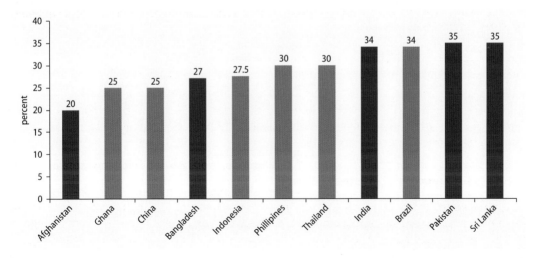

Source: World Bank 2011e.

creates distortions, because decisions about resource allocation, location, and investment are driven by tax considerations rather than underlying economic reasons. The cases of Bangladesh and Pakistan are discussed below.

Taxation in Bangladesh is characterized by low collections, highly complex rules, a heavy administrative burden, and poor compliance (World Bank 2008c). It has become the norm in Bangladesh to pay minimum taxes (by, for example, underreporting profits) or to avoid them altogether, because of both lax enforcement of laws (tax defaulters are rarely investigated) and the hassle and cost involved in dealing with tax authorities. Only 66 percent of metropolitan firms were required to pay corporate tax, and only 3 percent reported actually doing so. Furthermore, the variance in actual tax payments shows significant use of tax holidays and exemptions. The average firm paid taxes of about 16 percent of profits; the median firm paid only 7 percent. Among private unlisted firms, 25 percent paid 84 percent of the taxes collected (the bulk paid by foreign companies), and 13 percent paid no income tax. Among listed companies, 1.2 percent paid 53.3 percent of taxes, and the top 40 percent paid almost 100 percent. The top 10 percent of corporate taxpayers contributed 80 percent of total corporate income tax collection; the top 5 percent contributed 64 percent.

In Pakistan, average and marginal corporate tax rates vary widely by sector, with the bulk of the burden falling on large, formal manufacturing firms. Although formal manufacturing firms account for just 23 percent of output, they account for half of all federal taxes (World Bank 2009).

Annex 4C   Constraints facing nonbenchmark firms

FIGURE 4C.1   **Severity of constraints reported by benchmark firm and firm with 60 employees in the urban formal sector in Nepal and Sri Lanka**

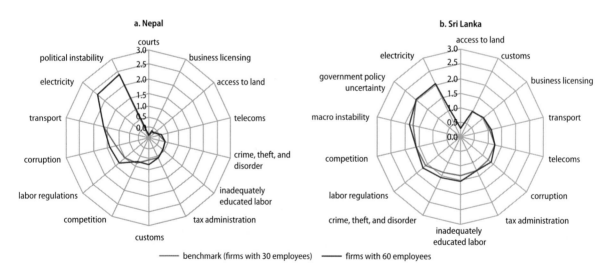

Source: Authors, based on Carlin and Schaffer 2011b (based on World Bank enterprise surveys).
Note: A benchmark firm is a medium-size manufacturing firm with 30 employees that is domestically owned, does not export or import, is located in a large city, and did not expand employment in the preceding three years. The firm with 60 employees is the same as the benchmark firm except for the firm size. Analysis is based on a pooled sample of enterprise surveys conducted in Nepal and Sri Lanka between 2000 and 2010. A point farther away from the origin indicates that the business constraint is considered more severe. The severity of constraint is rated by firms on a 5-point scale, with 0 being no obstacle, 1 being a minor obstacle, 2 being a moderate obstacle, 3 being a major obstacle, and 4 being a very severe obstacle. Access to finance and tax rates constraints are excluded.

FIGURE 4C.2 **Severity of constraints reported by benchmark (nonexporting) and exporting firm in the urban formal sector in South Asia and Bangladesh**

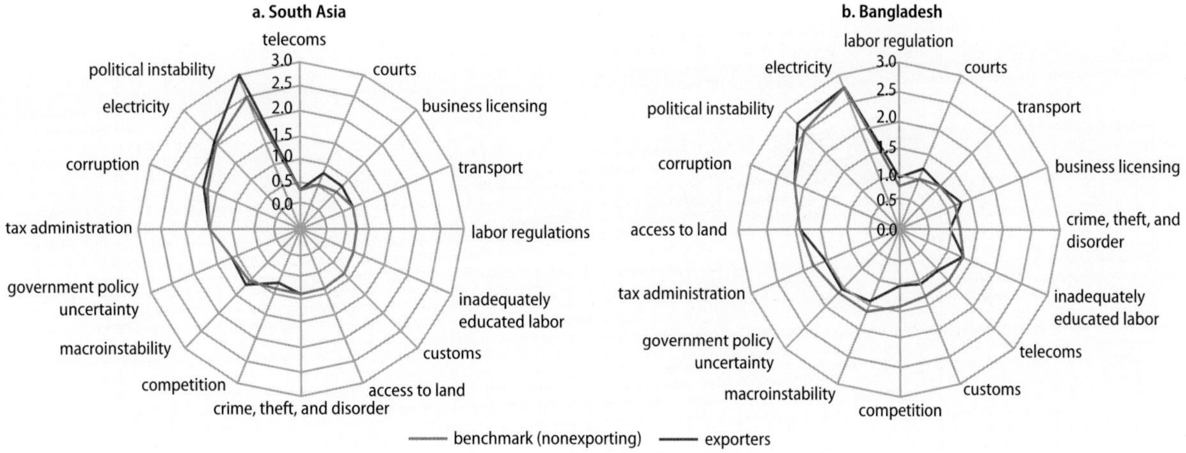

Source: Authors, based on Carlin and Schaffer 2011b (based on World Bank enterprise surveys).
Note: A benchmark firm is a medium-size manufacturing firm with 30 employees that is domestically owned, does not export or import, is located in a large city, and did not expand employment in the preceding three years. The exporter firm is the same as the benchmark firm except that it exports. Analysis is based on pooled sample of enterprise surveys conducted in South Asia and Bangladesh between 2000 and 2010. A point farther away from the origin indicates that the business constraint is considered more severe. The severity of constraint is rated by firms on a 5-point scale, with 0 being no obstacle, 1 being a minor obstacle, 2 being a moderate obstacle, 3 being a major obstacle, and 4 being a very severe obstacle. Access to finance and tax rates constraints are excluded.

Annex 4D   Access to finance as a constraint to firms

The reported severity of the access to finance constraint cannot be interpreted as evidence that access to finance is a binding constraint in South Asia. This annex looks at alternative indicators.

Cross-country comparison of reported severity

Figure 4D.1 shows the reported severity of the access to finance constraint for benchmark firms in different countries. It shows that in no country in South Asia do firms cite it as a greater obstacle than in firms in other countries with the same level of per capita GDP.

Financial depth

Financial depth measures the availability of financial resources for the economy and for firms. The financial markets in South Asia are not shallow by measures such as domestic credit to the private sector as a

percentage of GDP, and they are generally experiencing rapid growth. Indeed, financial depth has been increasing in all countries in South Asia except Sri Lanka.

In 2008, domestic credit to the private sector as a share of GDP was 29 percent in Sri Lanka and Pakistan, 30 percent in Bhutan, 39 percent in Bangladesh, 51 percent in India, and 56 percent in Nepal (Hoxha 2011). Compared with countries with similar levels of per capita GDP (which is positively correlated correlation with financial depth), only Bhutan is significantly below average.

Cost of finance

Using lending interest rates to assess the cost of finance is difficult, because there is a high level of state intermediation in many South Asian countries: interest rates in Bangladesh, India, and Pakistan are not freely set by the market. Nevertheless, lending rates in South Asia are not high compared with other countries at the same level of per capita GDP.

FIGURE 4D.1   **Cross-country comparison of reported severity of access to finance constraint**

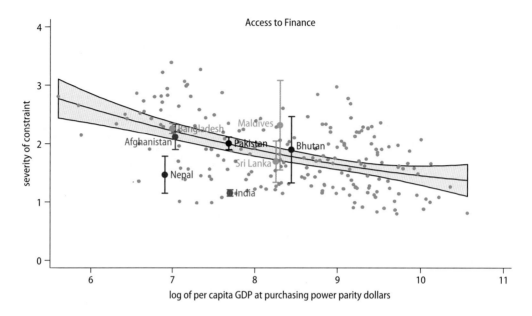

Source: Carlin and Schaffer 2011b (based on World Bank enterprise surveys).
Note: The cross-country regression line shows the relationship between the reported severity of the constraint for a benchmark firm and the log of per capita GDP. The shaded area is the 95 percent confidence interval band around the regression line. Vertical bars show confidence intervals of 95 percent around the reported severity of the constraint for countries in South Asia. The lack of overlap between the South Asian country confidence interval and the regression line confidence interval is a conservative test of the statistically significant difference between the reported severity of a constraint for the South Asian country and the average reported severity of constraint for countries at the same level of per capita GDP. The reported severity could still be significantly different even when there is an overlap. Analysis is based on pooled sample of enterprise surveys conducted between 2000 and 2010. The severity of constraint is rated by firms on a 5-point scale, with 0 being no obstacle, 1 being a minor obstacle, 2 being a moderate obstacle, 3 being a major obstacle, and 4 being a very severe obstacle.

Financial outreach and access

Outreach is a measure of financial inclusiveness; it is captured here by variables such as the percent of firms with access to a loan or other financial products. Enterprise surveys show large variation in access to external finance for firms both across and within countries, with smaller firms having less access, leading to claims of a small and medium-size enterprise finance gap, particularly in emerging economies, where larger enterprises are frequently the main beneficiaries of tax incentives and corporate subsidies and aid is targeted at microenterprises.[19]

Small firms in the urban formal sector in Afghanistan, Pakistan, and, to a lesser extent, India use external finance less than small firms in other countries (figure 4D.2). Only 2 percent of firms in Afghanistan and

5 percent of firms in Pakistan use banks to finance working capital compared with 36 percent in India, 43 percent in Bangladesh, and 52 percent in Sri Lanka. Small firms in Afghanistan and Pakistan finance a larger share of working capital (88–91 percent) from internal financial sources than large firms (63–88 percent).

Moreover, comparable survey data in Afghanistan, Bangladesh, and Pakistan show no clear trend in terms of the share of investment financed by internal funds (retained earnings); external finance (banks and nonbank financial institutions); and informal finance (family, friends, moneylenders) in the past five years for a benchmark firm in the urban formal sector. Internal funds continue to finance most investment.

Use of external finance is even lower among rural and informal firms, which are typically microenterprises, and often reflects lower

FIGURE 4D.2   Percentage of firms with credit line or loan from financial institution, by firm size and region

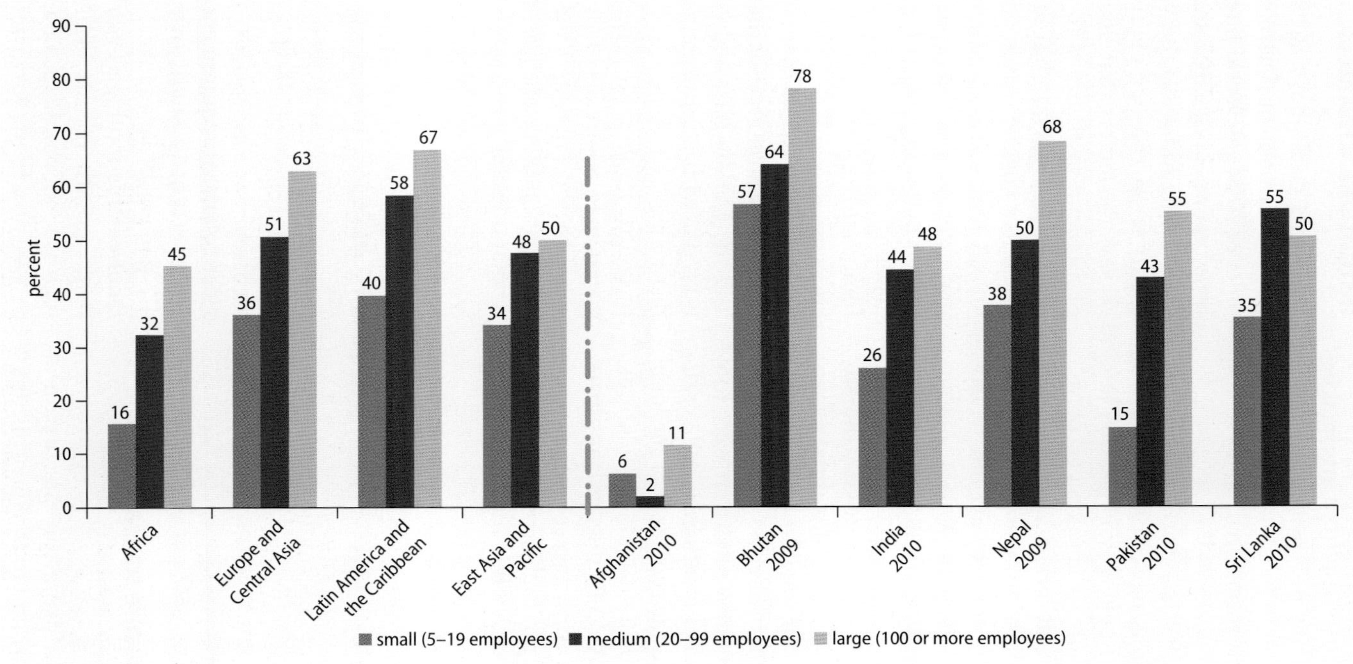

Source: Authors, based on World Bank enterprise surveys.

access to banking services. In Bangladesh, only 9 percent of firms in nonmetropolitan areas have bank accounts, compared with 95 percent in metropolitan areas, and only 6 percent of nonmetropolitan enterprises use formal finance.

In the informal sector in India, 89 percent of enterprises had bank accounts, but less than 20 percent had a loan (from informal or formal sources). Only 6–9 percent of informal firms had a loan from a financial institution (versus 26 percent of small firms in the formal sector).

In Pakistan, very few rural firms deal with the formal banking sector: only 10–12 percent of enterprises keep savings, and less than 10 percent maintain checking accounts. About 43 percent enterprises in villages and 58 percent in small towns made investments the year preceding the survey, but nearly 90 percent were made with savings. Among surveyed business owners in rural areas, 24–28 percent wanted to apply for a formal loan, but only 4–7 percent actually did so. Among firms in Pakistan that wanted a loan but did not apply for one, 40 percent cited loan procedures that were too complicated, 27 percent cited interest rates that were too high, 16 percent cited insufficient collateral, and 8 percent cited the shortness of the loan duration. Two-thirds of loan applications were approved. Among rejected applications, 36 percent were refused because of insufficient collateral. Eighty percent of formal loans require collateral, and the average

value of the collateral required was 132 percent of the loan amount. The most common forms of collateral were property/buildings and land. In summary, there is evidence of unmet demand for the rural nonfarm sector in Pakistan.

Institutional indicators

Creditors care about the broader institutional environment (Djankov, McLiesh, and Shleifer 2007). A World Bank (2008b) study, based on an April 2007 survey of commercial banks, addresses the issue of access to credit from the perspective of supply. It reviews the factors that limit the willingness of financial institutions to lend or increase their incentives to charge higher interest rates. Key concerns were problems with collateral registration and enforcement; limited information (the result of the lack of a well-functioning credit registry); and poor accounting and auditing practices, which limit verifiable financial information. Some countries in South Asia have weak legal and property rights, but the region as a whole performs better in this regard than Africa and the Middle East and North Africa and is on par with Latin America and the Caribbean and East Asia and Pacific. In terms of credit, public and private credit bureau coverage in South Asia is lower than in any other region, although the depth of credit information is better than in Africa and East Asia and Pacific.

Annex 4E   Policy options for increasing access to finance

This annex describes four policy areas that can increase access to finance, particularly for micro, small, and medium-size enterprises (Hoxha 2011).

Operationalize secure transactions registeries

Lack of credit information on customers and weak contract enforcement means

that banks are generally not willing to lend without secure collateral. Micro, small, and medium-size enterprises find it harder to meet collateral requirements: in Bangladesh 30.8 percent of small firms (compared to 4.2 percent of large firms) found collateral requirements too high (World Bank 2008c). Banks usually require immovable property, such as land, buildings, or an owner's assets, to secure a loan. Most micro, small, and medium-size enterprise firms' property and assets are vested in movable property, such as machinery and inventory.

For example, in India an immovable asset of the enterprise (60 percent of loans) or a personal asset of the owner (25 percent of loans) is usually required as collateral. Such assets account for a small percentage of the total asset value of unorganized firms. Moreover, in about half of cases, the collateral required was more than twice the amount of the loan (Ferrari and Dhingra 2009). In Sri Lanka, collateral in the form of land is especially important for rural enterprises, but high levels of public landownership, unclear ownership records, and widespread restrictions on the use and transfer of land make it difficult to use land as collateral (World Bank 2005).

In the absence of a secured transactions mechanism, lenders find it risky to accept movable property as collateral. A secured transactions mechanism facilitates lending by eliminating information asymmetries about collateral and reducing the risk of lending secured by movables.

Successful models of secured transactions registry include the creation of a registration database in which a public record of obligations secured by movable property can be made; the setting of priorities in case of multiple obligations of the same security giver as secured by the same collateral; and the establishment of a means to uniformly enforce secure interests in case the security giver defaults.

Deepen the reach of credit bureaus

Credit bureaus promote deeper financial systems by helping overcome adverse selection and moral hazard related to asymmetric information in credit markets (Djankov, McLiesh, and Shleifer 2007). As a result of the cost savings achieved through more efficient and accurate credit analysis and lower expected losses, lenders can increase their credit extension. Using cross-country firm-level survey data and survey data of credit bureaus, Love and Mylenko (2003) find that the existence of private credit bureaus is associated with lower financing constraints and a larger share of bank financing. In addition, small and medium-size enterprises tend to have a larger share of bank financing in countries where private registries exist. Currently, credit bureau coverage in South Asia is the lowest of any region. It is particularly low in Afghanistan, Bangladesh, Bhutan, Nepal, and Pakistan.

Downscale commercial banks and upscale microfinance institutions

Access depends not only on the terms and cost of finance but also on other barriers, such as eligibility criteria; procedural exclusions (high minimum loan size requirements, documentation requirements, days to process loans); and lack of appropriate financial products for micro, small, and medium-size enterprises.

A crucial function of financial intermediaries is to screen borrowers. The number of days it takes to process a loan application can be a de facto eligibility barrier, because some borrowers may be discouraged from applying for bank loans and seek financing elsewhere to avoid long waiting periods. Beck, Demirgüç-Kunt, and Peria (2007) find that on average loan applications by small and medium-size enterprise take more than a month to process in Bangladesh (43 days) and Pakistan (34 days). In contrast, the median number of days for the 60 countries in their sample was nine days.

Lack of documentation can create other eligibility barriers. Bangladesh and Nepal require at least four documents, including an identity card or passport, a recommendation letter, a wage slip, and proof of domicile. For the 60 countries Beck, Demirgüç-Kunt, and Peria examine, the average number of documents was two. Given the high degree of informality in South Asia, only a small proportion of potential borrowers can produce these documents.

Standard financial products offered by banks, such as lines of credit, are designed for large corporations (the traditional client for South Asian banks). They are inappropriate for many small businesses, which do not deposit their revenues in banks.

To serve small businesses well and profitably, banks need to simplify procedures for small business loans; design appropriate financial products for micro, small, and medium-size enterprises; reduce reliance on collateral and modernize lending based on risk and credit information; and use technology to reduce transaction costs and generate deal volume. Some banks have been successful in downscaling to the small and medium-size enterprise market, achieving high levels of outreach, scale, and sustainability (box 4E.1).

Microfinance institutions need to adapt their business model and product offerings to the small and medium-size enterprise market. One institution that has done so is BRAC Bank (box 4E.2).

BOX 4E.1   Successful approaches to small and medium-size business banking

ICICI Bank is the largest private sector bank in India. Its small and medium-size enterprise banking model is based on segmentation of the market by industry and business linkages; a proprietary risk evaluation covering financial and nonfinancial parameters to compensate for enterprises' lack of financial information; and a "beyond lending approach," which relies primarily on deposit products and other banking services (used by 95 percent of small and medium-size enterprise clients) rather than lending products (used by just 5 percent of such clients). Client servicing is done though multiple channels, including relationship managers, doorstep banking, branches, the Internet, and automatic teller machines.

In 2002, Standard Chartered Bank implemented a client-centric model on a global scale, creating a separate small and medium-size enterprise banking operation, with its own resources and credit processes, within its consumer bank unit. Today, this business unit operates in more than 30 countries. The bank follows three customer acquisition and servicing approaches: relationship managers handle larger medium-size enterprises; a portfolio team made up of salespeople and virtual relationship managers handle midsize small and medium-size enterprises; and branches handle smaller businesses, whose needs are similar to those of individuals.

BOX 4E.2   Scaling up microfinance institutions: The case of BRAC Bank

BRAC Bank Ltd. was established in Bangladesh in 2001, with a focus on the small business sector. Its small and medium-size enterprise banking unit goes beyond traditional banking, working with entrepreneurs as a business partner by building awareness, providing training, and arranging road shows to support and develop clients' businesses. BRAC Bank is the number one small business bank in Bangladesh in terms of loans outstanding, with nationwide coverage (44 percent of coverage is in rural areas). The bank's small business banking model empha-

sizes relationship banking and collateral-free lending of up to $14,000.

Upscaling relies heavily on support from international and domestic financial institutions in the start-up phase. Such support is particularly important in adapting microfinance institutions' lending technologies to serve the new clientele and in building the capacity of staff. BRAC Bank's second- and third-largest shareholders are Shorecap International Limited and the International Finance Corporation.

Commercial downscaling and microfinance institution upscaling should be led by banks themselves. Governments can facilitate the process by creating an enabling regulatory and institutional environment—by, for example, revising rules on provisioning and credit bureau reporting, which make it expensive to serve smaller firms. Governments can also look into using credit guarantee schemes and other financial products aimed at reducing the risk associated with lending to small and medium-size enterprises. Such schemes would address information asymmetries, the high costs of processing small credit transactions, and constraints in the enforcement of contracts.

Provide technical assistance and financial literacy training

Small and medium-size enterprises face several nonfinancial barriers that are related to their own capacity. Managers or owners of such firms usually perform a wider range of tasks than their managers or owners of larger firms. Moreover, small and medium-size enterprises cannot take advantage of economies of scale related to accounting, business planning, and market research to the same extent as large firms can. Enterprise survey data indicate that only 37 percent of small firms have their annual financial statement reviewed by an external auditor, compared with 58 percent of medium-size firms and 79 percent of large firms (Hoxha 2011). In Bangladesh, a quarter of smaller urban firms find the procedures for applying for a loan too complex (compared with only 1.2 percent of large urban firms) (World Bank 2008c). Only about 5 percent of village enterprises and 11 percent of small town enterprises in Pakistan prepare financial statements.

Technical assistance and financial literacy training can be provided to small and medium-size enterprises to increase their capacity to keep better accounts and develop and present bankable proposals. Doing so would ensure that such enterprises have the capacity to successfully apply for loans and effectively use loans for the growth of their businesses.

Notes

1. The first study sets out the methodological framework and tests predictions of how a firm's evaluation of the cost of constraints imposed by its external environment varies with the firm's characteristics. These tests confirm the predictions of the model and provide the empirical basis for using, in the second and third studies, the reported severity of constraints to assess which elements of the external environment are most problematic for firms across South Asia and in each country.
2. Eighteen constraints appear in the enterprise surveys: electricity; telecommunications; transport; access to land; inadequately educated labor; macroeconomic instability; government policy uncertainty; political instability; access to finance; competition; tax administration; tax rates; labor regulations; customs; business licensing; courts; corruption; and crime, theft, and disorder. Surveys in Afghanistan, Bhutan, and Nepal did not ask about macroinstability or government policy uncertainty. Surveys in India, Maldives, and Sri Lanka did not ask about political instability.
3. The World Bank enterprise surveys portal contains data on almost 120,000 urban formal firms (16,000 in South Asia) from more than 230 surveys in 126 countries conducted between 2000 and 2010 (see http://www.enterprisesurveys.org/).
4. The Bangladesh rural survey covered peri-urban areas, small towns, and rural villages. The Pakistan rural survey covered small towns and rural villages. The Sri Lanka rural survey covered rural areas as defined by the Department of Census and Statistics.
5. Only the 2001 survey was used in the formal analysis of the severity of constraints, because the constraint question in 2005 did not use the standard 0–4 scale. The ranking of constraints from the 2005 informal survey was used to check the results.
6. In addition, to facilitate better comparison, firms with more than 20 employees were dropped from the sample of urban formal firms.
7. The states were grouped based on net state domestic product per capita over the previous 10 years.
8. Empirical evidence on other developing regions indicates that because they lack the economies of scale to operate a power

generator efficiently, small and medium enterprises, which create a large share of new jobs, are the most affected in areas without access to electricity or an unreliable public grid (Aterido, Hallward-Driemeier, and Pagés 2007).

9. Results reported are from partial correlations with other indicators of firm productivity in the pooled sample of South Asian firms with country fixed effects and controls for firm size, sector, location, exporting and importing status, and ownership (Carlin and Schaffer 2011c).

10. Expanding firms in Afghanistan and Bangladesh firms report lower costs than the benchmark firm. A hypothesis on why this may be the case in Bangladesh is that expanding firms are located in export processing zones, which face especial conditions that lower the constraints.

11. This finding is consistent with a 2007 Organisation for Economic Co-operation and Development (OECD) economic survey of India that describes the service sector as being less dependent on electricity and less subject to labor regulations; the sector also faces lower indirect taxation and has access to better infrastructure and a more conducive business environment. The OECD survey makes the case that growth in the service sector has been more dynamic because these constraints are less binding.

12. The regression model assumes a linear relationship between firm characteristics and reported severity, so that if, on average, larger firms (more than 30 employees) report more severe constraints than the benchmark firm (30 employees), on average, smaller firms (fewer than 30 employees) will report less severe constraints.

13. Using the rural enterprise and household surveys, Deininger, Jin, and Sur (2007) find that the top five reported constraints among rural firms in Sri Lanka were also the most significant determinants of new nonfarm enterprise start-ups. In areas where electricity is a major constraint, the propensity to start up a firm is 14 percent lower. Distance to banks, poor road access, credit constraints, and lack of market demand are all negatively correlated with the probability of starting up a business.

14. Enterprises that sell to larger firms are less likely than enterprises that sell directly to local consumers to complain about low demand (World Bank 2008c).

15. About 305 urban manufacturing firms had subcontracting arrangements for input purchases, but only 1 percent purchased inputs from firms/distributors located in villages.

16. Other controls in the ordinary least squares regression include the number of urban centers in the district, the number of urban centers in a region, distance to district headquarters, the average height and slope of land, and the population density in the village.

17. The second Bangladesh investment climate assessment (World Bank 2008c) concludes that overall lending to the private sector had improved and was adequate in Bangladesh but that lending to small firms and nonurban firms remained inadequate because of lack of appropriate lending techniques and products for micro, small, and medium-size enterprises.

18. A procedure is defined as any interaction between the company founders and external parties (for example, government agencies, lawyers, auditors, or notaries). Cost is measured as a percentage of the economy's income per capita. It is measured in two ways: (a) all official fees and fees for legal or professional services if such services are required by law and (b) the amount the entrepreneur needs to deposit in a bank or with a notary before registration and up to three months following incorporation, as a percentage of the economy's income per capita.

19. A 2008 World Bank enterprise survey of more than 50,000 firms in more than 70 countries indicates that small and medium-size firms rank access to and cost of finance as one of their top constraints to growth.

References

Alby, P., J. J. Dethier, and S. Straub. 2010. "Firms Operating under Infrastructure and Credit Constraints in Developing Countries. The Case of Power Generators." Policy Research Working Paper 5497, World Bank, Washington, DC.

ADB (Asian Development Bank). 2009. *Enterprises in Asia: Fostering Dynamism in SMEs*. Manila.

———. 2010. *Bhutan Energy Sector: Sector Assistance Program Evaluation*. Manila.

Aterido, R., M. Hallward-Driemeier, and C. Pagés. 2007. "Business Climate and Employment Growth: The Impact of Access to Finance, Corruption and Regulation Across firms."

IZA Discussion Paper, Institute for the Study of Labor, Bonn.

Banerjee, A., and E. Duflo. 2008. "Do Firms Want to Borrow More? Testing Credit Constraints Using a Directed Lending Program." CEPR Discussion Paper 4681, Center for Economic and Policy Research, Washington, DC.

Banerjee, S. G., A. Singh, and H. Samad. 2011. *Power and People: The Benefits of Renewable Energy in Nepal*. World Bank, South Asia Sustainable Development, Washington, DC.

Banerji, D., and M. Mishra. 2010. "Power Sector to Lead Infra Investments in 12th Plan." *Business Standard*, December 29, New Delhi. http://www.business-standard.com/india/news/power-sector-to-lead-infra-investments-in-12th-plan/419972/.

Beck, T., A. Demirgüç-Kunt, and V. Maksimovic. 2005. "Financial and Legal Constraints to Firm Growth: Does Firm Size Matter?" *Journal of Finance* 60 (1): 137–77.

Beck, T., A. Demirgüç-Kunt, and M. Peria. 2007. "Banking Banking Services for Everyone? Barriers to Bank Access and Use around the World." Policy Research Working Paper 4079, World Bank, Washington, DC.

Besant-Jones, J. 2006. "Reforming Power Markets in Developing Countries. What Have We Learned?" Energy and Mining Sector Board Discussion Paper 19, World Bank, Washington, DC. http://siteresources.worldbank.org/INTENERGY/Resources/Energy19.pdf.

Bhatia, B., and M. Gulati. 2004. "Reforming the Power Sector: Controlling Electricity Theft and Improving Revenue." Note 272 Private Sector Development, World Bank, Washington, DC. http://rru.worldbank.org/documents/publicpolicyjournal/272bhatia_Gulati.pdf.

Bird, R., and M. Zolt. 2007. "Tax Policy in Emerging Countries." International Tax Program Paper 0707. University of Toronto.

Bruhn, M. 2008. "License to Sell: The Effect of Business Registration Reform on Entrepreneurial Activity in Mexico." Policy Research Working Paper 4538, World Bank, Washington, DC.

Carlin, W., and M. Schaffer. 2011a. "A Comparison of Business Environment Constraints between Formal Sector Firms and Rural and Informal Sector Firms." Background study conducted for this book.

———. 2011b. "Which Elements of the Business Environment Matter Most for Firms and How Do They Vary Across Countries?" Background study conducted for this book.

———. 2011c. "How Do Business Environment Constraints Vary with Firm Efficiency and Dynamism?" Background study conducted for this book.

Central Electricity Regulatory Commission. 2011. *Report on the State of Short-Term Power Market in India*. New Delhi.

Ceylon Electricity Board. 2009. "Statistical Digest 2009." Colombo, Sri Lanka.

CRISIL Risk and Infrastructure Solutions Limited. 2011. *The Study on Skill Gaps and Employment Opportunities in Power Sector in India*. Report submitted to World Bank, Washington, DC.

Deininger, K., S. Jin, and M. Sur. 2007. "Sri Lanka's Rural Non-Farm Economy: Removing Constraints to Pro-Poor Growth." *World Development* 35 (12): 2056–78.

De Mel, S., D. McKenzie, and C. Woodruff. 2011. "What Is the Cost of Informality? Experimentally Estimating the Demand for Formalization." Unpublished paper.

Devaiah, D. 2010. *Government of Gujarat: Jyotigram Yojana*. http://www.scribd.com/doc/33811921/Government-of-Gujarat-Jyotigram-Yojana.

Dininio, P., S. J. Kpundeh, and R. Leiken. 1988. *A Handbook on Fighting Corruption*. U.S. Agency for International Development (USAID), Center for Democracy and Governance, Washington, DC.

Djankov, S., C. McLiesh, and A. Shleifer. 2007. "Private Credit in 129 Countries." *Journal of Financial Economics* 8 (4): 299–329.

Economic Times. 2011. "Infra Sector Needs Rs 41 Lakh Cr Investment in 12th Plan Period: Economic Survey." February 25. http://articles.economictimes.indiatimes.com/2011-02-25/news/28634119_1_power-sector-national-forest-land-bank-land-acquisition.

Ferrari, A. and I.S. Dhingra. 2009. *India's Investment Climate Assessment: Voices of Indian Business*. World Bank, South Asia Region, Washington, DC.

Gill, J. B. S. 2003. *The Nuts and Bolts of Revenue Generation*. World Bank, Washington, DC.

Government of India. 2009. *Position Paper on Power Sector in India*. Department of Economic Affairs, New Delhi.

Government of Pakistan. 2010. *Economic Survey 2009–10*. Ministry of Finance, Islamabad. http://www.finance.gov.pk/survey_0910.html.

Hoxha, I. 2011. "Access to Finance in South Asia." Background study conducted for this book.

IDFC (Infrastructure Development Finance Company Limited). 2010. "India Infrastructure Report: Infrastructure Development in a Low-Carbon Economy." New Delhi.

IIP (Institute of Public Policy). 2009. *State of the Economy: Emerging from the Crises. Second Annual Report.* Beaconhouse National University, Lahore.

IMF (International Monetary Fund). 2010. World Economic Outlook Database, October. Washington, DC. http:www.imf.org/external/pubs/ft/weo/2010/02/weodata/index.aspx

Klapper, L., and I. Love. 2010. "The Impact of Business Environment Reforms on New Firm Registration." Policy Research Working Paper 5493, World Bank, Washington, DC.

KPMG. 2009. *Think BRIC: India. Key Considerations for Investors Targeting the Power Sectors of the World's Largest Emerging Economies.* Mumbai.

Love, I., and N. Mylenko. 2003. "Credit Reporting and Financing Constraints." Policy Research Working Paper 3142, World Bank, Washington, DC.

Mint. 2011. "Can't Erase State Power Firms' Losses at One Go." January 4.

Mishra, P. 2010. *Alleviating Energy Poverty through Innovation. The Case of Jytotigram Yojana of Gujarat.* http://www.worldenergy.org/documents/congresspapers/228.pdf.

OECD (Organisation for Economic Co-operation and Development). 2007. "OECD Economic Surveys: India." Paris.

Quah, John. 2007. *Combating Corruption Singapore-Style: Lessons for Other Asian Countries.* Maryland Series in Contemporary Asian Studies 2-2007 (189), University of Maryland School of Law, Baltimore, MD.

Transparency International. 2010. Corruption Perceptions Index 2010. http://www.transparency.org/policy_research/surveys_indices/cpi/2010/results.

Trimble, C., N. Yoshida, and M. Saqib. 2011. *Rethinking electricity tariffs and subsidy policy in Pakistan.* Report 62971-PK, World Bank, Washington, DC.

USAID (U.S. Agency for International Development). 2007. *Impact and Benefits of Power Trading in the South Asia Growth Quadrangle.* http://www.sari-energy.org/successdocs/ImpactBenefitsSAGQ.pdf.

Van, Sou Leng. 2011. "Competitiveness Partnerships: How the Cambodia Government Private Sector Forum (G-PSF) Helps the Garment Industry Grow." Presentation to the World Bank, April, Washington, DC.

World Bank. 2005. *Sri Lanka: Improving the Rural and Urban Investment Climate.* Washington, DC.

———. 2008a. *The Afghanistan Investment Climate Assessment.* Washington, DC.

———. 2008b. *Finance for All? Policies and Pitfalls in Expanding Access.* Washington, DC.

———. 2008c. *Harnessing Competitiveness for Stronger Inclusive Growth: Bangladesh Second Investment Climate Assessment.* Washington, DC.

———. 2009. *Pakistan Investment Climate Assessment.* Washington, DC.

———. 2010a. *Impact of the Global Financial Crisis on Investments in South Asia's Electric Power Infrastructure. India, Bangladesh, and Pakistan.* Report 56849-SAS. Washington, DC.

———. 2010b. *Sri Lanka: Environmental Issues in the Power Sector.* South Asia Sustainable Development, Washington, DC.

———. 2011a. *India Urbanization Review.* Washington, DC.

———. 2011b. *Perspectives on Poverty in India: Stylized Facts from Survey Data.* Washington, DC.

———. 2011c. PPI database. Washington, DC. http://www.ppi.worldbank.org.

———. 2011d. *Sri Lanka Infrastructure Assessment.* Washington, DC.

———. 2011e. *World Development Indicators.* Washington, DC.

Questions and Findings

Questions

- What are the dimensions of the education and skills challenge in South Asia?
- What are the policy priorities for improving the skills of graduates of education and training systems?

Findings

- Increasing wage premiums at the upper-secondary and tertiary levels of education signals increasing demand for more skilled workers. In addition to knowledge and specific technical skills for the job, analytical and behavioral skills are being demanded. Upper-secondary and tertiary education also sharply increase the ability of workers to access better jobs. Despite considerable recent gains, three main dimensions to the education challenge remain: increasing attainment beyond primary to secondary and tertiary education; including all groups in this effort; and going beyond attainment to ensuring that individuals are equipped with the skills demanded in the labor market.
- The targets and strategies of individual countries will depend on country-specific outcomes, constraints, resources, capacity, and political imperatives. Although specific targets will differ, there are two common priorities. All countries will need to improve the learning outcomes and skills of graduates of education and training systems at all levels and address market failures that lead to lower investment in human capital among disadvantaged groups.
- The biggest payoffs may come from addressing poor nutrition and other factors in early childhood—before children enter formal schooling—in order to prevent development problems that can hinder learning and contribute to early dropout, especially among children from poor families.
- Improving the quality of learning in primary and secondary schools calls for measures that strengthen incentives and capacity in the school system. Priorities include strengthening national assessment systems, improving capacity and accountability at the school level, and improving the quality and performance of teachers. Improving parents' understanding of the returns to education, reducing their budget constraints through conditional cash transfers, and providing subsidies to private providers to serve the poorest groups are some strategies that have succeeded in increasing education investments among disadvantaged groups in primary and secondary education.
- In tertiary education and preemployment training systems, priorities include providing information on outcomes and strengthening quality assurance; increasing the role of the private sector in providing training and education and in managing public institutions; providing public institutions with greater autonomy and incentives for improved performance; and increasing contributions from students able to pay while protecting those who cannot.

Opening the Door to Better Jobs by Improving Education and Skills | 5

Education and training systems have an important role to play in the labor market. They can influence the decisions of firms to invest, adopt new technologies or develop new products, and enter new markets—decisions that determine how the structure of the economy evolves as well as the number and productivity of the jobs that are created. There is a strong association between education and training, job creation, and firm innovation (see chapter 4). Job growth takes place in larger firms that are internationally engaged; these firms are also more likely to introduce new products and processes, engage in research and development, have more educated managers and workforces, and invest in the training of their workforce. Education and training systems also affect individuals' decisions to participate in the labor force, their ability to access productive and more secure employment, and their earnings and welfare.[1] Education is an important "sorter" in South Asian labor markets, with the less educated overwhelmingly work in agriculture, self-employment (mostly low-end own-account or unpaid family work), or precarious and irregular wage employment (see chapter 3).

This chapter takes a close look at the challenges confronting education and training systems in South Asia. These systems need to equip more than 10 million potential entrants a year into the labor force—including many from groups that have not been sufficiently included—with skills for productive employment.

The chapter is organized into eight sections. The first looks at skills in demand relative to those available in South Asian labor markets. The second looks at how education is connected to the ability of workers to access better jobs. The third discusses the dimensions of the education challenge in South Asia. The fourth looks at the potential evolution of educational attainment in South Asia's rapidly expanding labor force. The fifth looks at the role of early childhood development in preparing children for success in school and the labor market. The sixth looks at primary and secondary education. The seventh examines tertiary education and preemployment training systems. The last section examines the extent to which workers in South Asia's formal sector firms have opportunities to upgrade their skills through on-the-job-training.

Education and skills in South Asian labor markets

This section reviews employers' perceptions of skills constraints and wage premiums for different levels of education. It finds evidence of considerable gaps in the supply of skills in the labor force. Improving the skills of graduates requires building strong education and training systems and strengthening institutional capacity. It does not happen overnight.

Employers' perceptions of skills constraints

Inadequate skills of the labor force rank among the top five constraints enterprise managers face in Bhutan and Maldives, where it is the second-most important constraint, and India, where job-creating firms rank lack of skills fifth (comparable in severity to government policy uncertainty).[2] Firms in Afghanistan and Pakistan rate skills constraints among the least problematic. Although formal sector firms in five of the eight countries in South Asia do not report skills as a top constraint, the evidence on wage premiums for India, Nepal, Pakistan, and Sri Lanka suggests that demand for workers with secondary or tertiary education is increasing. Moreover, in focused surveys on skills, employers report dissatisfaction with skills.

Focused employer surveys in particular sectors in India and Sri Lanka suggest concerns with the skills of tertiary education graduates relative to skills in demand. A survey of employers hiring recent engineering graduates in India shows that 64 percent of employers are only somewhat satisfied or worse with the quality of their new hires (Blom and Saeki 2011). Employers evaluated the level of importance of a broad range of skills, including behavioral skills (such as teamwork, reliability, leadership, and willingness to learn); creative thinking and problem-solving skills; communication skills; and specific knowledge and technical skills needed for the job (figure 5.1). They reported that they considered most of these skills a

very important but that they were only somewhat satisfied with the graduates' skills.

A survey in Sri Lanka of the workforce in the information technology sector reveals a similar picture (table 5.1). Together the two surveys provide evidence on the importance of behavioral, creative thinking, problem-solving, communication, and knowledge and specific skills. Some of the largest perceived skills gaps are in these areas. The foundation for these skills is developed even before higher education, in primary and secondary education, as well as outside the education system.

Changes in demand: Trends in wage premiums and the skills content of labor

Some evidence from India suggests that the skills content of jobs is slowly changing, especially in urban areas, as demand for analytical and interactive skills increases. As countries develop and technologies evolve, new occupations appear and the skills demanded change.

Autor, Levy, and Murnane (2003) examine the evolution of the skills content of the U.S. labor force over a 40-year period beginning in 1960. They document the rise of nonroutine cognitive analytical and interactive skills ("new economy" skills) and the decline in routine cognitive and routine and nonroutine manual skills (see table 5.2).[3]

A similar analysis conducted for India between 1994 and 2010 for this book finds that the skills content remained fairly stable, although there was a slight decrease in the importance of routine and nonroutine manual skills. The lack of change is not surprising, given the large share of the workforce still employed in elementary, agricultural, and trade-related occupations. A closer look at the proportion of workers in occupations in which the content of "new economy skills" is high (4 or 5 on a 1–5 scale), however, suggests that the share of such occupations, although still modest, is increasing steadily (see annex table 5A.1). For urban wage earners, there has been a gradual increase in new economy and routine cognitive skills and a decline in manual skills (figure 5.2).

FIGURE 5.1   **Employers' perceptions of skills of recently graduated engineers in India**

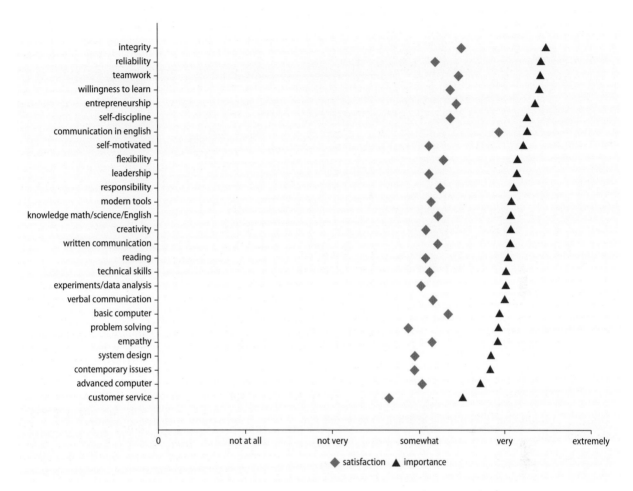

Source: Blom and Saeki 2011.

TABLE 5.1   **Perceived demand for and deficiency in skills in programming and software engineering in Sri Lanka**

| Rank | Skills in demand | | Skills deficient in employees |
	Essential skills	Complementary skills	
1	Programming	Team working	Communication skills
2	Systems Design	Communication skills	Creative thinking skills
3	.Net	Creative thinking skills	Systems design
4	Systems Analyst	Interpersonal skills	Proficiency in English
5	Visual Basic	C++	Programming
6	Java	SQL server	Team working
7	System testing	Professional ethics	Java
8	Business analysis	System testing	Interpersonal skills
9	Team working	XML	Professional ethics
10	Interpersonal skills	Systems design	.Net

Source: Sri Lanka Information Communication Technology Association 2007.

TABLE 5.2 **Routine and nonroutine skills categories**

Type of skill	Tasks	Examples of occupations requiring skills
Nonroutine cognitive: Analytical	Analyzing data/information Thinking creatively Interpreting information for others	Lawyers, professors, doctors, training and development managers
Nonroutine cognitive: Interpersonal	Establishing and maintaining personal relationships Guiding, directing, and motivating subordinates Coaching/developing others	
Routine cognitive	Repeating same tasks Being accurate Following tasks, priorities, and goals established for the job	Telephone operators, bookkeepers, accounting and auditing clerks, meter readers, cashiers
Routine manual	Importance to this job that the pace is determined by the speed of controlling machines and processes Making repetitive motions	
Nonroutine manual	Operating vehicles, mechanized devices, or equipment Using hands to handle or control objects or tools Using manual dexterity and spatial orientation	Industrial truck operators; machine setters, operators, and tenders; construction carpenters

Source: Acemoglu and Autor 2010.
Note: Acemoglu and Autor use the skills structure in the occupational information network database published by the U.S. Department of Labor, Employment and Training Administration to update the results in Autor, Levy, and Murnane (2003).

FIGURE 5.2 **Evolution of skills content of urban wage workers in India, 1994–2010**

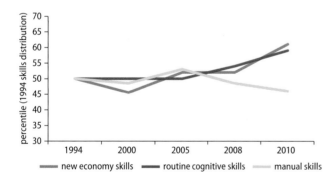

Source: World Bank staff, based on national labor force surveys.
Note: Data cover 21- to 60-year-old urban casual workers and regular wage or salaried workers. Changes in skills contents are assessed using the method proposed by Autor, Levy, and Murnane (2003) and the skills categories identified in the O*NET database, as suggested by Acemoglu and Autor (2010). The skills content level of every worker's job is assessed in each of the five skills categories, and a population distribution is created for each of the five skills categories. The process is repeated in each period surveyed. The skills content level for the median worker (50th percentile) in the distribution is identified, and the percentile corresponding to the same skills content level in the base year of 1994 is tracked. Thus, for example, the average intensity of new economy skills for the urban wage workers was around 10 centiles more in 2010 versus 1994. "New economy skills" is an aggregate of nonroutine cognitive analytical and nonroutine cognitive interpersonal skills. "Manual skills" is an aggregate of routine manual and nonroutine manual skills.

Consistent with these patterns, the wage premium associated with the more skilled occupations has increased relative to elementary occupations (figure 5.3). Sharp increases are evident in changes in the premium for skilled occupations over elementary occupations between 1994 and 2010. This pattern is consistent with the picture above, which suggests gradually increasing demand for more skilled occupations. It is also consistent with the finding below on increasing returns for higher levels of education, especially tertiary education.

The wage premium increased for higher levels of education in several countries, even as the supply of educated workers increased. The premiums shown in figure 5.4 reflect the differential between a particular level of educational attainment and the level of attainment just below. The pattern is one in which the premium to lower levels of education has been falling while the premium for

FIGURE 5.3   **Wage premiums over elementary occupations in India, 1994–2010**

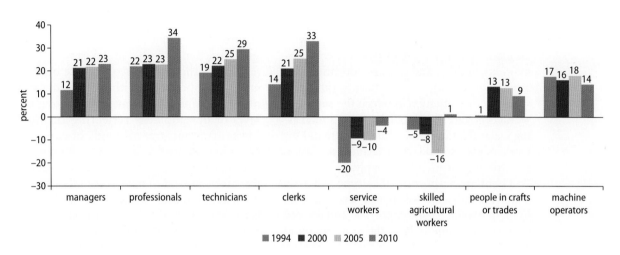

Source: Authors, based on data from national labor force surveys.
Note: The bars represent the wage premiums of each occupation relative to elementary occupations. The wage premiums are obtained as the coefficients in a regression of log hourly wage on a number of individual characteristics such as age, education, occupation, caste, and so on. The omitted occupation category is elementary occupations.

FIGURE 5.4   **Wage premiums in selected South Asian countries, by level of education**

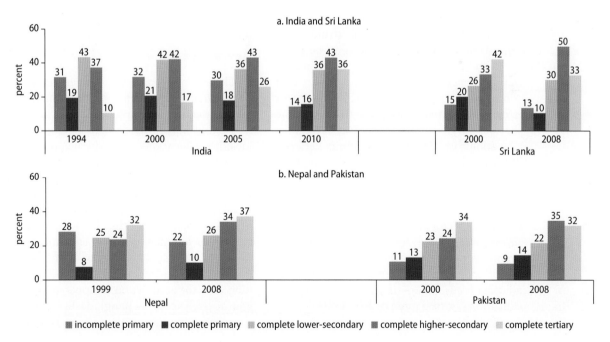

Source: Authors, based on data from national labor force and household surveys.
Note: The first bar for each country-year pair reflects the wage premium for even some primary education relative to no education; the last bar reflects the wage premium for completing tertiary relative to completing upper-secondary education. The wage premiums represent the differences in the coefficients of a regression of log hourly wage on basic controls (the highest level of education completed, experience, and experience squared). The qualitative results are robust to other specifications with additional controls.

upper-secondary and tertiary education has been increasing. This trend is taking place in a context in which the educational attainment of the labor force has been generally rising, with an increase in the share of workers with primary, secondary, and tertiary education (see annex figure 5A.1). This pattern is thus consistent with a situation in which the supply of workers at lower levels of education is increasing faster than demand while the demand for workers with secondary or tertiary education is outpacing the increased supply.

There are important differences across countries. India and Nepal have seen increases in the premium to both upper-secondary and tertiary education. Indeed, the wage premium for tertiary education more than doubled in India between 2000 and 2010, despite an increase in the share of the labor force with tertiary education from 1 percent to 8 percent over this period. This increase is seen in both the public and private sectors, in urban and rural areas.[4] In Nepal, the largest relative increases in the wage premium were at the upper-secondary level, suggesting that demand increases at this level were greater than the small increases in supply (from 2 percent of the labor force to 3 percent) between 1999 and 2008. In Sri Lanka, wage premiums for upper-secondary education increased substantially, signaling significant increases in demand relative to supply at this level. The share of the labor force with lower-secondary education rose 10 percentage points between 2000 and 2008; the increase in the supply of workers with upper-secondary and tertiary education was much smaller.

In Pakistan, trends in wage premiums in the private sector are different from the trends shown in figure 5.4. In the private sector, the premium to tertiary education over upper-secondary increased, whereas the premium to all other levels fell or—in the case of primary education—stayed more or less stable.

Educational attainment of the labor force

With the exception of Afghanistan, for which data are available only for 2008, and Sri Lanka, where primary attainment has long been high, most countries in the region have seen rapid declines in the share of the labor force that does not have any education (figure 5.5). Declines were particularly sharp in Nepal, Bangladesh and Pakistan.

Despite this progress, the share of workers in the labor force without any education at all remains high relative to the region's level of development reflecting relatively lower attainment at all levels of education (see annex figure 5A.2). (The main exception is primary attainment in Sri Lanka.) Educational attainment of men in the labor force is higher than that of women, but in Afghanistan, Bhutan, and Pakistan, the share of the male labor force with no education is high compared with other countries at similar income levels. In the case of women, more than half of the labor force in all countries other than Sri Lanka and Maldives lacks any education at all. Much of this difference reflects gaps in educational attainment of earlier generations, but gender gaps remain even in young cohorts of the population in many countries (see annex figure 5A.6).

Education and access to better jobs

There is a strong link between education and type of employment. A multinomial logit model was used to explore the link between household and individual characteristics—including education—and whether and where individuals work. It reveals that in all countries, an individual's education level is typically the most important determinant.

For both working men and women in rural and urban areas, the likelihood of being in a better job increases with education, particularly with secondary and higher levels (figure 5.6). The increases are sharpest beginning with the completion of upper-secondary education, except in Bangladesh, where the sharpest increases occur at the tertiary level (other exceptions include male workers in urban India, where the increases are not as sharp at upper-secondary, and female workers in urban Pakistan, where sharp increases occur even with completion of lower-secondary school). Disaggregation within

FIGURE 5.5 **Share of South Asian labor force with no education, with international comparisons**

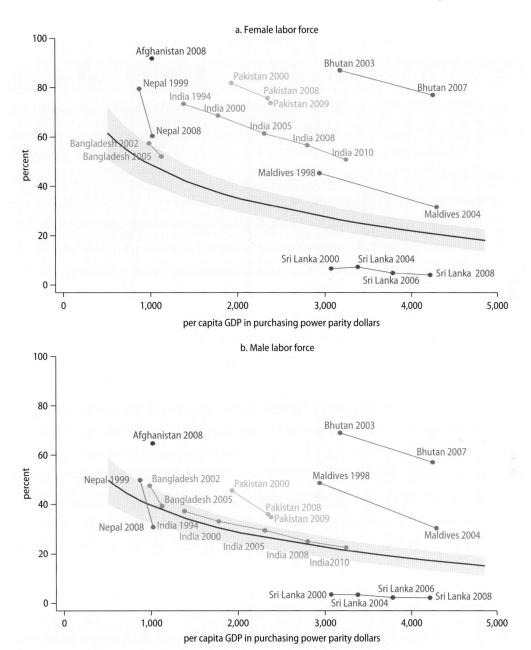

Sources: Authors, based on data from World Bank 2011b and national labor force and household surveys.
Note: The dark line shows the predicted values of the share of the labor force with no education by per capita GDP, based on a cross-country regression (excluding high-income countries). The shaded area is the 95 percent confidence interval band around the regression line. GDP = gross domestic product.

rural areas (not shown in figure) indicates that this pattern primarily reflects the fact that workers with secondary or higher levels of education are much more likely to work in nonfarm self-employment or regular wage or salaried jobs. Among male workers in Bangladesh, Nepal, and Pakistan, the likelihood of being in casual nonfarm employment increases with some primary education and falls at higher levels of education.

FIGURE 5.6 **Predicted probability of working in rural nonfarm and urban regular wage jobs in selected South Asian countries, by level of education and gender**

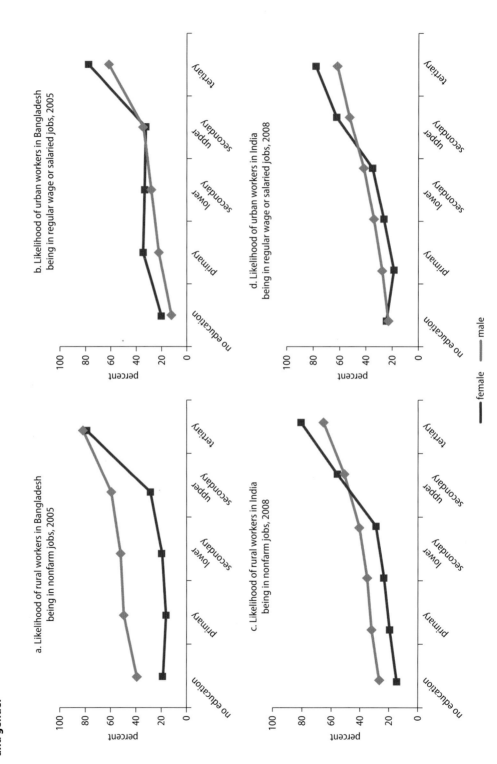

a. Likelihood of rural workers in Bangladesh being in nonfarm jobs, 2005

b. Likelihood of urban workers in Bangladesh being in regular wage or salaried jobs, 2005

c. Likelihood of rural workers in India being in nonfarm jobs, 2008

d. Likelihood of urban workers in India being in regular wage or salaried jobs, 2008

female   male

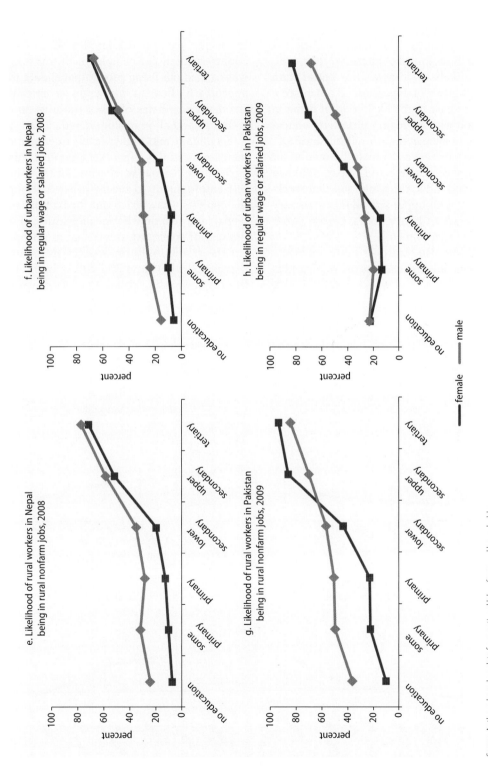

e. Likelihood of rural workers in Nepal being in rural nonfarm jobs, 2008

f. Likelihood of urban workers in Nepal being in regular wage or salaried jobs, 2008

g. Likelihood of rural workers in Pakistan being in rural nonfarm jobs, 2009

h. Likelihood of urban workers in Pakistan being in regular wage or salaried jobs, 2009

female   male

Source: Authors, based on data from national labor force and household surveys.
Note: The likelihood of workers being in a particular sector or type of employment is the predicted share of workers in a particular sector or type of employment from a multinomial logit regression of occupational choice on household and individual characteristics.

Working women with less than upper-secondary education (lower-secondary in Pakistan) are generally less likely than men to hold better jobs. The main exception is in urban Bangladesh, where women who work are likely to do as well or better than men at all levels of education. Women see a sharper increase in the likelihood of being in a better job with secondary or tertiary education than do men: at these levels of education, women are at least as likely to be in a better job. In rural Bangladesh and Nepal, unlike in Pakistan and India, the likelihood that working women with upper-secondary or tertiary education are in better nonfarm jobs is not higher than that of men.

Education also improves labor mobility. Multinomial logit regressions provide insights into the distribution of workers' employment type with varying educational levels among a cross-section of workers, but panel data are needed to provide a picture of labor mobility. In the absence of panel data for South Asian countries, analysis of employment transitions was carried out using pseudo-panel data (see appendix B). Education emerges as one of the strongest correlates of labor mobility in all countries and all years considered.

Secondary and higher levels of education increase the ability of workers to move out of agriculture, casual wage jobs, and low-end self-employment to better jobs. Although the analysis was carried out for Bangladesh, Nepal, and two time periods for India, in the interest of space, figures 5.7 and 5.8 present the results only for worker transitions between 2004/05 and 2007/08 in India. The figures show the probability of transition

FIGURE 5.7   **Conditional probability of moving into and out of better jobs in rural India, by education and gender, 2005–08**

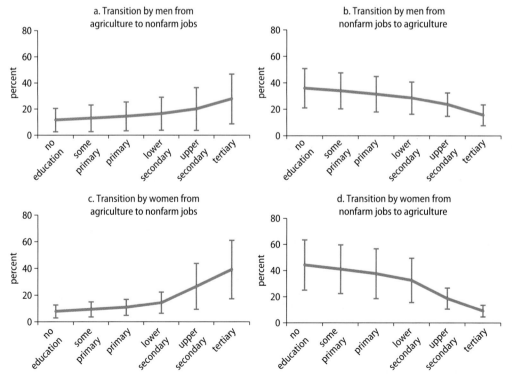

Source: Authors, based on data from national labor force and household surveys.
Note: The probability of transition is conditional on being in a specific type of employment in the first period (e.g., panel a shows the estimated probability that a rural male worker who was in agriculture in the first period is working in a nonfarm job in the second period). The probability differs by the level of education of the worker. Upper and lower bounds of the estimated probabilities are shown. The blue lines are drawn through the midpoints of the bounds.

FIGURE 5.8   **Conditional probability of moving into and out of better jobs in urban India, by education and gender, 2005–08**

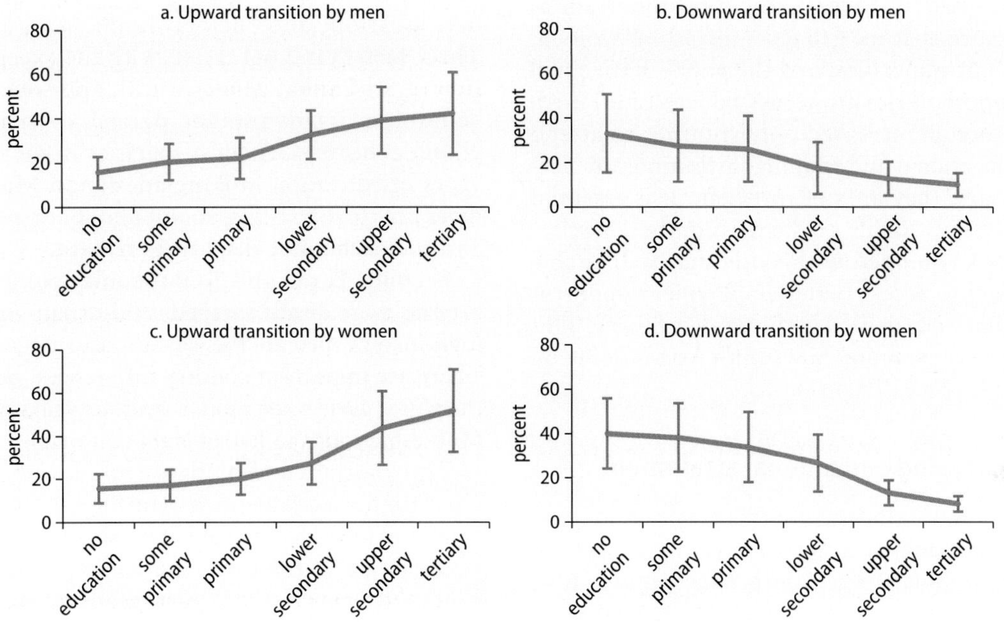

Source: World Bank staff, based on data from national labor force and household surveys.
Note: See note for figure 5.7. An upward transition in the urban context is a move from casual wage work or low-end self-employment to regular wage or salaried work or high-end self-employment. A downward transition is a move from regular wage or salaried work or high-end self-employment to casual wage work or low-end self-employment.

between the first and second period conditional on type of employment in the first period, by education and gender.[5] Three interesting findings emerge:

- Rural workers who were in agriculture and urban workers who were in casual or low-end self-employment in the first period were more likely to be able to make the transition to a better job (nonfarm employment in rural areas and high-end self-employment or regular wage or salaried jobs in urban areas) if they had secondary or higher levels of education (panels a and c of figures 5.7 and 5.8). This mobility is typically greater for workers with completed upper-secondary education (in Bangladesh for workers with tertiary education).[6] Workers with lower levels of education were more likely to transition out of better jobs (for example, from nonfarm employment to agriculture in rural areas) than workers with higher levels of education.

- Workers with higher levels of education were much more likely to move to better jobs than they were to lose them, as shown in the lower levels of the transition bars for higher levels of education in panels b and d of figures 5.7 and 5.8 than in panels a and c. Workers with lower levels of education were more likely to lose better jobs than they were to gain them, as shown in the higher levels of the transition bars for lower levels of education in panels b and d than in panels a and c.
- These patterns appear to be sharper for women in both urban and rural areas, suggesting that education may play a stronger role in worker mobility for women.

The education challenge

The analysis described in the previous sections suggests three dimensions to the education challenge in South Asia. First, there is a need to increase the educational attainment of the labor force beyond primary to secondary and higher levels of education, where the payoffs in worker mobility and earnings are greatest. Second, it will be important to ensure that all groups—including women, ethnic minorities, and the poor—have equal opportunities to access education. Third, although increased opportunities to attend educational and training institutions are necessary, they are not sufficient. It is essential that individuals graduate from these institutions equipped with skills that will enable them to access better employment opportunities and succeed in the world of work. This section examines how South Asia is doing on these three dimensions.

Increasing educational attainment

Despite significant progress by young cohorts, educational attainment in young cohorts of the population in South Asia remains low, reflecting low attainment of upper-secondary and tertiary education in all countries and of primary education in Afghanistan. The average years of education of young cohorts of the population (age 15–34) has increased in all countries since the late 1990s or early 2000s (annex table 5A.2). It is still low in most countries, however, ranging from 2.5 years in Afghanistan to 10.2 years in Sri Lanka. About 80 percent of youth complete primary education in all South Asian countries except Afghanistan, Nepal, and Pakistan (figure 5.9; see annex figures 5A.6 and 5A.7 for a break-out by gender). Primary attainment is especially low in Afghanistan, where only a third of youth complete primary school. Considerable progress has been made in most countries in lower-secondary attainment, although less than 60 percent of recent cohorts completed lower-secondary in all countries except India, Maldives, and Sri Lanka. Completion of upper-secondary and tertiary by young cohorts remains low in all countries in the region, with only 21–23 percent completing upper-secondary even in India, Maldives, and Sri Lanka.[7] In all countries, less than 10 percent of youth have completed tertiary education.

Including all groups

Figure 5.10 shows mean years of education of young cohorts of the population by gender, location, and socioeconomic group.[8] Three facts stand out. First, with the exception of Sri Lanka, gender, rural, and socioeconomic disadvantages persist even in young cohorts. Gender disparities in mean years of education in Bangladesh and Maldives are close to being eliminated, but rural and socioeconomic disparities remain.[9]

Second, rural and low-income women are the most disadvantaged, and urban and high-income men are the least disadvantaged. There are important country differences, but the gap is close to or more than four years on both dimensions in five of eight countries.

Third, urban and higher-income women have higher educational attainment than rural and low- income men in most countries, suggesting that the rural and income disadvantage dominates the gender disadvantage.

Ethnic minorities and disadvantaged castes also have lower educational attainment, even among younger cohorts. In India, scheduled castes and tribes and Muslim minorities have significantly lower educational attainment. In Nepal, the Dalits and Muslims are among the most disadvantaged. Ethnic differences in education outcomes are also observed in Sri Lanka (see annex figure 5A.8). These disadvantages by gender, location, and socioeconomic status reflect both a still low likelihood of starting school and a high likelihood of dropping out, with variations across countries (see annex figure 5A.9.)

Education disadvantages by gender, socioeconomic status, and ethnicity play out in the labor market and are an important reason for the small number of workers from disadvantaged groups holding better jobs (see chapter 3).

Equipping children with skills

Children in school in South Asia have very low levels of learning, with large numbers of children acquiring no more than basic literacy. No systematic studies enable comparison of

FIGURE 5.9   Share of young cohorts with completed primary, secondary, and tertiary education in South Asia, by country

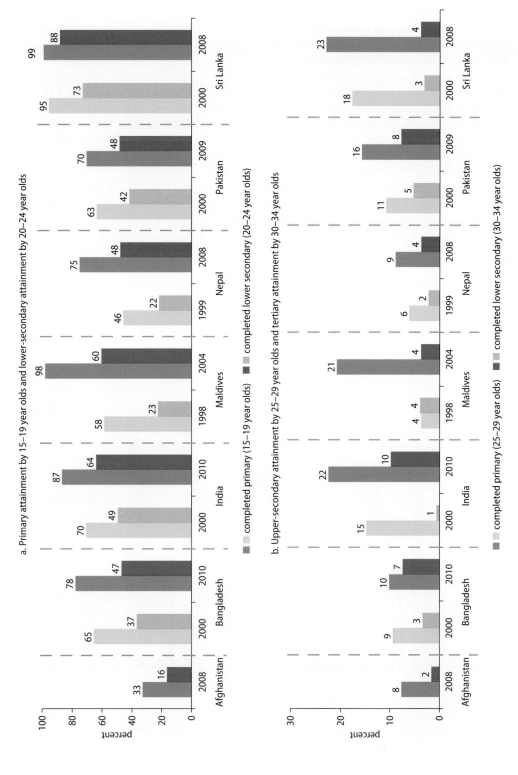

a. Primary attainment by 15–19 year olds and lower-secondary attainment by 20–24 year olds

■ completed primary (15–19 year olds)   ■ completed lower secondary (20–24 year olds)

b. Upper-secondary attainment by 25–29 year olds and tertiary attainment by 30–34 year olds

■ completed primary (25–29 year olds)   ■ completed lower secondary (30–34 year olds)

Source: Authors, based on data from national labor force and household surveys.

183

learning outcomes in primary, secondary, or tertiary education across South Asian countries or over time. There is also limited reliable information on learning from national assessment systems, particularly on trends over time within countries. However, as discussed below, evidence from several in-country studies and surveys suggests that the low level of learning is perhaps the greatest challenge facing the education and training systems in all countries. For example, 62 percent of children in class 4 in India and Pakistan could read only at the expected level for class 1: after four years of schooling, they could at most read a short paragraph. Results in math in both countries are also poor (figure 5.11).

In Bangladesh, the vast majority of children who complete grade 9 attain only grade 5 competency in math (93 percent in oral math, 80 percent in written math) (Asadullah and others 2009). In India and Pakistan, learning levels are significantly below curriculum standards (Das, Pandey, and Zajonc 2006). There is also evidence that children have difficulties with conceptual thinking and problem-solving skills. In Pakistan, less than 2 percent of students in a representative national sample (in the 2006 national assessment) were able to reason in settings involving the application of concept definitions, relationships, or representations of either, and less than 1 percent were able to demonstrate the choice and application of mathematical processes in different situations. Similar evidence is available from India from a sample of elite private schools,

FIGURE 5.10   **Mean years of education of 15–34 year olds in South Asia, by gender and country**

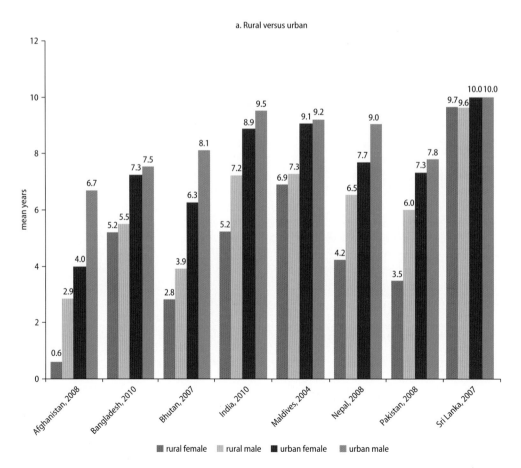

FIGURE 5.10   (continued)

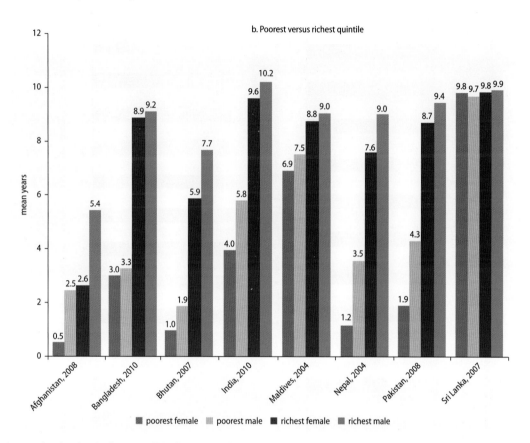

b. Poorest versus richest quintile

■ poorest female   ■ poorest male   ■ richest female   ■ richest male

Source: Authors, based on data from national labor force and household surveys.
Note: Socioeconomic group is based on per capita consumption quintile of the household.

suggesting that concerns of quality are not limited to public or low-cost private schools (EI 2006).

Two common priorities

The strategies and targets of countries will depend on country-specific outcomes, constraints, resources, capacity, and political imperatives. In the face of multiple dimensions to the education challenge, countries will determine their own priorities and targets. For example, achieving completion of primary remains a priority in Afghanistan and in some other countries in the region, whereas Bangladesh is concerned about providing equal opportunities for boys and girls from low-income households in primary and secondary school.

Except in Bangladesh and Pakistan, average public education expenditures in South Asia are comparable to or higher than in East Asia (figure 5.12).[10] Although countries may chose to increase budgetary allocations to meet the education challenge, there is also considerable room to increase the efficiency with which existing resources are used. The solid progress in improving educational attainment in recent years in South Asia has been achieved by the combined efforts of governments, households, and the nongovernment and private sector—in the face of resource and capacity constraints. These efforts will continue to be important and, indeed, may be leveraged further.

Although country's strategies and targets will differ, all countries share two priorities. First, what is ultimately critical for labor market success is what individuals learn. Research

FIGURE 5.11   Reading and arithmetic achievement in rural India and Pakistan, by class, 2010

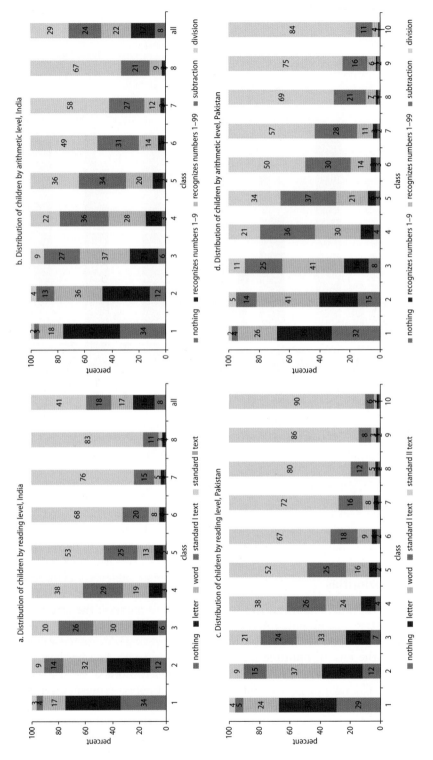

a. Distribution of children by reading level, India

b. Distribution of children by arithmetic level, India

c. Distribution of children by reading level, Pakistan

d. Distribution of children by arithmetic level, Pakistan

Source: Pratham 2010.

FIGURE 5.12   **Public expenditure on education as a share of GDP, in South Asia and other regions**

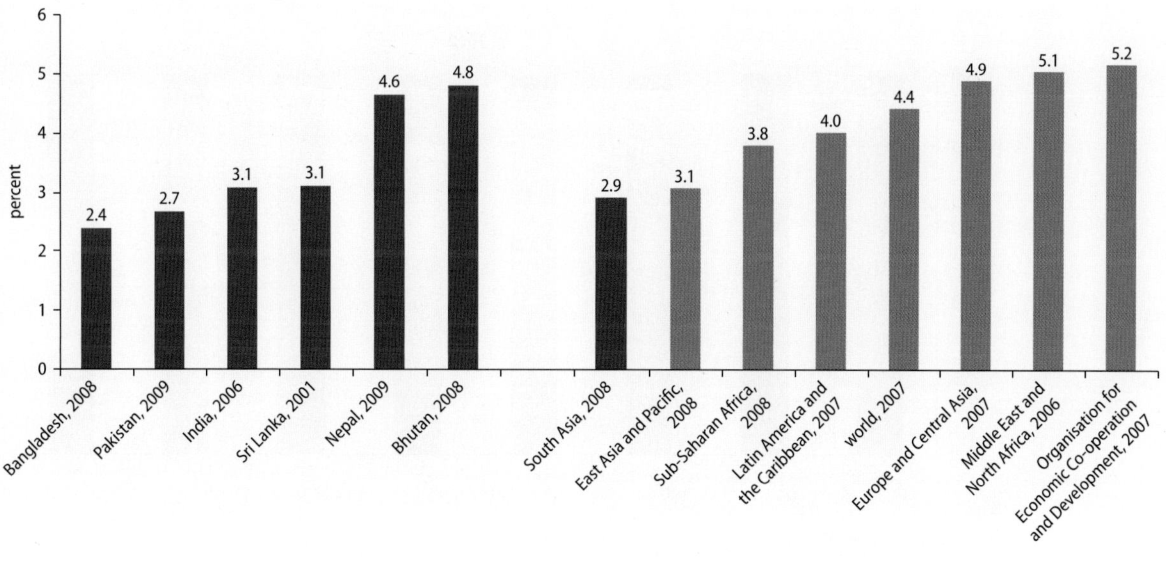

Source: World Bank 2011b.
Note: Public expenditure on education is reported to be about 11 percent of GDP in the Maldives (not shown in figure). GDP = gross domestic product.

suggests that the level of skills—as measured by performance on international student assessments such as the Programme for International Student Assessment (PISA) and the Trends in International Mathematics and Science Study (TIMSS)—predicts economic growth far better than do average schooling levels (Hanushek and Woessman 2008).[11] Thus an important focus for governments is to establish and strengthen the systems that will lead to improved learning outcomes and skills of graduates at all levels. Second, governments have an important role to play in addressing market failures that lead to lower investment in human capital among disadvantaged groups.

The next 20 years: Can South Asian countries improve the educational attainment of their labor forces?

Should all South Asian countries increase education attainment at the highest pace observed among countries in the region, the composition of the labor force could change

dramatically. Figure 5.13 shows the composition of the labor force in 2010 and what it could look like under an optimistic but feasible scenario of progress in educational attainment in 2030[12] (see annex 5B for assumptions and more details). This scenario corresponds to one in which primary attainment of young cohorts is based on the six best-performing South Asian countries over the previous 10 years and secondary attainment follows the trends of a smaller subset of countries in South Asia with the highest progression.[13]

With effort, South Asian countries could dramatically improve educational attainment of their workforces over the next 20 years. Many countries should be able to more than halve the share of the labor force with no education; in all countries, the percent of the labor force with only primary education or less will fall. The share of individuals with at least some secondary education could rise dramatically. Under this scenario, the percentage of the labor force with some secondary education could reach almost 30 percent in Afghanistan and over 50 percent in India, Nepal, and Sri Lanka. Tertiary attainment

FIGURE 5.13   **Educational attainment of the South Asian labor force in 2010 (estimated) and 2030 (projected), by country**

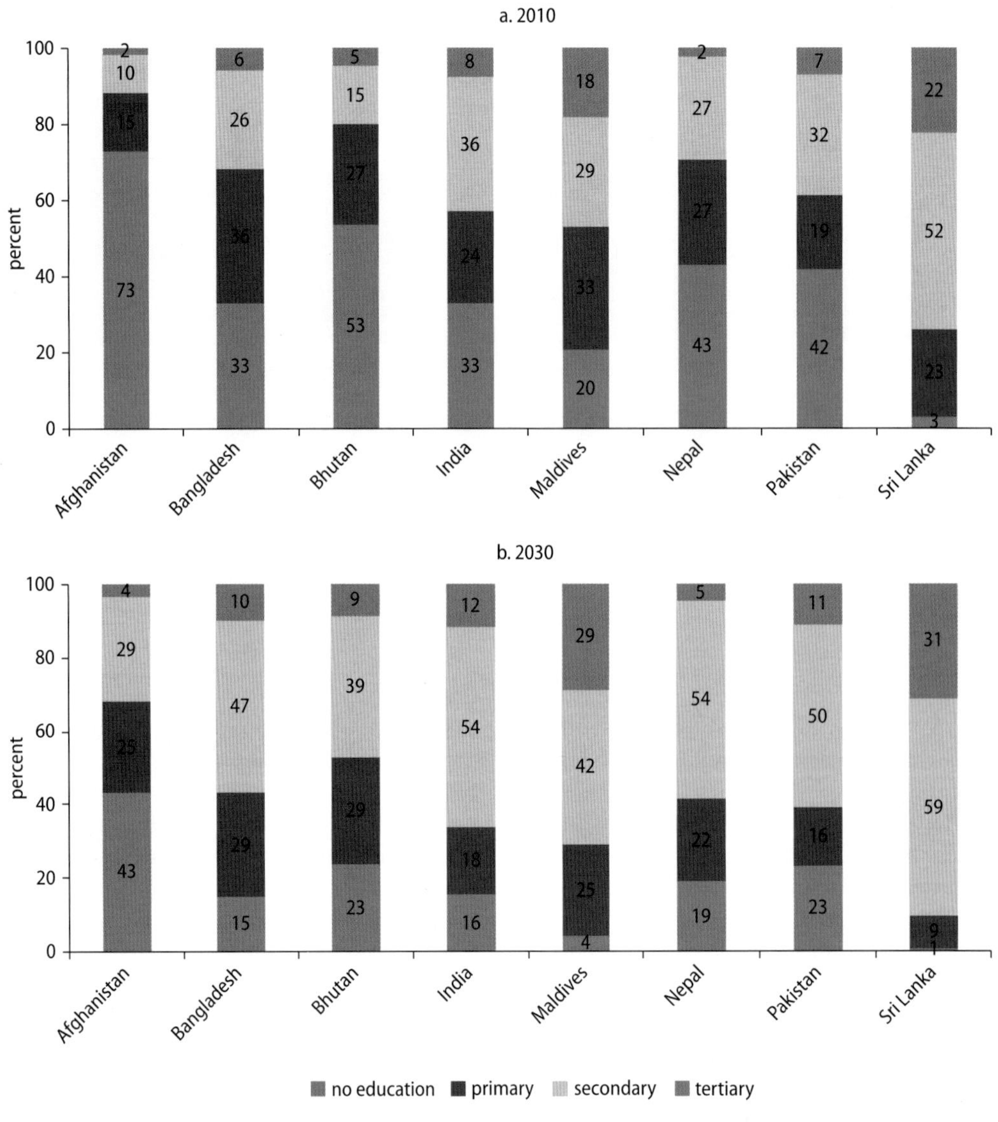

a. 2010

b. 2030

■ no education   ■ primary   ■ secondary   ■ tertiary

Sources: Authors, based on data from national labor force and household surveys; UN 2009, 2010; KC and others 2010.

remains under 12 percent in all countries except Maldives and Sri Lanka, although under a more ambitious scenario, most countries could raise the percentage of the labor force with tertiary education to at least 20 percent (see annex table 5B.2).

Progress will be made by younger cohorts and new labor market entrants; a large stock of prime-age and older workers will still have lower levels of education. Except in Sri Lanka, the majority of prime-age (35–49) and oldest (50–64) adults in the labor force will continue to have no more than primary attainment in 2030 (figure 5.14). The share of prime-age adults with primary attainment or below ranges from 30 percent of the labor force in Sri Lanka to 88 percent in Afghanistan; the picture is worse in rural areas. These

FIGURE 5.14 **Projected shares of prime-age (35–49) and oldest (50–64) labor force participants in South Asia with no education or only primary attainment in 2030, by country**

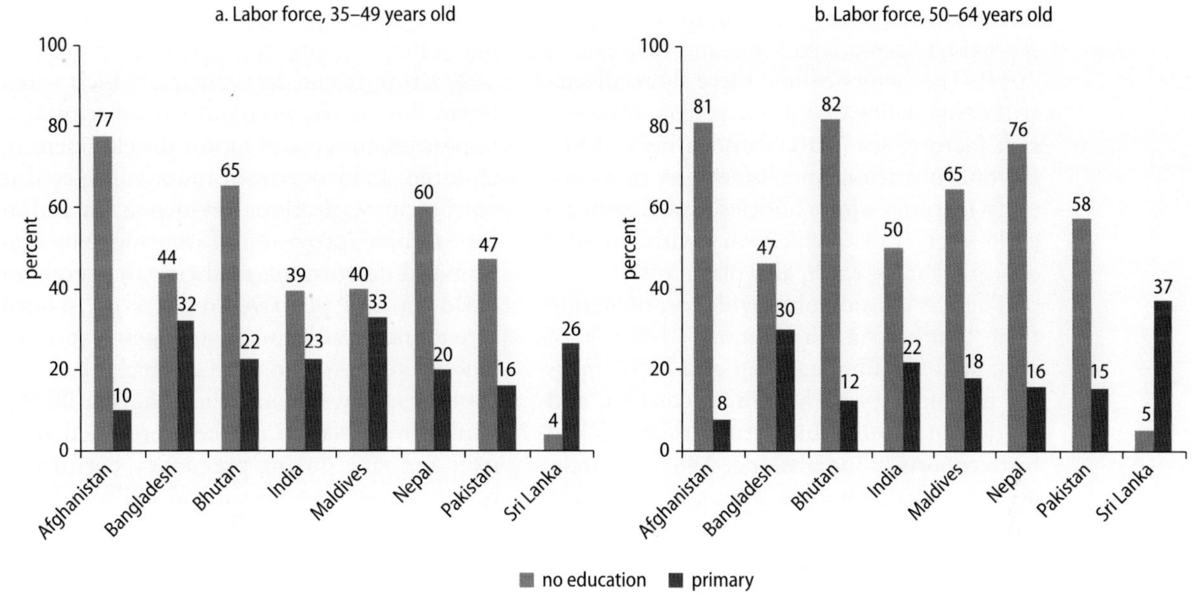

a. Labor force, 35–49 years old

b. Labor force, 50–64 years old

■ no education ■ primary

Sources: Authors, based on data from national labor force and household surveys; UN 2009, 2010; KC and others 2010.

poorly educated will be likely hold informal jobs, with lower earnings and higher labor market risks. (Chapter 6 discusses programs that can help informal workers adjust to labor market shocks and improve their productivity and future earnings potential.) Policy options and promising interventions for improving the skills of potential new entrants into the labor force (from education and training systems), and including individuals from disadvantaged groups in these efforts, are discussed in the next few sections of this chapter. Some of the constraints education and training systems face in improving the skills of potential new entrants into the labor force and policy options and promising interventions for addressing them are discussed later in this chapter.

Addressing disadvantages before school: The role of early childhood development

The first years of life—long before formal schooling begins—are a key period for building human capital.[14] The benefits

of health and nutrition early on can have effects that persist throughout life; damage from childhood disease and malnutrition can be difficult to undo.

There are critical periods in childhood for acquiring different skills.[15] Three types of outcomes in early years are critical for future development: physical growth and well-being, cognitive development, and socioemotional development. The context in which a child develops and is either stimulated or shocked can have a significant influence on how much of his or her potential is eventually realized.

Developmental delays often begin early in life and accumulate quickly over time, especially for the poorest children. Low levels of cognitive development in early childhood are often strongly correlated with low socioeconomic status, as measured by wealth, parental education, and malnutrition. Evidence from Cambodia, Ecuador, Nicaragua, Madagascar, and Mozambique shows that children from low-income households begin to fall behind on various measures of cognitive development starting from about 36 months (Nadeau and others 2011). Falling behind is evident not only in language development but also in behavioral (sometimes termed "noncognitive") abilities, such as sustained attention (Fernald, Galasso, and Ratsifandrihamanana 2011). The factors behind these shortfalls are still being delineated (for a recent review of risk factors, see Walker and others 2011). Beyond nutrition and infectious diseases, early learning opportunities and caregiver-child interactions, which vary with parental education and wealth, also play a role.

There is considerable evidence, including from South Asia, that improved nutrition enhances lifetime learning and labor market productivity (Behrman, Alderman, and Hoddinott 2004). In a study that tracked birth cohorts of Indians since 1969, researchers conclude that both birthweight and weight gain in the first two years of life are strong predictors of schooling outcomes (Martorell and Horta 2010).[16] A study of Pakistan finds that malnourished girls—but not boys—were less likely to enter school (Alderman and others 2001). Consistent with these findings, a study from Guatemala finds that adult men and women who were better nourished in the first three years of life (having received nutritional supplements) had significantly higher schooling attainment, higher scores on cognitive tests, and greater likelihood of employment in higher-paying and white collar jobs and were less likely to live in poor households (Hoddinott and others 2011). These and a number of other studies indicate high returns to preventing malnutrition.

Micronutrient deficiencies, which often begin during the prenatal period, can also impair cognitive and motor development in children. Evidence from India and Nepal is consistent with global evidence. In India, for example, provision of iron supplementation and deworming medicine to preschool children had positive impacts on school attendance, with much stronger responses among children who were anemic at baseline (Bobonis, Edward, and Puri-Sharma 2006). Children of Nepali mothers provided with iron and zinc during pregnancy performed better on cognitive measures as well as on tests of working memory, inhibitory control, and fine motor functioning (Christian and others 2010). Addressing micronutrient deficiencies long before school begins, often with prenatal micronutrient fortification or supplementation, is often the most efficient response.

South Asia has some of the highest rates of malnutrition in the world as well as high levels of anemia and iodine deficiency. It has the highest prevalence of malnutrition in children under five across all indicators (figure 5.15).[17] Indeed, malnutrition rates are higher than in

FIGURE 5.15   Percentage of children under five with malnutrition, by region and country

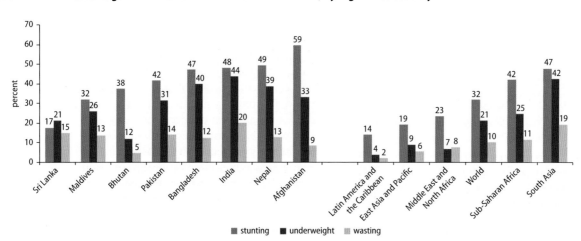

Source: Authors, based on data from World Bank 2011b.

Africa. Rates of malnutrition, anemia, and iodine deficits decrease with wealth, but only modestly (annex figure 5A.10).

Three conclusions can be drawn from this evidence. First, high malnutrition and micronutrient deficiencies are likely important contributors to developmental delays in low-income groups in South Asia. Second, they may also be important factors for overall cognitive development of the broader population. Third, income growth alone will not eliminate malnutrition; focused attention is needed.

Insufficient cognitive stimulation among low-income children in South Asia may also be a factor. Some evidence from Bangladesh and Sindh (Pakistan) suggests that mothers' limited understanding of when children respond to communication, for example, and low levels of learning materials and involvement could be contributing factors.[18] In Bangladesh, parents have been found to be more interactive with their sons than their daughters, even at a very young age. Lack of time and maternal depression can also limit stimulation.

Many children in South Asia come to school with significant disadvantages, which hinder learning, contribute to early drop out, and can be difficult or costly to reverse in later years. Although outcomes and activities at home play a key role, they can be enhanced by programs in health and education that take place in communities and preschools.

Most countries in South Asia do not have integrated policy frameworks for early childhood development. Early childhood interventions—nutrition, hygiene, early cognitive stimulation, preschool programs—are among the most cost-effective investments to improve the quality and efficiency of basic education, as well as labor market outcomes. Table 5.3 provides an overview of the key issues for early childhood development policy and some types of programs that can help prepare children for school.

National nutrition policies and programs in Bangladesh and some aspects of public health campaigns related to nutrition in Pakistan have contributed to improvements in nutrition. Neither country has a national policy on early childhood development, however.

India has the region's strongest enabling policy framework, which derives it foundation from the constitution. Its centrally sponsored Integrated Child Development Services (ICDS) program, which emanated from the Fifth Five-Year Plan (1969–79), remains the cornerstone for implementing its early childhood development policy. ICDS is one of the few programs at scale in the region that seeks to integrate early childhood interventions. The program—one of the largest

TABLE 5.3 **Main issues, interventions, and expected outcomes in early childhood development**

Main issue/age	Key nutrition/early childhood development interventions	Expected outcomes
Lack of nutrition, health, and cognitive stimulation (0–3) • Protein-energy malnutrition and deficiencies in key micronutrients • Infectious diseases and parasites	• Promotion of good nutritional practices, including feeding and personal hygiene • Deworming and provision of micronutrients for young children (vitamin A, zinc, iodine) and their mothers (iron folate) • Provision of micronutrients through food fortification	• Better physical well-being and health • Preschool readiness • Improved cognitive and noncognitive development
Lack of cognitive stimulation and parental interaction (0–5)	• Parental enrichment training • Home visits in high-risk cases	• Improved cognitive and noncognitive development
Insufficient age-appropriate stimulation and development of social skills (4–5)	• Preschool programs with appropriate curricula	• School readiness • Improved cognitive and noncognitive achievement • Lower dropout

Source: Alderman 2011.

child development programs in the world—
integrates health and nutrition services, early
stimulation and learning, and nonformal pre-
school education. Although well conceived
as an approach to holistic child development,
the program has not had the desired impact
on promoting cognitive development or
improving child nutrition. Inadequate coverage of children under three, an overempha-
sis on food supplementation, and substantial
operational challenges (such as inadequate
program stewardship and delivery capacity,
weak monitoring and evaluation and supervision, and the lack of community ownership)
have undermined its potential impact. There
is, however, wide variation in implementation of the program across states, with some
states having demonstrated good results. Several localized innovations have the potential
to be scaled up.

In part, the absence of programs at scale
reflects still limited understanding of what
constitute cost-effective designs in South
Asia. Several pilot projects can serve as a laboratory for designing cost-effective programs,
but many lack careful plans for evaluation.
Potentially promising efforts are under way,
however. Pilots run by the International Center for Diarrheal Disease Research (ICDDR)
in Dhaka, for example, have stronger evaluation designs and have proven the feasibility of
promoting better parenting and mother-child
interactions through home visits. The Lady
Health Workers Programme in Pakistan, a
community-based preventive care government
program, holds promise for promoting nutrition and child care through scaling up of carefully evaluated cost-effective pilot designs.

Primary and secondary education

This section begins by examining constraints
to—and priorities for—strengthening primary and secondary education systems in
order to improve the quality of learning of
graduates. It then discusses some innovative
interventions that have had increased investment in primary and secondary education of
disadvantaged groups.

Improving the quality of learning

Improving the quality of learning in primary and secondary school calls for measures that strengthen incentives and capacity
in the school system. Poor quality, particularly in public schools, can be attributed to
several governance challenges. First, underdeveloped assessment systems limit monitoring by stakeholders on what children learn
and the extent to which they master needed
competencies. This lack of information is a
serious constraint to introducing reforms to
improve quality. Second, with some notable
exceptions—such as the community-based
management of schools in Nepal—education
systems are still very centralized; decision-
making authority, especially at the school
level, is limited. Third, neither government
education management nor parents hold
schools accountable for education outcomes.
The potential of efforts to increase local
autonomy and accountability has not been
fully realized, as a result of limited capacity
and information of school and village management committees. Fourth, financing of
providers is not typically based on objective
measures of performance; it tends to be historical and based on inputs. Fifth, political
interference in teacher hiring and still underdeveloped career and pay incentives may be
affecting teacher performance. This human
resource management challenge extends
beyond teachers to education management.

Information, capacity, and incentives can
also be important for private provision. The
private sector is playing a significant role in
providing even primary education in many
countries; it has already contributed to significant expansion in enrollments (figure
5.16).[19] Private provision offers the potential for increasing access at lower cost, often
with comparable or better outcomes than
public schools.

A study in two states in India shows that
although private schools do not always achieve
higher learning outcomes than public schools
(especially after controlling for observable
differences in children) and achievement gaps
vary between states, private schools are more
cost-effective than public schools (Goyal and

FIGURE 5.16   **Share of primary and secondary enrollments in public and private institutions in selected South Asian countries**

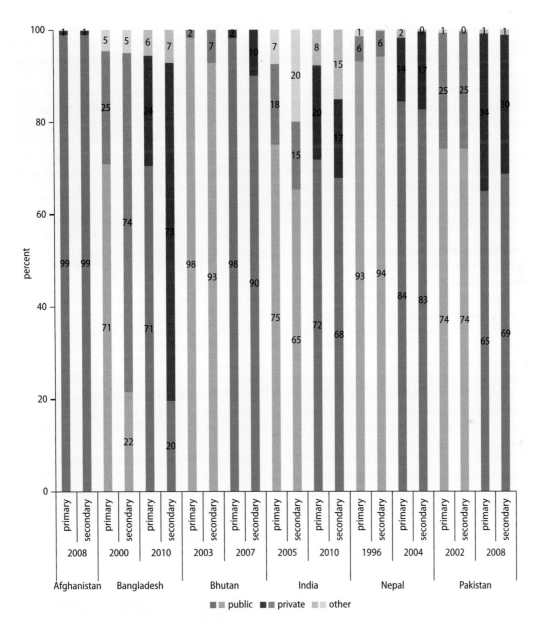

Source: Authors, based on national labor force and household surveys.
Note: "Other" includes private-aided schools in India; technical schools in Nepal; and madrasas in Afghanistan, Bangladesh, and Pakistan. Public schools in Nepal are, for the most part, under community management.

Pandey 2009b).[20] A study in rural Punjab (Pakistan) finds that private school students' test scores are 1.5–2.5 years ahead of their public school counterparts and that a significant achievement gap remains even after controlling for the fact that more affluent

children attend private schools (Andrabi and others 2007). In Bangladesh, where secondary education is almost entirely provided by the private sector with government financing, the majority of financing is on the basis of inputs, and serious concerns about quality remain. Insufficient attention has been paid in most South Asian countries to developing quality assurance systems for the public and private sectors and strengthening incentives and capacity in the school system as a whole.

The global knowledge base on interventions to improve quality is still being built. More is known on how to improve access and to include disadvantaged groups. An ongoing regional study on the quality of education in South Asia will provide a more comprehensive look at the region's education systems and a more in-depth discussion of interventions to improve quality. Addressing governance challenges will need to be at the center of all country strategies, as discussed below.

Improving governance and accountability through information
A key missing element in the accountability regimes in the region is data on student learning outcomes. Only India, Pakistan, and Sri Lanka have national systems of student assessment, and even they are at the primary level only. Only India has participated in an international assessment of student achievement (two Indian states participated in the Programme for International Student Assessment [PISA 2009+], the results of which will be available at the end of 2011). Although all countries have an extensive system of public examinations at the end of secondary education and often also at the end of primary education, the tests are usually not a good basis for accountability.[21]

Even on a sample basis, national assessments can yield important information about the strengths and weaknesses of the system, which provides guidance for policy makers and other institutional actors (such as teacher training institutions) in designing interventions. Establishing such assessment is a priority area for education systems in South Asia. Countries with assessment systems are working on strengthening them. India, for example, is modernizing its system to bring it to international standards. Nongovernmental organizations (NGOs) such as Pratham have played a key role in contributing to the education debate in India (and now in Pakistan)

through their annual status of education reports (Pratham 2010).

Providing information to local stakeholders on roles, responsibilities, and learning outcomes can improve accountability and outcomes in schools. Many countries (including Bangladesh, India, and Pakistan) are increasing efforts to address the limited information and capacity of school management committees and to increase the involvement of parents and communities. Rigorous evaluations of some pilot interventions suggest that such efforts hold promise, although capacity building requires sustained effort and results can take time.

In India, a study in 12 districts in 3 states evaluated the impact of an intervention that provided information to villagers about the roles and responsibilities of school or village management committees. Although the magnitude and channels of impact (for example, increased knowledge, engagement, and monitoring) varied across states, math competencies increased 10–30 percent and teacher absenteeism fell 9–12 percent (Pandey, Goyal, and Sundararaman 2009).

In Pakistan, school report cards were distributed to parents and teachers, and discussion groups took place to ensure that participants understand the information reported. Average test scores increased in villages in which report cards were distributed. Increased local competition appeared to have spurred the poorest-quality private schools to improve (Andrabi, Das, and Khwaja 2009).

Strengthening school management
Most South Asian countries have started devolving greater responsibilities to schools, although the extent of the devolution varies across countries. Nepal has undertaken the most sweeping reforms. Bangladesh, India, Pakistan, and Sri Lanka have all begun to engage school committees in the school planning process, increase the availability of funds to schools, and strengthen the role of school leadership. Although the global evidence on school-based management reforms is still limited, studies find that they can change

the dynamics of the school, because parents become more engaged, teachers' behaviors change, or both. The studies document a positive impact on repetition and failure rates, although evidence on learning outcomes is mixed (Bruns, Filmer, and Patrinos 2011).

The evidence from initiatives in South Asian countries is promising. In Nepal, where the devolution of responsibility for managing schools to communities is one of the most extensive in the world, positive impacts include increased participation of disadvantaged children and improved grade progression (see box 7.5 in chapter 7). Sri Lanka's Program for School Improvement empowers school management committees to develop and implement school improvement plans. The program, which has improved math and English language test scores of grade 4 students, is expected to be expanded nationally.

Improving the quality and performance of teachers

Recruiting, motivating, and supporting the right teachers have to be critical components of any strategy to improve education outcomes. South Asian countries have started taking bold steps to reduce the politicization of recruitment and placement, improve the quality of teachers recruited, and increase motivation through various approaches, such as incentive pay and the development of career paths.

Moving away from patronage-based recruitment to merit-based recruitment of teachers is key. Political interference in recruitment and school postings reduces the quality and accountability of teachers, affecting student attendance and learning. In the past few years, the region has made considerable progress toward transparent and merit-based recruitment of teachers. Bangladesh developed a teacher registration and certification authority, which administers examinations to certify teachers, who are then assigned on the basis of demand from schools. Pakistan introduced new policies in various provinces requiring the use of transparent and merit-based criteria and school-specific contracts (box 5.1).

Some studies from South Asia suggest that well-designed schemes that provide incentives

---

BOX 5.1   **Recruiting teachers based on merit in Sindh, Pakistan**

Patronage-based hiring of teachers has long been prevalent throughout South Asia. In Sindh, Pakistan's second most populous province, hiring has historically been patronage based, potentially compromising the quality of incoming teachers and their accountability, as evidenced by rates of teacher absenteeism estimated as high as 25 percent. Teacher absenteeism further undermines the regularity and quality of teaching, and, in turn, student attendance and learning.

To improve the quality of incoming teachers, the government of Sindh is administering a program for transparent merit-based recruitment. In a major shift from past recruitment policies and practices, the government now first screens candidates through an externally developed and administered content-based examination. Higher priority in placement is given to candidates who score higher on the entrance exam and have better academic and professional qualifications, candidates who live close to the proposed placement, and women. Qualifying candidates are then placed in understaffed schools under school-specific and fixed-term contracts in an effort to enhance accountability, reduce absenteeism, and place teachers according to need.

About 13,500 teachers have been hired over two rounds of recruitment. The first round emphasized merit-based recruitment; the second round also introduced needs-based placement. Both rounds were validated by an external third party. Early findings show the rate of absenteeism of newly recruited teachers to be 16 percent, compared with 22 percent for regular teachers. A rigorous impact evaluation of the program is underway to determine the effects of the program on teaching and learning quality.

Source: World Bank staff reports.

through the nature of the contract or pay can lead to learning gains. There are a few good studies from developing countries, but the knowledge base is still limited. Moreover, evidence on incentive pay varies across countries and scheme designs (see annex table 5A.3). The evidence is still based on relatively short periods of time, with much less known on longer-term impacts.

These caveats notwithstanding, some studies show promising results. The use of contract teachers appears to have led to learning gains for students in India, in part because contract teachers exhibit more effective work habits, such as better attendance and greater effort (Duflo, Hanna, and Ryan 2010;

Muralidharan and Sundararaman 2010). These improved outcomes come at considerable savings, as the cost of hiring teachers on civil service terms and conditions is four to seven times greater than the cost of recruiting contract teachers (Goyal and Pandey 2009a). Few countries have figured out how to create career paths for contract teachers; doing so will be important for ensuring the sustainability of such policies.

Evaluations from the states of Rajasthan (Duflo, Hanna, and Ryan 2010) and Andhra Pradesh (Muralidharan and Sundararaman 2011) show positive impacts of teacher incentives on attendance and student learning. Box 5.2 provides additional information on the

---

BOX 5.2   Teacher incentives schemes in Andhra Pradesh

In a statewide representative sample of 500 schools, four different approaches to improving learning were tried. The schemes included two incentives schemes (an individual teacher bonus and a group teacher bonus) and two input schemes (provision of an additional contract teacher and provision of a block grant to the school) as well as a comparison group of 100 schools. All schools, including the control schools, were monitored, with students tested at the beginning and end of the school year. Teacher bonuses were awarded on the basis of average improvement of student test scores over each school year. In the group incentive schools, bonuses were awarded on the basis of the average gains of all students in the school, and were equally distributed among teachers. In the individual incentive schools, the bonuses were awarded to each teacher on the basis of the average gains in scores of students taught by that particular teacher.

After two years, all four schemes improved student learning. However, the schools receiving the teacher incentive programs improved their test scores by significantly more than those receiving additional inputs. Students in incentive schools scored 0.27 standard deviations higher in math, and 0.16 standard deviations higher in language than students in the control schools (while the students in input schools scored 0.09 and 0.08 standard deviations higher in math and language than those in control

schools). The main mechanism for the effectiveness of the teacher incentive program was not higher teacher attendance in the incentive schools, but greater teacher effort conditional on attendance (teachers report that they assigned more homework, held extra classes, gave practice tests, and helped weaker students).

After two years, the individual incentive schools performed better than the group incentive schools. Averaged across subjects, students in individual incentive schools scored 0.28 standard deviations higher than the control group, while students in group incentive schools scored 0.16 standard deviations higher. However, because the bonuses were paid as a function of actual improvement in test scores, the bonuses paid out under the group incentive program were lower, and so the cost per unit of increase in test scores of the two programs was similar (though the individual incentive program was more cost effective after including fixed administrative costs).

Although there was no incentive for performance in science and social studies, scores in these subjects also rose. It seems likely that weak literacy and math skills were preventing students from doing well in other subjects, and the results suggest positive spillovers from gains in math and language to other subjects.

Source: Murlidharan and Sundararaman 2011.

intervention in Andhra Pradesh and the relative cost-effectiveness of various interventions.

Countries in South Asia are taking steps to improve incentives and performance through capacity building linked to career progression of teachers. Although this is still an underdeveloped area of reform in South Asia, recent initiatives by several governments suggest that they recognize the importance of this issue. For example, to address the serious deficiencies in teacher education and professional development, the Sindh government is gradually implementing a comprehensive teacher education development program. The program envisions an integrated and coherent system for preservice and systematic in-service training (continuous professional development) linked to entry and career progression. Reforms in Nepal are focusing on developing separate professional career paths for basic and secondary-level teachers and provision of preparatory and in-service training. The plan is to link career progression to pedagogical effort/time, seniority, qualification, training, and student achievement.

Increasing human capital investment in disadvantaged groups

In addition to strengthening the school system to improve the quality of learning, governments have a role to play in addressing market failures that lead to lower investment in human capital in disadvantaged groups. On the demand side, inadequate information and budget constraints are two reasons for low investment in human capital among low-income households. There is some evidence that inaccurate perceptions on returns reduces investment in education. Direct and indirect costs associated with schooling also reduce investment (distance to schools is a problem for girls in Afghanistan and Pakistan). On the supply side, in many remote and rural parts of South Asia, latent demand for schooling is going unmet in underserved communities. The following sections discuss some innovative interventions on the demand and supply sides that have shown promise in increasing participation among disadvantaged groups.

Increasing demand from households
As the demand for more educated workers increases, improving parents' understanding of the returns to education can lead to increased investment in the education of their children. In a study of three states in India, Oster and Millet (2011) show that opening an information technology–enabled service center increased knowledge of improved job opportunities and perceived returns from higher schooling, leading to a 5.7 percent increase in the number of children enrolled in a primary school. They find that the very localized effects were a result of limited information diffusion outside the areas where the call centers were opened, suggesting that policies that improve understanding of job opportunities could play an important role in increasing enrollments. Consistent with this finding, an intervention that provided three years of recruiting services for business process outsourcing opportunities for women in randomly selected rural villages in India was associated with large increases in enrollment as well as subsequent employment (Jensen 2010).

Reducing the costs of schooling or otherwise reducing household income constraints can also contribute to increased participation. In Afghanistan, and Pakistan, reducing indirect costs by reducing distance to school has increased enrollment, especially for girls. In Afghanistan, enrollment of girls in communities randomly selected to receive schools increased by 15 percent more than overall enrollment (a 50 percent increase for all students versus a 65 percent increase for girls) (Burde and Linden 2010). After six months, girls in villages with community schools also reported far higher test scores than boys.

Around the world and in South Asia, conditional cash transfer programs, which help households address budget constraints, have a strong record in increasing enrollment (Fishbein and Schady 2009). Enrollment and attendance of girls in secondary schools increased substantially in Bangladesh after the government introduced cash stipends to rural girls under the Female Secondary School Stipend (FSSS) program in the 1990s. Female enrollment rates in lower secondary (grades 6–10) rose from about 25 percent in 1991 to about 60 percent by 2008, leading to gender parity at this level. A follow-up program is targeting poor children. Early evaluation of this program shows an estimated average net increase in retention of 20 percentage points (Asadullah and others 2011).

In Pakistan, both Sindh and Punjab provinces have large-scale conditional cash transfer programs targeting girls in secondary grades in government schools. Evaluations of the program in Punjab find enrollment gains (of about 9 percent), delayed marriage and pregnancy, and no negative spillover effects on boys' enrollment (Adam, Baez, and del Carpio 2011; Chaudury and Parajuli 2010).

Providing accountability-based subsidies to private providers
Public-private partnerships (PPPs) are proving to be a cost-effective means of reaching underserved children. Although low-cost private schools are emerging, including in rural

areas, they are less likely to locate in the most underserved areas or to serve the poorest groups. Governments in the region are therefore innovating with programs that use subsidies to address this market failure.

A PPP program in Punjab (Pakistan) provides per student subsidies to low-cost private schools for enrolling and raising learning levels among children from low-income households. An evaluation of the program finds large effects (of 0.3–0.5 standard deviation) on student learning—far greater than the 0.1–0.2 standard deviation gains from most interventions that have been evaluated in the literature—across two different tests, suggesting that teaching to the test is likely not at play (Barrera-Osorio and Raju 2010). In Sindh, Pakistan, a pilot program that offers public per student subsidies to support the set-up and operation of private coeducational primary schools in underserved rural communities increased school participation by 51 percentage points in program communities. The growth in school participation was

---

BOX 5.3   The Reaching Out-of-School Children project in Bangladesh

The Reaching Out-of-School Children (ROSC) project has increased access to learning opportunity for out of school children ages 7–14 in about 60 targeted *upazilas* (subdistricts). It combines accountability-based subsidies to providers (learning centers) with demand-side financing of students (stipends). Key features include public financing of stipends and grants to learning centers, community management of learning centers, and public-private partnerships (of community, government, and NGOs) in implementation. Grants to learning centers are provided on a per capita basis, and continuation of financing of learning centers as well as stipends is contingent on achieving minimum levels of student attendance and performance. The community-driven approach focuses on establishing learning centers through a functional center management committee that is directly accountable to parents and

students, with support from NGOs as implementation partners. Operational program delivery differs from the norms in primary schools in order to cater to specific needs of students (through, for example, flexible school timing, multigrade teaching, and entry at an older age).

Initial findings from an independent impact evaluation find that ROSC has succeeded in targeting intended beneficiaries (children from the poorest households); reducing the proportion of out-of-school children; and improving learning levels, as measured by student test scores in math and language (Bangla). Compared with the regular primary schooling system, the ROSC project is achieving similar outcomes in access and equity at less than half the per student spending, implying impressive cost-effectiveness.

Source: Asadullah and others 2011.

larger for girls than for boys, eliminating the gender gap. The cost for this intervention of inducing a 1 percent increase in school participation lies at the bottom of the range of estimates for interventions in developing countries subject to rigorous evaluations (Barrera-Osorio and others 2011). Early results indicate learning gains of two standard deviations. Bangladesh has also demonstrated the potential of innovative partnerships with the private sector (box 5.3).

Tertiary education and preemployment training systems

Preemployment vocational training provides an alternative for students who do not pursue tertiary education. It is provided in institutions outside the general schooling system, often targeting early school leavers with the objective of directly preparing participants for the labor market. Preemployment training includes formal accredited courses and can be part of a national qualification framework requiring a minimum entry qualification. It is typically provided in specialized training centers, training colleges, or polytechnics.

Minimum entry qualifications vary across countries. In most countries, premployment training requires completion of grade 10; it starts after grade 8 in Bangladesh and Pakistan and after grade 9 in Afghanistan and Sri Lanka. Depending on entry qualifications, courses can range from less than a year to five years, with multiple entry and exit points. Courses range from those aimed at future tradespeople and technicians to those providing higher levels of skills.

Tertiary education refers to academic and professional degree and diploma courses provided by universities, colleges, and professional schools (such as medical schools). The minimum entry qualification is completion of higher-secondary education or its equivalent.

This section discusses the challenges and priorities for strengthening preemployment training and tertiary education systems. Although the students targeted by these two systems are different, as is the focus of the knowledge and technical skills, many of the challenges are similar. Three countries in the region—Bangladesh, India, and Pakistan—also have small vocational education streams within the secondary school system (box 5.4).

Policy makers are keen to expand the small preemployment training and tertiary education systems. Participation in preemployment training ranges from about 1.0 percent of secondary enrollment in Afghanistan to 8.1 percent in Sri Lanka. India ranks second in the region, with 4.5 percent (see annex figure 5A.4). Gross enrollment rates for tertiary education range from 4 percent in Afghanistan to about 13 percent in India and 12–21 percent in Sri Lanka (depending on whether external degree programs are included) (see annex figure 5A.5). In most South Asian countries, policy makers see expansion of these sectors as an important element of their strategy for increasing the skills of the large number of new entrants into the labor force. Bhutan seeks to increase the number of its preemployment training graduates by a factor of 12 by 2013. India is targeting training 500 million people over the next 10 years through a combination of preemployment training, in-service training, and tertiary education (Government of India 2009). Nepal and Pakistan are also significantly increasing their investments in preemployment training. All South Asian countries are targeting substantial expansion of their tertiary education systems.

Expansion should not come at the expense of strengthening the systems for better outcomes. As with concerns about skills of graduates of tertiary education discussed earlier, there are concerns with the quality and relevance of preemployment training. A 2006/07 tracer study of labor market outcomes for graduates of preemployment training in Bangladesh finds that only 9.7 percent of male participants and just 5.2 percent of female participants were employed (World Bank 2008). A tracer study conducted by the International Labour Organization in three states in India in 2002/03 notes very low employment of graduates of the

BOX 5.4   Vocational education provided in the public school system

In Bangladesh, India, and Pakistan, students who do not fare well in the general (academic) education stream are often tracked into vocational education streams, typically at the senior-secondary level (and sometimes earlier). Vocational schools are supposed to equip students with skills that will allow them to join the labor market or preemployment training programs.

The experience with secondary vocational programs in South Asia, as in many other regions, has been poor. In India, for example, studies show that 60–70 percent of graduates fail to obtain employment even two to three years after graduation (World Bank 2007).

Despite these poor outcomes, policy makers remain keen to expand vocational secondary education. Bangladesh has targeted 20 percent and India 25 percent of secondary education to be vocational. There is also a desire to make general secondary education more vocational. As in other parts of the world, this desire is motivated by the concern that large numbers of students complete primary and secondary education with no occupational skills and the assumption that having occupational skills improves prospects in the labor market.

Such strategies may not be appropriate for the following reasons:

- Vocationalizing education is difficult. It requires specially trained instructors, preferably with work experience in the types of skills being taught. Teachers with these qualifications are hard to recruit and retain.
- Vocationalizing education is costly. Most variants of vocational training cost more per student class period than general education subjects, primarily because classes are smaller and facilities, equipment, and consumables cost more.
- Private sector involvement in running vocational education systems, setting course content and curricula, or managing vocational schools is very limited.
- Time spent on vocational skills training can detract from the teaching of basic academic skills, which provide the foundation for future learning and are increasingly essential for labor market success.

A better alternative to expanding vocational training in the school system would be to make general secondary schools more relevant and better able to cater to a wider range of students.

Expanding or retargeting secondary vocational programs is not justified unless a model is found that substantially improves outcomes. One such model is Chile's Corporación de Desarrollo Social del Sector Rural (CODESSER) program. CODESSER is a non-profit organization created by the National Society of Farmers in 1976. Initially, it administered four schools with weak reputations that found it difficult to attract students. Today, some of these schools receive more than 300 applications for 45 first-year openings, and schools have been added to accommodate growing demand. Recent figures show that more than 75 percent of graduates from agricultural schools hold mid level management positions in agriculture.

CODESSER has the following features, which embody some of the principles for reforming the vocational education system:

- Private sector players participate in management. A directorate of seven farmers or industrial entrepreneurs oversees each school. Their participation ensures better job skill matches, a direct connection to the labor market for graduates, and an effective medium for bringing about organizational and productive innovations.
- Teachers are hired as private sector employees. Personnel policy (including selection and promotion criteria and new contracts) conforms to the labor code that regulates private sector employees. Teachers' salaries are about 50 percent higher than in municipal schools. There has been a consistent effort to upgrade teacher training.
- The focus is on general education. Schools provide basic general knowledge in humanities and sciences, prepare students to work in various occupations, teach students to be problem solvers, and encourage them to continue learning. They emphasize general growth and the development of responsibility, leadership, and personnel management.
- The curriculum is regularly revised. CODESSER conducts periodic surveys of job requirements in the areas around each school. The surveys are used to adjust vocation-specific components in the curriculum.
- Schools developed independent sources of funding. The real value of public subsidies fell in the early 1980s; it declined by another 15 percent between 1987 and 1991. In 1982, the public subsidy represented the bulk of schools' budgets; it is now less than 50 percent.

Source: Chhoeda, Dar, and Tan 2010.

preemployment training system (ILO 2003). According to the study, formal sector employment of graduates from both public and private industrial training institutions was very low. In none of the states did more than half of graduates find wage employment, become self-employed, or work in a family business (figure 5.17).

Pressure to expand will continue, as more and more students complete secondary education. A key priority for government is to strengthen systems to improve quality while leveraging partnerships with a variety of stakeholders. Also important will be addressing market failures that prevent children from low-income households from progressing to and graduating from higher levels of education. In what follows, some of the key challenges facing these systems and approaches to addressing them are examined.

Strengthening policy and regulatory oversight

Fragmented system management blurs the roles of various agencies and reduces policy coherence. Responsibility for policy direction, leadership, and regulation of and accountability for implementation is often diffused across different levels of government or multiple ministries and agencies. In Bangladesh, for example, both the Ministry of Education and the Ministry of Labor are responsible for preemployment training, and about 10 other ministries run training institutes. Financing and regulation of tertiary education institutions in medicine is also the domain of multiple agencies.

Two main problems result from this administrative overlap. The first is a lack of clarity and duplication of functions. The second is a tendency to emphasize the delivery of training by multiple agencies at the cost of ensuring quality standards. It is important for governments to transition from a preoccupation with provision and financing to a stronger stewardship role.

There is a need for governments to take on a stronger stewardship role and clarify the functions of various agencies. It may be appropriate to entrust one body with playing

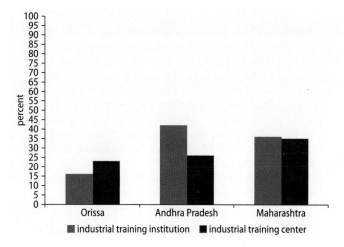

FIGURE 5.17 **Percentage of graduates from public and private industrial training institutions employed in the organized sector in three states of India, 2002/03**

Source: ILO 2003.

the stewardship role, setting policy, ensuring coordination between ministries, overseeing financing, developing curriculum, handling certification and accreditation, and providing information on the quality and effectiveness of institutions. Critical to the success of such a body is the role of employers. Unless they are given a prominent role in the policy and decision-making process, provision may not be adjusted sufficiently to meet their needs.

Australia provides a successful example for preemployment training and tertiary education (box 5.5). Some interesting initiatives are also underway in tertiary education in South Asia. If implemented well, for example, establishment of the National Council of Higher Education and Research (NCHER) could improve policy coordination and regulation of tertiary education and research in India. The existing tertiary education bodies—the University Grants Commission, the All India Council of Technical Education, the National Council of Teacher Education, the Distance Education Council, and related academic councils—are expected to come under the umbrella of the NCHER.

In the medium term, the establishment of a national qualifications framework can make programs more coherent and clarify the roles of various players. Sri Lanka has a

---

BOX 5.5 **Learning from Australia's systemic reforms of training and tertiary education**

Australia's federal and state governments created the Australian National Training Authority (ANTA) in the 1990s. The agency was overhauled over time.

On July 1, 2009, the government formed a Ministerial Council for Tertiary Education and Employment (MCTEE) to oversee skills development. Membership in the council includes federal, state, and territory ministers with responsibility for tertiary education, preemployment training, and employment. MCTEE is chaired by the federal government minister.

MCTEE has overall responsibility for skills development. Its functions include the following:

- Setting national priorities and the strategic policy directions for the tertiary education sector and preemployment training to meet the skills needs of the Australian economy
- Establishing streamlined arrangements for national consistency and harmonization of tertiary

education and preemployment training (while respecting the mission of each sector)
- Funding the national training system
- Maintaining strong industry leadership of and engagement in preemployment training and tertiary education
- Overseeing the work of the Australian Qualifications Framework Council in strengthening the Australian Qualifications Framework
- Engaging with all associated bodies, councils, and ministerial committees to ensure the effectiveness of policy and strategies for tertiary education and preemployment training
- Responding to business, industry, and stakeholder advice on issues affecting tertiary education and preemployment training
- Setting national research priorities for skills development.

Source: Skills Australia 2011.

---

qualifications framework for preemployment training (the National Vocational Qualifications Framework), which is being implemented. The government is also working on a full national qualifications framework that will cover primary, secondary, and tertiary education, as well as preemployment training. India plans to establish a standards-based national vocational qualifications framework that will permit individuals who follow different learning pathways to certify their skills through testing and facilitate advancement to higher diplomas and degrees. Taking advantage of a still nascent tertiary education and training system, the government of Afghanistan is setting up a national qualifications authority and a national qualifications framework with which to better coordinate and articulate between the general education, tertiary education, and training systems, as well as between the various players responsible for implementing tertiary education and preemployment training.

A key role for governments is the provision of information and the strengthening of quality assurance mechanisms. Limited information, especially on quality and outcomes, is an important deterrent to improving effectiveness—and to students and employers making the right choices. Limited information about privately provided programs can lead to public sector crowding out private providers by entering areas where there is already a private supply. To address these issues, most countries in the region have started establishing education management information systems in tertiary education to provide information on participation and completion, transition from college to work, and finance. Bangladesh, India, and Nepal have begun to work on establishing information systems for preemployment training. It is important that these systems collect and disseminate information on outcomes (such as the quality of graduates and their employability). Toward this end, some countries have begun to conduct employer surveys and tracer studies of graduates (in India and Sri Lanka), and student and faculty surveys (in Bangladesh and India).

South Asian countries have also begun developing quality assurance and accreditation systems in tertiary education. Although there is still a long way to go, and a need to increase transparency and strengthen capacity of accreditation agencies, the region has been moving toward developing these systems. India has a formal accreditation system, but only 15 percent of its more than 20,000 institutions are accredited (Agarwal 2009). Nepal is in the process of establishing an independent quality assurance and accreditation council/board. Pakistan established the Quality Assurance Agency in 2005 as a monitoring and regulatory body to facilitate quality assurance in both public and private institutions. Nine accreditation councils have accredited 60 programs, and quality enhancement cells are being established within institutions to undertake internal quality assurance. Sri Lanka is developing a quality assurance review process covering 60 percent of all universities.

Strengthening institutional governance and accountability

Politicization and insufficient representation of key stakeholders in governing bodies undermines institutional accountability and effectiveness. Vice chancellors of public universities are often politically appointed. In addition, many colleges and universities in South Asia do not have a board of governors with representation of key stakeholders. This failure undermines the transparency of decision-making process and accountability to beneficiaries, particularly students, parents, and employers. Governing bodies of preemployment training institutions are less politicized. A key omission in both systems is the lack of representation of the private sector in the governing bodies.

Some countries have initiated reforms in this regard. India has begun to ban politicians from serving as chairs of the governing

bodies of tertiary education institutions in engineering. It has established qualification criteria for their selection and mandated greater transparency in the selection process (Government of Maharashtra 2009; Government of India 2010). Private sector involvement in institutional management of public tertiary education and training institutions is also increasing. Industry associations and individual employers are increasingly represented on governing boards. In India, the two largest industrial associations—the Federation of Indian Chambers of Commerce and Industry and the Confederation of Indian Industries—are represented and actively participate in the management committees of tertiary education and training institutions. In Sindh (Pakistan), private sector representatives now head the institutional management committees of training institutions. Bangladesh and Nepal are moving in this direction.

Involving employers in management will yield positive results only if governments are willing to provide institutions with greater autonomy. This means letting institutions administer themselves and keep the funds they raise through fees and other sources. Administrative regulations and budgeting rules provide scant incentives for efficiency and innovation. Possibly to counter the lack of local oversight, many governments in the region have highly specific rules on hiring, firing, and rewarding faculty (administrative autonomy) and managing revenues, including fee setting and expenditures (financial autonomy). In Afghanistan, Bangladesh, and several states of India, teachers are hired centrally, removing the power of institutional leaders to hire or promote teachers. In Afghanistan, all revenue generated by universities, including fees, has to be returned to the Ministry of Finance.

Elements of autonomy are also being introduced in the region. In India, public training institutions and engineering colleges, in consultation with employers, decide on their own training programs, have the freedom to hire part-time teachers, and retain part of the revenues generated by selling goods and services. Nepal's tertiary education system is also moving in this direction, albeit slowly. The move toward greater autonomy and accountability needs to be accompanied by measures to increase awareness among and strengthen the capacity of members of oversight committees and governing boards.

In most cases, funding mechanisms still provide limited incentives to institutions to improve performance. As countries develop, funding mechanisms for tertiary education gradually shift from incremental budgeting (historically negotiated budgets) to performance-based approaches (table 5.4). This transition has not yet occurred in South Asia. Training institutions are typically guaranteed continued funding irrespective of performance, with levels of finance allocated to poorly performing institutions with high drop-out rates equal to those allocated to institutions that maintain a high quality of teaching and performance.

Since about 2000, several governments in South Asia have laid a cornerstone by allocating some tertiary education funding through competitive or innovation funds. These funds transparently finance investments in public and private tertiary education based on objective policy goals, such as improved quality and relevance of undergraduate programs. One example is the Quality Enhancement Fund for Higher Education in Sri Lanka, launched in 2005, which is progressively being strengthened based on experience.

Financing systems for training are also seeing reforms. Bangladesh and Nepal are introducing performance grants to training institutions that meet agreed upon performance criteria (such as the pass rate for students or the employment rates of students six months after graduation). In Pakistan, continued funding under the Benazir Bhutto Shaheed Youth Development Program (BBSYDP)

TABLE 5.4   Mechanisms for funding tertiary education in South and East Asia, by economy

Economy	Historically negotiated budget	Formula funding	Competitive funding	Performance-based contracts
High-income				
Hong Kong SAR, China		•		
Japan			•	•
Korea, Rep.		•		•
Singapore		•		•
Middle-income				
China	•	•		
Indonesia	•	a	•	
Malaysia	•	•		
Philippines	•	•		
Thailand	•	•		
Low-income				
Cambodia	•			
Lao PDR	•			
Vietnam	•		•	
South Asia				
Bangladesh	•		b	
India	•		b	
Nepal	•		b	
Pakistan	•		b	
Sri Lanka	•		•	

Sources: Authors, based on data on East Asia from World Bank 2011a and data on South Asia from sector staff.
Note: a = Formula funding incorporating performance indicators has been piloted in five autonomous universities (and some nonautonomous universities).
b = Government projects financed by the World Bank have started competitive funding for selected institutions and disciplines.

now requires training providers to achieve minimum levels of job placement.

Increasing the role of the private sector

Private provision of education is significant in South Asia, particularly in preemployment training, and is growing. Enrollment in private preemployment institutions ranges from 6 percent of total enrollment in Afghanistan to 82 percent in Nepal; in tertiary education, the figures range from less than 5 percent in Afghanistan and Bhutan to more than 50 percent in Bangladesh (figure 5.18). Even in Afghanistan, where formal institutes are still very much under government domain, strong private and NGO–based initiatives are developing.

Easing barriers to entry and leveling the playing field can generate a stronger private sector response. Private providers in some South Asian countries identify lack of access to credit and financing of initial investments

as key constraints to setting up new and upgrading existing institutions.[22] Although not uniform across countries, other concerns include excessive barriers to entry and government bureaucracy in registering institutions and accrediting and certifying courses.

International experience suggests that when private providers are not discouraged by stringent regulations, rapid industrial growth can be accompanied by strong private sector response in supply. Streamlining the process of registration/licensing based on clear merit-based criteria is critical. Imposing strict consequences for malpractice by bureaucrats can also help improve the environment for private providers. In India, where the private sector is more heavily engaged in training in commercial areas than in other countries, up to 15 percent of all providers now provide technical training, indicative of private sector response despite the higher initial investment costs for technical fields. Enabling private institutions to compete for public resources

FIGURE 5.18 **Share of preemployment training and tertiary education enrollment in public and private institutions in South Asia, by country**

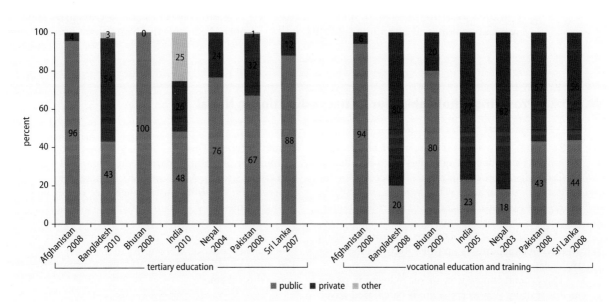

Sources: Authors, based on data from Chhoeda, Dan, and Tar 2010 for vocational education and training; labor force and household surveys for tertiary education for all countries except Bhutan and Sri Lanka; Thinley 2009 for Bhutan; World Bank 2009 for Sri Lanka.
Note: "Other" includes private-aided schools in India and *madrasas* in Bangladesh and Pakistan. For Sri Lanka, enrollment in external degree programs—which accounts for 58 percent of total tertiary enrollment—is included in public enrollment. If shares in the public and private sectors are computed excluding enrollment in external degree programs, private enrollment represents 28 percent of total tertiary enrollment.

on a level playing field, particularly in priority education and training areas, could reduce barriers. The recent trend toward competitive funding is a promising step in this direction.

PPP arrangements are just being initiated in the region. Potential models include the private sector investing in and managing defunct public institutions as a concession or setting up new institutions in underserved areas with public subsidies. Early experience suggests several lessons for making PPPs work, including the importance of sound project fundamentals; attention to the timing, scope, and duration of transaction; high-quality advisors; a strong government implementation team; and transparency throughout the process (based on unpublished presentation by the International Finance Corporation 2010).

Diversifying the resource base

Until recently, little attention was paid to exploring ways to enhance the resource pool to finance expansion and improvements. Throughout the world, the unit costs of both preemployment training and tertiary education are significantly higher than those of general education. In the face of competing demands and limited fiscal space, significant expansion and enhancing quality will

be possible only by diversifying the resource base.

One important mechanism is tuition, which is being increased in public tertiary and preemployment training institutions in Bangladesh, India, Nepal, and Pakistan. The much higher fees being paid at private institutions demonstrates both the demand for services and the willingness of better-off segments to pay. Governments can offset the adverse impact of such fees on equity by providing targeted scholarships to low-income groups, as Bangladesh, India, Nepal (box 5.6), and Pakistan are doing. Student loans can help ease liquidity constraints. Student loan schemes for tertiary education have been implemented in India and are being developed in Pakistan.

On-the-job training

Formal on-the-job training can be an important channel through which workers can build human capital. Although this chapter focuses primarily on education and training that takes place before entry into the labor force, a significant part of human capital accumulation takes place in the work place.

As analysis of business enterprise data in South Asia reveals, firms that innovate, are

---

BOX 5.6   Providing scholarships for tertiary education in Nepal

In 2003/04, only about 1 percent of children in each of the two poorest quintiles were enrolled in tertiary education compared to 88 percent in the richest quintile. To address the problem, in 2009 the government initiated a scheme to provide financial support for meritorious and needy students through scholarships. These scholarships finance education and living expenditures up to Rs 40,000 ($530) for the duration of study.

The crucial innovation of the scheme is proxy means testing. A poverty score is calculated based on a set of observable household characteristics (for

example, types of walls, roof, cook stove, and toilet; number of siblings; parent education; and caste and ethnic group). All household characteristics are observables; information can therefore be verified through household visits to prospective beneficiaries. The calculation gives preference to disadvantaged castes and ethnic groups. A minimum share of beneficiaries must be women. As of February 2010, 176 undergraduate students had received benefits under this scheme.

Sources: Nepal Living Standards Survey 2003/04 and World Bank 2010.

internationally engaged, and have a more educated workforce are also more likely to invest in the training of their workforce. This finding is consistent with the strong links found in the international literature between on-the-job training and individuals' and firms' productivity. Despite econometric challenges associated with identifying the impact of on-the-job training on wages and firm productivity (see Almeida, Behrman, and Robalino 2011 for a review of the evidence), there is convincing evidence, particularly from developed countries, of the positive effects of training. It may be the case that on-the-job training may be more critical in producing skilled workers in developing countries than in developed countries, in view of the considerable skills gaps of graduates of education and preemployment training systems in these countries.

The incidence of formal on-the-job training is lower in South Asia than in any other region (figure 5.19). Across the world, small and medium-size firms are less likely to train, but even holding firm size constant, the incidence of training in South Asia is relatively low. In East Asia and Latin America and the Caribbean, for example, more than 70 percent of the largest firms and 30 percent of the smallest firms provide training to their workers. In South Asia, less than 40 percent of the largest firms train their workers, and only about 5 percent of the smallest firms do so.

Training incidence also varies with worker characteristics. It is lowest among workers with less schooling, confirming complementarities between investments in general schooling and on-the-job training. Evidence from India also shows distinct differences across industries in their propensity to offer formal in-service training, with industries such as textiles, garments, leather products, food processing, automobile parts, and metal products less likely to train and

FIGURE 5.19   **Percentage of firms providing on-the-job training in regions and selected South Asian countries, by firm size**

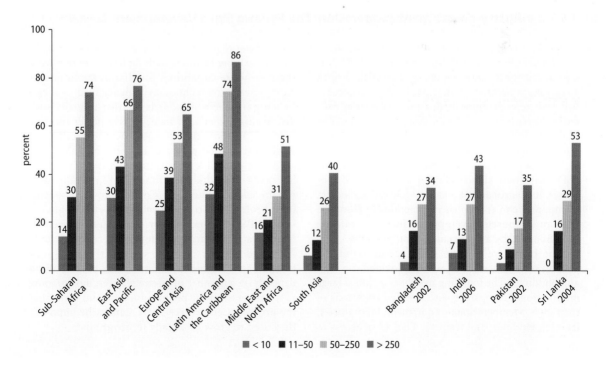

Source: World Bank staff, based on establishment survey data compiled by Almeida and Aterido 2010.

industries such as chemicals, pharmaceuticals, machine tools, electrical white goods, electronic products, and software more likely to do so. In-house programs (offered by 23 percent of all firms) tend to be more common than external programs (offered by 14 percent of firms). This evidence is consistent with the notion that workforce training can complement general skills of workers, with training tailored to the production and technological requirements of individual enterprises (Riboud, Savchenko, and Tan 2007).

The low incidence of formal training does not necessarily imply the need for public intervention. For many firms in developing countries, investment in on-the-job training may not be necessary, given technological choices, the skills components of most of their jobs, or their reliance on informal training. Other firms, however, may face severe informational constraints in, for example, identifying relevant training programs, recruiting training experts, or financing programs. Market failures associated with the risk of other firms

poaching trained employees could also lead to suboptimal investments. Policies should be designed to address the primary source of market failure.

International evidence suggests three main reasons why employers do not train workers. Responses of managers in enterprise surveys suggest that in the majority of firms, formal training may not be needed (informal training is considered sufficient or the technology does not require training) (Almeida, Behrman, and Robalino 2011; Batra and Stone 2004). High worker turnover or fear of poaching (or the ability to hire workers from elsewhere), lack of financing, and information barriers also appear to be factors. Improving the investment climate should improve incentives for employers to invest in both physical and human capital. Policies that improve access to new technologies and funding for investments in technology and skills upgrading would also increase firms' demand for training.

PPPs and collective industry action can strengthen the in-house training capabilities of firms. Firms, industry associations, buyers

BOX 5.7   Industry-government cooperation: The Penang Skills Development Centre

The Penang Skills Development Centre (PSDC) is a joint corporate training center established with government support. It has evolved to become a full private continuing education institution providing certificate and diploma-level training. The Malaysian government invests in the center and uses it to conduct public training programs.

With more than 100 member companies, the PSDC runs both standardized and customized programs. It charges at cost and is largely self-financing. Companies can recoup their expenditure from the Human Resource Development Fund, a training fund financed by a 1 percent levy on payrolls.

The initiative for the PSDC came from the Penang state government, which provided the land and buildings. The founding members included large multinational companies with training traditions of their own. Members donate equipment, laboratories, training modules, and trainers. They have access to

shared training facilities without having to duplicate their in-house capability. Small and medium-size enterprises enjoy technology transfer from and can benchmark their standards against multinationals. Multinationals, in turn, receive better support services. Vendors donate equipment to familiarize workers with their products and promote sales.

Although still a joint training center, the PSDC has taken on institutional functions to provide training for school-leavers, thus moving toward becoming a professional training entity in its own right.

The PSDC is not easily replicated. Eleven of Malaysia's 16 states and federal territories have launched similar centers, with varying degrees of success. The success of this sort of enterprise depends on a number of circumstances, most important among them the people initiating and managing the process. Centers like PSDC cannot be imposed; they need to grow in already fertile ground.

and equipment suppliers, and private training institutes are an important means of expanding the resources available for developing workforce skills.

Successful examples of such collective action—a potential response to the externalities associated with poaching—are in place in the region. The Chittagong Skills Development Centre is the first industry-led, nonprofit skills training center in Bangladesh. It is modeled on the successful Penang Skills Development Center (box 5.7). The center provides skills training to corporate members and other private companies. Its high-quality, cost-saving advantage stems from its corporate members' willingness to share their training resources, technologies, costs, trainers, space, and equipment, which ensures demand-driven, timely, and calibrated training without the overhead investment and delay of building a new center.

Numerous training programs, especially in the information and communications technology sector in India, are meeting industry needs. A randomized field experiment that provided five months of intensive management consultancy to help poorly managed textile firms adopt standard internationally used systems (for quality, inventory, and production control) found gradual but significant improvements in management practices and firm performance (Bloom and others 2011). Possible reasons for poor initial management included informational constraints (firms were not aware of many modern management practices).

Annex 5A   Additional tables and figures on education and skills

TABLE 5A.1   Share of Indian labor force requiring high concentration of nonroutine cognitive analytical and interpersonal skills, 1994–2010
(percent)

Type of nonroutine cognitive skill	1994	2000	2005	2008	2010
Analytical					
Analyzing information	3.9	5.0	4.2	9.5	11.8
Thinking creatively	3.3	4.3	3.9	6.5	9.5
Interpreting information for others	1.3	1.1	1.0	1.4	1.3
Interpersonal					
Establishing and maintain relationships	6.9	7.4	7.9	11.9	13.2
Guiding, directing, and motivating subordinates	1.7	2.9	2.7	4.6	8.2
Coaching and developing others	1.2	1.0	1.1	1.3	1.2

Source: Authors, based on national labor force surveys.
Note: High concentration of a skill in an occupation is when the content of the skill in the occupation is valued at 4 or 5 on a 1–5 scale.

TABLE 5A.2   Mean years of education of 15–34 year olds in South Asia, by gender and country

Country (period studied)	All		Male		Female	
	Earliest year	Most recent year	Earliest year	Most recent year	Earliest year	Most recent year
Afghanistan (2008)	—	2.5	—	3.7	—	1.4
Bangladesh (2000–10)	4.5	5.9	5.2	6.1	3.9	5.8
Bhutan (2003–07)	3.0	4.5	3.8	5.2	2.4	3.9
India (2000–10)	5.3	7.1	6.4	7.9	4.3	6.3
Maldives (1998–2004)	7.2	7.8	7.5	8.1	7.0	7.6
Nepal (1999–2008)	3.2	5.7	4.5	7.1	2.2	4.8
Pakistan (2000–09)	4.7	5.9	6.0	6.9	3.5	4.9
Sri Lanka (2000–08)	8.7	10.2	8.5	9.9	8.9	10.4

Source: World Bank staff, based on national labor force and household survey data.
Note: — = Not available.

TABLE 5A.3   Summary of randomized experiments on teacher incentives

Study	Description	Level of incentive	Strategy of estimation	Impact	Unintended effects
Duflo, Hanna, and Ryan (2010)	Local program (113 schools, 57 treated) in India monitors teachers' presence at school and provides rewards for reduction in absenteeism.	School and teacher	Randomized experiment	Reduction of teacher absence by 21 percentage points Increase in instructional time of 30 percent Positive impact on test scores (0.17 standard deviation) Effects come from incentives and not from monitoring	None
Glewwe, Ilias, and Kremer (2008)	Local program (100 schools, 50 treated) in Kenya provides cash rewards to teachers for reducing dropouts and increasing test scores.	School	Randomized experiment	No change in homework or pedagogy No impact on test linked to incentives Short-term impact on scores linked to test No impact on dropout rate	Teaching to the test (for example, strategies for not leaving blank multiple choice questions); encouragement of students to take and prepare for the test
Lavy (2002)	Local program (involving more than 62 schools) conducts tournament, offering prizes to top third of schools.	School: secondary schools (grade 7–12); all teachers receive prizes	Regression discontinuity: schools in same community	Positive impact on average test score and average credits Increase in proportion of students for matriculation certificate (especially among low-income groups) Reduction in dropout rate	None
McEwan and Santibáñez (2005)	Global program (all public teachers) provides rewards based on student test results.	Individual teachers (all levels, all grades)	Regression discontinuity: schedule of points	No impact on test scores	Permanent increases in wages without any benefit
Muralidharan and Sundararaman (2011)	Program in Andhra Pradesh provides bonuses to schools and individual teachers tied to student achievement (200 schools including 100 in group bonus program, 100 in individual bonus program, and 100 controls).	Group bonus scheme covered all teachers in school; individual bonus scheme covered teachers who taught grades tested	Randomized experiment	Increase in test score of 0.15 standard deviation in first year, 0.22 in second year in both programs Impacts fairly robust across grades, test difficulty levels, and most baseline school and student characteristics Higher impacts in math than language; impacts also observed on subjects not included for bonus After two years, impact of individual bonuses larger than group bonuses	None cited

Source: World Bank staff compilation.

FIGURE 5A.1 **Educational attainment in the labor force in South Asia, by country**

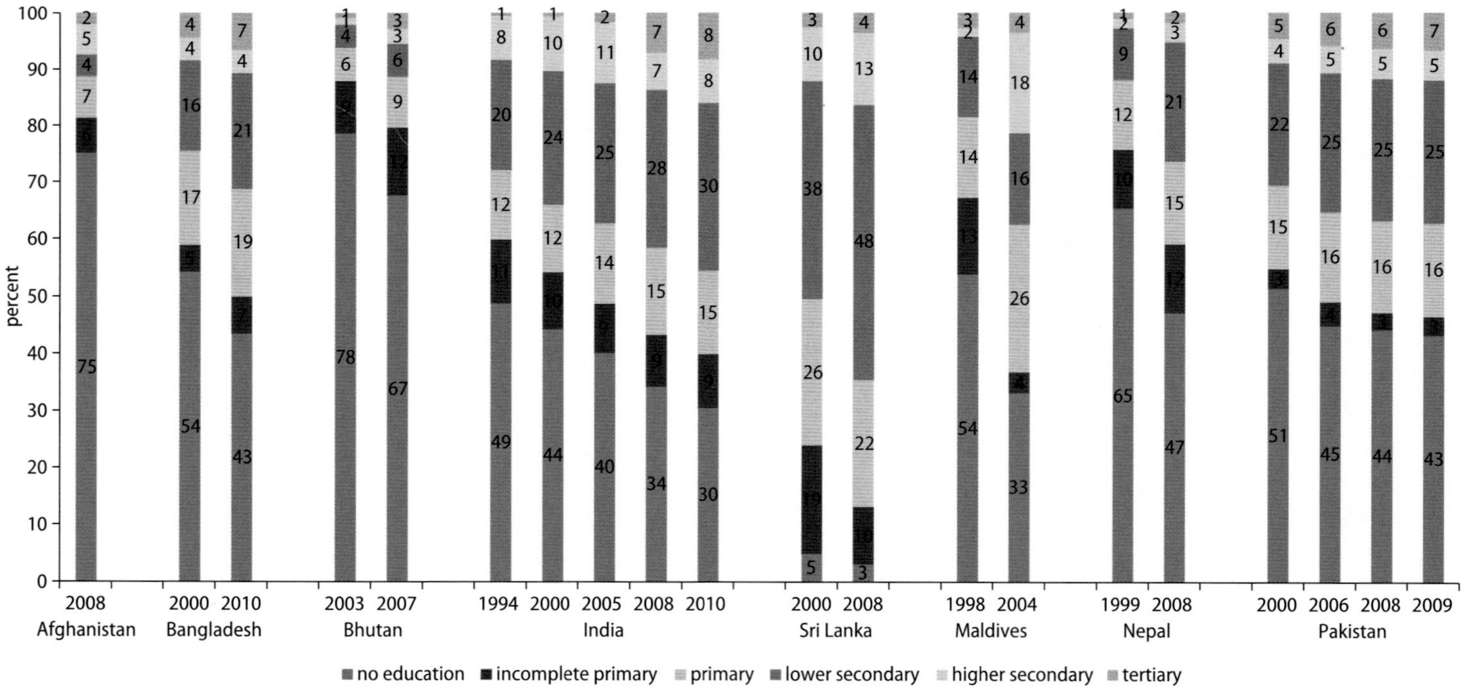

percent
100
90
80
70
60
50
40
30
20
10
0
2008
Afghanistan
2000 2010
Bangladesh
2003 2007
Bhutan
1994 2000 2005 2008 2010
India
2000 2008
Sri Lanka
1998 2004
Maldives
1999 2008
Nepal
2000 2006 2008 2009
Pakistan
no education
incomplete primary
primary
lower secondary
higher secondary
tertiary

Source: Authors, based on data from national labor force and household surveys.

FIGURE 5A.2   Share of labor force with at least primary, upper-secondary, and tertiary education, in South Asia and international comparators

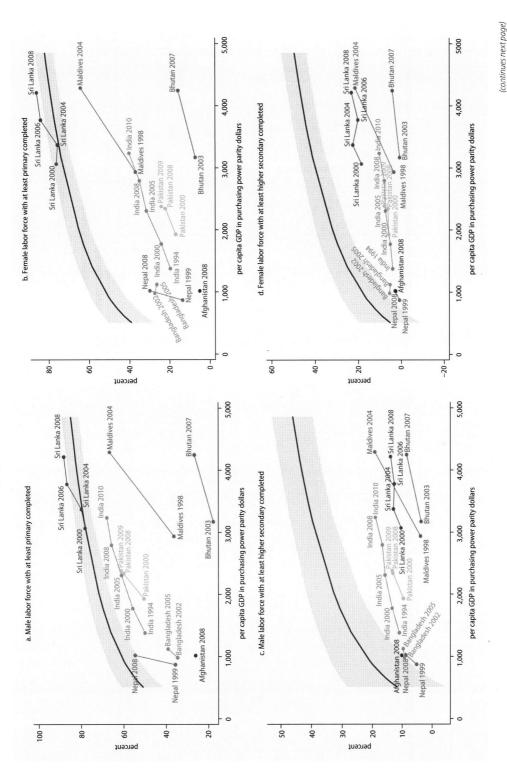

(continues next page)

213

FIGURE 5A.2   Share of labor force with at least primary, upper-secondary, and tertiary education, in South Asia and international comparators (continued)

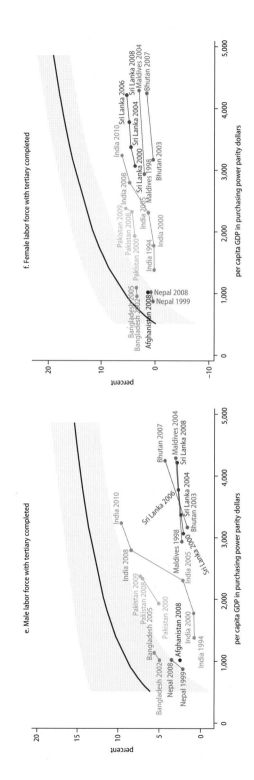

Sources: Authors, based on data from World Bank 2011b and national labor force and household surveys.

Note: The dark line shows the predicted values of the share of the labor force with completed primary, upper-secondary, and tertiary education by per capita GDP. Predicted values are obtained from cross-country regressions (excluding high-income countries) of the share of the labor force with completed primary, upper-secondary, and tertiary education on the log of per capita GDP. The shaded area is the 95 percent confidence interval band around the regression line.

FIGURE 5A.3   Gross and net enrollment rates in primary and secondary education, by region and country

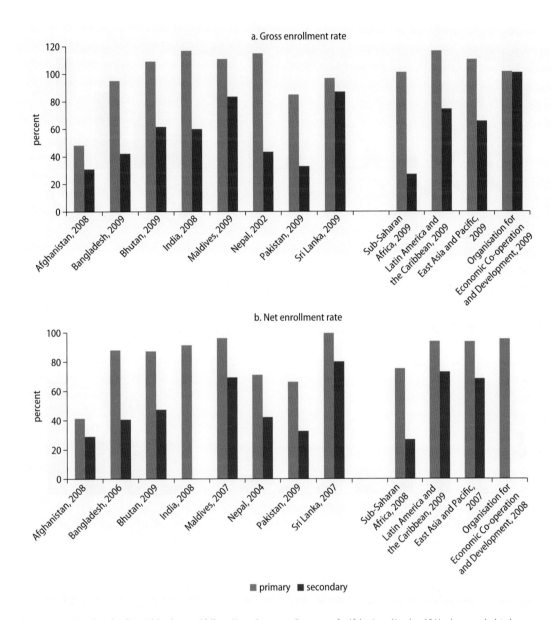

Sources: Authors, based on data from UIS Database and EdStats. Net and gross enrollment rates for Afghanistan, Nepal, and Sri Lanka were calculated using national household surveys.
Note: For Afghanistan, primary grades are 1–6 (ages 6–12) and secondary grades 7–12 (ages 12–18). For Nepal and Sri Lanka, primary grades are 1–5 (ages 5–10) and secondary grades are 6–12 (age 11–18).

FIGURE 5A.4   Enrollment in vocational education and training as a share of secondary enrollment, by region and country

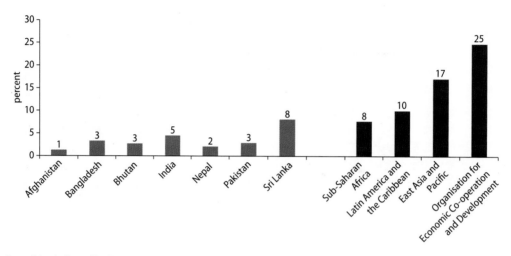

Source: Chhoeda, Dar, and Tan 2010.
Note: Data are for latest year available. They primarily reflect preemployment training for South Asian countries. Although vocational education provided by the public school sector is also included, this sector is absent in many South Asian countries and is very small in others.

FIGURE 5A.5   Gross enrollment rate in tertiary education, by region and country

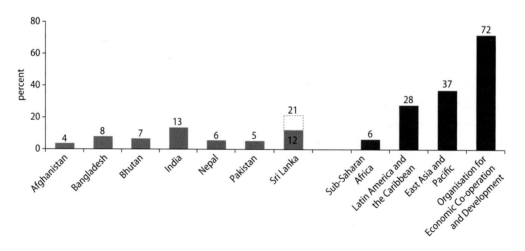

Sources: Authors, based on data from UNESCO 2011 and World Bank 2011b.
Note: Data are for latest year available. Gross enrollment of 21 percent in Sri Lanka includes students enrolled in external degree programs, some of whom may be only nominally enrolled. Gross tertiary enrollment excluding external degree enrollment is about 12 percent.

FIGURE 5A.6   Share of young cohorts with completed primary and lower-secondary education in South Asia, by gender and country

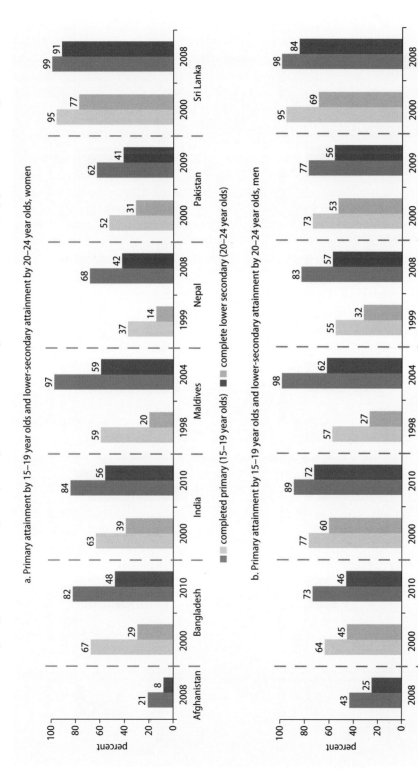

a. Primary attainment by 15–19 year olds and lower-secondary attainment by 20–24 year olds, women

b. Primary attainment by 15–19 year olds and lower-secondary attainment by 20–24 year olds, men

■ completed primary (15–19 year olds)   ■ complete lower secondary (20–24 year olds)

Source: Authors, based on data from national labor force and household surveys.

FIGURE 5A.7   Share of young cohorts with completed upper-secondary and tertiary education in South Asia, by gender and country

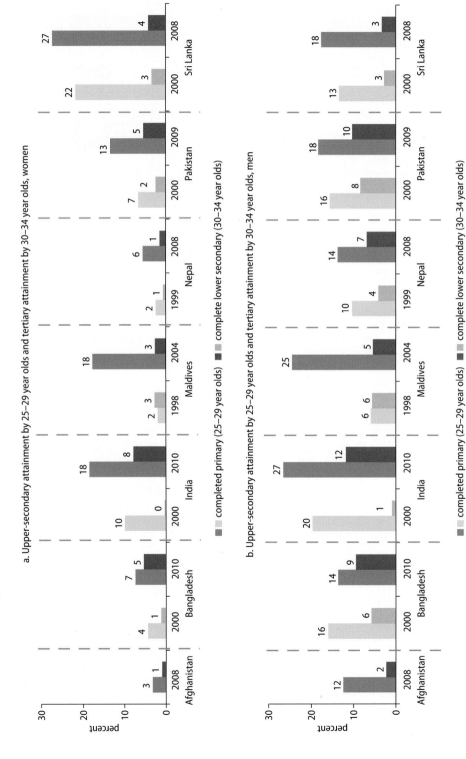

a. Upper-secondary attainment by 25–29 year olds and tertiary attainment by 30–34 year olds, women

b. Upper-secondary attainment by 25–29 year olds and tertiary attainment by 30–34 year olds, men

■ completed primary (25–29 year olds)   ■ complete lower secondary (30–34 year olds)

Source: Authors, based on data from national labor force and household surveys.

FIGURE 5A.8 **Mean years of education of 15–34 year olds in selected South Asian countries, by caste/ethnicity**

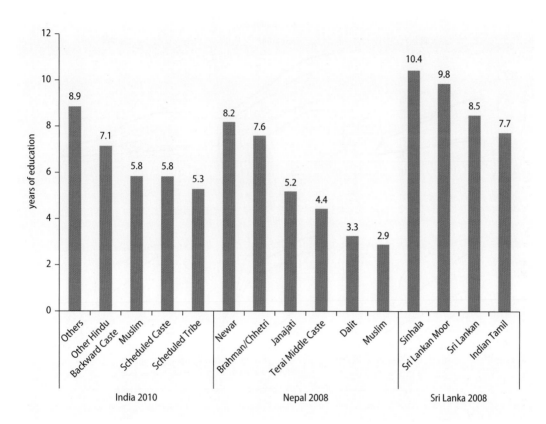

Source: Authors, based on data from national labor force and household surveys.

FIGURE 5A.9   **Share of 20–28 year olds in Afghanistan and Nepal with different years of education completed in Afghanistan (2008) and Nepal (2004), by gender and socioeconomic status**

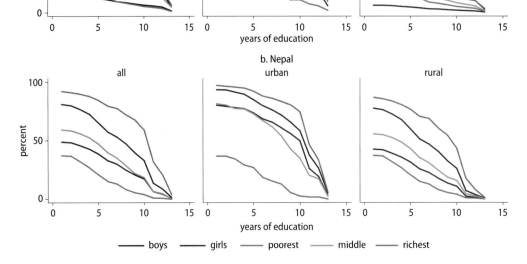

Source: Authors, based on national household surveys.

FIGURE 5A.10   **Percentage of children under age 5 with stunting in selected South Asian countries, by socioeconomic status**

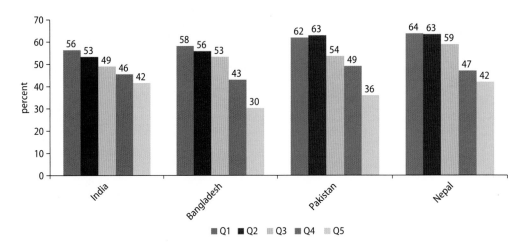

Source: Van De Poel and others 2008.
Note: Bars indicate income quintile.

Annex 5B   Projections of the educational attainment of South Asia's population and labor force

The projections used in this book are based on an adaptation of the international projections by KC and others (2010) to South Asia. Projections of educational attainment were made under three scenarios, a baseline scenario and two optimistic scenarios. The assumptions under the three scenarios are summarized in table 5B.1.

Projections for the male and female labor force for 2030 were obtained by explicitly factoring in trends in educational attainment and urbanization. Various sources of data were used: population projections by gender and five-year age groups are from *World Populations Prospects: The 2008 Revision (UN 2010)*; urban and rural projections are from the UN's *World Urbanization Prospects: The 2009 Revision (UN 2011)*; and educational attainment projections by age and gender are adapted from KC and others (2010). Labor force participation rates for each age/sex/ educational attainment/rural-urban group were calculated from the latest national labor force and household surveys. They were then applied to the educational attainment projections of the population to obtain projections on the educational attainment of the labor force. The assumption is that there would be no behavioral change in labor force participation, that current participation rates for each cell would hold in 2030. Changes in labor force participation are therefore driven by trends in urbanization and educational attainment of the population. Table 5B.2 shows current and projected attainment of the labor force under various educational scenarios.

TABLE 5B.1   Assumptions underlying scenarios used to project educational attainment of population in South Asia

Scenario	Primary education (age 10–14)	Secondary education (age 20–24)	Tertiary education (age 30–34)
Baseline SA–GET (SA8)	Primary attainment over past 10 years in all South Asian countries	Global Education Trend (GET), based on trends from 120 countries	GET
Optimistic SA-GET (SA6)	Primary attainment over past 10 years in all South Asian countries except Pakistan (stalled) and Maldives (universal)	Rate of increase for secondary age cohorts whose gains were higher than the GET in past 10 years	GET
Fast Track (FT1)	99 percent by 2020	60 percent by 2030, 100 percent by 2040	Tertiary progression following Singapore rate

Source: Authors.
Note: GET scenarios as in KC and others 2010. SA = South Asia.

TABLE 5B.2   Educational attainment of the South Asian labor force in 2010 (estimated) and 2030 (projected) under various scenarios, by country

(percent)

Country	2010				2030											
					SA8				SA6				FT			
	No Education	Primary	Secondary	Tertiary	No Education	Primary	Secondary	Tertiary	No Education	Primary	Secondary	Tertiary	No Education	Primary	Secondary	Tertiary
Total																
Afghanistan	73.1	15.3	9.6	2.0	43.1	33.4	20.1	3.5	43.1	24.8	28.6	3.5	33.3	30.0	23.0	13.7
Bangladesh	32.9	35.6	25.6	6.0	14.6	37.5	38.1	9.9	14.5	28.9	46.6	9.9	14.3	28.4	32.1	25.2
Bhutan	53.3	26.9	15.2	4.6	23.7	39.0	28.5	8.8	23.4	29.1	38.7	8.7	24.3	28.9	25.4	21.4
India	33.0	24.0	35.5	7.5	15.4	23.3	49.5	11.7	15.5	18.3	54.3	11.9	14.9	18.8	41.7	24.6
Maldives	20.4	32.6	28.8	18.2	4.3	29.9	36.9	28.9	4.3	24.6	42.4	28.7	4.0	24.5	32.9	38.5
Nepal	43.2	27.2	27.4	2.2	18.9	29.9	46.6	4.5	19.0	22.2	54.2	4.6	18.4	23.1	45.3	13.2
Pakistan	41.8	19.5	31.6	7.1	22.8	22.3	43.7	11.2	22.9	16.0	49.6	11.4	19.8	18.3	38.1	23.9
Sri Lanka	2.9	23.2	51.9	22.1	0.8	12.4	55.5	31.4	0.8	8.9	58.9	31.5	0.8	8.6	40.1	50.5
Male																
Afghanistan	64.3	20.3	13.1	2.4	34.8	36.8	25.1	3.3	35.0	28.0	33.7	3.4	27.3	34.6	26.1	11.9
Bangladesh	28.8	37.3	27.4	6.6	13.9	37.6	38.5	10.0	13.9	29.5	46.5	10.1	14.0	29.5	32.9	23.6
Bhutan	45.7	32.4	16.2	5.7	20.2	42.7	27.7	9.3	20.2	35.0	35.5	9.4	20.8	35.0	23.8	20.5
India	24.7	25.4	41.4	8.5	10.9	22.3	54.7	12.1	10.9	18.1	58.8	12.2	10.5	18.6	45.5	25.4
Maldives	19.5	33.8	29.5	17.2	4.2	30.8	38.1	26.9	4.2	25.8	43.1	26.9	3.9	25.9	33.3	36.9
Nepal	26.8	33.3	36.3	3.6	10.5	30.3	52.6	6.6	10.5	24.7	58.2	6.6	9.6	25.6	46.4	18.4
Pakistan	33.9	21.8	36.8	7.5	17.9	23.4	48.0	10.7	17.9	17.6	53.6	10.8	15.7	19.9	42.0	22.4
Sri Lanka	2.4	25.9	55.3	16.5	0.8	15.2	62.0	22.0	0.8	11.1	66.0	22.1	0.8	11.1	43.8	44.4
Female																
Afghanistan	91.5	4.9	2.3	1.2	62.8	25.1	8.3	3.9	62.3	17.3	16.5	3.9	47.2	19.3	15.7	17.8
Bangladesh	46.0	30.1	19.7	4.1	16.7	37.1	36.8	9.5	16.4	27.2	47.1	9.4	15.0	25.5	29.7	29.8
Bhutan	64.6	18.8	13.7	2.9	28.8	33.5	29.7	8.0	28.0	20.8	43.4	7.8	29.4	20.3	27.6	22.7
India	56.5	20.0	18.8	4.7	29.7	26.6	33.1	10.6	30.4	18.9	39.8	10.9	28.6	19.1	30.0	22.3
Maldives	21.8	30.5	27.8	19.9	4.5	28.7	35.0	31.8	4.4	22.8	41.4	31.4	4.2	22.5	32.3	41.0
Nepal	60.4	20.8	18.0	0.8	28.5	29.5	39.8	2.2	28.8	19.5	49.5	2.3	28.4	20.2	44.2	7.2
Pakistan	73.7	10.1	10.6	5.5	46.6	16.7	22.8	13.8	47.6	8.0	29.9	14.4	38.4	10.7	20.0	30.9
Sri Lanka	3.7	18.5	46.1	31.7	0.9	7.9	44.9	46.4	0.9	5.3	47.4	46.5	0.8	4.9	34.7	59.7

Sources: Authors, based on data from national labor force and household surveys; UN 2009, 2010; and KC and others 2010.
Note: See text for descriptions of scenarios. FT = fast track, SA = South Asia.

Notes

1. Access to education is a basic human right. It also has considerable value beyond its role in the labor market: it enables individuals to be better parents, more responsible citizens, and more effective stewards of the natural environment. This book focuses on the skills imparted and how they play out in the labor market.

2. Other constraints are more binding for formal sector firms in the region as a whole. Enterprise surveys provide information only about the constraints facing existing enterprises. They are not useful in understanding constraints perceived by potential firms that did not enter in the first place.

3. Autor, Levy, and Murnane (2003) argue that as a result of computerization, the shift in demand for labor has contributed to the secular increase in the premium for tertiary education in the United States.

4. The increase in the public sector likely reflects adjustments in wages to reduce wage compression. In India, the premium for upper-secondary

relative to lower-secondary increased in both the private and the public sector.

5. Instead of point estimates, the probabilities of worker mobility are estimated as upper and lower bounds. The lines shown in the figures link the midpoints of the bounds; they primarily show how the bounds vary with education. The midpoints of the bounds should not be interpreted as true point estimates.

6. These transition probabilities are conditional on being in a particular state in the initial year. The likelihood of a worker with tertiary education being in agriculture or in casual employment is relatively low.

7. Annex figure 5A.3 shows enrollment rates at primary and secondary. Annex figure 5A.5 shows enrollment at tertiary institutions in South Asia and other regions.

8. For all countries, this section uses the multi-purpose household surveys that permit analysis by consumption quintiles (see appendix A to the report). The only exception is India, where the Labor Force Survey is used.

9. Between 2000 and 2008, young female cohorts in Bangladesh still had lower attainment at the upper-secondary and tertiary levels, but they made significantly larger gains at the primary and lower- secondary levels, surpassing young men. In Maldives, primary attainment among young female cohorts was comparable to that of males, but attainment at higher levels was still lower. In Sri Lanka, educational attainment among young female cohorts was higher than of males at all levels of education (see annex figures 5A.6 and 5A.7).

10. Private expenditures by households are also high in some countries. In India, for example, they are equal to 1.4 percent of gross domestic product (Tilak 2009).

11. Hanushek and Woessman find that an increase of one standard deviation in student reading and math scores (roughly equivalent to improving a country's performance ranking from the median to the top 15 percent) is associated with a 2 percentage point increase in annual gross domestic product per capita growth.

12. The scenario discussed here is the SA6 scenario in annex 5B.

13. Projections are based on a methodology used for global projections; as a result, there are differences in the definitions of educational attainments by level used in this section. In the projections in this section, "primary" combines incomplete and complete primary; "secondary"

is a broad category that combines lower-secondary and completed upper-secondary.

14. This section benefited from the draft chapter on early childhood development and preschool prepared for the ongoing regional study on the quality of learning in South Asia (Alderman 2011).

15. A growing neuroscience literature provides insights into biologically determined windows in childhood for these processes. For example, the number of neurons devoted to language peaks before a child turns one and then declines, implying that children lose plasticity even before they engage in rudimentary conversations.

16. Martorell and Horta (2010) find that weight gain during the first two years of life has the strongest association with schooling, followed by birthweight. A one standard deviation increase in birth weight (about 0.5 kilograms) is associated with 0.21 years more schooling and an 8 percent decrease in the risk of grade failure. A one standard deviation increase (about 0.7 kilograms) in conditional weight gain in the first two years of life is associated with 0.43 years more schooling and a 12 percent reduction in the risk of grade failure. Gains in education as a result of weight gain were particularly large for babies who were born small.

17. Wasting, stunting, and underweight indicators refer to the proportion of children under five whose weight for height, height for age, and weight for age are more than two standard deviations from the medians of an international reference population recognized by the World Health Organization. Low height for age (also termed *stunting*) is a measure of chronic malnutrition. Progress toward the Millennium Development Goal is tracked based on underweight. Trends in underweight and stunting tend to move together. Although underweight has a somewhat higher risk of mortality, stunting is more strongly associated with long-term development (human capital and economic) outcomes.

18. These findings are based on indicators developed by the United Nations Children's Fund, including "family care indicators," an index of inputs and resources, and more comprehensive "home observations for measurement of the environment" (HOME), which can be adapted to household surveys. Family care indicators have been validated as a predictor of cognitive development in diverse settings. See Alderman (2011) for a discussion.

19. The role of the private sector varies greatly across countries. Whereas almost all secondary schools in Afghanistan are government schools, almost all secondary schools in Bangladesh are private.

20. Some caution should be exercised in interpreting these results, as these studies may not take into account all the characteristics that influence the choice of public or private school. Desai and others (2008) control for the endogeneity of school choice in India. They find modest gains in math and reading scores in private schools compared with government schools, with higher gains for children from lower economic strata.

21. These tests do not typically measure important skills and knowledge against established learning standards, tending instead to rely heavily on rote learning and multiple choice answers. In addition, the results are generally not comparable across years.

22. Technical training is costly to set up, causing private entrepreneurs to shy away from this kind of training. Commercial training (in languages and secretarial skills, for example), which costs less to provide, attracts more private providers.

References

Acemoglu, D., and D. Autor. 2010. "Skills, Tasks and Technologies: Implications for Employment and Earnings." In *Handbook of Labor Economics,* vol. 4B, ed. O. Ashenfelter and D. Card. 1043–72. Amsterdam: Elsevier.

Agarwal, P. 2009. *Indian Higher Education: Envisioning the Future.* New Delhi: Sage Publications.

Alam, A., J. Baez, and X. del Carpio. 2011. "Does Cash for School Influence Young Women's Behavior in the Longer Term? Evidence from Pakistan." Policy Research Working Paper 5669, World Bank, Washington, DC.

Alderman, H. 2011. "Early Childhood Development and the Role of Pre-school." Background paper prepared for Regional Quality of Education Study, South Asia Region, Human Development Unit, World Bank, Washington, DC.

Alderman, H., J. Behrman, V. Lavy, and R. Menon. 2001. "Child Health and School Enrollment: A Longitudinal Analysis." *Journal of Human Resources* 36 (1): 185–205.

Almeida, R., and R. Aterido. 2010. "Investment in Job Training: Why Are SMEs Lagging So Much Behind?" Policy Research Working Paper 5358, World Bank, Washington, DC.

Almeida, R., J. Behrman, D. Robalino. 2011. *The Right Skills for the Job? Rethinking Effective Training Policies for Workers.* World Bank, Social Protection. Human Development, Washington, DC.

Andrabi, T., J. Das, and A. Khwaja. 2009. "Report Cards: The Impact of Providing School and Child Test Scores on Educational Markets." Working Paper, Kennedy School of Government, Harvard University. http://www.hks.harvard.edu/fs/akhwaja/papers/RC_08Oct09Full.pdf.

Andrabi, T., J. Das, A. Khwaja, T. Vishwanath, T. Zajonc, and the LEAPS Team. 2007. "Learning and Educational Achievement in Punjab Schools (LEAPS): Insights to Inform the Education Policy Debate." *The LEAPS Project.* Punjab.

Asadullah, M. N., N. Chaudhury, D. Parajuli, L. R. Sarr, and Y. Savchenko. 2011. *Reaching Out-of-School Children (ROSC) Project: Evaluation Report.* World Bank, South Asia Region, Human Development Unit, Washington, DC.

Asadullah, M. N., N. Chaudhury, D. Parajuli, L. R. Sarr, Y. Savchenko, and S. R. Al-Zayed. 2009. "Bangladesh Secondary Education Quality and Access Enhancement Project: Baseline Report." World Bank, South Asia Region, Human Development Unit, Washington, DC.

Autor, D., F. Levy, and R. Murnane. 2003. "The Skill Content of Recent Technological Change: An Empirical Exploration." *Quarterly Journal of Economics* 118 (4): 1279–33.

Barrera-Osorio, F., D. S. Blakeslee, M. Hoover, L. L. Linden, and D. Raju. 2011. "Expanding Educational Opportunities in Remote Parts of the World: Evidence from a RCT of a Public Private Partnership in Pakistan." Paper presented at the Third Institute for the Study of Labor (IZA) workshop, "Child Labor in Developing Countries," Mexico City. http://www.iza.org/conference_files/childl2011/blakeslee_d6783.pdf.

Barrera-Osorio, F., and D. Raju. 2010. "Short-Run Learning Dynamics under a Test-Based Accountability System: Evidence from Pakistan." Policy Research Working Paper 5465, World Bank, Washington, DC.

Batra, G., and A. Stone. 2004. *Investment Climate, Capabilities and Firm Performance: Evidence from the World Business Environment Surveys.* World Bank, Investment Climate Department, Washington, DC.

Behrman, J., H. Alderman, and J. Hoddinott. 2004. "Hunger and Malnutrition." In *Global Crises, Global Solutions,* ed. B. Lomborg, 363-420. Cambridge: Cambridge University Press.

Blom, A., and H. Saeki. 2011. "Employability and Skill Set of Newly Graduated Engineers in India." World Bank Policy Research Working Paper, Washington, DC.

Bloom, N., B. Eifert, A. Mahajan, D. McKenzie, and J. Roberts. 2011. "Does Management Matter?" World Bank Policy Research Working Paper 5573, Washington, DC.

Bobonis, G., M. Edward, and C. Puri-Sharma. 2006. "Anemia and School Participation." *Journal of Human Resources* 41 (4): 692–721.

Bruns, B., D. Filmer, and H. A. Patrinos. 2011. *Making Schools Work: New Evidence on Accountability Reforms.* Washington, DC: World Bank.

Burde, D., and L. Linden. 2010. "The Effect of Village-Based Schools: Evidence from a Randomized Controlled Trial in Afghanistan." Working Paper, J-PAL, Cambridge.

Carlin, W., and M. Schaffer. 2011. "Which Elements of the Business Environment Matter Most for Firms and How Do They Vary across Countries?" Background study conducted for this book.

Chaudury, N., and D. Parajuli. 2010. "Conditional Cash Transfers and Female Schooling: The Impact of the Female School Stipend Programme on Public School Enrolments in Punjab, Pakistan." *Applied Economics* 42 (28): 3565–83.

Chhoeda, T., A. Dar, and H. Tan. 2010. *Vocational Education and Technical Training in South Asian Countries: Summary of Issues and Recommended Policy Reforms.* World Bank, South Asia Region, Human Development Unit, Washington, DC.

Christian, P., L. E. Murray-Kolb, S. K. Khatry, J. Katz, B. A. Schaefer, P. M. Cole, S. C. LeClerq, and J. M. Tielsch. 2010. "Prenatal Micronutrient Supplementation and Intellectual and Motor Function in Early School-Aged Children in Nepal." *Journal of the American Medical Association* 304 (24): 2716–23.

Clarke, P. 2005. "Technical and Vocational Education Systems in Australian and India:

An Experiment in Cross-Cultural Learning." Working Paper, World Bank, South Asia Region, Human Development Unit, Washington, DC.

Das, J., P. Pandey, and T. Zajonc. 2006. "Learning Levels and Gaps in Pakistan." Policy Research Working Paper, World Bank, Washington, DC.

Desai, S., A. Dubey, R. Vanneman, and R. Banerji. 2008. "Private Schooling in India: A New Educational Landscape." Brookings–National Council of Applied Economic Research (NCAER) India Policy Forum, New Delhi.

Duflo, E., R. Hanna, and S. Ryan. 2010. "Incentives Work: Getting Teachers to Come to School." Working Paper, Department of Economics, Harvard University, Cambridge, MA. http://www.hks.harvard.edu/fs/rhanna/Incentives_Work_30may2010.pdf.

EI (Educational Initiatives). 2006. "Student Learning in the Metros." Working Paper 2, Ahmedabad, India.

Fernald, L., E. Galasso, and L. Ratsifan-drihamanana. 2011. "Socioeconomic Gradients and Child Development in a Very Low-Income Population: Evidence from Madagascar." *Developmental Science* 14 (4) 1–16.

Fishbein, A., and N. Schady. 2009. *Conditional Cash Transfers: Reducing Present and Future Povery.* Washington, DC: World Bank.

Gill, I., F. Fluitman, and A. Dar, eds. 2000. *Vocational Education and Training Reforms: Matching Skills to Markets and Budgets.* Oxford: Oxford University Press.

Glewwe, P., N. Ilias, and M. Kremer. 2008. "Teacher Incentives in the Developing World." In *Performance Incentives: Their Growing Impact on K–12 Education,* ed. Matthew Springer, 295–326. Washington, DC: Brookings Institution Press.

Government of India. 2009. *National Policy on Skills Development.* Ministry of Labour and Employment, New Delhi.

———. 2010. *Project Implementation Plan for the Second Phase of the Technical Education Quality Improvement Project.* National Project Implementation Unit, Noida.

Government of Maharashtra. 2009. "May 2009 Amendment to the Maharashtra University Act 1994." Mumbai

Goyal, S., and P. Pandey. 2009a. *Contract Teachers.* Washington, DC: World Bank.

———. 2009b. "How do Government and Private Schools Differ? Findings from Two Large Indian States." Working Paper 30, World

Bank, South Asia Region, Education Sector, Washington, DC.

Gustabo, B., C. Puri-Sharma, and E. Miguel. 2006. "Anaemia and School Participation." Working Paper 337, *eSocial Sciences*. http://www.esocialsciences.com/articles/displayArticles.asp?Article_ID=337.

Hanushek, E., and L. Woessmann. 2008. "The Role of Cognitive Skills in Economic Development." *Journal of Economic Literature* 46 (3): 607–68.

Hoddinott, J., J. Maluccio, J. Behrman, R. Flores, and R. Martorell. 2008. "Effect of a Nutrition Intervention during Early Childhood on Economic Productivity in Guatemalan Adults." *Lancet* 371 (February 2): 411–16.

Hoddinott, J., J. Maluccio, J. R. Behrman, R. Martorell, P. Melgar, A. R. Quisumbing, M. Ramirez-Zea, A. D. Stein, and K. M. Yount. 2011. "The Consequences of Early Childhood Growth Failure over the Life Course." IFPRI Discussion Paper 01073, International Food Policy Research Institute, Washington, DC.

ILO (International Labour Office). 2003. "Industrial Training Institutes in India: The Efficiency Study Report." Subregional Office for South Asia, ILO, New Delhi.

International Finance Corporation. 2010. "Public Private Partnerships in Education: Sharing IFC's Experience." Presentation to the National Summit on Higher Education, New Delhi, India.

Jensen, R. 2010. "Economic Opportunities and Gender Differences in Human Capital: Experimental Evidence for India." NBER Working Paper 16021, National Bureau of Economic Research, Cambridge, MA.

KC, S., B. Barakat, A. Goujon, V. Skirbekk, W. Sanderson, and W. Lutz. 2010. "Projection of Populations by Level of Educational Attainment, Age, and Sex for 120 countries for 2005–2050." *Demographic Research* 22 (15): 383–472.

Lavy, V. 2002. "Paying for Performance: The Effect of Teachers' Financial Incentives on Students' Scholastic Outcomes." CEPR Discussion Paper 3862, Center for Economic and Policy Research, Washington, DC.

Martorell, R., and B. Horta. 2010. "Weight Gain in the First Two Years of Life Is an Important Predictor of Schooling Outcomes in Pooled Analyses from Five Birth Cohorts from Low- and Middle-Income Countries." *Journal of Nutrition* 40 (2): 348–54.

McEwan, P. J., and L. Santibáñez. 2005. "Teacher and Principal Incentives in Mexico." In *Incentives to Improve Teaching: Lessons from Latin America*, ed. E. Vegas, 213–53. Washington, DC: World Bank.

Muralidharan, K., and V. Sundararaman. 2010. "Contract Teachers: Experimental Evidence from India." Paper presented at the Massachusetts Avenue Development Seminar, Washington, DC, May 24.

———. 2011. "Teacher Performance Pay: Experimental Evidence from India." *Journal of Political Economy* 119 (1): 39–77.

Naudeau, S., S. Martinez, P. Premand, and D. Filmer. 2011. "Cognitive Development among Young Children in Low-Income Countries." In *No Small Matter: The Interaction of Poverty, Shocks, and Human Capital Investment,* ed. H. Alderman, 9–50. Washington, DC: World Bank.

Oster, E., and B. Millet. 2011. "Do Call Centers Promote School Enrollment? Evidence from India." Working Paper, Department of Economics, University of Chicago.

Pandey, P., S. Goyal, and V. Sundararaman. 2009. "Community Participation in Public Schools: Impact of Information Campaigns in Three Indian States. " *Education Economics* 17 (3): 355–75.

Pratham. 2010. *Annual Status of Education Report. Rural 2010.* New Delhi.

Riboud, M., Y. Savchenko, and H. Tan. 2007. "The Knowledge Economy and Education and Training in South Asia." World Bank, South Asia Region, Human Development Unit, Washington, DC.

SAFED (South Asia Forum for Education and Development). 2010. *Annual Status of Education Report 2010.* Lahore, Pakistan.

Skills Australia. 2011. "Ministerial Council for Tertiary Education and Employment (MCTEE) Industry Forum." Canberra. http://www.skillsaustralia.gov.au/MCTEEIndustryForum.shtml.

Sri Lanka Information Communication Technology Association. 2007. *Rising Demand: The Increasing Demand for IT Workers Spells a Challenging Opportunity for the IT Industry.* Colombo.

Thinley, K. 2009. "Higher Education in the Kingdom of Bhutan: Cherishing Dreams and

Confronting Challenges." Report prepared for UNESCO, Paris.

Tilak, J. 2009. *Household Expenditure on Education and Implications for Redefining the Poverty Line in India*. Government of India, Planning Commission, New Delhi.

UN (United Nations). 2009. *The World Populations Prospects: The 2008 Revision*. Department of Economic and Social Affairs, Population Division, New York.

———. 2010. *World Urbanization Prospects: The 2009 Revision: Highlights*. Department of Economic and Social Affairs, Population Division, New York.

UNESCO (United Nations Education, Scientific and Cultural Organization). 2011. Data from UNESCO Institute for Statistics, Montreal.

Van de Poel, E., A. Hosseinpoor, N. Speybroeck, T. Van Ourti, and J. Vega. 2008. "Socioeconomic Inequalities in Malnutrition in Developing Countries." *Bulletin of the World Health Organization*. 86 (4) 282–91.

Walker, S., T. Wachs, S. Grantham-McGregor, M. Black, C. Nelson, S. Huffman, H. Baker-Henningham, S. Chang, J. Hamadani, B. Lozoff, J. Gardner, C. Powell, A. Rahman, and L. Richter. 2011. "Inequality Begins in Early Childhood: Risk and Protective Factors for Early Child Development." *Lancet*.

World Bank. 2007. *Skills Development in India: The Vocational Education and Training System*. Washington, DC.

———. 2008. *The Bangladesh Vocational Education and Training System: An Assessment*. South Asia Region, Human Development Unit, Washington, DC.

———. 2009. *The Towers of Learning: Performance, Peril, and Promise of Higher Education in Sri Lanka*. Washington, DC.

———. 2010. *Nepal: Second Higher Education Project: Implementation Status Results Report*. Washington, DC.

———. 2011a. *Skills and Research for Productivity and Growth: Higher Education in East Asia*. Washington, DC: World Bank.

———. 2011b. *World Development Indicators*. Washington, DC: World Bank.

CHAPTER 6   The Role of Labor Market Regulations, Institutions, and Programs

Questions and Findings

Questions

- What is the role of labor market policies and institutions in encouraging job creation and protecting workers in the formal and informal economy?
- How can South Asian countries increase access of informal sector workers to programs that help them manage labor market shocks?
- What are the directions for labor market policies moving forward?

Findings

- Employment protection rules create disincentives for expanding employment in the formal sector, especially in India, Nepal, and Sri Lanka. Job security laws are often too restrictive, compliance too complicated, and enforcement too weak and discretionary. Labor regulations also tend to fall short of their intended goal of protecting workers, because most workers fall outside the coverage of these rules and employers search for ways to circumvent regulations.
- South Asian countries need to reorient their labor market policies from protecting jobs to protecting workers. Doing so calls for coordinated strategies that relax statutory protections (especially the procedures and costs associated with dismissals) and build up the income support and active labor market programs available to workers. The distributional effects imply political economy challenges to this approach, but the aggregate welfare gains could be substantial. One policy, especially relevant in Sri Lanka, is to transform the current severance system into an unemployment benefit scheme, perhaps through the creation of funded worker accounts. Simultaneously, cost-effective employment services and retraining programs need to be ramped up to help workers adjust to changes in the labor market.
- In the short run, shifting strategy in this way would benefit only those informal sector workers who find jobs in the formal sector. Policy makers need to pay attention to the vast majority of workers in South Asia—disproportionately poor and vulnerable—who will not. Universal social insurance schemes that cover all informal sector workers may not be feasible, but coverage could grow organically by encouraging the most effective among the plethora of plans sponsored by government and civil society.
- Public works, self-employment assistance, and training programs are also important. All of these instruments are already in place throughout the region. The priority is to improve their administration and delivery, thereby expanding access and increasing cost-effectiveness.

The Role of Labor Market Regulations, Institutions, and Programs | 6

Labor market regulations, programs, and institutions can have important effects on creating jobs, increasing productivity and earnings, and helping workers manage risks of unemployment and low and uncertain earnings. However, any assessment of the labor market framework in South Asia must be based on the reality that the region is still dominated by informal and casual employment. The prevalence of low-income, precarious, and informal employment reflects the stage of development characterizing much of South Asia. Strong growth could gradually change the quality of employment in the region, but this process is slow, and the experience of other regions suggests that the relationship between development and the formalization of the labor market is not as linear as it was once thought to be.

Given this reality, the policy challenge is to reform regulations to encourage the creation of better jobs while broadening the access of all workers to programs that help them manage labor market shocks. Doing so will require choices on regulation of the labor market and design of social protection programs for workers that are well adapted to the South Asian context. These interventions can be seen as a system that includes promotion (for example, activation programs), prevention (for example, social insurance), and protection (for example, social assistance).

The focus of this chapter is on policies, regulations, and programs that cover the first two of these functions.[1] The discussion recognizes the distinctions between the formal and informal sectors. How are policies affecting the size and quality of employment in each sector and movement between them? How much access do workers in the two sectors have to programs that could help them improve their position in the labor market and manage labor market-related risks? This chapter considers the formal and informal sectors separately, beginning with the formal sector.

Labor market institutions, policies, and programs in the formal sector

Labor laws and social security programs apply largely to regular wage or salaried workers in nonagricultural employment. Although the structure of South Asia's economies is changing, the labor force is still predominantly rural and agricultural. A majority of workers are either self-employed or work in family enterprises.[2] Formal sector workers make up only a small minority of the workforce.

Nonetheless, the institutional and policy framework still has a significant impact on the region's labor markets. Where they are enforced, labor laws can protect the rights of workers. Job security rules, wage regulations, and the financing of social insurance can provide important benefits to workers, but they also affect the cost of labor and, thus, employment levels in the formal sector. Reform of labor law and the strengthening of employment programs could improve incentives for formal sector employment while increasing the real protection available to workers.

Who is covered by worker protection?

Wage employment accounts for less than half of employment in all South Asian countries other than Maldives and Sri Lanka. Even in the wage sector, nonregular or casual work remains very important. None of these workers is typically covered by social protection programs. In fact, formal social security and labor laws cover less than 10 percent of the workforce in most South Asian countries and only a fraction of wage employees. Coverage of formal social insurance (based on pension coverage) is low not only in absolute terms but also relative to per capita gross domestic product (GDP) in all countries except Sri Lanka (figure 6.1). Even in Sri Lanka, which has the most extensive social protection system in the region, only about a third of all workers are covered by formal social security, reflecting the high share of self-employed, temporary, and casual workers (social security covers about 9 percent of workers in India and 4 percent of workers in Nepal).

Figure 6.2, based on household survey data, takes a closer look at social security coverage within the wage sector in Sri Lanka and India. In Sri Lanka, coverage is high, except among casual wage employees. India's profile is more typical of the region as a whole, with only a small fraction of workers benefiting from formal protection, especially

in the private sector. In contrast, coverage is high among regular wage or salaried workers in the public sector. In addition to noncontributory pension schemes, workers in this sector enjoy considerable job security and, in some countries, significantly higher earnings (see Palacios and Whitehouse 2006 for pension schemes; see chapter 3 for wage differences). Coverage of labor laws that set out basic rights of workers, define minimum working conditions, and specify contractual requirements can be expected to be even lower than coverage of formal social insurance programs, because most labor regulations apply only to firms above a minimum size threshold.[3, 4]

Wages, working conditions, and social protection for workers can also be determined through collective bargaining. Collective agreements negotiated at the firm, industry, or national level can exist in parallel with legislation, potentially establishing more generous provisions than stipulated by law.

Unions and collective bargaining play a limited role outside the public sector in most South Asian countries.[5] Figures 6A.1–6A.3 in the annex provide estimates of trade union membership in India, Pakistan, and Sri Lanka, based on administrative data. Combined with information on total employment these estimates suggest that less than 1 percent of workers in Pakistan (2008), about 2 percent in India (2005), and just below 10 percent in Sri Lanka (2008) are unionized. Although there are problems with these data, alternate sources provide a consistent message.[6] For countries on which data are available, coverage of collective bargaining is even lower. For example, based on a questionnaire administered to the Ministry of Labor in Sri Lanka, an estimated 4 percent of the workforce is covered by a collective agreement. Union membership is higher in the public sector than the private sector (see annex figure 6A.4 for India). Although their overall numbers may be relatively low, where unions are present, they can play important roles in negotiating benefits and protection of members,

FIGURE 6.1   **Percentage of workforce not covered by formal pension scheme**

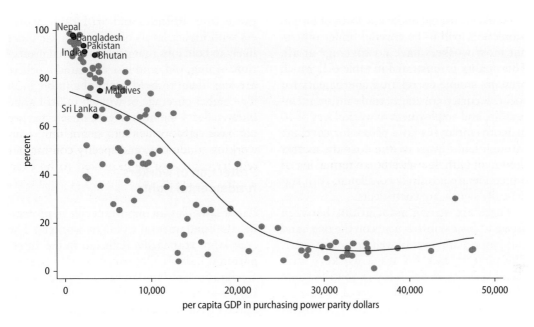

Sources: Authors, based on data from Loayza, Servén, and Sugawara 2010; World Bank 2011c.
Note: Data are for latest year available.

FIGURE 6.2   **Percentage of wage employees in India and Sri Lanka covered by social security, by type of worker**

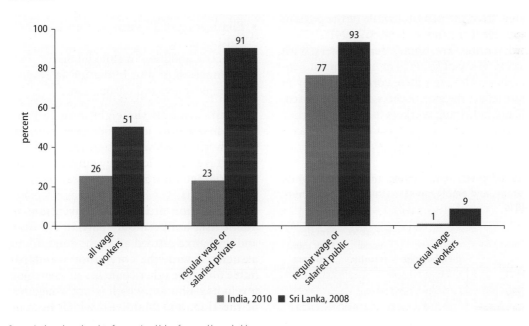

Source: Authors, based on data from national labor force and household surveys.
Note: Social security coverage in India includes eligibility for pension or provident fund only or in combination with other benefits, such as gratuity (a lump sum payable to an employee on termination of employment), health care, and maternity benefits. Coverage in Sri Lanka includes employers' contributions to the pension scheme or provident fund on workers' behalf. The category of casual workers includes temporary workers in Sri Lanka. In India and Sri Lanka, questions about social security coverage were asked only of wage workers.

increasing compliance, and influencing the more general policy debate.

Workers covered under one form of formal protection tend to be covered under others, but most workers have no coverage at all. This duality is illustrated in table 6.1, which presents simple correlation coefficients for social security coverage, trade union membership, and employment in workplaces of 10 or more employees (as a proxy for coverage through labor laws) in India. As the matrix shows, all of these indicators of formal social protection are positively correlated, with statistically significant coefficients.

There are strong associations between access to formal instruments on the one hand and poverty and overall welfare on the other. The poverty rate for wage workers with social security is much lower than the rate for workers who are not covered (4 percent versus 24 percent in India in 2005; 3 percent versus 29 percent in Nepal in 2003/04). The poverty rate for nonunion workers (22 percent) in India was more than twice the rate for union members (10 percent) in 2010. In Sri Lanka, nearly one-third of the workers covered by the employment protection law come from the richest quintile of the population (Heltberg and Vodopivec 2004).

Earnings are higher for workers with access to social security or employment protection.[7] Although these correlations may in part reflect the effectiveness of formal instruments in helping workers manage risk, they also reflect the greater likelihood of high-productivity workers finding jobs that offer protection. In India and Sri Lanka, workers with higher levels of education are more likely to hold jobs that provide formal protection; young, old, and less educated workers are less likely to hold such jobs (table 6.2). The higher coverage of women in Sri Lanka likely reflects the high degree of selection of more educated women into better jobs.

Protection of workers' fundamental rights

Labor laws play an important role in protecting the fundamental rights of workers. The core labor standards, reflected in the International Labour Organization (ILO) 1998 Declaration on Fundamental Principles and Rights at Work, represent an internationally agreed upon group of basic rights relevant regardless of the level of development.[8] The declaration covers four principles and rights, each covered by two ILO conventions:

- Freedom of association and the effective recognition of the right to collective bargaining
- Elimination of all forms of forced or compulsory labor
- Effective abolition of child labor
- Elimination of discrimination in respect of employment and occupation.

Ratification of the eight core conventions does not by itself imply implementation, but it does signal political will. As such, it is a useful metric by which to assess countries' commitment to protecting basic worker rights.

Ratification of the core conventions in South Asia has been only partial. Pakistan and Sri Lanka ratified all of the conventions associated with the core labor standards (table 6.3). The other countries in the region (excluding Bhutan, which is not a member of the ILO, and Maldives, which became an ILO member only in 2009) have ratified some but not all standards. The conventions on freedom of association and collective bargaining and on abolition of child labor have

TABLE 6.1   **Correlation coefficients among union membership, social security coverage, and employment in firms with 10 or more employees, India, 2010**

	Union membership	Access to social security	Firm size of 10 or more workers
Union membership	1.00		
Access to social security	0.51[a]	1.00	
Firm size of 10 or more workers	0.19[a]	0.42[a]	1.00

Source: Authors, based on data from the 2009/10 National Sample Survey.
Note: Social security coverage includes pensions and provident funds only. Union membership includes registered trade unions, memberships in associations of owners, and self-employed workers. It is not possible to isolate trade union membership.
a. Pearson correlation coefficient significant at the 1 percent level.

TABLE 6.2   **Percentage of workers with access to formal protection instruments in India and Sri Lanka, by worker characteristic**

(percentage of workers)

Worker characteristic	India					Sri Lanka	
	2005			2010		2008	
	Social security coverage	In workplace of 10+ employees	Union membership	Social security coverage	In workplace of 10+ employees	Social security coverage	In workplace of 10+ employees
All	29	22	11	26	24	51	28
Male	29	22	13	25	24	44	26
Female	28	19	7	27	24	63	31
15–24 years	6	16	5	8	20	42	42
25–44 years	30	22	12	25	25	54	30
45–54 years	54	27	16	42	27	54	20
55–64 years	47	18	12	42	20	39	14
Primary or below	9	14	6	6	15	30	20
Secondary	41	27	14	26	24	58	31
Tertiary	76	57	36	67	50	93	60
Regular wage	45	50	31	44	53	95	87
Casual wage	2	26	5	1	23	10	39
Public	83	70	57	77	67	93	—
Private	12	16	8	12	19	34	60

Source: Authors, based on national labor force and household surveys.
Note: — = Not available.

TABLE 6.3   **Year of ratification of International Labour Organization core conventions, Declaration on Fundamental Principles, and Rights at Work, by country**

Country	Freedom of association and collective bargaining		Elimination of forced and compulsory labor		Elimination of discrimination in respect of employment and occupation		Abolition of child labor	
	Convention 87	Convention 98	Convention 29	Convention 105	Convention 100	Convention 111	Convention 138	Convention 182
Afghanistan	a	a	a	1963	1969	1969	2010	2010
Bangladesh	1972	1972	1972	1972	1998	1972	a	2001
India	a	a	1954	2000	1958	1960	a	a
Nepal	a	1996	2002	2007	1976	1974	1997	2002
Pakistan	1951	1952	1957	1960	2001	1961	2006	2001
Sri Lanka	1995	1972	1950	2003	1993	1998	2000	2001

Source: ILOLEX database, http://www.ilo.org/ilolex/.
Note: Bhutan is not a member of the ILO. Maldives became a member in 2009 and has not yet ratified any core conventions. a = Not ratified.

the poorest ratification records. Most countries have indicated their intention to ratify all outstanding core conventions, but some difficulties remain.[9]

Even in countries that have not ratified all conventions, the constitution, national policy, or national legislation may broadly recognize the principles and rights reflected in them.[10] In practice, however, limited enforcement capacity and large informal sectors, among other factors, make protecting the basic rights of workers a challenge in South Asia.[11]

Employment protection legislation and its effect on labor market outcomes

Employment protection legislation refers to the rules governing the initiation and termination of employment. These rules cover the kinds of contracts permitted, the conditions under which workers can be terminated, and the procedures for termination.[12] Employment protection arrangements are often characterized along a continuum, ranging from protective to unregulated (or rigid to flexible). A stylized characterization of this continuum is presented in figure 6.3.

Employment protection rules provide job security—but not without controversy. Legislation can provide protection by restricting the ability of employers to hire workers on an explicitly nonpermanent basis or by making dismissal costly. Controversies surround employment protection legislation because of sharp differences in views about the costs and benefits of these policies.[13] One perspective sees restrictions on nonpermanent hiring and employer dismissal rights as providing important social protection for workers. Increased employment security can also encourage longer working relationships and the accumulation of firm-specific human capital. An opposing perspective emphasizes that these regulations raise the cost of labor, discouraging job creation and favoring privileged "insiders." The impacts of employment protection legislation are discussed later in this section.

Most countries in South Asia have flexible hiring rules, although there are exceptions.

Table 6.4 summarizes the rules for fixed-term contracts, based on the World Bank's Doing Business database.[14] Most countries in the region take a flexible approach, allowing the use of fixed-term contracts for permanent tasks and imposing no limits on the duration of such contracts.

Although the Doing Business database indicates no restrictions in India, the situation with respect to fixed-term contracting is actually more uncertain. The Contract Labor (Regulation and Abolition) Act of 1970 is intended to prevent denial of job security where it is feasible (for example, situations that warrant longer-term employment). In this regard, it empowers the appropriate government to prohibit contract labor in some situations. In practice, states in India adopt different stances toward contract labor.[15] Pakistan is the most restrictive country in the region, prohibiting fixed-term contracts for permanent activities and limiting their duration to nine months.[16]

In contrast, dismissal procedures in much of the region are among the most onerous in the world. A number of countries rely on high administrative and financial costs of dismissal as the principal means of protecting permanent workers. India, Nepal, and Sri Lanka stand out in that they require not only notification but prior approval by the state to lay off workers (see table 6.4).[17] The three countries are among only 33 of 183 countries worldwide that require prior approval for individual dismissals and among only 42 that require prior approval for collective dismissals

FIGURE 6.3   The continuum of employment protection legislation

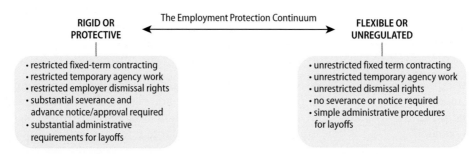

Source: Authors.

TABLE 6.4 Selected hiring and redundancy rules in South Asia, by country

| Country | Hiring rules | | | Redundancy and severance rules | | | | | |
| | Fixed-term contracts prohibited for permanent tasks | Maximum length of fixed-term contracts | | Coverage of severance pay | Notification required | | Approval required | | Average notice period for redundancy dismissal (months) |
		Single contract	Renewals	Excluded categories	1 worker	9 workers	1 worker	9 workers	
Afghanistan	No	No limit	No limit	—	Yes	Yes	No	Yes	4.3
Bangladesh	Yes	No limit	No limit	Firms with fewer than five workers, managerial positions	Yes	Yes	No	No	4.3
Bhutan	No	No limit	No limit	—	Yes	Yes	No	No	5.3
India	No	No limit	No limit	Firms with fewer than 50 workers	Yes	Yes	Yes	Yes	4.3
Maldives	No	24 months	24 months	—	No	No	No	No	4.3
Nepal	Yes	No limit	No limit	Firms with fewer than 10 workers	Yes	Yes	Yes	Yes	4.3
Pakistan	Yes	9 months	9 months	Firms with fewer than 20 workers	No	No	No	No	4.3
Sri Lanka	No	No limit	No limit	Firms with fewer than 15 workers, members of cooperatives	Yes	Yes	Yes	Yes	4.3

Sources: Authors, based on data in World Bank 2011a and Holzmann and others 2011.
Note: The notice period for redundancy dismissal is 4.3–10.3 months in Bhutan and 2.0–8.7 months in Maldives for workers with tenures of 9 months–20 years. For Bhutan and Maldives, figures show notice period for workers with one year of tenure. For other countries, the notice period is the same irrespective of tenure length. — = Not available.

(World Bank 2011a). In addition, severance pay requirements, which typically require minimum tenure and increase with seniority, are high in Bangladesh, Nepal, Pakistan, and particularly Sri Lanka (figure 6.4).

Indeed, Sri Lanka has one of the most costly severance pay systems in the world, though workers do not always benefit from it. Sri Lanka's Termination of Employment of Workmen Act (TEWA), which governs nondisciplinary termination in private firms with more than 14 workers, has heavy reporting demands and requires official authorization for intended layoffs.[18] Retrenchment costs are extremely high by international standards (see figure 6.4), as well as complicated.[19] TEWA requires that workers be paid 0.5–2.5 months' salary for each year of service, depending on the number of years of service. The maximum compensation payable is 48 months (capped at Rs 1.25 million), although only very rarely do workers fulfill

the requirements for maximum compensation. Although statutory severance rights are generous, nonpayment or partial payment is common (as it is in some other South Asian countries).[20]

Benchmarking by the Organisation for Economic Co-operation and Development (OECD) suggests that India's level of statutory employment protection is considerably higher than that of most OECD member countries as well as most other major emerging economies.[21] In terms of dismissal protection for permanent workers, India's labor laws are stricter than all OECD countries except Portugal and all non-OECD countries except Indonesia (figure 6.5). Indian employers in establishments with 100 or more workers cannot lay off any worker (or close down operations) without permission from the appropriate government. In addition, unfair dismissals can lead to reinstatement by the court following lengthy court procedures

FIGURE 6.4 **Weeks of wages required to be paid in severance in regions, country income groups, and selected South Asian countries, by length of service**

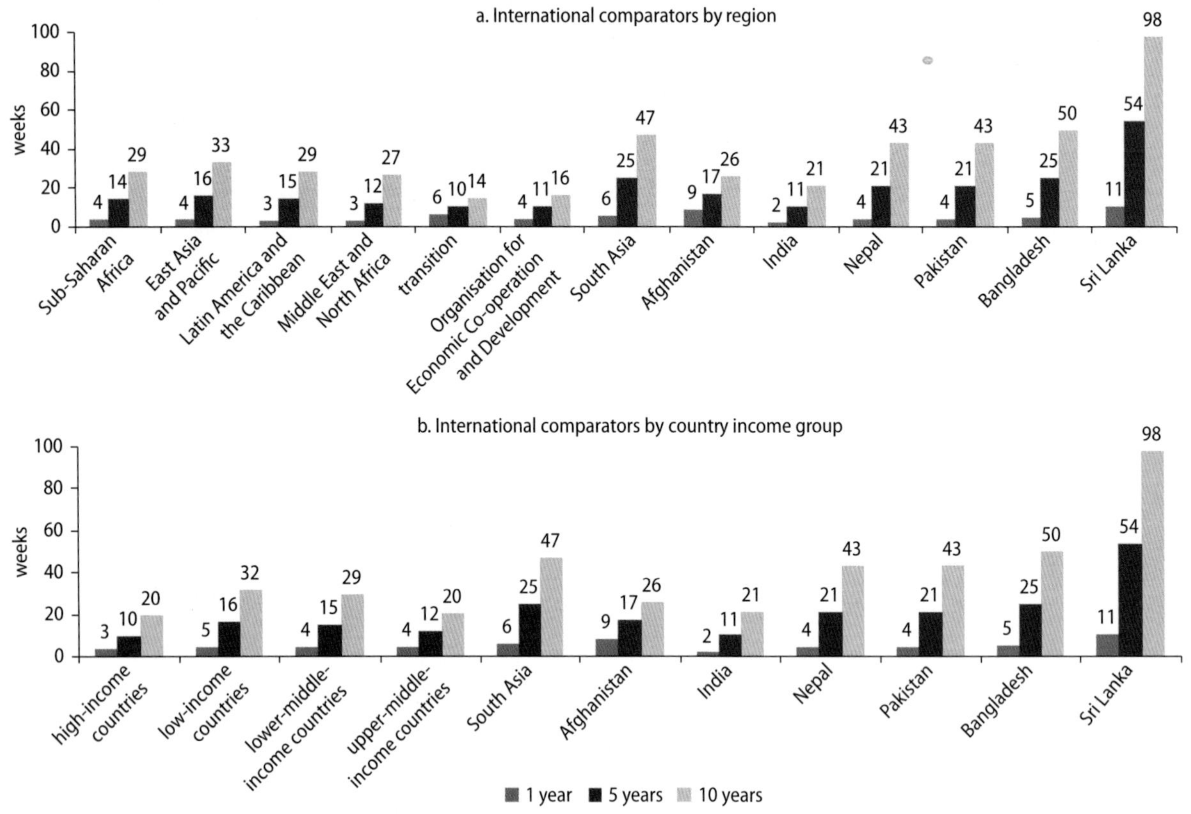

a. International comparators by region

b. International comparators by country income group

■ 1 year ■ 5 years ▨ 10 years

Source: Holzmann and others 2011.

(see annex table 6A.1).[22] Although there are no additional costs or notification requirements/regulations for collective dismissals, the effective costs of dismissals (the sum of costs for individual dismissals and any additional costs for collective dismissals) puts India, together with Indonesia, among the top third of countries included in the OECD benchmarking. India's employment protection legislation for temporary and fixed-term contracts, though more relaxed, is just above the OECD mean.

The effects of employment protection legislation on labor market outcomes have been extensively researched, especially in OECD countries (for overviews of this literature, see OECD 2006, 2007b). Studies conducted in developing countries, particularly in Latin America, reach broadly similar conclusions

(see Freeman 2009). This research finds modest impacts on employment and unemployment, often statistically insignificant in the case of unemployment. The empirical findings are stronger in the case of dynamic effects: in general, more restrictive employment protection legislation is associated with lower labor turnover, job creation, and destruction; longer job tenure; and longer unemployment duration. The research also suggests that there are distributional impacts of strong employment protection rules, with prime-age males and skilled workers benefiting and women, youth, and unskilled workers losing.

Studies on the impact of labor laws in South Asia have concentrated on India.[23] A generally robust set of conclusions emerges: states with more protective legislation have significantly lower output, employment,

FIGURE 6.5 Employment protection indicators in selected countries

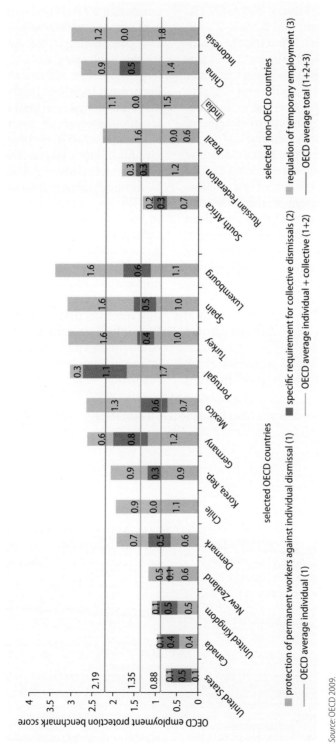

Source: OECD 2009.
Note: The OECD employment protection indicators cover three aspects of employment protection: individual dismissal of permanent workers, regulation of temporary employment, and specific requirements for collective dismissal. Each subindicator ranges from 0 to 6, with 0 the least restrictive and 6 the most restrictive. The overall indicator—the sum of the three subindicators, weighted at 5/12, 5/12, and 2/12—also ranges from 0 to 6.

number of establishments, investment, and labor productivity in the formal manufacturing sector and higher output in informal manufacturing (see Ahsan and Pagés 2009; Gupta, Hasan, and Kumar 2009; OECD 2007a). Gupta, Hasan, and Kumar (2009) find that output growth following the significant deregulation of the 1980s and 1990s was higher in labor-intensive industries in states with more flexible labor regulations. Gains in employment generation were higher in states with more flexible regulations, irrespective of the labor intensity of the industry.

Ahsan and Pagés (2009) find evidence of strong complementarities across labor laws in India. They find that the output and employment costs of employment protection legislation are higher in states and time periods in which it is more difficult to resolve disputes and not very important when such costs are low. Workers do not benefit from these laws, because any gains in employment protection are more than offset by the decline in employment, resulting in a decline in the total wage bill (Ahsan and Pagés 2009; Besley and Burgess 2004).

Evidence from India and Sri Lanka on job turnover suggests efficiency costs of labor legislation. Using urban enterprise survey data for the early 2000s, Gunatilaka and Vodopivec (2010) find that Sri Lanka has very low job flows relative to other countries (see annex figure 6A.5) and suggest that its stringent job security legislation may be a significant contributing factor. Analysis carried out for this book using a newly available panel of large (more than 100 employees) manufacturing firms in India finds higher rates of job creation and destruction (and therefore job reallocation/turnover) for contract labor relative to permanent workers (annex table 6A.2).[24] It also finds higher job turnover for states with more flexible labor regulations (figure 6.6).

Although labor regulations are not binding on all firms in the region, enterprise managers in India, Nepal, and Sri Lanka cite them as an important constraint to the operation and growth of their businesses. Job-creating firms report that labor regulations are the third most important constraint in Bhutan, the fourth most important constraint in India, and the fifth most important constraint in Nepal and Sri Lanka. In contrast, formal sector firms in Afghanistan and Bangladesh rate labor regulations as among the least problematic. Labor regulations generally become more costly to

FIGURE 6.6   Job turnover rates and labor regulations in Indian states

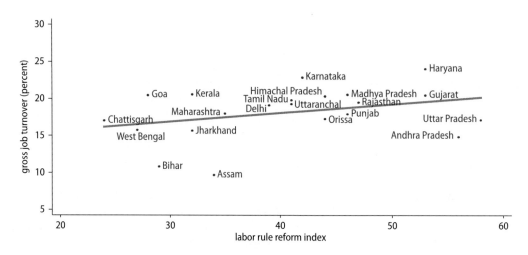

Sources: Authors, based on various sources. Gross job turnover data are calculated from the Annual Survey of Industries panel data for 2000–08 for firms with more than 100 employees. The Labor Rule Reform Index is the OECD index of state-level reform in India, developed on the basis of data collected through a customized survey instrument (Dougherty 2008; OECD 2007a). The proportional index, which captures the state's share of total reforms, is used here.
Note: Higher values of the reform index reflect a greater degree of change in procedures to reduce transactions costs (such as limiting the scope of the regulation, providing greater clarity with regard to application, and simplifying compliance procedures in eight specific labor law areas).

FIGURE 6.7   **Cross-country comparison of reported severity of the labor regulation constraint**

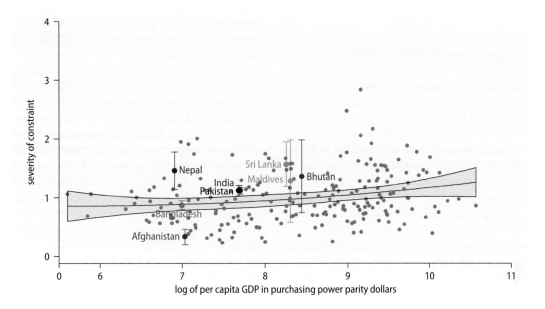

Source: Carlin and Schaffer 2011 (based on World Bank enterprise surveys).
Note: The cross-country regression line shows the relationship between the reported severity of the constraint for a benchmark firm and the log of per capita GDP. The shaded area is the 95 percent confidence interval band around the regression line. Vertical bars show confidence intervals of 95 percent around the reported severity of the constraint for countries in South Asia. The lack of overlap between the South Asian country confidence interval and the regression line confidence interval is a conservative test of the statistically significant difference between the reported severity of a constraint for the South Asian country and the average reported severity of constraint for countries at the same level of per capita GDP. The reported severity could still be significantly different even with overlap. Analysis is based on pooled sample of enterprise surveys conducted between 2000 and 2010. The severity of constraint is rated by firms on a 5-point scale, with 0 being no obstacle, 1 being a minor obstacle, 2 being a moderate obstacle, 3 being a major obstacle, and 4 being a very severe obstacle.

firms as GDP per capita rises (figure 6.7). India, Nepal, and Sri Lanka report higher levels of this constraint than other countries at their level of development.[25]

In India, labor regulations were markedly more problematic in 2010 than in 2005. Firms in high-income states report greater severity and ranking of the labor regulations constraint than low-income states. Nearly 30 percent of Indian firms that perceive labor regulations as a major or severe constraint report that restrictions on dismissal are a constraint to hiring, about 25 percent report that restrictions on employing casual work are constraints, and about 20 percent complain about restrictions on temporary work.

Compensation and minimum wages

Government policy can affect compensation—and thus employment—through various channels, including the rules determining collective bargaining, pay equity policies intended to eliminate wage discrimination, and minimum wages. Another way in which public policy can affect compensation is through rules mandating contributions by employers, employees, or both to social insurance (such as pension plans and health insurance) and other benefits. The quality and efficiency of the insurance and benefits financed by such contributions are in themselves major policy issues. However, from the perspective of this book, the relevance of these nonwage labor costs pertains to their labor market implications. Depending on the details of the contributions and who ultimately pays for them, these contributions can affect total labor costs incurred by the employer (and thus labor demand) or net earnings of the employee (and thus labor supply).

Where social contributions are large, employment impacts can be substantial. Labor economists typically measure the magnitude of social contributions through the "tax wedge"—the difference between total labor costs and net earnings.[26] Most South Asian countries have tax wedges that are below the international average (see annex figure 6A.6). However, the tax wedges in India, Nepal, and Sri Lanka are high enough that any policy reforms must take into consideration the potential employment disincentives of further increases.

Social insurance systems can also affect worker mobility. The lack of portability of benefits in some countries (including India, Nepal, and Sri Lanka) with multiple schemes could inhibit the movement of workers between the public and private sector. In 2010 (for the public sector) and 2011 (for the private sector), Maldives introduced a new contributory pension scheme that is designed to address this issue. The design of defined benefit schemes can also penalize movement out of covered employment (for example, for workers covered by India's employee pension scheme).

Minimum wage rules are another intervention with potentially important employment effects. Like employment protection rules, minimum wages can provide security to workers adversely affected by market failures. When they are set too high, however, they can have the unintended consequence of reducing employment and encouraging informality.

For the most part, the international literature finds the employment effects of minimum wages to be modest or negligible (Card and Krueger 1997; Neumark and Wascher 2006). In developing countries, it suggests that minimum wages often raise the pay of low-paid workers in the formal sector and can even have a spillover effect on the pay of informal sector wage workers.[27] However, the impacts of minimum wages vary considerably, with examples of negative employment effects in some countries and groups of workers within countries.

All countries in South Asia have minimum wage rules; some have multiple minimum wages (see annex table 6A.3). It is important to consider local labor market conditions in assessing whether the level set for the minimum wage strikes the right balance between protection and efficiency. In India, where states set the minimum wage, there is wide variation in how it relates to market wages, although overall the level is low. In a number of Indian states, for example, the minimum wage is less than 20 percent of the median formal wage. It is highest in Dadra and Nagar Haveli and Delhi, but even in those states it was less than 40 percent of the median wage in the formal sector in 2008. In most states, the minimum wage is below the median wage for casual workers (see annex figure 6A.7). In Nepal, Pakistan, and the manufacturing sector of Sri Lanka, it is higher as a proportion of the median formal sector wage (46–61 percent) (figure 6.8). In Nepal and Pakistan, it is at or above the median wage for casual labor, suggesting that the majority of these wage workers are unlikely to find formal sector employment. Although minimum wages in Nepal, Pakistan, and Sri Lanka are not high by international standards, they approach the level at which lower-productivity workers will be effectively excluded from formal wage employment, suggesting caution with respect to further increases.

FIGURE 6.8   Minimum wages as a proportion of median formal sector wages in Nepal, Pakistan, and Sri Lanka

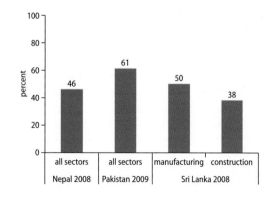

Sources: Authors, based on national sources for minimum wages and labor force surveys for median wages.

The main concern regarding minimum wages in South Asia involves the institutional arrangements used to implement them. Labor regulations typically indicate that there should be a minimum wage but do not define the mechanisms to set its level or enforce it. Regulations are also often silent about the structure of the body in charge of setting minimum wages, the role of employers and employees, and the mechanism to adjust the minimum wage over time, creating uncertainty for both employees and employers.

Compliance and dispute resolution

Lack of compliance weakens the impact of labor market rules.[28] Firms employ various strategies to circumvent statutory rules, reducing de facto the regulation of labor markets. Incentives for noncompliance can be particularly strong where compliance can be costly, as in the case of dismissals. Strategies firms use include increasing the use of contract and temporary workers (India, Pakistan, Sri Lanka), using voluntary retirement schemes for collective dismissals (India, Sri Lanka), fragmenting production and "leasing" production to smaller firms through subcontracting (India, Sri Lanka), using disciplinary grounds to justify firing a worker or harassing workers to make them quit (Sri Lanka), adopting capital-intensive technologies (India), locking out workers (India); employing foreign workers instead of local workers (Nepal), and terminating workers during the period of probation (Pakistan).[29, 30]

Weak enforcement is another factor. One problem is that the administrative machinery for enforcement is inadequate. Bangladesh and Nepal, for example, suffer from shortages of inspectors. Nepal faces challenges of terrain and transport.

Another problem is the sheer complexity of compliance. This problem is especially severe in India, with its multitude of labor laws, which are often poorly specified and interpreted as well as contradictory; its requirements to maintain registers and file returns under each law; and the lack of a single system of inspection for labor legislation (Debroy 2011).

Enforcement is also weakened by collusion between and corruption of inspectors and employers. According to World Bank enterprise surveys, 50–60 percent of firms in India (2005) and Pakistan (2007) report that inspectors expect gifts. About 20 percent of managers in India in 2002 reported that inspectors responded to unofficial payments by reducing the number of visits to their establishments.[31]

Implementation is further hampered by inefficient procedures for resolving disputes. In India, Pakistan, and Sri Lanka, options for resolving disputes and grievances through negotiation appear to be limited, and the legal framework favors adjudication over negotiation or collective bargaining. In India, for example, the Industrial Disputes Act sets the conciliation, arbitration/mediation, and adjudication procedures to be followed in industrial disputes. If conciliation fails, the government may refer the case to the industrial tribunal or a labor court, which normally leads to a long litigation process.[32] The backlog means that an average adjudication takes three to five years (some cases have been pending for more than a decade). In Pakistan, unfair dismissal cases can involve protracted processes at labor courts and appeals to high courts. In Sri Lanka, the process of inquiry in unfair dismissal cases can take a substantial amount of time and is often arbitrary and nontransparent. Although a 2003 amendment to the TEWA mandated a 4:3:2 month formula for labor tribunal cases, arbitration, and decisions by the commissioner, the process still takes a long time, and most cases drag on for two to three years. Poorly resourced institutions and weak capacity are evident in most countries.

Strengthening enforcement and dispute resolution capabilities are necessary for improving compliance, but they require complementary measures. There is consensus in most countries on improving the efficiency of inspections and strengthening enforcement capabilities. Inspection must play a key role in enforcement, but the sheer number of firms (especially small firms) limits the impact it can have. Improving inspection must therefore be complemented by other strategies, including strengthening complaint and grievance redressal mechanisms and streamlining and addressing the lack of clarity and consistency in laws and regulations. Options to reduce firms' incentives to circumvent legislation include reducing the stringency of such legislation. These options, on which there is typically less consensus, are discussed below.

Shifting protection from jobs to workers

Easing protective regulations would improve labor market outcomes but weaken job security for formal sector workers. Less restrictive regulations, especially pertaining to dismissal, could create incentives for formal sector job creation; benefit certain groups, including women; and encourage compliance with the law. The minority of workers that currently benefit from these regulations would lose from such a reform, especially in India, Nepal, and Sri Lanka, where job security rules are strongest.

Better tools to protect workers, such as income support and active labor market policies, would provide a more broadly effective mechanism for achieving social and employment objectives than the current focus on protecting jobs. The strategy of protecting workers is based on allowing the labor market to function more freely than it does in regimes with strong job protection but giving workers better access to active and passive programs that help them adjust to market fluctuations and increase their future employability.

Table 6.5 contrasts the different approaches to worker protection. The challenge for countries in South Asia—like other low-income countries with small formal sectors and indeed many middle-income countries—is to move from the lower-right-hand cell in table 6.5 upward and to the left.

Reducing job protection for formal sector workers is difficult, because it increases the prospects of layoffs and dismissals from previously protected jobs. Many countries—including several transition economies of Central and Eastern Europe—have taken this difficult step by combining it with the introduction of better programs to protect workers (Holzmann and others 2011; see Vodopivec, Wörgötter, and Raju 2005 for a discussion of the reform paths and challenges in these countries).

One aspect of this shift is to extend the legality of nonpermanent contracts. Most countries have reasonably flexible contracting rules. Bangladesh, Nepal, and Pakistan set limits on the use of fixed-term contracts,

TABLE 6.5 Stylized characteristics of protecting workers versus protecting jobs

		Protecting jobs (employment protection legislation)	
		Low	**High**
Protecting workers (income support, active labor market policies)	**High**	• Broad coverage of social protection • Positive impact on job creation • High incidence of short-term and temporary employment • High adjustment flows handled through active and passive programs	• Some duplication in social protection • High cost (regulation plus taxes) • Incentives for informal activity and low compliance • Encourages tenure and human capital investment • Strict regulation has negative effects on labor market dynamism and protects insiders
	Low	• Little protection offered • Positive impact on job creation • Precarious employment and weak safety net • Unfavorable for productivity growth	• Little social protection support for outsiders • Incentives for informal activity and low compliance • Encourages tenure and human capital investment • Strict regulation has negative effects on labor market dynamism and protects insiders

Source: Authors.

however, and in India, lack of clarity has led to widely different interpretations, regulations, and practices across states. Opening up the use of fixed-term contracting runs the risk of encouraging employers to use this form of employment to avoid obligations of permanent contracts, but it can also have the positive effect of shifting workers from casual employment relationships (without contracts) to more formal contracted positions. If countries also reduce some of the procedural and financial costs associated with dismissal (as discussed below), incentives for avoiding permanent contracts in legitimately long-term employment relationships could be minimized and formalization of casual employment could be the more dominant effect.

Combined with strengthened enforcement, minimum income security provisions for contract workers can be improved. Although pools of temporary contract and casual workers are generally similar—with women and young, old, and poorly educated workers overrepresented in both groups—data from India's 2010 National Sample Survey show that social security covers more than twice as many contract workers (28 percent) as casual workers (12 percent). Indeed, increasing protection of contract labor by extending minimum wage and social security requirements, as well as regulating the conditions of work, is an important objective of India's Contract Labor Act. Noncompliance with requirements for minimum wage and social security benefits is widespread, however (NCEUS 2009). Opening up the use of contract labor and improving enforcement of basic provisions of income security could increase the share of workers with effective basic protection.

Reducing the costs of dismissal is an important aspect of reform, but it would need to be accompanied by improvements in support for the unemployed. Many stakeholders support reducing severance pay (in Sri Lanka) and termination-related procedural costs (in India, Nepal, and Sri Lanka) in order to bring them more in line with international arrangements. More universal support would require steps to ensure protection of workers

who currently benefit from job security rules. One option would be to grandfather existing beneficiaries while adjusting provisions for new entrants. Another would be to combine this measure with some form of income support in the event of unemployment and active programs that help unemployed workers find new jobs.

The design of such income support programs needs to draw on international experiences while making adjustments for income and administrative conditions in South Asia. A number of countries, especially in the OECD and Latin America, have introduced funded unemployment accounts (box 6.1). Some countries in Eastern Europe have implemented flat unemployment benefits, which are relatively simple to implement and monitor. Studies by the World Bank have looked at design principles, particularly those suited for Sri Lanka, a higher-income country with some administrative capacity (box 6.2). A key design question involves how income support programs are financed. If financing is through social insurance contributions, countries need to be careful that these contributions do not increase the tax wedge to the point that employment is negatively affected.

Income protection could be complemented by strengthened active labor market programs, including cost-effective training and employment services. Active labor market programs can enhance labor supply, create labor demand, and improve the functioning of the labor market, potentially increasing employment, productivity, and earnings. They can be tools for helping unemployed workers. However, the evaluation literature underscores the fact that programs often do not meet their intended objectives and are often not cost-effective (see, for example, Betcherman and others 2004, 2007). Careful design and implementation matter.

If it is responsive to the real needs of the labor market, training could potentially be an important support for unemployed formal sector workers. Training can help unemployed workers upgrade their skills or learn new ones. However, programs in many countries are not responsive to the

BOX 6.1   Severance reforms in Austria and Chile

In 2003, Austria converted its severance pay to a fully funded, contributory system. The reform extended entitlement to workers with short tenures and removed obstacles to worker mobility, granting full portability and allowing the accumulation of benefits from the beginning of the employment spell. Employers contribute 1.5 percent of the payroll to each worker. Resources are held in a central account and invested in the capital market. Laid-off workers with job tenure of three or more years can withdraw accumulations from their accounts or keep them and claim them upon retirement. (Workers who separate voluntarily and workers with tenures of less than three years are denied the right of immediate withdrawal.)

In 2002, Chile introduced a new unemployment insurance system that combines social insurance with self-insurance. Both workers and employers pay contributions. Unemployment contributions are split between individual accounts and a common solidarity account, which is partly financed by the government.

This scheme has reduced employers' severance payment obligations, which are being partly replaced by the new unemployment insurance system. The system is effectively funded with individual accounts managed by a freestanding administrator selected through a competitive tender. To stimulate reemployment, the scheme requires benefit recipients to first draw resources from their own accounts; when they deplete these funds, they draw from the solidarity account. Withdrawals from individual accounts are triggered by separation from the employer, regardless of the reason. Withdrawals from the common fund are triggered by insufficient resources in individual accounts. Claimants must satisfy the usual eligibility conditions under unemployment insurance (not working and being available and searching for a job). They are limited to two withdrawals over a five-year period. Benefits are linked to past earnings, with a declining schedule.

Source: Holzmann and others 2011.

occupational demands of the labor market, and curricula are often not in tune with the requirements of firms. International experience has shown that training and retraining programs need to have a strong connection to the employer community for design and implementation. Establishing such a connection can be done in various ways, including promoting competition among trainers, creating performance incentives through outcome-based fees for suppliers, and involving employers in the planning of training, the supervision of trainers, and the direct provision of training.

South Asian countries have a variety of training programs for unemployed workers. Training is delivered by government training institutes, enterprises, nongovernmental organizations (NGOs), and commercial training companies. Many programs, particularly those funded by governments and international donors, seek to improve the

livelihoods of the poor (these programs are discussed in the next section). No serious evaluation evidence exists on the impact of training programs in the region, but there appear to be many obstacles that likely affect their success. Many programs are more about life skills and basic job readiness than vocational skills training (Rahman and Shamsunnahar 2011). Another concern is the lack of correspondence between the training provided and the needs of employers. To strengthen the relevance of training, some countries have initiated public-private partnerships. The most prominent example is India's National Skill Development Corporation, which provides gap financing to trainers in 21 key manufacturing and service sectors.

Employment services have generally been found to be a cost-effective active labor market policy. These services include job brokerage, labor market counseling, testing

---

BOX 6.2 Unemployment benefit proposals for Sri Lanka

Analysis by Vodopivec (2004) and Abidoye, Orazem, and Vodopivec (2009) identifies design principles for moving to a more effective protection system for the unemployed in Sri Lanka. Their proposals take into account short-term political economy needs as well as the need for a longer-term transition to an unemployment benefit program. Key elements include the following:

- Starting eligibility conditions and coverage would be essentially the same as under the Termination of Employment of Workmen Act, with retrenched workers in firms with more than 14 workers receiving both severance and unemployment benefits. (Workers whose employers went bankrupt would at least get unemployment benefits, even if they were unable to get TEWA benefits.)
- The continuing eligibility requirements (other than employment in the formal sector) found in OECD programs would be eliminated. Recipients would be automatically entitled to a maximum amount of benefits, paid as a lump sum. This feature takes into account Sri Lanka's large informal sector, in which workers self-protect through informal employment, and the associated challenges and costs of monitoring.
- Employee or a combination of employer and employee contributions would be made to individual worker accounts, which are transferrable across enterprises, based on a modest level of

benefits (for example, a maximum potential duration of 6–10 months, with a replacement rate of about 50 percent), to take into account the fact that potential beneficiaries would be from better-off segments of the population.
- Workers would be able to access their accounts on becoming unemployed.
- Existing administrative systems—such as the Employees Provident Fund network—would be used to pay out benefits into beneficiaries' accounts (to address the administrative costs of setting up new systems).
- Unused funds remaining in individual accounts on retirement would be transferred to pension accounts.
- Employment services would be provided (through JobsNet, for example).

In the long run, employers' obligations under TEWA could be fully transformed into their regular monthly contributions to the individual accounts of workers and coverage extended to all workers covered by the Employees Provident Fund scheme, which does not have a size-related threshold. The insurance function could be improved through the addition of a social insurance component to supplement individual savings for workers who exhaust their accounts (see the example from Chile in box 6.1).

Sources: Abidoye, Orazem, and Vodopivec 2009; Vodopivec 2004.

---

and assessment, and job search assistance. Evaluations from developed and developing countries suggest that employment services are among the most cost-effective mechanisms, especially under favorable economic conditions (Betcherman and others 2004). When labor demand is sluggish, employment services need to be combined with other interventions. In developing countries, where employment agencies are weak and most hiring is done through informal channels, considerable capacity needs to be built for public employment agencies to be effective. The market for private employment agencies also needs to be further developed.

There is considerable room for improving the effectiveness of national employment services. India's national employment service runs almost 1,000 employment exchanges, which register job seekers, notify them about vacancies, collect and disseminate labor market information, and provide vocational guidance to students and youth. The limited information available suggests that most (but not all) of these exchanges—like exchanges elsewhere—are of limited effectiveness (World Bank 2010). In Nepal, the Department of Labor and Employment Promotion operates skills development offices for registering job applicants and provides labor market information.

There are promising models and emerging good practices in the region, all of which include a central role for information technology in reaching jobseekers and employers and in providing detailed information for employers to review. There has also been an increase in job fairs, which enable employers and workers to engage directly. Employment exchanges in Gujarat, India, and in Sri Lanka have strong linkages with private employers. In Gujarat, a group of NGOs provides local labor market information.

The state of Karnataka has set up India's first employment exchange based on a public-private partnership. Under this arrangement, the state government and TeamLease Services, a staffing solutions company, have created the Karnataka Employment Center.

In Sri Lanka, JobsNet—which intends to set up a wide network of job service centers and is one of the largest active labor market services in terms of registrations—provides intermediation, career guidance and counseling, and job search assistance. It is financed by a commission of employers. It receives special funds from the government treasury for programs that target youth and internally displaced people. JobsNet's board of directors—which has representation from government, the private sector, and trade unions—is responsible for framing policy priorities and overseeing the implementation of programs. Several private firms are involved, as both job providers and providers of private sector perspectives on industry needs. A transparent database facilitates monitoring of the program.

Labor market institutions, policies, and programs in the informal sector

Labor market regulations, institutions, and programs are important even in sectors that are informal: public works, self-employment assistance including microfinance, and many training programs are oriented to workers who are outside the formal sector. These and other types of programs may be financed or delivered by government, donors, NGOs, or the private sector. Indeed, South Asia has a rich mix of informal worker associations and trade unions, self-help groups, and other membership- and community-based organizations, all of which play important roles in the labor market (box 6.3). The role of labor market institutions and programs in the informal sector is of great relevance in South Asia, given that this sector employs the vast majority of workers.

The social protection challenge in low-income countries is how to cover the gap in protection for informal sector workers while not constraining incentives for creating income from informal activities. This gap covers all aspects of the social protection system, including activation programs, which promote opportunities for workers; social and self-insurance plans, which prevent declines in income from shocks; and safety net programs, which protect against destitution.

Countries in South Asia rely on three types of programs to support workers in the informal sector: public works, training, and support for self-employment/small business.[33] These interventions play both an activation (promotion) and a safety net (protection) role. There are also efforts to extend social insurance (prevention) options to informal workers—the thrust of proposals made by the National Commission for Enterprises in the Unorganised Sector for minimum universal social security in India (NCEUS 2009), for example. The different approaches need to be considered in terms of their effects on adequacy of protection, efficiency, functioning of the labor market, and productivity.

Public works

Public works have a long history in South Asia and continue to be an important instrument for activation, insurance, and safety nets in the region. A global review of public works programs finds that South Asia has more participants than any other region (del Ninno, Subbarao, and Milazzo 2009). Most countries in the region have public works programs, which provide cash or food in

---

BOX 6.3   Nongovernment players in South Asia's informal labor market

An impressive range of NGOs provides various forms of protection to workers in informal labor markets in South Asia, carrying out functions that are typically the responsibility of government agencies and trade unions in the formal sector. Informal worker associations, microfinance institutions, self-help groups, and other membership- and community-based organizations are involved in the full range of worker protection activities. They promote income-generating activities, largely through microfinance services and training, and mitigate labor market–related shocks, through social and self-insurance plans and by advocating for the basic rights of informal workers. Programs target the poor and vulnerable, often with a focus on women.

Some of South Asia's organizations are well known internationally. Grameen Bank has been a pioneer in microfinance, offering credit and related banking services to the poor in Bangladesh since the

1970s. BRAC, the largest NGO in the world, has an extensive microfinance operation as part of its wide-ranging development activities. India's Self-Employed Women's Association (SEWA) is a leading example of an organization devoted to improving the security and self-reliance of workers in the informal sector. The organization—actually a registered trade union—provides a broad range of services, including microfinance and banking services, training, insurance, housing, and lobbying and negotiating for better wages and working conditions.

These (and some other) organizations operate on a very large scale and have major impacts. Many smaller organizations also provide services to the hundreds of millions of South Asian workers who work beyond the reach of labor laws, statutory social insurance programs, and formal collective agreements.

Source: Authors.

---

return for work on projects typically developed by governments (at the national, subnational, or local level); donors; or NGOs.

Various public works designs exist across the region (table 6.6). Public works are an important tool in the reconstruction of Afghanistan, for example, where programs include food-for-work programs, supported by the World Food Programme, and the National Rural Access Program, which reconstructs and maintains rural infrastructure. Nepal has implemented a range of public works activities, some reaching out to the remote communities. In some cases (for example, the Poverty Alleviation Fund), public works have been part of larger programs with various components. The Rural Community Infrastructure Works Program is a food-for-work program operated jointly with the World Food Programme. Pakistan and Sri Lanka have provided some public works programs, but public works have been used less there than elsewhere in the region.

Bangladesh and India, where public works are most prominent, have been using public

works since the 1950s. Bangladesh has five programs that directly create employment through public works. The emphasis is on the rural poor. The program with the largest number of participants is Employment Generation for the Hard Core Poor, which served 1.8 million beneficiaries between October 2009 and May 2010. This program operates in 16 poor districts, with the objectives of creating temporary employment, reducing poverty, and contributing to rural development. The program provides up to 100 days of wage employment to one person per poor family. This model is similar in some ways to India's Mahatma Gandhi National Rural Employment Guarantee Act (MGNREGA). Bangladesh also has a food-for-work program, which has the largest budget of all public works programs.

India has had a succession of public works programs over the past half century. The national and state governments, NGOs, and the private sector have all been, and continue to be, involved. The most prominent program is the Mahatma Gandhi National Rural Employment Guarantee Program, created

TABLE 6.6   Selected public works programs in South Asia, by country

Country	Program	Target population	Benefits	Number of participants (latest year available)
Afghanistan	Protracted Relief and Recovery Operations (with World Food Programme)	Food insecure in rural areas, women, internally displaced people, excombatants	Food, basic education, and training for girls and women	700,000
	National Rural Access Program	Rural unemployed	Short-term employment, training for excombatants	1,435,000 labor days
Bangladesh	National Service Program	Unemployed rural youth and women with secondary education and above	Wages and training	13,000
	Rural Employment Opportunities for Public Assets	Poor rural female household heads	Wages (portion put into savings account for future self-employment)	5,000
	Employment Generation for the Hard Core Poor	Rural poor	Wages	1,800,000
	Rural Employment and Road Maintenance Program	Poor rural women	Wages (portion put into savings account for self-employment in future), training, other supports for self-employment	10,000
	Food for Work	Food insecure in rural areas; people affected by disasters	Food	56,000
India	National Rural Employment Guarantee Program	Rural poor	Wages	41 million rural households
	Swarna Jayanti Shahari Rozgar Yojana (Urban Wage Employment Program)	Urban poor and unemployed	Wages	71 million person-days under wage program
Nepal	Rural Community Infrastructure Works	Food insecure in rural areas	Food	30,000 households from food-insecure regions
	Support Activities for Poor Producers of Nepal (SAPPROS)	Households affected by drought	Food	30,000
	Social Safety Net Project	Households in chronically food-insecure districts	Food	168,000
Pakistan	People Works Program	Poor and unemployed youth	Wages	228,000

Source: Authors' compilation.

in 2006 under MGNREGA. With its rights-based design—which guarantees 100 days of work annually for any rural household willing to perform unskilled manual labor, at a rate no more than the wage specified by the scheme—MGNREGA is being watched with interest (box 6.4).

MGNREGA has created much more employment than other Indian public works programs have, but the employment guarantee has not been fully implemented. In 2009/10, the program provided employment to about one-fourth of rural households (table 6.7). Although the number of days of

work has been higher than other programs, qualitative evidence and field studies indicate that there is substantial unmet demand for MGNREGA work in some states.[34] About one-fifth of rural households who sought work in the program did not get it (table 6.7). This evidence, together with field monitoring reports from the Professional Institutional Network, suggests that the employment guarantee does not always operate in the way set out in the act.[35, 36]

Evidence suggests that MGNREGA beneficiaries tend to be poor and that the program is largely successful in targeting the

---

BOX 6.4   Key features of India's Mahatma Gandhi National Rural Employment Guarantee Act

Under India's Mahatma Gandhi National Rural Employment Guarantee Act, the government guarantees 100 days of work per rural household per year. Each rural household is entitled to a free job card with photographs of all adult members living in it. A job card holder may then apply for employment. The government must provide employment within 15 days. If it fails to so, a daily unemployment allowance has to be paid to the applicant. Work must be provided within five kilometers of the applicant's residence. If it is not, the worker receives a 10 percent premium over the scheme wage. How the household distributes the 100 days among its members is entirely the household's decision. The scheme is therefore completely self-targeted and follows a demand-driven, rights-based approach.

The central government in the union budget of 2009/10 promised to provide a real wage of Rs 100 a day (indexed to state-specific inflation) for work performed under MGNREGA. Payment is based on a rural schedule of rates that depends on the amount of work performed by a person. This schedule of rates should be set such that able-bodied workers should be able to produce the output that could earn them the program wage.

Wages are paid in cash—a departure from previous public works programs, which typically included a food component. In a move to counter corruption in forging job cards and tampering with muster rolls (registries of eligible households) and improve transparency in wage payment, the government announced that as of April 1, 2008, all MGNREGA wages would be paid directly into worker bank or post office accounts, opened free of charge. The idea was that separating the implementing agency from the payment mechanism would reduce room for fraud and harassment.

Adequate worksite facilities are to be provided. To facilitate manual labor, the act mandates provision of certain basic facilities at the worksite, including provision of shade, drinking water, crèches for children, and first-aid facilities.

Several provisions of the act favor the participation of women. The act mandates that one-third of workers be women. It ensures equal wages for men and women, with women typically having to perform less work to earn the program wage. The act also provides for childcare facilities for children under six if more than five such children are present at a worksite. Together with the provision that the job be within five kilometers of the worker's residence, these features make MGNREGA work a feasible option for women.

The act focuses on labor-intensive rural development works, with a focus on water and irrigation activities as well as connectivity. In addition to the list of specific types of works allowed under the act, there is a provision for other types of works based on consultations between the state and the central government. Overall, the scheme maintains a 60:40 labor to capital ratio. Contractors and machines are explicitly banned.

Panchayati Raj institutions (PRIs) and communities play a central role in implementing MGNREG. Unlike previous public works and social protection programs, PRI leaders and communities are supposed to identify the list of works through discussions in the *gram sabha* (village council). PRIs also participate in implementation (at least half of works by value are to be implemented through the *gram panchayat* [local self-governments in villages and small towns]), supervision, and monitoring of works (including through social audits). This program feature represents a significant shift from earlier public work schemes which were based on central rules, with PRIs involved only in supportive implementation or distribution functions.

To implement MGNREG, the act calls for dedicated administrative structure. Unlike previous public works programs, there is a specific provision of administrative costs, which are borne by the center and supplemented by states. There is also provision for a dedicated cadre of MGNREGA officials and functionaries at the district, block, and *gram panchayat* level responsible for implementing the program.

The act emphasizes accountability, through the use of information and communication technology tools and reliance on communities and third-party monitoring. Management information systems have been established to handle administrative data on employment generated and assets created at the lowest level. Field-based monitoring is supposed to be performed by national field-level monitors

(continues next page)

BOX 6.4 **Key features of India's Mahatma Gandhi National Rural Employment Guarantee Act** (continued)

reporting to the central ministry, as well as local vigilance and monitoring communities. Some states are also using community-based monitoring through social audits.

The central government bears 90 percent of the total cost of the program. It covers all wage costs and three-quarters of the nonwage component (materials and most administrative expenses, subject

to a maximum limit), working on an assumed 60:40 labor to capital ratio. States are responsible for providing unemployment allowances should they fail to provide work within 15 days of it being demanded. This penalty is designed to create a strong incentive for the state government to provide work.

Source: World Bank 2011b.

TABLE 6.7 **Participation in the Mahatma Gandhi National Rural Employment Guarantee Program, by consumption quintile, 2010**
(percentage of households, except where otherwise indicated)

Quintile	Holds MGNREGA job card	Reports working in MGNREGA program	Sought but did not obtain MGNREGA work	Mean person days for households that worked in MGNREGA program	Mean person days for all rural households
1 (poorest)	47	34	25	34	11
2	41	30	22	36	11
3	39	27	21	38	10
4	33	23	18	40	9
5	22	14	14	40	6
All	35	24	19	37	9

Source: Authors' estimates, based on the 2009/10 National Survey Sample.

disadvantaged.[37] Nationally, households in poorer quintiles are considerably more likely than households in richer quintiles to be registered with and report employment through the program (table 6.7).[38] Rural households in the poorest quintile report about twice as many days of MGNREGA work as households in the richest quintile. However, a small but nontrivial share of MNREGA work opportunities go to better-off households, and the number of days of work is actually higher for participants from richer quintiles.[39]

Administrative data show that women account for almost half of work days funded by MGNREGA (figure 6.9). Although households determine who will participate, the program sets targets for the share of jobs held by women (box 6.4). To achieve this target, MGNREGA encourages states

and localities to design projects that are accessible to women. Scheduled castes and tribes are also well represented in the program, although there is some evidence that their share of total work declined in recent years.[40]

The design of MGNREGA partially addresses some of the traditional problems with public works, including the lack of community participation, the leakage of funds and related forms of corruption, and the lack of monitoring and evaluation (see box 6.4). However, an implementation review reveals problems with the issuance of job cards; manipulation of program data; discrimination against women, scheduled castes and tribes, and people with disabilities; fraudulent payments and anomalies; and slippage in execution of work undertaken (NCAER–PIF 2009). Moreover, concerns remain about the poor quality of the assets created, which critics cite as indicative of a primary focus on employment generation at the expense of the creation of productive assets and improved future livelihood opportunities.[41] The effectiveness with which MGNREGA has been implemented has varied considerably across states.

MGNREGA has potentially important effects on the functioning of rural labor markets. A concern is that it may be affecting labor supply by offering wages above what would normally be offered for unskilled labor. Given the scale of the program, this issue is important. Although there is anecdotal evidence that in some areas MGNREGA wages may be discouraging labor supply outside the program (in, for example, labor-importing states like Punjab and Haryana [Wall Street Journal 2011]), there is no systematic evidence with which to rigorously assess this claim. This issue should be carefully analyzed.

Public works can provide an effective safety net for poor and vulnerable households. The evidence both internationally and in the region suggests that public works can have a positive impact on beneficiaries' (short-term) income and ability to smooth consumption (del Ninno, Subbarao, and Milazzo 2009).

The cost-effectiveness of public works as a safety net is enhanced when a number of design and implementation-related features are incorporated. These features include encouraging self-targeting (by setting the wage or in-kind rate appropriately); establishing the optimal labor intensity; responding to seasonality variations; exhibiting gender sensitivity; maintaining transparency and accountability; and ensuring community involvement in project selection. (See del Ninno, Subbarao, and Milazzo 2009 for an elaboration of these points.)

Less clear is whether and how public works can be an effective "activation" strategy that helps workers improve their employability and income-earning potential. The limited evaluations on the effects of public works on employability suggest that participation improves postprogram employment

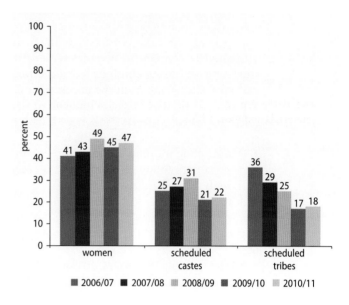

FIGURE 6.9 **Participation of women and members of scheduled castes and tribes in the Mahatma Gandhi National Rural Employment Guarantee Program, 2006/07–2010/11**
(share of person days of employment provided)

Sources: World Bank 2011b and MGNREGA website (http://nrega.nic.in).

chances for about half of participants but does not improve earnings (Betcherman and others 2004).[42]

Could these programs play a greater role in enhancing the labor market prospects of participants? Some programs attempt to activate participants in various ways. One way is to combine work with training. Another, used in a few programs in Bangladesh, is to allocate a portion of wages to a savings account used to support future self-employment.

The lack of evaluation evidence makes it difficult to empirically establish whether these, or other, design features are associated with success. In any event, policy makers need to be cautious in choosing the employability-related objectives they establish for public works programs. Experimenting with different activation designs would be worthwhile, especially in urban labor markets as the region continues to urbanize. Better monitoring and evaluation will be essential to identify and then disseminate good practices.

Training

Even under optimistic scenarios of educational attainment, the majority of prime-age and older workers in South Asian countries other than Sri Lanka will continue to have only primary education or less over the next 20 years (see chapter 5). Workers with little education will likely continue to hold informal jobs, suggesting both the importance of developing initiatives to help workers in the informal sector and the challenge of doing so with workers with a low skills base.

Most public training agencies and private sector trainers focus on the formal sector. Although some initiatives are in place that seek to improve the skills of informal workers, until recently they have been ad hoc in nature, making it difficult to estimate the number of workers they cover.

Many training initiatives do cover informal sector workers, but the numbers involved are small. In Afghanistan, vibrant private sector and NGO training activities exist for the informal sector, although it is extremely difficult to assess the size of these efforts. In India, several initiatives provide skills to the informal sector. Community polytechnics provide skills training within communities, with no entry prerequisites. The Jan Shikshan Sansthan (Institute for People's Education) focuses on unskilled workers in both rural and urban areas, offering courses ranging from candle and incense stick making to sewing and embroidery to computers. India's National Institute of Open Schooling provides skills training to disadvantaged youth. The Ministry of Labor and Employment's Modular Employable Skills program is also geared toward the informal sector. It provides vocational training to school leavers, existing workers, graduates of industrial training institutes, and others to improve their employability by optimally using the training infrastructure available in public and private institutions and within industry. Nepal's Department of Cottage and Small Industries and the Small Industry Development Board provide skill-oriented training programs and assistance in the operation of small enterprises and income-generating activities (such as textile manufacturing, tailoring, knitting, carpentry, batik painting, plumbing, house wiring, and radio and TV maintenance). Pakistan's Training for Rural Economic Empowerment program offers vocational, entrepreneurial, managerial, and literacy/numeracy skills to 2,400 trainees.

Training institutions play a limited role in improving skills in the informal sector. In most of South Asia, the mandate of formal training institutions includes training workers for the informal sector, but evidence shows that they are rarely successful in doing so. In India, for example, only 12 percent of graduates of formal training institutions enter the informal sector (World Bank 2007). Although similar numbers are not available from other countries, anecdotal evidence from Bangladesh and Nepal suggests that they face a similar situation.

Overall, current efforts through formal programs and training institutions are inadequate to meet the training needs of the large workforce in the informal sector, many of whom have never been to school. Because of its entry requirements and concentration in urban areas, the formal training system is not designed to offer skills to low-educated people, particularly people in the rural non-farm sector.

What distinguishes some informal sector employment from formal wage employment is the breadth of tasks that need to be performed, especially by self-employed workers, who typically need to complete specific jobs by themselves, from beginning to end (table 6.8). These self-employed workers must perform a variety of functions, including conducting initial market surveys, maintaining cost and quality control, and handling financing and marketing. Technical and business skills are important in enhancing productivity and the quality of goods and services produced. Improving skills will strengthen the ability to compete. Complementary services (access to credit, technology, markets, and information) appear to lead to better outcomes.[43]

Reorienting public training institutions is probably not the best solution to meeting the

TABLE 6.8 **Skill requirements in the informal sector**

Skill area	Training needs
Technical	• General upgrading of technical skills used in trade • Improved knowledge of materials used in trade • Practical ways to reduce waste of materials • Basic reading of designs and drawings • Repair of own equipment • Skills required for new product designs • Understanding of more advanced equipment and improved technologies • Basic knowledge of industrial production techniques
Management	• Costing, pricing, and related aspects of financial administration • Various aspects of marketing, including rudimentary market research • Customer relations, including creation of a customer data base • Division of labor in the workshop and personnel management • Input stock planning • Quality control • Workshop layout • Legal and fiscal regulations
Literacy and numeracy	• Functional language skills and higher educational attainment (to enhance trainability)
Other	• Knowledge of recent technological developments in the trades • Improvement in the teaching skills of master craftspeople (to increase the effectiveness of the training) • Ability to work cooperatively (why and how to work together, informally, or as a trade association)

Source: Johanson and Van Adams 2004.

training needs of the informal sector. Public institutions would find it difficult to make the changes and serve both the formal and informal sectors. Major investments would be needed to upgrade facilities and equipment, develop and retain new staff, and design curricula and materials to provide the package of skills described above. Such improvements would require far greater resources than are currently provided as public subsidies. Increased training fees would not generate much income in view of the lack of clear benefits of past training and constraints on family incomes of the target groups.

Trainers from local NGOs are often more effective in providing services that meet the needs of the informal economy. Anecdotal evidence on the impact of these programs is positive, although only a few programs have been evaluated.

One such program that has been carefully evaluated is the Afghanistan Skills Development Program. In view of its own inability to provide services in hard to reach and insecure rural provinces, the government contracted

with NGOs to provide skills training in diverse areas (such as business development, horticulture, food processing, and livestock) to farmers, underemployed youth, and poor women. In almost all provinces, people who received training reported significantly higher wages than those who did not. These positive impacts likely reflect the fact that the NGOs are providing tailor-made training catering to the needs of the local labor market.

A significant—and undocumented—amount of training in the informal sector occurs through informal apprenticeships and learning by doing. The model for this training is a simple one: an experienced tradesperson or master craftsperson teaches a trade to younger apprentices and workers.

More young people acquire competence through traditional (informal) apprenticeships than would be possible through the formal education system. Although data for South Asian countries are not available, figures for other countries with informal sectors of similar size suggest that 50–70 percent of employees in microenterprises in India may have obtained their skills through apprenticeships (World Bank 2007).

Effective informal apprenticeships have several advantages. They provide trainees with flexible and dynamic skills, are self-regulating, cost the government virtually nothing, and require little initial skill or experience, just a willingness to be trained by a master, often a relative. But they also have important limitations. They are based on traditional technologies and ideas from previous generations, and the quality of training is only as good as the skills of the master and his or her willingness and ability to pass them on. The theoretical aspect of learning is weak or absent; only the simplest skills are learned, resulting in low-quality products or services. Apprentices also often lack exposure to modern training systems and technologies as well as the innovative aspect of learning. The range of skills taught tends to be narrow, limited to a particular product or phase in production. These skills may quickly become outdated in rapidly changing labor markets.

Governments may not be the best deliverers of training for informal workers, but they have an important role to play as facilitators. Instead of delivering training themselves, governments could focus on creating an environment to support nonpublic providers by performing the following roles:

- Establishing a policy framework (regulations and incentives)
- Supporting curriculum development, the training of trainers, and competency-based skills testing
- Stimulating investment through tax incentives or financial support, in order to increase the capacity and the quality of training
- Revising apprenticeship acts that are outdated and contain regulations that hamper enterprise-based training.

An interesting concept in this regard is India's National Skills Development Corporation (NSDC), set up in 2009 as a nonprofit company to promote private sector involvement in skills development.[44] NSDC will perform three key functions:

- Stimulate private sector training providers, by providing seed capital and viability gap funding.
- Facilitate the direct involvement of private sector firms in the development of training programs and curricula, in part by supporting sector skills councils in priority sectors
- Focus on the informal sector, underprivileged segments of society, and "backward" areas, in which residents have not received adequate opportunities to acquire skills.

Although evidence is sparse on effective training programs for informal workers, some international experiences show some promise. One successful approach has been Mexico's Integral Quality and Modernization Program (CIMO, later renamed PAC and then PAP). Like India, Mexico is dominated by small and medium-size firms. The program shows that partnerships between the public and private sector to provide training and a range of support services can enhance the productivity of workers in the informal sector (box 6.5). The program was successful not only because the government facilitated the provision of training to small and medium-size enterprises but also because enterprises were provided with an integrated package of services, including information on technology, new production processes, quality control techniques, marketing, and how to run a business.

Some public-private partnerships have improved the quality of informal apprenticeships. Their strategy focuses on upgrading both the technical and management skills and the pedagogical skills of masters. Traditional apprenticeships can be linked with specialized training providers or master craftspeople, with the government acting as facilitator. There are examples of innovative financing as well, as exemplified by Kenya's Jua Kali project, in which vouchers for training are distributed to informal sector entrepreneurs (box 6.6).

BOX 6.5 Mexico's proactive approach to supporting small and medium-size enterprises

Mexico's Integral Quality and Modernization program, known as CIMO, is a good example of a comprehensive program that assists small and medium-size enterprises and has a sound embedded monitoring and evaluation effort. Launched in 1987, CIMO was one of several Mexican programs targeting small and medium-size enterprises. It focused on training and consulting by specifying its goal to improve productivity by increasing training levels, helping design training plans, and expanding the availability of training.

The program, administered by the Ministry of Labor, was decentralized to the state level in 2002 under the name Training Support Program (Programa de Apoyo a la Capacitación [PAC]) and in 2009 under the name Productivity Support Program (Programa de Apoyo para la Productividad [PAP]). There was also a change in the design of the program: before 2000, all training was provided by the private sector; after 2000, the program used only public providers. With an estimated budget of about $75 million, CIMO/PAC trained about 1.6 million workers between 2001 and 2006 and benefited more than 226,000 firms.

Before its decentralization, one of the unique features of CIMO was its comprehensive approach to addressing training. Because small and medium-size enterprises face multiple constraints, training alone may not enhance their productivity. In recognition of those constraints, CIMO provided an integrated package of training and consulting services through independent private instructors (while promoting firms' participation in defining their own training) as well as a range of industrial extension services.

Another noteworthy feature of the CIMO/PAC program is its monitoring, evaluation, and data collection. The collection of panel data allows for rigorous evaluation of these interventions. Evaluations of CIMO before its decentralization find that it was effective in improving the performance of targeted companies. Compared with firms in a control group, CIMO firms increased investments in worker training, had higher rates of capacity use, and were more likely to adopt quality control practices. These improved outcomes were associated with an increase in net productivity of 6–11 percent for CIMO participants. Evaluations of the program's performance after 2000 do not find significant effects on firms' productivity, although they do find an increase in worker training and the use of quality control practices.

Sources: López-Acevedo and Tinajero 2010; Tan and López-Acevedo 2005.

Support for self-employment and microenterprises

Interventions that support self-employment or microenterprise development can help informal sector workers improve their potential for generating income. Financial assistance has been the primary means of encouraging income-generating activities in most South Asian countries. In fact, since the 1970s and the founding of the Grameen Bank, South Asia has been at the forefront of the microfinancing movement, which has become prominent in international development.[45] Almost half of the people worldwide who use microfinance services live in South Asia (World Bank 2009). In contrast to other regions—particularly Latin America, where microfinance focuses on linking microentrepreneurs to the formal credit market—microfinance in South Asia focuses on reducing poverty.

Microfinance providers in South Asia reach more than 50 million clients.[46] Coverage of microfinance services ranges from 0.1 percent of the population in Afghanistan to more than 20 percent in Bangladesh (table 6.9). Demand for microcredit services far outstrips supply. Microfinance in the region has concentrated on women in rural areas, although in Bangladesh, and increasingly India, the share of urban clients is growing.

The principle underlying microcredit is activation: providing credit to individuals without access to formal banking services

---

BOX 6.6   Training informal workers: Kenya's Jua Kali experience

The Jua Kali (informal sector) project, funded by the International Development Association, aimed to upgrade skills and technology for about 25,000 informal sector manufacturing workers, increase the access of informal sector entrepreneurs to services, and improve the policy and institutional environment by removing restrictive laws and policies. A key feature of the project was a voucher program intended to introduce consumer choice, enabling informal sector operators to purchase the training they want wherever they want. Intermediaries (allocation agencies) were selected by competitive tender to market, allocate, and redeem vouchers in a decentralized way throughout Kenya. Allocation agencies received a fee equal to 3 percent of the value of vouchers issued. Vouchers could be used for any kind of training from any registered training provider.

Over the course of the project in the 1990s and the earlier part of the last decade, about 700 training providers prequalified for providing training. By early 2001, some 18,000 training vouchers had been issued.

The impact of the project on beneficiaries, evaluated through two tracer studies, has been highly positive. Employment among graduates was 50 percent higher than employment before training, and the income of surviving enterprises increased 50 percent. According to anecdotal evidence, some participants who received a voucher for basic training paid the full cost of more advanced training.

Lessons from this project include the following:

- The use of a voucher mechanism enabled the project to stimulate demand for training, technology, management, and marketing consultation by micro and small enterprises. A supply response was generated and a training market established to address these firms' needs.
- An unexpected impact of the voucher training program was the emergence of skilled craftspeople as the leading providers of training. In the first phase of the project, 85 percent of all vouchers went to pay for their services; only 15 percent went to training institutions. Entrepreneurs preferred receiving training from master craftspeople to training in formal institutions. This training was usually well adapted to entrepreneurs' need for short, practical training.
- Implementation experience underscores the importance of appropriate management arrangements. A project for the private sector is best managed by the private sector, with government playing a facilitating role.

Source: Johanson and Van Adams 2004.

TABLE 6.9   Coverage of microfinance in South Asia, by country, 2009/10

Country	Population 2010 (millions)	Number of microfinance borrowers 2009/2010 (millions)	Percentage of population
Afghanistan	31	0.3	0.1
Bangladesh	149	30.0	20.2
India	1,225	22.6	1.8
Nepal	30	1.8	6.0
Pakistan	174	1.9	1.1
Sri Lanka	21	2.5	12.0

Sources: Authors, based on data on number of microfinance clients from South Asian Microfinance Network (http://www.samn.eu/?q=microfinance-asia) and population figures from UN 2010.
Note: Data on number of clients are for 2010 for Afghanistan and Pakistan and 2009 for other countries (http://esa.un.org/unpd/wpp/unpp/panel_population.htm). With the exception of a few limited efforts to provide microcredit services as part of integrated development projects, Bhutan and Maldives do not have specific microfinance sectors.

in order to enable them to initiate or expand productive activities, usually in the form of self-employment or a household enterprise. An important limiting factor is the level of human capital among entrepreneurs. For this reason, adding training, counseling, and various forms of technical assistance to microfinance ("microfinance plus") is key to promoting business development among small-scale entrepreneurs. A key challenge from an activation perspective is to develop instruments that allow providers of microfinance to identify the entrepreneurs most likely to benefit from credit or associated subsidies.

The institutional structure of microfinance programs varies widely. NGOs, nonprofit microfinance institutions, and community-based organizations, including cooperatives, account for most of the outreach of financial services available to the poor in the region. The retail operations of development and commercial banks; post office banks; and, less often but increasingly, insurance companies provide a small amount of additional lending services. Commercial banks are less important to microfinance than they are in some other regions, such as Latin America, although in all countries except Afghanistan and Bangladesh, microfinance does have significant commercial bank linkages (EDA and APMAS 2006).[47]

This diverse set of institutional arrangements of microfinance programs is mirrored by a diversity of delivery systems. The Grameen model refers to a methodology first applied by the Grameen Bank of Bangladesh. Borrowers have to be a part of a small group that gets together with 7–10 other groups from the same village or neighborhood, forming a "center." By aggregating liabilities within each center, this model reduces the likelihood of default. This delivery system is the dominant methodology in Bangladesh. All retail development banks in Nepal, some institutions in Afghanistan and Pakistan, and some leading microfinance institutions in India also use this system.

The self-help group is the main approach to microfinance in India. It is based on the principle of revolving members' own savings. Savings thus precedes borrowing by members. Groups, made up of 15–25 members, operate a revolving fund that is supplemented with external financial assistance.

Another mode of delivery is cooperative programs, in which microfinance institutions provide financial services to individual clients organized into credit and savings cooperatives. All borrowers need to be members of the cooperative. Sri Lanka, with its large number of cooperative banks, relies heavily on this approach. India and Nepal have similar initiatives.

One of the main issues facing microfinance institutions relates to financial sustainability. A small number of gradually more efficient institutions account for a large share of the market; the majority of institutions are relatively weak, sustained mainly by the high level of subsidies provided by donors or governments (World Bank 2009). In Bangladesh, three of the top four microfinance institutions—ASA, BRAC, and Grameen Bank—show positive returns. These organizations account for some 11 million of an estimated 16 million clients.

India has a large number of loss-making microfinance institutions and relatively few viable ones. Political and social restrictions have inhibited many microfinance institutions from setting actuarially neutral interest rates, which affects their performance.

In Pakistan, the provision of microfinance on a sustainable basis is particularly challenging, partly as a result of substantial pressure from government officials, elected representatives, and the press to charge low interest rates. To date, the only microfinance institution that has become fully sustainable is the Kashf Foundation.

In Sri Lanka, the schemes under the Samurdhi program offer subsidized interest rates. They face default rates of 30–50 percent.

South Asia has numerous programs involving not only microfinance but other forms of assistance to support self-employment and microenterprise development. Table 6.10 lists some of these programs.

Both internationally and within the region, there is little evidence on the impact on employability and earnings of programs that support self-employment.[48] The few studies that exist suggest that the provision of services to support entrepreneurs often results in higher rates of business success and higher earnings (Betcherman and others 2004, 2007). In general, a combination of access to credit and support services, such as counseling, seems to have the best outcomes.

Few evaluations use rigorous methods or try to calculate cost-benefit ratios. One exception is a recent evaluation of a Sri Lanka program that uses training and financial support to encourage women to create and expand businesses (box 6.7).

TABLE 6.10   Selected programs supporting self-employment and microenterprises in South Asia, by country

Country/program	Institutional set-up	Target population	Services
Bangladesh			
Vulnerable Group Development for Ultra Poor	Directorate of Women's Affairs; funded by the European Union	Poor, landless women	Subsistence allowance, training
Employment Guarantee Scheme for Hard-Core Poor in Northern region	Bangladesh Rural Development Board (BRDB)	Poor	Training assistance in organizing income-generating activities
Urban-Based Marginal Women's Development Agency	Jatio Mahila Sangstha	Poor, assetless women	Training, financial assistance
India			
Swarnjayanti Gram Swarozgar Yojana (now the National Rural Livelihoods Mission)	Ministry of Rural Development	Poor families in rural areas	Financial assistance, training, support for self-help groups
Swarna Jayanti Shahari Rojgar Yojana	Ministry of Housing and Urban Poverty Alleviation	Urban unemployed or underemployed	Financial assistance, training, support for self-help groups
Prime Minister's Employment Generation Programme	Khadi and Village Industries Commission	Unemployed youth	Credit and subsidies
Rajiv Gandhi Udyami Mitra Yojana	Ministry of Micro, Small, and Medium Enterprises	Potential first- generation entrepreneurs	Technical assistance, counseling
Nepal			
Great Himalayan Trail Development Program	Ministry of Tourism and Civil Aviation, in partnership with Stichting Nederlandse Vrijwilligers (a Dutch development organization), local authorities, industry associations, and communities	Local communities	Skills training, support for entrepreneurs
Production Credit for Rural Women	Ministry of Local Development, various banks; funded by the International Fund for Agriculture Development	Poor women	Microcredit
Rural Self-Reliance Fund	Nepal Rastra Bank	Poor and specified vulnerable groups	Wholesale provision of microcredit
Microenterprise Development Programme	Ministry of Industry, multilateral donors	Poor and specified vulnerable groups	Training, microcredit
Poverty Alleviation Fund	Board reports to prime minister, community-based organizations, and NGOs; funded by International Development Association	Rural poor and vulnerable groups	Training, technical assistance
Development Project Service Center (DEPROSC) Nepal	Executive director reports to seven-member board; implementation follows guidelines of Nepal Rastra Bank	Poor women	Microcredit, training, entrepreneurial development
Pakistan			
Rural Support Programs	National and provincial Rural Support Programs	Poor people, especially women	Microcredit, microinsurance, training
Khushali Bank	Created under Rural Support Programs; four banks are shareholders	Poor people, particularly women	Microcredit
Khasf Foundation	Pakistan Poverty Alleviation Fund, U.K. Department of International Development, and Agha Khan Foundation provided core funding	Women from low-income households	Microcredit

(continues next page)

TABLE 6.10 (continued)

Country/program	Institutional set-up	Target population	Services
Sri Lanka			
Samurdhi Authority	Ministry of Economic Development	Low-income groups	Microcredit
Small Enterprise Development Division	Ministry of Youth Affairs	Youth, especially dropouts	Microcredit
	Ministry of Labour Relations	Unemployed	Microcredit
Sarvodaya Economic Enterprise Development Services	SEEDS (NGO), donors	Poor people, women and girls, migrants	Microcredit

Source: Authors' compilation, based on country research on active labor market programs.

BOX 6.7 **Business training and financial support for self-employed women in Sri Lanka**

Self-employment is a potentially important form of employment for women in South Asia. However, most women-owned enterprises are small and barely generate a subsistence-level income for their owners. Policy efforts have sought to enhance the likelihood of women owning small businesses and increase the earnings of women business owners.

Business training programs are a popular policy used for this purpose. Preliminary results from a randomized experiment in Sri Lanka offer insight into whether such training works and whether it can complement financial assistance.

The study worked with two random samples, of about 600 women each. One sample included women operating subsistence enterprises. The second included women who were out of the labor force but interested in starting a business. Both samples were randomly divided into three groups: a control group; a group invited to attend a seven- to nine-day business training course based on the International Labour Organization's "Generate, Start, and Improve Your Business" programs; and a group invited to receive this training and receive a cash grant of Rs 15,000 ($130) upon completing the training.

Business training sped up the creation of new businesses, but it did not ultimately lead to more new businesses. Women who were out of the labor force were more likely to have a business 4 months and 8 months after the training program, but by 16 months the control group had the same rate of business ownership. Receiving cash in addition to training led to even larger short-run effects but no difference in business ownership after 16 months.

Although training did not seem to lead to more businesses, it did result in more successful businesses

for the sample of women who had been out of the labor force. Firms created by women who received training earned higher profits 16 months later than firms created by women in the control group. These results suggest some success for business training among women interested in opening a business who currently do not work.

For women already operating businesses, training alone led to some improvement in business practices (they were more likely to implement some of the ideas taught in the training course), but it did not lead to any improvement in profits, sales, or capital stock. In contrast, the combination of business training and the cash grant led to large and significant improvements in business performance for these enterprises, with profits rising 36–50 percent and capital stock increasing by about the amount of the grant. As previous work with female microenterprises finds little return to capital alone, the authors of this study argue that the results suggest important complementarities between training and access to capital.

Together with other recent experiments with women-owned microenterprises (Bruhn and Zia 2011; Gine and Mansuri 2011), these results suggest that it is much easier to get women to start enterprises than it is to get these enterprises to grow. Only 1–2 percent of the enterprises started by women who underwent business training employed any paid workers who were not family members. Female self-employment is thus largely a means to increase income and provide a living for enterprise owners themselves rather than a means of generating additional jobs for others.

Source: de Mel, McKenzie, and Woodruff 2011.

There is more evaluation evidence on microfinance programs. The focus of these studies has typically been on the antipoverty effects and effects on microenterprise creation and survival, but studies have also considered other outcome variables (for example, health, education, empowerment of women). Longer-run labor market outcomes (for example, employability and earnings) have been included less often.

There is a some controversy over the impact of microfinance, but, on balance, evaluations point to positive effects.[49] Findings are heterogeneous, with welfare effects ranging from nonexistent to significant (Armendáriz de Aghion and Morduch 2004). Many evaluations use flawed methodology, with selection bias and other issues confounding results (EDA and APMAS 2006).

Many concerns can be addressed with random experimental designs, which tend to be rare in the study of microfinance. One exception is a randomized evaluation in Hyderabad that found that the opening of branches of a microfinance institution had significant and positive impacts on business start-ups and the profitability of existing businesses, but no impact on average household consumption. The results led the authors to conclude that "microcredit therefore may not be the 'miracle' that is sometimes claimed on its behalf, but it does allow households to borrow, invest, and create and expand businesses" (Banerjee and others 2009, p. 21).

Extension of social insurance to informal workers

A key question for labor market policy in South Asia is whether social insurance models can be extended to protect informal workers from risks related to income and employment and to provide a vehicle for pension, disability, and health coverage. Efficient programs with adequate benefits and wide coverage play an important prevention function, by reducing the vulnerability of workers and their families to the negative impact of various shocks. They

also fill a promotion function, by providing workers with more room to maneuver in making human capital investments and transitioning to better employment opportunities.

Bismarkian social insurance systems linked to formal employment relationships have limited scope in South Asia. In the absence of extensive formalization, the key question is whether the formal social insurance model can be modified and adapted to the realities of informal sector workers in the region.

Plans to extend social insurance to informal workers need to take into account possible effects on the incidence of informality itself. Employers may be more likely to seek ways to opt out of formal contributory systems if they know employees can access social protection in other ways. Depending on how programs are financed, workers themselves may prefer to remain informal. Although the extension of social insurance (for example, for pensions, health, and disability) would address the vulnerability problem associated with informality, other problems, including the fiscal and productivity disadvantages of large informal sectors, would remain. Thus, although there would be benefits to extending social protection coverage beyond the formal sector, the tradeoffs should not be ignored.

Various social insurance schemes for informal workers have been introduced in the region. To encourage informal sector participation, the new pension law in Maldives provides for matching contributions for informal sector workers such as fishers. Sri Lanka has voluntary pension schemes for informal farmers, fishers, and the self-employed. NGOs also provide microinsurance schemes that protect against specific risks.

India has been active in trying to extend social insurance to informal sector workers. Numerous welfare funds and insurance schemes exist nationally, at the state level (in, for example, Kerala and Tamil Nadu), and by occupation (covering, for example, workers making hand-rolled cigarettes). Informal worker associations, self-help groups, and other organizations have also been active in this area (IHD 2011).

Proposals have been made—by, for example, the National Commission for Enterprises in the Unorganised Sector (NCEUS)—to institute a national minimum social security. The NCEUS proposal sought to guarantee minimum coverage for health, death and disability, and pension benefits for all workers, organized and unorganized, earning less than Rs. 6,500 in 2005. Benefits were to have been financed through equal contributions, at least notionally, from government, employers, and employees. In fact, the burden would have been greatest on government, as it would have had to cover the employer share when an employer could not be identified and the employee share in the case of the poor. Although the NCEUS proposal was the spark behind the Unorganised Workers Social Security Act of 2008, that bill was much more modest in scope (IHD 2011).[50]

The limited scope of the Unorganised Workers Social Security Act underlines the difficulties of implementing an overarching policy framework for social insurance in the informal sector. Given the heterogeneity of informal workers, it seems more likely that broader coverage could be achieved by creating and expanding different programs with different design features—programs that run alongside existing contributory programs for the formal sector.[51]

The potential for extending social insurance to the informal sector depends heavily on financing and the degree to which individuals are able to contribute. Workers in the informal sector fall into three broad categories, with the first accounting for only a very small share of the population:

- High-income individuals (for example, professionals and large landowners), who are able to protect themselves through savings and insurance schemes already available in the market
- Middle-income individuals, who may be able to benefit from insurance and pension coverage and could afford to pay for a significant portion of the required contributions
- Low-income individuals, who are unable to make any contributions beyond a very marginal level.

Given the high prevalence of individuals with no or limited capacity to contribute, coverage can be expanded only if governments are willing to provide significant subsidies. The level of subsidies needs to be determined in light of the mandate of the programs, and the subsidies need to be allocated and financed in ways that minimize labor market distortions.

Annex 6A   Additional tables and figures on labor market regulations and institutions

FIGURE 6A.1   **Trade union membership in India, 1987–2006**

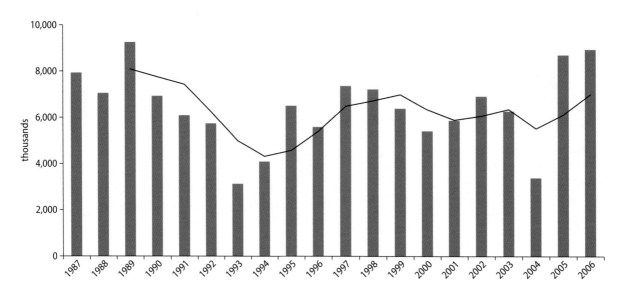

Source: Indiastat.com.
Note: Trend line indicates three-year moving average of membership in workers' unions submitting returns in India.

FIGURE 6A.2   **Trade union membership in Pakistan, 1999–2008**

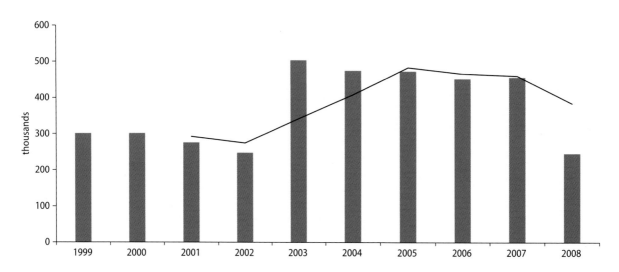

Source: Federal Bureau of Statistics Pakistan 2011.
Note: Trend line indicates three-year moving average of membership in reporting unions.

FIGURE 6A.3   Trade union membership in Sri Lanka, 1987–2006

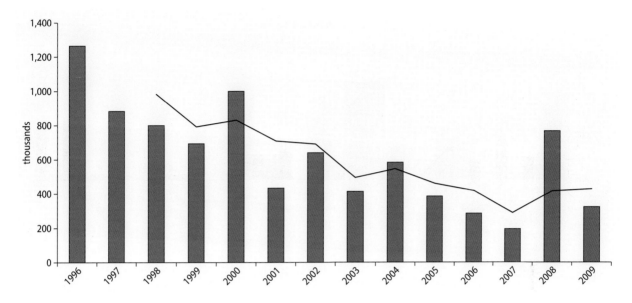

Source: Department of Labour, Sri Lanka.
Note: Fluctuation in total membership is a result of poor reporting by unions. Trend line indicates three-year moving average.

FIGURE 6A.4   **Percentage of unionized workers in India, by employment status and sector, 1994 and 2000**

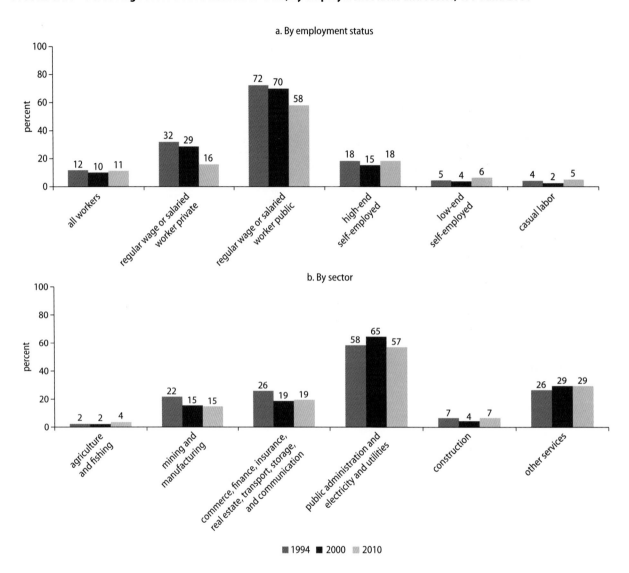

Source: Authors, based on data from various rounds of National Sample Survey.
Note: Union membership, based on household data, includes not only registered trade unions but also membership in associations of owners, self-employed workers, and any association whose objective is to look into the interests of its members. It is not possible to break membership down into trade unions and other associations.

FIGURE 6A.5   Job creation and destruction flows in Sri Lanka and selected groups of countries

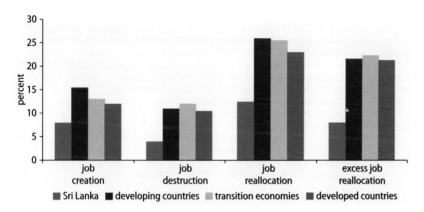

Source: Gunatilaka and Vodopivec 2010 (based on 2003 Sri Lanka urban enterprise survey using employment data for three years in the early 2000s).
Note: Transition economies include Estonia (1997–2000), Hungary (1994–2000), Latvia (1994–99), Romania (1994–2000), and Slovenia (1992–2000). Developed countries include Canada (1985–97), Denmark (1982–94), France (1991–96), Finland (1989–98), Germany (1978–99), Italy (1988–93), Portugal (1984–94), the Netherlands (1994–97), the United Kingdom (1987–98), and the United States (1989–97). Developing countries include Argentina (1997–2001) and Mexico (1987–2000). Job reallocation is the sum of job creation and job destruction, where job creation is the sum of new jobs in firms that expanded during the previous year, and job destruction is the sum of employment losses in firms that contracted. Another measure, net employment growth, is the difference between the job reallocation and net employment growth. Using these measures, excess job reallocation computes the difference between job reallocation and net employment growth. This indicator measures the extent of job flows over and above what is needed to accommodate a needed change in net employment; hence, it reflects the intensity of enterprise restructuring. All variables are expressed as a percentage of the average of the stocks at the beginning and end of the period.

FIGURE 6A.6   **Tax wedges in South Asian and international comparator countries**

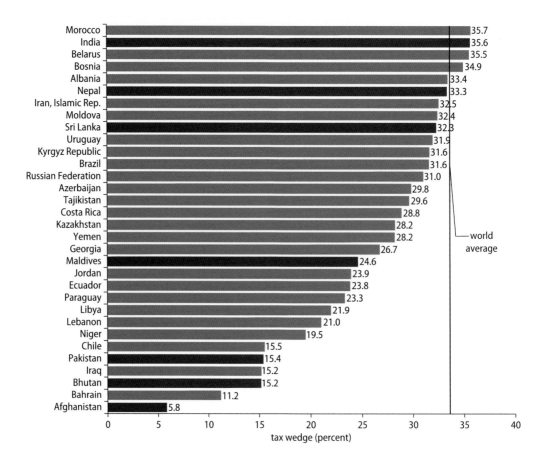

Sources: Authors, based on latest data on social security contributions available from the International Social Security Administration. Data on average wages and income taxes were collected by staff at the country level.

FIGURE 6A.7   **Ratio of minimum wage to median casual and formal sector wage, by states in India, 2008**

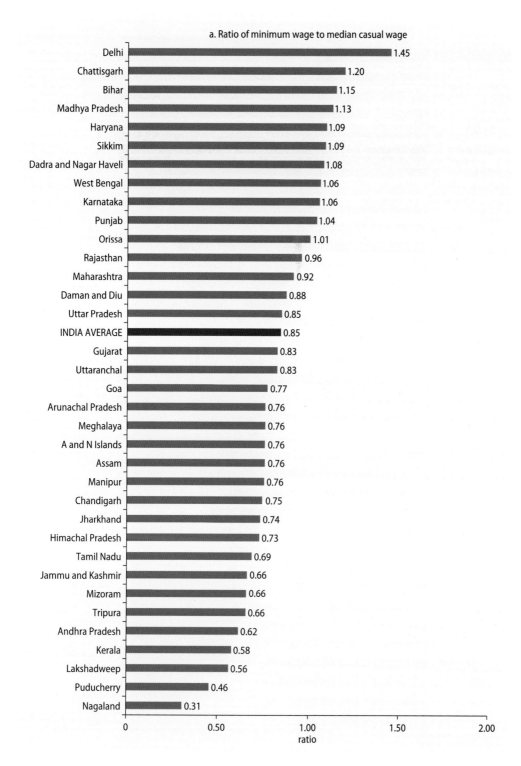

(continues next page)

FIGURE 6A.7   Ratio of minimum wage to median casual and formal sector wage, by states in India, 2008 (continued)

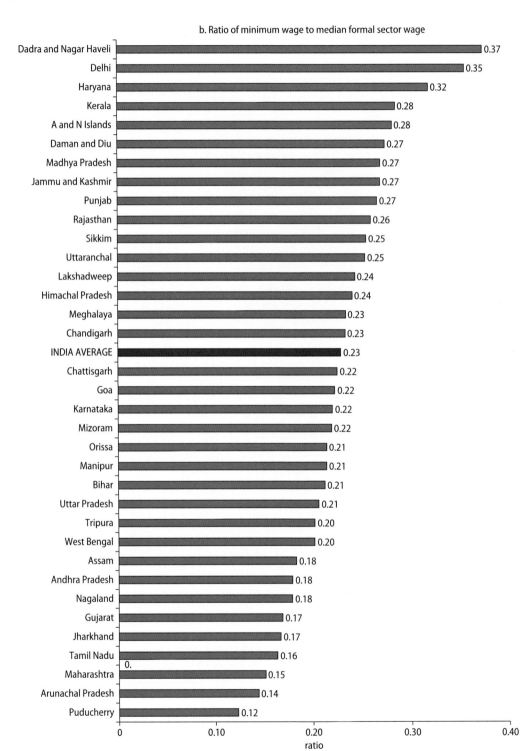

b. Ratio of minimum wage to median formal sector wage

State	ratio
Dadra and Nagar Haveli	0.37
Delhi	0.35
Haryana	0.32
Kerala	0.28
A and N Islands	0.28
Daman and Diu	0.27
Madhya Pradesh	0.27
Jammu and Kashmir	0.27
Punjab	0.27
Rajasthan	0.26
Sikkim	0.25
Uttaranchal	0.25
Lakshadweep	0.24
Himachal Pradesh	0.24
Meghalaya	0.23
Chandigarh	0.23
INDIA AVERAGE	0.23
Chattisgarh	0.22
Goa	0.22
Karnataka	0.22
Mizoram	0.22
Orissa	0.21
Manipur	0.21
Bihar	0.21
Uttar Pradesh	0.21
Tripura	0.20
West Bengal	0.20
Assam	0.18
Andhra Pradesh	0.18
Nagaland	0.18
Gujarat	0.17
Jharkhand	0.17
Tamil Nadu	0.16
Maharashtra	0.15
Arunachal Pradesh	0.14
Puducherry	0.12

ratio

Sources: Authors, based on data on minimum wages and state GDP per capita from IndiaStat.com and data on wages from labor force survey.

TABLE 6A.1   Selected aspects of employment protection in India

Type of employment protection	Legal provisions
Procedures for individual notification and dismissal	• Written notice to employee • Employee given sufficient warning and opportunity to respond • Employers with at least 100 workers must give government 60 days' notice before dismissing worker and await its approval before doing so
Notice period for individual dismissals	• Workers small firms with 4 or more years of tenure: 1 month • Workers at large firms with at least 20 years of tenure: 3 months
Severance pay for individual dismissals	• Workers with 4 or more years of tenure: 2 months • Workers with at least 20 years of tenure: 10 months
Economic reason as valid reason for dismissal	• Permitted, but in absence of agreement between worker and employer, last person to be employed in category should be one dismissed
Maximum time to make complaint of unfair dismissal	• No time limit
Compensation for unfair dismissal	• Court orders reinstatement in most cases (with or without back pay) • In extreme cases, court may order compensation instead of reinstatement • Typical compensation for employee with 20 years of tenure is 42 months' wages • Typical three to four years for labor courts to settle disputes and make award
Definition and notification requirements or additional procedures for collective dismissals	• No special regulations or additional costs
Valid cases for fixed-term contracts	• Limited for work of temporary nature likely to be finished within a limited time • Some industries (information technology, business process outsourcing); export processing zones, and special economic zones in some states are exempted
Maximum number of fixed-term contracts	• No limits on number of renewals or maximum duration
Temporary agency work	• Allowed in noncore activities; prohibited in some industries or firms • No limits on durations or renewals • Contractors and firms with more than 20 employees required to obtain license (renewable every 12 months) and pay fees before engaging contract workers • Contractors required to report changes in number of workers or conditions of work to licensing authority • Wages and conditions of work of contract worker must be same as direct employees performing same type of work

Source: Authors' compilation, based on information in OECD 2009.

TABLE 6A.2 **Job creation and destruction rates in large manufacturing firms in India, by employment type, 2001–08**
(percent)

Type of worker/year	Job creation rate	Job destruction rate	Net job growth rate	Job reallocation rate	Job excess reallocation rate
Contract workers					
2001	15.3	18.7	−3.3	34.0	30.7
2002	19.1	19.1	0.0	38.2	38.2
2003	18.2	16.0	2.2	34.1	32.0
2004	21.3	16.2	5.2	37.5	32.3
2005	21.4	14.5	6.9	35.9	29.0
2006	24.8	14.5	10.3	39.3	28.9
2007	22.9	14.0	8.9	36.8	28.0
2008	23.6	13.8	9.9	37.4	27.5
Total	24.5	15.6	8.9	40.1	31.2
Noncontract workers					
2001	6.5	10.1	−3.6	16.6	13.0
2002	7.6	10.1	−2.4	17.7	15.3
2003	7.5	9.0	−1.5	16.5	15.0
2004	8.2	10.0	−1.8	18.2	16.4
2005	9.5	7.9	1.6	17.4	15.8
2006	9.7	7.9	1.8	17.6	15.8
2007	11.5	7.4	4.1	18.9	14.8
2008	11.9	6.7	5.2	18.6	13.4
Total	9.1	9.8	−0.7	18.9	18.1
All employees					
2001	6.6	10.2	−3.6	16.7	13.2
2002	7.8	9.8	−2.0	17.7	15.6
2003	7.9	8.8	−0.9	16.7	15.8
2004	8.9	9.3	−0.4	18.2	17.8
2005	10.1	7.4	2.7	17.6	14.8
2006	10.9	7.1	3.8	18.0	14.3
2007	12.2	7.0	5.2	19.2	14.0
2008	13.0	6.6	6.4	19.6	13.3
Total	9.8	8.6	1.2	18.4	17.1

Source: Authors, based on data from various rounds of the Annual Survey of Industries.
Note: See figure 6A.5 for definitions.

TABLE 6A.3   Minimum wage policies in South Asia, by country

Country	Minimum wage setting	Coverage	Latest available minimum wage	Year of last update of minimum wage
Afghanistan	One minimum wage set for public sector workers.	Public sector workers	Af 4,000 a month	2009
Bangladesh	Three-person national minimum wage board convenes every five years to set minimum wages by industry.	Minimum wage does not apply to categories of workers excluded from general coverage of the Labor Act of 2006 under §1(4) (for example government offices, small establishments run by family members).	Sectors not covered by industry-specific minimum wages: Tk 1,800 a month Garment industry: Tk 3,000 a month Shrimp industry: Tk 2,510 a month	Garment industry: 2010 Shrimp industry: 2009
Bhutan	Ministry of Labor and Human Resources, in consultation with the government, employers, and employees, fixes minimum wage or wages.	National coverage	Nu 3,000 a month	2010
India	Minimum wage set at state level by scheduled sectors and occupations.	Workers in sectors/occupations categorized as scheduled sector/ occupation in a particular state	National minimum wage (nonbinding): Rs 115 a day	2011
Maldives	One minimum wage for public sector.	Public sector is covered. Employment Act of 2008 provides a mechanism to establish a minimum wage in the private sector.	Rf 2,600 a month	2008
Nepal	Government sets monthly minimum wage set for four skill categories (unskilled, semiskilled, skilled, and high skilled). Daily minimum wage set for daily wage workers. Separate provisions made on industry basis.	Private sector workers and employees in enterprises of more than 10 workers and enterprises operating in industrial districts established by the government.	Minimum monthly wage for unskilled workers: NPR 6200 Minimum daily wage: NPR 231	2011
Pakistan	Federal government sets minimum wages for unskilled workers at the national level, through an ordinance. Provincial governments then adjust federal minimum wage to account for regional differences and skill levels.	Workers in agricultural sector and people employed by federal or provincial governments are not covered by minimum wage legislation.	PRs 7,000 a month	2010
Sri Lanka	Minister of Labour may set up wages boards by trade (occupation), sector, or region to recommend minimum wages by grade levels of jobs within each category.	Bases on scope of wage boards.	Agriculture (average for plantation sector): SL Rs 235.15 a day Manufacturing: SL Rs 247.04 a day Construction: SL Rs 292.50 a day	2009

Sources: Authors, based on data from ILO database; U.S. Department of State; national labor force and household surveys.

Notes

1. Labor market and social protection interventions often straddle these functions. For example, public works can play both an activation and a safety net role. This chapter does not address wider aspects of social protection, such as the provision of pension benefits and health care services, except in terms of how they may affect job creation and the functioning of the labor market.
2. As discussed in this chapter, voluntary social security schemes have begun to emerge for informal sector workers, but they cover only a small share of them. The various schemes in India are estimated to cover less than 10 percent of the unorganized labor force (World Bank 2011b). In Sri Lanka, voluntary social security schemes cover an estimated 0.5 million members of the workforce of roughly 7.5 million (Gunatilaka 2011).
3. For example, India's 1948 Factories' Act, one of the main laws governing working conditions, applies to manufacturing establishments with at least 10 workers if the establishment uses power and at least 20 workers if it does not. See table 6.4 for coverage of laws that protect workers against redundancy in South Asian countries.
4. IHD (2011) and NCEUS (2009) provide estimates of the intended coverage of various labor laws in India. They estimate that 12 million workers were covered by the Factories Act in 1999/2000. The Ministry of Labor estimates coverage (generally based on enterprises that have submitted returns under the act) of 8.8 million workers the same year. The first estimate translates into 3 percent of the total workforce; the second translates into 2.2 percent of the total workforce. Together, they suggest coverage of about three-quarters of the workers intended to be covered.
5. The possible exception is Nepal, where estimates of union density in the private sector range from about 29 percent of the workforce (for firms in the formal sector surveyed in the 2009 enterprise surveys) to 75 percent of the formal work force in 2010 (http://www.state.gov/g/drl/rls/hrrpt/). In Sri Lanka, the corresponding estimates are 11 percent of the nonagricultural private labor force and 26 percent of the workforce of firms included in the 2004 enterprise survey sample.
6. Data are typically based on returns filed by unions. Unions may not file returns in a timely manner or not at all. They can therefore provide an unreliable picture especially on trends. Statistics cited in the 2010 U.S. Department of State Country Reports on Human Rights Practices at http://www.state.gov/g/drl/rls/hrrpt/ give a similar picture—with estimated union membership of 13–15 million in India, and estimated union densities of approximately 10 percent in Sri Lanka, under 1 percent in Nepal, 3 percent in Pakistan, and 4 percent in Bangladesh. In India, where household data for 2010 provide information on union membership, the estimated density is higher (11 percent) (see annex figure 6A.4), but the figure includes self-employed workers and members of associations of owners and other associations whose objective is to look after the interests of their members.
7. Median monthly earnings in for wage workers with social security were Rs. 5,332 in India (2010), NPR 5,128 in Nepal (2008), and SL Rs7,881 in Sri Lanka (2008). These earnings exceeded those of workers without coverage by a factor of 3.1 in India, 1.9 in Nepal, and 1.7 in Sri Lanka. Wage workers who were members of unions had mean/median monthly earnings that were about 2.5 times those of nonunion members in India (National Sample Survey 1999/2000). Heltberg and Vodopivec (2004) estimate that the earnings of wage workers in Termination of Employment of Workmen Act (TEWA) jobs were 11–12 percent higher than those of workers in informal jobs in 1999/2000 after taking into account differences in education and other characteristics.
8. See http://www.ilo.org/declaration/lang--en/index.htm.
9. Afghanistan has signaled its intention to ratify its three conventions that are outstanding, but the government has indicated the need for ILO assistance to ensure and support this process. Nepal has delayed ratification of C.87, citing political instability and the period of political transition as reasons for delay. Bangladesh identifies difficulties in addressing the large informal sector where child labor is engaged as an obstacle in ratifying C. 138 in 2001. India has cited various issues complicating ratification of the collective bargaining and freedom of association and child labor conventions. For details on ratification status by country, see http://www.ilo.org/declaration/
10. In Afghanistan, India, and Nepal, the basic legal provisions on freedom of association

and collective bargaining are provided in the constitution as well as in national legislation; in India, judicial decisions have also upheld these rights. In Bangladesh, the Labor Act of 2006 not only establishes minimum age requirements, it also strengthens the labor administration for enforcement. In addition to the constitution, about a dozen pieces of legislation provide the basic legal provisions on child labor in India. In Nepal, the principle of and rights to freedom of association and collective bargaining are enshrined in the 2007 interim constitution as well as national legislation.

11. See http://www.ilo.org/declaration/ and http://www.state.gov/g/drl/rls/hrrpt/.

12. Particularly relevant are the rules governing whether and how workers can be dismissed for "economic" reasons (shrinking markets, increasing competitiveness, and so forth). This class of terminations stands in contrast to dismissals for "noneconomic" reasons, such as job performance.

13. Freeman (1993) characterizes these two perspectives as the "institutionalist" and "distortionist" views. For an updated interpretation, see Freeman (2009).

14. Cross-country comparisons of employment protection rules need to be viewed with some caution, especially because of the importance of enforcement, which is difficult to take into account. National settings can matter as well. The Doing Business database includes almost all employment protection legislation. Its indicators are based primarily on laws and regulations, with country scores calculated by local experts. See www.doingbusiness.org for scores and methodological details.

15. The main sources of uncertainty related to the legislation arise from interpretation and court judgments on what constitutes "core" or "perennial" activities, for which contracts are prohibited, and pressure to absorb contract labor into permanent employment. Andhra Pradesh has relaxed the use of contract labor in "core" activities; Goa has tightened the prohibition of contract labor in "noncore" activities.

16. The relevant legislation is the West Pakistan Industrial and Commercial Employment (Standing Orders) Ordinance of 1968. Fixed-term contracts can be used only in "objectively defined cases."

17. In Sri Lanka, prior approval is necessary only when the worker does not consent in writing to the lay-off. This is different from India, where Chapter VB of the Industrial Dispute Acts requires establishments with 100 or more workers to gain prior approval from government even if workers give their consent. Under Chapter VA of the act, which applies to enterprises employing 50 or more workers, employers are obligated to inform the government of dismissals rather than ask for their consent. The clause does not specifically mention worker consent. However, if workers do not consent, they resort to dispute resolution.

18. Employers need the authorization of the commissioner of labor for each intended layoff if the employee worked for at least 180 days the year before termination and does not give written consent to the termination. The commissioner has the power to grant or refuse permission to terminate services.

19. The level of pay is determined by two variables: years of service with the employer (past service) and the age of the worker (denied future service). It is relatively high for young workers and those with short service, exceeding the average for all the regions of the world. For older workers and those with long service, the severance pay determined by the formula is more in line with international practice (Vodopevic 2004).

20. "Nonperformance" is a generic problem with unfunded severance systems: employers' liabilities rise when they are likely to be in financial difficulty. This problem becomes most acute during recessions. During the recent economic crisis, labor authorities took unprecedented steps to enable firms to weather the crisis. Employers were allowed to temporarily lay off workers for a period of three months on half pay on application to and approval by the commissioner of labor. If after three months the employer was still unable to resume operations as normal, he or she was required to apply for a second temporary lay-off (Gunatilaka 2011).

21. The OECD measure calculates strictness of employment protection legislation based on 21 indicators covering three areas of employment protection: dismissal protection for individual workers with regular contracts, additional costs for collective dismissals, and regulations governing temporary contracts. Summary

scores for each area are calculated as weighted averages of the relevant indicators. An overall employment protection legislation measure is calculated as a weighted average of the three summary scores. For details, see http://www .oecd.org/employment/protection.

22. Since the Industrial Disputes Act was amended in 1965, any nonmutual layoff, retrenchment, or closure becomes an industrial dispute, going first to the Ministry of Labor for conciliation and then, if conciliation fails, to tribunals of courts, which often order reinstatement.

23. The more recent research builds on the work of Besley and Burgess (2004), who exploit variations across Indian states and over time in amendments to central legislation. The Besley-Burgess index of state employment protection legislation has been controversial (see Ahsan and Pagés 2009; Gupta, Hasan and Kumar 2009; and OECD 2007 for criticisms and approaches to addressing them).

24. Analysis of the full sample of manufacturing firms in the Annual Survey of Industries data for 2000–08 shows increases in formal sector manufacturing beginning in 2005 in both large (100 or more employees) firms and smaller firms. Large firms account for 70 percent of formal manufacturing employment. The analysis also shows rapid growth in the use of contract labor: the share of contract labor increased from 12 percent of total formal manufacturing employment in 1999 to 24 percent in 2008. The biggest increases were in large firms (100 or more employees), but the share also increased (from 12 percent to 19 percent) in smaller firms. The job creation/ job destruction analysis, which relies on panel data, uses all firms for which two consecutive years of data are available. This analysis is possible only for firms with more than 100 employees. Results for contract workers should be treated with some caution, as a zero for contract workers in one year could simply reflect nonreporting and hence lead to artificially large job creation or destruction figures.

25. Comparisons of enterprise survey results over time are not shown in figure 6.7, which pools all surveys for individual countries.

26. Many countries in the Europe and Central Asia region have large tax wedges, with unfavorable employment consequences (Rutkowski 2007).

27. See Freeman (2009) for a more detailed review. Minimum wages are not an effective antipoverty tool.

28. The discussion of compliance and dispute resolution draws on Kyloh (2008) for Nepal, World Bank (2006) for Pakistan, and Gunatilaka (2011) for Sri Lanka.

29. Information for India suggests that payoffs under voluntary retirement schemes are far above the severance pay provided in the Industrial Disputes Act and that average observed costs place India among the most costly in the world for dismissals (Debroy 2011; OECD 2007a). Use of golden handshakes does require approval by trade unions.

30. Labor legislation may be only part of the story. In Sri Lanka, for example, it is difficult to disentangle the effects of TEWA, the Payment of Gratuity Act, and the Inland Revenue Act, as all three kick in at a firm size threshold of 14 workers (Gunatilaka 2011). Gunatilaka and Vodopevic (2010) find suggestive evidence that all three are likely responsible for the irregular size distribution of firms and limited growth of firms with 14 workers. Abidoye, Orazem, and Vodopivec (2009) test this hypothesis by applying a difference-in-differences method to a panel data set of formal sector firms. They distinguish between firms in export processing zones (EPZs), which enjoy tax exemptions and other incentives offered by the Board of Investment, and others. They find that non-EPZ firms at or below the threshold are less likely to increase employment than non-EPZ firms above the threshold. Above the threshold, non-EPZ firms are more likely to shed workers, and EPZ firms are more likely to add workers. At all sizes, EPZ firms are more likely to add workers than non-EPZ firms.

31. Firms reporting incidents reported that on average, making informal payments cut the number of visits and time spent in dealing with inspections by about half.

32. Conciliation normally succeeds in cases in which an agreement could have been arrived at without conciliation (NCEUS 2009).

33. Information on these programs comes from country studies of active labor market programs commissioned for this book.

34. Drèze and Khera (2009) find considerable latent demand for public works in their study of six northern states. In other states, such as Kerala, field studies report a lack of demand (Jacob and Varghese 2006).

35. The Professional Institutional Network of the Mahatma Gandhi National Rural Employment Guarantee Act (http://www.nrega.net/pin) is a

network of institutions, including the Indian Institutes of Management, the Indian Institutes of Technology, the National Institute of Rural Development, agriculture universities, the Administrative Staff College of India, think tanks, civil society organizations, and other professional institutes. It was created by the Ministry of Rural Development as an integrated structure for monitoring, appraising, diagnosing implementation constraints, and recommending remedial action and sustainable interventions to enhance the quality of the program.

36. Moreover, there is little evidence that state-funded unemployment benefits are always made.

37. In their survey of 100 MNREGA worksites spread across six northern states, Drèze and Khera (2009) find that a majority of people employed in the program come from the most disadvantaged segments of society.

38. An important question to be examined is the extent to which this national picture applies at the state level, where there are important differences in implementation.

39. A more detailed picture of participation in MGNREGA and a fuller evaluation of the program should be obtained from special purpose surveys designed to assess the program.

40. These shares of participation by social group from administrative data for 2010 are consistent with those obtained from the 2009/10 National Sample Survey.

41. See Ambasta, Shankar, and Shah (2008) and CSE (2008) for a discussion of the quality of assets.

42. At the time of this review, nine rigorous evaluations of public works programs in developing countries were identified. Of these, five found that participants had higher post-program employment rates than nonparticipants in the control group, and four found no effect. None of the three studies that looked at earnings found any positive effect.

43. Some training programs in South Asia are also beginning to reorient themselves to the nature of informal employment. In Nepal, for example, the recently introduced Adolescent Girls Employment Initiative targets unemployed girls and girls working in the informal sector. In addition to providing technical training, the initiative also provides job placement services and life-skills training (covering a range of life skills most

likely required by young women in their households, communities, and the labor market, such as negotiation skills, dealing with discrimination, workers' rights education, reproductive health, basic financial management, control over the use of their own income, and mentoring). About 60 percent of the first round of trainees has been gainfully employed after completing training (Employment Fund 2010).

44. NSDC is jointly owned by the private (51 percent) and public (49 percent) sectors. It was established as a nonprofit company under Section 25 of the Indian Companies Act.

45. Microfinance services include microcredit, deposit services, money transfer services, and microleasing.

46. See http://www.samn.eu/?q=microfinance-asia.

47. These linkages are miniscule from the point of view of the banks (EDA and APMAS 2006).

48. For reviews of the limited evaluation evidence on self-employment programs in developing countries, see Betcherman and others (2004, 2007).

49. Some of the controversies relate to issues that are tangential to this book, including the role of commercial banking institutions in microfinance, the interest rates charged on microloans, the debt accumulated by poor people through microloans, and the politicization of some programs. There is also a claim that the benefits of microfinance have been oversold. Although these are important concerns, they do not speak directly to the question of whether microfinance can be an effective instrument for helping informal workers manage labor market–related risks.

50. In effect, the act provides for the formulation by the central and state governments of social insurance schemes for unorganized workers. It does not establish a universal minimum social insurance program.

51. The design of the benefit side of social insurance programs is beyond the scope of this book. Promising initiatives exist throughout the region. One prominent example is India's recently introduced national health insurance scheme, Rashtriya Swasthya Bima Yojana (RSBY), designed to provide hospitalization coverage to households below the poverty line. For more details on the program and its early implementation experience, see World Bank (2011b).

References

Abidoye, B., P. Orazem, and M. Vodopivec. 2009. "Firing Cost and Firm Size: A Study of Sri Lanka's Severance Pay System." Social Protection Discussion Paper 0916, World Bank, Washington, DC.

Ahsan, A., and C. Pagés. 2009. "Are All Labor Regulations Equal? Evidence from Indian Manufacturing." *Journal of Comparative Economics* 37 (1): 62–75.

Ambasta, P., P.S. Vijay Shankar, and M. Shah. 2008. "Two Years of NREGA: The Road Ahead." *Economic and Political Weekly* 43 (8): 41–50.

Armendáriz de Aghion, B., and J. Morduch. 2004. "Microfinance: Where Do We Stand?" In *Financial Development and Economic Growth: Explaining the Links,* ed. C. Goodhart 135–48. London: Palgrave.

Banerjee, A., E. Duflo, R. Glennerster, and C. Kinnan. 2009. "The Miracle of Microfinance? Evidence from a Randomized Evaluation." Department of Economics and Abdul Latif Jameel Poverty Action Lab Working Paper, Massachusetts Institute of Technology, Cambridge, MA.

Besley, T., and R. Burgess. 2004. "Can Labor Regulation Hinder Economic Performance? Evidence from India." *Quarterly Journal of Economics* 119 (1): 91–134.

Betcherman, G., A. Dar, A. Luinstra, and M. Ogawa. 2004. "Active Labor Market Programs: Policy Issues for East Asia." Social Protection Discussion Paper 0005, World Bank, Washington, DC.

Betcherman, G., M. Godfrey, S. Puerto, F. R. Rother, and A. Stavreska. 2007. "Global Inventory of Interventions to Support Young Workers: Synthesis Report." World Bank, Social Protection Unit, Washington, DC.

Bruhn, M., and B. Zia. 2011. "Stimulating Managerial Capital in Emerging Markets: The Impact of Business and Financial Literacy for Young Entrepreneurs." Policy Research Working Paper 5642, Development Research Group, Finance and Private Sector Development Team, World Bank, Washington, DC.

Card, D., and A. Krueger. 1997. *Myth and Measurement: The New Economics of the Minimum Wage.* Princeton, NJ: Princeton University Press.

Carlin, W., and M. Schaffer. 2011. "Which Elements of the Business Environment Matter Most for Firms and How Do They Vary across Countries?" Background study conducted for this book.

CSE (Centre for Science and Environment). 2008. *An Assessment of the Performance of The National Rural Employment Guarantee Programme in Terms of its Potential for Creation of Natural Wealth in India's Villages.* New Delhi.

de Mel, S., D. McKenzie and C. Woodruff. 2011. "Business Training and Female Enterprise Start-up and Growth in Sri Lanka." Development Economics/Finance and Private Sector Development, World Bank, Washington, DC.

Debroy, B. 2011. "India's Labour Market: Laws, Regulations and Reforms." Background study conducted for this book.

del Ninno, C., K. Subbarao, and A. Milazzo. 2009. "How to Make Public Works Work: A Review of the Experiences." Social Protection Discussion Paper 48567, World Bank, Washington, DC.

Dougherty, S. 2008. "Labour Regulation and Employment Dynamics at the State Level in India." OECD Economics Department Working Paper 624, Organisation for Economic Co-operation and Development, Paris.

Drèze, J., and R. Khera. 2009. "The Battle for Employment Guarantee." *Frontline* 26: 1.

Dutta, K. 2011. "Active Labor Market Programs in India." Background study conducted for this book.

EDA (EDA Rural Systems Pvt Ltd), and APMAS (Andhra Pradesh Mahila Abhivruddhi Society). 2006. *Self-Help Groups in India: A Study of the Lights and Shades.* Gurgaon and Hyderabad, India.

Employment Fund. 2010. *Employment Fund Half Annual Report (January–June 2010).* Kathmandu. http://www.employmentfund.org.np/annual-reports.html/.

Federal Bureau of Statistics Pakistan. 2011. *Pakistan Statistical Year Book 2011.* Islamabad.

Freeman, R. 1993. "Labor Market Institutions and Policies: Help or Hindrance to Economic Adjustment?" Proceedings of the *World Bank Annual Conference on Development Economics*, ed. M. Bruno and B. Pleskovic, 117–44. Washington, DC: World Bank.

———. 2009. "Labor Regulations, Unions, and Social Protection in Developing Countries: Market Distortions or Efficient Institutions?" NBER Working Paper 14789, National Bureau of Economic Research, Cambridge, MA.

Gine, X., and G. Mansuri. 2011. "Constraints to Female Entrepreneurship: Ideas or Capital." World Bank, Development Research Group, Washington, DC.

Gunatilaka, R. 2011. "Institutional Constraints to Decent Job Growth in Sri Lanka's Segmented Labour Market." Background study conducted for this book.

Gunatilaka, R., and M. Vodopivec. 2010. "Labor Market Institutions and Labor Market Segmentation in Sri Lanka." In *The Challenge of Youth Unemployment in Sri Lanka,* ed. R. Gunatilaka, M. Mayer, and M. Vodopivec, 49–68. Washington, DC: World Bank.

Gupta, P., R. Hasan, and U. Kumar. 2009. "Big Reforms but Small Payoffs: Explaining the Weak Record of Growth and Employment in Indian Manufacturing." MPRA Paper 13496, Munich Personal RePEc Archive, University Library of Munich.

Heltberg, R., and M. Vodopivec. 2004. *Sri Lanka: Unemployment, Job Security, and Labor Market Reform.* http://ssrn.com/abstract=1208662.

Holzmann, R., Y. Pouget, M. Vodopivec, and M. Weber. 2011. "Severance Pay Programs around the World: History, Rationale, Status, and Reforms." Social Protection Discussion Paper 62726, World Bank, Washington, DC.

IHD (Institute for Human Development). 2011. *Human Development in India: Emerging Issues and Policy Perspectives.* New Delhi.

IPS (Institute of Policy Studies of Sri Lanka). 2011. *Review of Active Labor Market Programs (ALMPS) in Sri Lanka.* Colombo.

Jacob, A., and R. Varghese. 2006. "NREGA implementation 1: Reasonable Beginning in Palakkad, Kerala." *Economic and Political Weekly* 2 (December): 4943–45.

Johanson, R., and A. Van Adams. 2004. *Skills Development in Sub-Saharan Africa.* World Bank, Regional and Sectoral Studies, Washington, DC.

Kyloh, R. 2008. *From Conflict to Cooperation: Labour Market Reforms That Can Work in Nepal.* International Labour Office, Geneva, and Academic Foundation, New Delhi.

Loayza, N., L. Servén, and N. Sugawara. 2010. "Informality in Latin America and the Caribbean." In *Business Regulation and Economic Performance,* ed. N. Loayza and L. Servén, 157–96. Washington, DC: World Bank.

López-Acevedo, G. and M. Tinajero. 2010. "Impact Evaluation of SME Programs Using Panel Firm Data." Policy Research Working Paper 5186, World Bank, Latin America and the Caribbean Region, Poverty and Gender Unit, Washington, DC.

Munshi, F. 2011. "Labor Regulations in Bangladesh: Constraints to More and Better Jobs?" Background study conducted for this book.

NCAER–PIF (National Council of Applied Economic Research–Public Interest Foundation). 2009. *Evaluating Performance of National Rural Employment Guarantee Act.* New Delhi.

NCEUS (National Commission for Enterprises in the Unorganized Sector). 2009. *The Challenge of Employment in India: An Informal Economy Perspective. Final Report of the National Commission for Enterprises in the Unorganised Sector.* Government of India, New Delhi.

Neumark, D., and W. Wascher. 2006. "Minimum Wages and Employment: A Review of Evidence from the New Minimum Wage Research." NBER Working Paper 12663, National Bureau of Economic Research, Cambridge, MA.

OECD (Organisation for Economic Co-operation and Development). 2006. *Employment Outlook.* Paris.

———. 2007a. *Economic Survey of India.* Paris.

———. 2007b. *Employment Outlook.* Paris.

———. 2009. *Indicators of Employment Protection.* Paris.

Palacios, R., and E. Whitehouse. 2006. "Civil Service Pension Schemes around the World." Social Protection Discussion Paper 0602, World Bank, Washington, DC.

Rahman, R., and N. Shamsunnahar. 2011. "A Review of Active Labour Market Programs in South Asian Countries: Bangladesh." Background study conducted for this book.

Rifaqat, S. 2011. "A Review of Active Labor Market Programs in Pakistan." Background study conducted for this book.

Rutkowski, J. 2007. "Taxation of Labor." In *Fiscal Policy and Economic Growth in ECA,* ed. C. Gray, T. Lane, and A. Varoudakis, 281–313. Washington, DC: World Bank.

SAMN (South Asian Microfinance Network). 2010. "Microfinance in the South Asian Countries: Quick Facts." New Delhi. http://www.samn.eu/?q=microfinance-asia.

Tamiru, K. 2011. "Active Labor Market Policies Inventory Review for Afghanistan." Background study conducted for this book.

Tan, H., and G. López-Acevedo. 2005. "Evaluating Training Programs for Small and Medium Enterprises: Lessons from Mexico." Policy

Research Working Paper 3760, Latin America and the Caribbean Region, Poverty Sector Unit, World Bank, Washington, DC.

UN (United Nations). 2010. *World Population Prospects: The 2010 Revision.* New York.

U.S. Department of State. 1999–2010. *Human Rights Report.* Washington, DC.

Vodopivec, M. 2004. *Introducing Unemployment Benefits to Sri Lanka.* Washington, DC: World Bank.

Vodopivec, M., A. Wörgötter, and D. Raju. 2005. "Unemployment Benefit Systems in Central and Eastern Europe: A Review of the 1990s." *Comparative Economic Studies* 47 (4): 615–51.

Wall Street Journal Asia. 2011. "India's Guaranteed Joblessness." July 27. http://online.wsj.com/article/SB1000142405311190359110457 6467562817474174.html.

World Bank. 2006. *Pakistan Labor Market Study: Regulation, Job Creation and Skills Formation in the Manufacturing Sector.* South Asia Region, Finance and Private Sector Development, Washington, DC.

———. 2007. "Skill Development in India: The Vocational Education and Training System." South Asia Region, Human Development Unit, Washington, DC.

———. 2009. *Financing the Bottom of the Pyramid: Microfinance Strategy for South Asia.* South Asia Region, Washington, DC.

———. 2010. *India's Employment Challenge: Creating Jobs, Helping Workers.* India: Oxford University Press.

———. 2011a. *Doing Business Database.* Washington, DC: World Bank.

———. 2011b. *Social Protection for a Changing India.* South Asia Region, Human Development Unit, Washington, DC.

———. 2011c. *World Development Indicators.* Washington, DC: World Bank.

Questions and Findings

Questions

- How does armed conflict affect labor markets?
- What are the key constraints to job creation in conflict-affected areas of South Asia?
- What are the policy priorities for creating more and better jobs in conflict-affected areas?

Findings

- Even when it is over, armed conflict remains a serious obstacle to job creation in South Asia. Conflict affects both the demand for and the supply of labor. It affects demand by reducing both the incentives and the ability of firms to invest and create jobs. Lack of security, inadequate infrastructure and services, and a weak governance and regulatory environment are the most significant deterrents for private sector job creation in conflict-affected areas. Loss of skills, migration, fluctuations in family income, and demographic changes also affect the nature of the workforce in conflict zones. Conflict-affected areas in South Asia remain more rural, more dependent on agriculture, and more isolated than low-intensity conflict areas. They also remain less likely to have private employers, more likely to have low-skilled workers, and more likely to have vulnerable jobs.

- In the initial postconflict phase, labor market programs and policies can play important roles in providing and promoting employment, through such efforts as disarmament, demobilization, and reintegration programs and broader-based public works. Governments also need to take initial steps to attract the private sector (such as reforming business regulations, issuing temporary tax breaks, and forging public-private partnerships) so that the private sector can eventually become a more significant provider of jobs. International organizations and foreign governments have important roles to play in providing funding and building capacity in these early stages, particularly in cases of nationwide conflict.

- Policy makers should plan three important transitions for policies and programs over the medium term: increasing the role of the private sector; refocusing attention from the agricultural sector toward facilitating higher-productivity employment in other sectors; and moving from targeted programs for vulnerable groups (such as excombatants, at-risk youth, war victims, and displaced people) to broad-based employment generation.

Creating Jobs in Conflict-Affected Areas | 7

Armed conflict represents a major challenge to job creation. Conflict destroys communities, institutions, and physical and human capital and leaves the affected population living in insecurity and often without sources of livelihood. More than 58,000 people worldwide died directly as a result of armed conflict in 2009—more than a third of them in South Asia (IISS 2010). Most countries in South Asia are immersed in—or only recently emerged from—armed conflict, ranging from the insurgencies in Afghanistan and Pakistan and low-level localized insurgency in India to the recently ended civil wars in Nepal and Sri Lanka.[1] Some of these conflicts have officially ended, but even in these cases sustainable peace is not guaranteed.

The creation of more and better jobs should be at the center of any recovery plan for conflict-afflicted areas, as the literature suggests that poor economic conditions and labor market prospects increase the likelihood of conflict. At the same time, a minimal level of security is essential to economic recovery and to the success of policies and programs that encourage job creation. Jobs and sustainable peace can therefore positively reinforce each other, as long as programs and policies are inclusive and sensitive to the grievances

that led to conflict in the first place. Household surveys and focus group discussions in conflict-affected areas in Afghanistan and Sri Lanka show that economic recovery and the restoration of livelihoods are people's main priorities after the cessation of hostilities (World Bank 2010a). The fact that millions of new entrants will enter the South Asian labor force in the next two decades further increases pressure to create more and better jobs, especially in postconflict environments and areas at risk of new or renewed violence.

This chapter describes the key challenges to job creation in conflict-affected environments and outlines what governments in the region can do to overcome them.[2] The next section discusses the characteristics and intensity of armed conflict in South Asia. The second section discusses the constraints to labor demand and labor supply in conflict-affected areas. The third section takes a closer look at the profile of labor markets in conflict-affected areas in South Asia. The fourth section focuses on the role the private sector can play in creating jobs in conflict-affected areas, the main constraints it faces, and the lessons international experience yields regarding effective interventions. The fifth section discusses education delivery in conflict situations. The sixth section focuses on the role of labor market policies and programs. The last section discusses some of the key transitions needed in conflict-affected areas if job creation is to be sustainable. It identifies the main actors, the key sectors to focus on, and the groups to target.

Characteristics and intensity of armed conflict in South Asia

South Asia has experienced one of the highest levels of armed conflict in the world. On average, countries in the region experienced armed conflict for half of the years since 2000, as measured by the incidence of at least 25 battle-related deaths a year (figure 7.1). This is the highest incidence of conflict in absolute terms and the second-highest proportion of deaths from armed conflict in the world. Among the top 10 countries in terms of direct deaths from armed conflict in 2008, 4 (Afghanistan, Pakistan, India, and Sri Lanka) were in South Asia (figure 7.2).[3]

This chapter focuses on internal armed violence against the state—violent incidents perpetrated by a relatively organized group

of nonstate actors and directed against the apparatus of the state or with the intent of destabilizing the state. This definition of internal conflict is used in the Uppsala Conflict Data Program and Centre for the Study of Civil War at the International Peace Research Institute (UCDP/PRIO) conflict database. It is similar to the definition of *terrorism* adopted in most incident-level data sets dealing with internal conflict. The definition excludes interstate conflicts and violence between individuals.

The focus in this chapter is on internal conflict against the state for two main reasons. First, internal armed conflict directed against the state arguably poses the greatest challenge to the ability of the state to implement policies and programs conducive to employment generation. Second, the majority of conflicts in the developing world, including South Asia, are internal conflicts. Since World War II, internal conflicts have resulted in three times as many deaths as interstate wars (Fearon and Laitin 2003).

The nature, duration, and intensity of internal armed conflicts vary across South

FIGURE 7.1 **Proportion of country-years in armed conflict, by region, 2000–08**

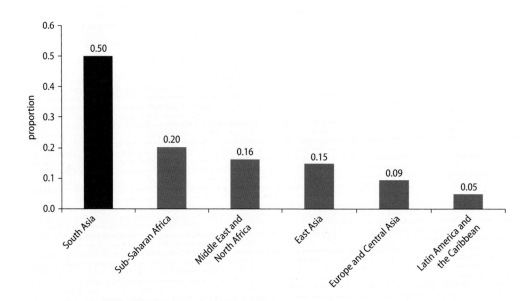

Source: UCDP/PRIO Armed Conflict Dataset version 4-2009 (http://www.prio.no/CSCW/Datasets/Armed-Conflict/UCDP-PRIO/Armed-Conflicts-Version-X-2009/).
Note: Armed conflict refers to internal armed conflicts between the government of a state and one or more internal opposition groups that result in at least 25 battle-related deaths a year.

FIGURE 7.2 **Top 15 countries in number of deaths from armed conflict, 2008**

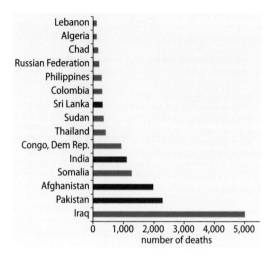

Source: National Counterterrorism Center 2009, based on the Worldwide Incidents Tracking System (WITS), which contains details about incidents of violence against civilians and noncombatants from publicly available information.

Asian countries. Ongoing conflicts in the region include the conflicts in Afghanistan and Pakistan, the long-running insurgency movements in India's northeastern regions, and the escalating violent activities of left-leaning groups in the eastern and central parts of India. Table 7.1 provides information on the major internal armed conflicts in South Asia over the past decade (see Iyer 2009 for a discussion of these conflicts).

The challenges posed by armed conflict vary significantly with the type of conflict. The focus here is on two dimensions of conflict of particular importance for job creation: the geographic scope and the stage of the conflict. Geographic scope refers to whether the conflict is nationwide or localized. The stage of the conflict refers to whether the conflict is ongoing or has ended. A conflict is classified as having ended if there has been a clear military victory or a peace agreement

TABLE 7.1 **Major internal armed conflicts in South Asia since 1978**

Country/region	Approximate start and end dates	Estimated number of fatalities (2000–09)	Outstanding number of internally displaced people
Afghanistan			
Nationwide	1978–	51,580	More than 235,000
Bangladesh			
Nationwide	2005–07	93	—
India			
Assam	1990–	3,838	257,000
Manipur	1982–2008	2,712	180,000
Nagaland	1992–2007	710	62,000
Tripura	1978–2006	1,708	—
Eastern and central states	1980–	5,290	60,000
Nepal			
Nationwide	1996–2006	13,592	60,000
Pakistan			
Baluchistan	2004–	1,294	80,000
North West Frontier Province (renamed Khyber Pakhtunkhwa in 2010) and the Federally Administered Tribal Areas	2002–	20,261	900,000
Sri Lanka			
Northern and Eastern Provinces	1980–2009	51,815	320,000

Source: Authors, based on start and end dates from the UCDP/PRIO Armed Conflict Dataset version 4-2009 (http://www.prio.no/CSCW/Datasets/Armed-Conflict/UCDP-PRIO/Armed-Conflicts-Version-X-2009/) and number of fatalities and displaced people from the Armed Conflict Database compiled by the International Institute for Strategic Studies, based on data from the Internal Displacement Monitoring Centre (http://www.iiss.org/publications/armed-conflict-database/).
Note: — = Not available.

TABLE 7.2 **Armed conflicts in South Asia, by conflict stage, geographic scope, and number of casualties per thousand people**

		Conflict stage	
		Ongoing	Postconflict
Geographic scope	Nationwide	Afghanistan (1.80)	Nepal (0.475)
	Localized	Pakistan (0.130) India (0.013)	Sri Lanka (2.570)

Sources: Authors, based on data on casualties from the armed conflict database compiled by the International Institute for Strategic Studies (http://www.iiss.org/publications/armed-conflict-database); population data from World Development Indicators; and Afghanistan population estimate from the CIA Factbook.
Note: Figures in parentheses are estimates of number of casualties per 1,000 people between 2000 and 2009. The classification of conflict stage is based on the status as of December 2010.

FIGURE 7.3 **Effects of conflict on demand for and supply of labor**

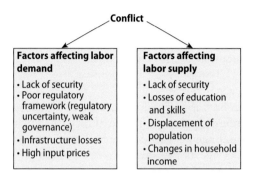

Source: Authors.

between the warring parties and the number of conflict-related deaths has declined significantly as a result.

The conflicts in South Asia between 2000 and 2010 show considerable variation along both of these dimensions (table 7.2). Armed conflicts in Afghanistan and Nepal were widespread in almost all parts of the country. In Afghanistan, the conflict continues. In Nepal, the conflict was formally brought to an end by a comprehensive peace agreement in 2006.

Constraints to job creation in conflict-affected areas

Armed conflict affects the demand for labor, because firms and businesses are reluctant to invest in the face of significant threats to the security of life and property (figure 7.3). Inadequate or confusing regulations and the poor quality of governance in affected areas also discourage firms from investing. The presence of warring parties and fragile states adds to uncertainty regarding both what the regulations are and who is enforcing them. Infrastructure losses and unreliable access to key services, such as electricity and transport, restrict the scale of firm activity, and the absence of markets increases input prices. At the height of the armed conflict in northern Sri Lanka in 2007, for example, the price of a bag of cement was more than four times higher in Jaffna (Northern Province) than in other parts of the country (World Bank 2010c).

Conflict also affects the capacity of the population to supply labor, as well as the quality and composition of the workforce. Security concerns in traveling to work can be a major constraint to labor supply. Disruptions to education and the loss of job-related skills and training reduce the quality of the workforce in conflict areas, with potentially long-term effects. Population displacement and migration, as well as the challenges posed by the reintegration of returnees after the end of conflict, place further restrictions on the availability of skilled labor. Finally, labor supply will also be affected by changes in household income resulting from the conflict as, for example, women start working to supplement the family's income in the absence of male family members who join the fighting.

Although all of these constraints apply in some degree to all conflict situations, poor governance and inadequate infrastructure are more likely to be severe constraints in areas of nationwide conflict, because regional conflict typically coexists with a functioning state in the rest of the country. This means that the government has a tax base on which to draw, the ability to provide public services and infrastructure, and functioning institutions (army, police forces, bureaucracy, judicial system), which can be extended to the conflict-affected region when the conflict ends.

In contrast, nationwide conflicts often involve the building up or complete reform of state institutions when the conflict ends. As discussed in the *World Development Report 2011* (World Bank 2011c), building institutions is a long-term affair that generally takes a generation. Policy makers in countries emerging from nationwide conflict face the additional challenge of reestablishing connectivity with the rest of the world or neighboring countries, in addition to rebuilding internal connectivity. The lack of such external connectivity can significantly affect access to foreign goods and capital, access to foreign markets, and the ability of international agencies to deliver humanitarian and other assistance.

Internal migration to safer parts of the country is likely to be significant in cases of localized conflict. In Pakistan, for example, an estimated 60 percent of workers in the Federally Administered Tribal Areas (FATA) leave their tribal area to find employment (World Bank and ADB 2010).[4] Migration can help households access more and better jobs and send home money that can be used for human capital investments or business start-ups. The presence of large numbers of internal migrants and displaced people raises an important policy question related to job creation, however: should jobs for internal migrants be created in their current areas of residence, or should the focus be primarily on creating jobs in conflict-affected areas, thereby providing incentives for the displaced to return?

When the conflict is ongoing, it may not pay to rebuild infrastructure, which could be damaged during fighting. In postconflict situations, the intensity of violence has decreased, allowing better planning and reducing uncertainty in investment and resource allocation decisions. But violence also characterizes many postconflict situations. Peace is very fragile: historically, 40 percent of postconflict situations have reverted to conflict within a decade (Collier, Hoeffler, and Söderbom 2008).

Armed conflict and labor markets

Labor market indicators (such as lack of jobs for young people and low wage growth) are important predictors of the likelihood of conflict (Collier, Hoeffler, and Sambanis 2005; Hoeffler 2011; Smith 2004; World Bank 2011). But how does conflict change labor markets in conflict zones?

This section begins by briefly discussing the impact of armed conflict on aggregate economic growth and unemployment. It then analyzes the impact of conflict on employment, unemployment, sectoral composition, and the types of jobs, using national household and labor force surveys. Multiple rounds of household data were used to compare trends in high-conflict and low-conflict areas of India, Nepal, and Sri Lanka (see annex 7A for definitions of high- and low-conflict areas). Within-country variation in the intensity of armed conflict was exploited to better understand the relationship between conflict and labor markets.

Two caveats should be heeded in interpreting the results. The first refers to interpreting results as causal. Labor market characteristics may be different in conflict areas because of the conflict itself or because of preexisting conditions. Where information for more than one point in time is available, the data can be interpreted as caused by the conflict, to the extent that the two types of areas would have followed similar trends in the indicators of interest in the absence of the armed conflict.[5] For Afghanistan, where household data for only one year are available, results should be interpreted with more care.

The second caveat refers to the potential bias in the sample composition, as areas affected by conflict are often underrepresented in household surveys. If these areas were included in the surveys, it is possible that labor market conditions in conflict-affected areas would look even worse, as the worst-affected areas are probably omitted. Annex 7B describes the difference in trends for South Asian countries for employment and unemployment, disaggregated by gender.[6]

Conflict, growth, and the peace dividend

Conflict can have aggregate effects on economic growth and therefore on the quantity and quality of jobs the economy is able to generate.[7]

Assessing the economic costs of armed conflict is empirically complicated, because it is difficult to specify an appropriate counterfactual, data are not available from conflict-affected countries or regions, and different methodologies often yield widely different results (Gardeazabal forthcoming). For example, in 1998 the macroeconomic impact of the civil war in Sri Lanka was officially estimated at 2–3 percent of gross domestic product (GDP) growth a year since its start (Central Bank of Sri Lanka 1998). More recent estimates for the period 1984–96 put the annual cost at 10.8–15.8 percent of 1996 GDP (Arunatilake, Jayasuriya, and Kelegama 2001).

Cross-country estimates find that countries that experienced civil war between 1960 and 1999 saw their annual GDP growth rate reduced by 2.4 percentage points on average (Hoeffler and Reynal-Querol 2003). Even for countries with some conflict during 1980–2008, growth was 1.2 percentage points higher, on average, in years of peace than in years of conflict. In South Asia as well, periods with more conflict have usually been periods of slow growth (figure 7.4).

This evidence suggests that the peace dividend for growth and job creation is potentially large. Chen, Loayza, and Reynal-Querol (2007) analyze 41 countries that experienced civil war between 1960 and 2003. They find that once the war ended, recovery in economic performance, health, education, and political development was significant.

Once violence ceased, conflict-affected communities also experienced a faster reduction in poverty than communities less directly exposed to the conflict within the same country. Poverty reduction was particularly high in Sri Lanka, where it fell 40 percent in conflict-affected areas (the average decline elsewhere in the country was 34 percent) (World Bank 2010a).[8] During the ceasefire that lasted from 2002 to 2004, unemployment fell from 13.0 percent to 9.2 percent in the Northern Province and from 15.9 percent

FIGURE 7.4   Annual growth in GDP and number of battle deaths in India and Nepal, 2000–08

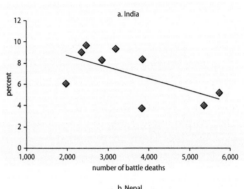

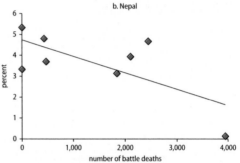

Source: Authors, based on data from World Bank 2011b.
Note: Each data point represents a single year.

FIGURE 7.5   Unemployment rates in the Northern and Eastern provinces of Sri Lanka, 1997–2001 and 2002–04

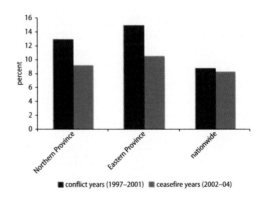

Source: Annual Reports of the Central Bank of Sri Lanka.

to 10.5 percent in the Eastern Province, at a time when the national unemployment rate decreased only slightly, from 8.8 percent to 8.3 percent (figure 7.5).

Employment rate

Armed conflict seems to be associated with an increase (or a smaller reduction) in high-conflict areas in the share of the working-age population that is economically active and employed.[9] In Afghanistan, the share of the working-age population that was employed was 55.6 percent in low-conflict provinces and 68.3 percent in high-conflict areas. In India, employment rates in conflict-affected areas fell less than in peaceful areas. In Nepal, the proportion of the working-age population that was employed increased about 2 percentage points between 1996 (preconflict) and 2004 in low-conflict areas and more than 4 percentage points in high-conflict areas (figure 7.6). This evidence suggests that conflict could increase labor supply even in the face of decreased demand.[10] Together these forces are likely to reduce equilibrium wages in conflict areas over time, leading to a decline in living standards.

Increased labor force participation and employment in conflict zones seems to arise primarily from the increase (or smaller reduction) in employment of women. In Afghanistan, for example, the proportion of men employed is 4 percentage points higher in high-conflict areas, but the proportion of working-age women employed is 19 percentage points higher. The difference in employment patterns over time is statistically insignificant for men in India and Nepal; among women, the likelihood of being employed increases with the intensity of the conflict in both countries. In high-conflict areas of Nepal, for example, the proportion of working-age men increased about 3 percentage points between 1996 (preconflict) and 2004, whereas the proportion of women increased almost 6 percentage points (figure 7.7).

There are two potential reasons for the increased participation of women. One is the "added-worker" effect, whereby additional members of the household enter the labor force in response to economic necessity or the absence of key earning members. Both of

FIGURE 7.6 **Percentage of working-age population employed in high-conflict and low-conflict areas of India and Nepal**

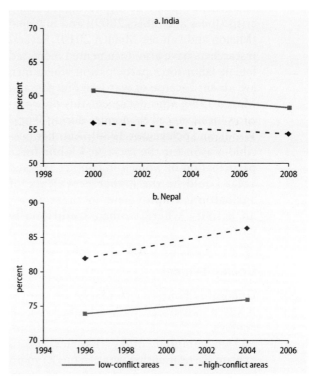

Source: Authors, based on national household and labor force surveys.

FIGURE 7.7 **Percentage of working-age population employed in high-conflict areas of Nepal, by gender, 1996–2004**

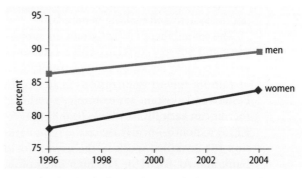

Source: Authors, based on data from Nepal Living Standard Measurement Study Surveys.

these conditions are likely to apply in conflict-affected areas, given that men often leave to fight and economic conditions in the household usually worsen as a result of the conflict.

A rise in employment among women during difficult economic times has been documented in cross-country studies (Bhalotra and Umana-Aponte 2010); during the Asian crisis (Jones and others 2009); and in Nepal (Menon and van der Meulen 2010). Several researchers have also documented increased female labor force participation where men are absent because of war (see Finegan and Margo 1994, who document this phenomenon for advanced economies during World War II, and Schweitzer 1980). Another possible reason for the increased labor force participation of women in conflict-affected areas could be the higher prevalence of agricultural employment in these areas, an activity where women traditionally participate.[11]

Unemployment

Unemployment, particularly of youth, is often associated with a higher risk of conflict.

Two complementary theories try to explain the relationship between (male) youth unemployment and armed conflict. The first, the youth bulge theory, states that when a large proportion of the population consists of young men who are marginalized from political and economic opportunities, countries are more vulnerable to instability, and violence becomes a rational option for engaging the system and making demands.

The second theory is that youth unemployment and poverty correlate with the onset of armed conflict because the opportunity cost of joining rebel organizations is lower. In Peshawar, Pakistan, for example, a militant recruit can earn PRs 15,000–20,000 ($176–$235) a month—nearly twice the remuneration for unskilled work in the area (World Bank and ADB 2010). The high unemployment among people 15–24 (close to 10 percent in Bangladesh, India, and Pakistan; 16 percent in Maldives; and almost 20 percent in Sri Lanka) bodes ill for the possibility of conflict.

Some cross-country empirical evidence finds a positive correlation between the likelihood of armed conflict on the one hand and youth unemployment and other indicators of economic opportunities on the other (Collier, Hoeffler, and Sambanis 2005; Urdal 2006). A similar result is obtained across states in India, especially when combined with slower wage growth in rural areas (Urdal 2008). There is also evidence that young adolescents are the optimal target of rebel forces (Beber and Blattman 2010).

Other work has failed to find econometric evidence of a relationship between youth unemployment and armed conflict. The evidence overall remains mixed, as discussed in the *World Development Report 2011* (World Bank 2011c).

In South Asia, some limited evidence supports the hypothesis that male youth unemployment may be a risk factor for conflict. In Nepal, where labor market information before the violence started is available, pre-conflict unemployment rates among men 15–35 years old were 2.4 percentage points higher (almost twice as high) in districts where the conflict started (in the midwestern hills) than in the rest of the country, even after accounting for differences in poverty, location (urban or rural), and education levels.[12] In South Asia as a whole, the more important question is likely to concern the relationship between the quality of jobs available to youth and conflict, as open unemployment is generally low.

The evidence from South Asia on the impact of conflict on overall unemployment is mixed. In Nepal, the conflict seems to have been associated with a reduction in the unemployment rate in high-conflict areas. In India and Sri Lanka, the difference is not statistically significant (see annex 7B). There is also no clear pattern across countries in relative unemployment rates before the start of the conflict (see annex 7B).[13]

Employment patterns by location and sector

Conflict-affected countries tend to be less urbanized, in part because the mountainous and forested terrain is usually favorable for rebellion (see Collier and Sambanis 2005; Do and Iyer 2010). At the global level, 58 percent of the population in conflict-affected countries lives in rural areas—a proportion that is 11 percentage points higher than the average in nonconflict countries (World Bank 2011b). Jobs in conflict areas are therefore more likely to be in rural areas and the agricultural sector.

In South Asia, too, the workforce in high-conflict areas is also significantly more likely to be in rural areas. In Afghanistan, for instance, 22 percent of the working-age population lives in urban areas in low-conflict areas; the corresponding figure for high-conflict areas is 5 percent. Work is primarily in agriculture: 71 percent of workers in high-conflict areas work in this sector, compared with 52 percent in the rest of Afghanistan. In India, the share of employment in agriculture was 61 in high-conflict and 58 percent in low-conflict areas. In Nepal, 87 percent of workers in high-conflict and 78 percent in low-conflict countries work in agriculture.

Conflict delays urbanization and the structural transformation of the economy. The proportion of the workforce located in urban areas increased by 10 percentage points in low-conflict areas of Nepal between 1996 (preconflict) and 2004 but by only 4 percentage points in the high-conflict areas (figure 7.8). To the extent that urban areas are able to provide better jobs and better access to public services, this pattern reflects a slowdown in the improvement of household welfare. The same pattern is evident in India.

In India and Nepal, armed conflict seems to have also delayed the transition of the workforce out of agriculture. In India, for example, the share of workers employed in agriculture fell throughout the country between 2000 and 2007, but the decline was 3 percentage points lower in conflict-affected areas. In Nepal, agriculture fell in all districts between 1996 and 2004, but the average decline was 2 percentage points lower in high-conflict areas (see annex 7B). These results echo findings in other settings, including

FIGURE 7.8   **Urban workers as share of all workers in India and Nepal**

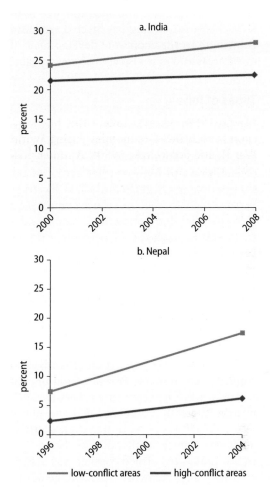

Source: Authors, based on national household and labor force surveys.

Mozambique, Rwanda, and Uganda (Brueck 2004; Deininger 2003; McKay and Loveridge 2005).

Economic activities outside of agriculture are very limited in conflict-affected areas in South Asia, as evidenced by the small share of the workforce employed by a third party and the limited presence of manufacturing, construction, and commercial activities (see annex 7B). This finding is important, because the international evidence shows that diversified economies experience less conflict than those that rely on a few sectors (Collier, Hoeffler, and Sambanis 2005). It is especially relevant for countries like Afghanistan and Nepal, which remain overwhelmingly agrarian. Fostering small and medium-size non-farm enterprises in conflict-affected areas can contribute to the economic development of those areas and may also contribute to peace.

Types of jobs

Jobs in high-conflict are more likely to remain vulnerable as a result of the conflict, for two main reasons. First, the dearth of employers in high-conflict areas means that people are significantly less likely to become regular wage or salaried employees. In Nepal, the share of regular wage or salaried workers increased 1.2 percentage points between 1996 and 2004 in low-conflict districts but dropped in high-conflict districts. In India, the share of workers in regular wage or salaried jobs increased 3 percentage points in low-conflict areas, but the increase was only 1 percentage point in high-conflict areas (see annex 7B).[14]

Second, a larger proportion of workers in conflict areas remains dependent on unpaid family work. The share of workers engaged in unpaid family labor declined sharply in low-conflict areas of India; high-conflict areas saw a much smaller decline (figure 7.9). In Sri Lanka, the armed conflict was associated with an increase of 7 percentage points in the likelihood of being an unpaid family worker. This pattern partly reflects the higher concentration of employment in agriculture, but it is also evident in urban areas.

The patterns on casual wage work are mixed, with conflict associated with lower shares of wage work in casual activities in Afghanistan and Nepal, higher shares in Sri Lanka (possibly because of the sizable expansion of the construction sector), and no apparent association in India. A mixed picture also emerges for informal work. It is perhaps not surprising that the evidence on vulnerability of jobs is stronger in the context of unpaid family workers than for casual wage work, as casual wage work typically requires third-party employers.

Education

Levels of education are significantly lower in the areas of South Asia most affected by conflict. In Afghanistan in 2008, for instance, the share of the working-age population with no education was 68 percent in low-conflict areas and 82 percent in high-conflict areas. In every South Asian country, a smaller proportion of the workforce had completed secondary education in conflict-affected areas than in low-conflict or peaceful areas, with the differences both pre-dating the conflict and resulting from the conflict (figure 7.10). (For a breakdown of the working-age population by education level, see annex 7B.) The difference in education levels is not related only to lower urbanization: differences are smaller but remain when urban and rural areas are analyzed separately.

These effects take place through the impacts of conflict on supply and demand factors that affect schooling decisions. On the supply side, armed conflict may lead to the destruction of schools or complementary infrastructure and the absence or death of teachers. In Nepal, for example, almost 5 percent of all victims of the civil war have been identified as teachers or students (INSEC 2010). In Pakistan's North West Frontier Province, 8 percent of schools were destroyed between 2002 and 2009 (World Bank 2009b). The availability

FIGURE 7.9   Percentage of workforce employed in unpaid family labor in India, 2000–08

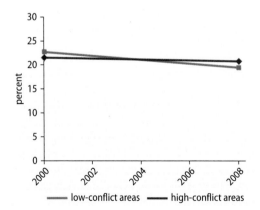

Source: Authors, based on labor force surveys.

and quality of school facilities has been associated with student attendance and achievement (Glewwe 2002).

Several factors—including the decline in household income and job opportunities, increased security risks, and lowered expected returns to education—can reduce demand for schooling in conflict areas:

- Increased pressure to supplement household income (or join the conflict) can lead to children dropping out of school.[15]
- Lack of security makes it more difficult for students to reach school, and schools may be attacked. In Afghanistan, for instance, threats of sexual violence reportedly keep many girls at home (Amnesty International 2003).
- Conflict potentially reduces the expected returns to education by reducing job opportunities for educated people. Between 2000 and 2008, the rate of emigration among South Asians with tertiary education was 4.7 percent in nonconflict-affected countries and 14.8 percent in conflict-affected ones (World Bank 2011b).
- Population displacement makes it difficult to continue schooling.

The literature reveals mixed results on the direction in which conflict has a causal effect on schooling and skill acquisition. Using detailed household and individual surveys, several researchers find a significant loss of education and experience for children and youth exposed to conflict (see Verwimp and Van Bavel 2010 on Burundi; Akresh and de Walque 2008 on Rwanda; Shemyakina 2011 on Tajikistan; Blattman and Annan 2010 on Uganda). Research by Stewart, Huang, and Wang (2001), however, suggests that countries with favorable institutions are able to maintain enrollment rates during armed conflict or recover quickly to their preconflict enrollment levels once the conflict is over. In particular, they find that primary school enrollment fell in only 3 of 18 African countries affected by internal conflict and actually improved in 5 (it is important to note that the authors lacked appropriate counterfactuals in their exercise). Lopez and Wodon (2005)

FIGURE 7.10 **Percentage of working-age population with completed lower-secondary education in low- and high-conflict areas of selected South Asian countries**

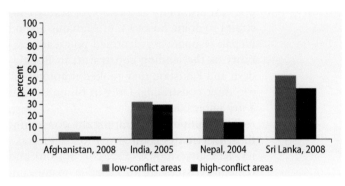

Source: Authors, based on data from national household and labor force surveys.

find that in Rwanda, where the conflict was short but intense, school enrollment rates returned to their preconflict levels within five years of the end of the violence. In Nepal, as discussed later in this chapter, important progress in education was made in conflict-affected areas during the civil war.

In summary, labor markets in conflict-affected areas present unique features. Overall, conflict-affected areas tend to be more rural and more dependent on agriculture, rely less on regular wage or salaried employment and more on unpaid family work, and have workforces that are significantly less educated. In most cases, these characteristics reflect both the conflict and conditions predating it. These characteristics of the labor markets in conflict-affected areas mean that job creation efforts need to initially focus on agriculture or other low-skilled sectors, such as construction. Additionally, providing inputs such as finance, infrastructure, and training needs to be tailored to the informal and casual sector, in addition to the formal sector.

Facilitating private sector job creation

Armed conflict, even conflict that has ended, is a serious obstacle to job creation in South Asia. Chapter 4 showed that political instability is one of the three most common binding constraints for formal urban and rural nonfarm firms in South Asia. Almost 60 percent of formal firms in South Asia included in the World Bank's enterprise surveys rank political instability as a major or severe constraint to doing business. In Afghanistan and Nepal, respondents identified political instability as the leading constraint; in Bangladesh and Pakistan, they ranked it among the top three constraints. Only in Bhutan was it a negligible concern.[16]

The second most important constraint to firm activities is the provision of electricity. Key governance (e.g., corruption) and regulatory issues are also cited as major constraints. These issues—insecurity, inadequate infrastructure, and a poor regulatory framework—are precisely the factors that are likely to be exacerbated in conflict situations.

In Afghanistan's 2008 enterprise survey, for example, firms located in areas where conflict was most violent reported that they were more severely constrained than firms in more peaceful areas in most aspects of the business environment. The biggest differences between high- and low-conflict areas were reported in infrastructure (electricity and transport); the governance and regulatory environment (corruption, business licensing, courts, land); security (crime and political instability); and skills (figure 7.11). The data on other South Asian countries do not allow for a similar analysis, because too few firms operating in conflict-affected areas were included in the enterprise surveys. The rest of this section discusses each of these constraints to job creation, focusing on ways in which different actors—the state, international donors, nongovernmental organizations (NGOs), local communities—can address them.

FIGURE 7.11   **Severity of business environment constraints (average) reported by firms in low-conflict and high-conflict areas of Afghanistan, 2008**

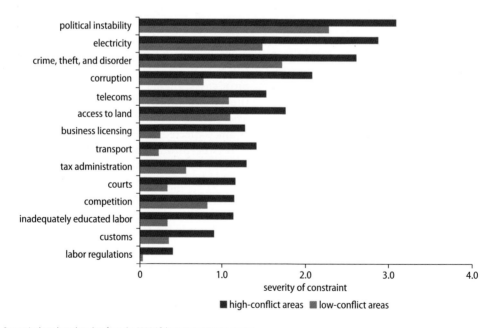

Source: Authors, based on data from the 2008 Afghanistan enterprise survey.
Note: High-conflict provinces are defined as provinces in which the number of deaths per 1,000 population caused by terrorist incidents in 2007 was greater than 0.1. By this definition, Baghlan, Ghazni, Farah, Helmand, Kandahar, Khost, Kunarha, Nimroz, Paktika, Paktya, Panjsher, Takhar, Urozgan, Wardak, and Zabul are high-conflict areas. Only differences that are statistically significant at at least the 5 percent in an ordinary least squares regression including firm size and industry fixed effects are shown.

Improving security

Security risks, which affect the economic returns to investment, persist even after armed conflict officially ends, putting both facilities and workers at risk. Firms need additional funds to ensure security by hiring private security or paying off the warring sides in a conflict.

Firms also experience difficulties in obtaining supplies for production. Farmers do not plant crops or go fishing when they live in fear. The lack of security may also manifest itself in the hesitation of the local community to take part in economic activities led by the private sector (or the government for that matter).

Even after a conflict has officially ended, considerable risks to security remain. Nepal, for instance, witnessed 514 deaths attributed to groups other than the Maoists and the government in 2007, after the peace agreement had been signed, an increase over the 327 such deaths in 2006 (INSEC 2008). Continued violence is attributable largely to the inability of a fragile state to provide effective security to all parts of the country; it highlights the risk that armed conflict can transform itself into other forms of violence or instability, as discussed in the *World Development Report 2011* (World Bank 2011c). Once firms leave, they often do not come back. In Assam, India, and Sri Lanka, for example, communities affected by armed conflict report that factories and plantations that shut down during conflict did not reopen when security improved (World Bank 2010a).

Governments can manage some of the security risks in conflict situations, by, for instance, implementing disarmament, demobilization, and reintegration (DDR) programs (discussed later in this chapter) and creating "safe" economic zones. Together with the private sector, the government can also involve local communities in security arrangements. The first two options are more likely to be successful when violence has been significantly reduced and an end to the conflict is in sight.

Special economic safe zones

Special economic safe zones are modeled after special economic zones (SEZs).[17] SEZs typically provide duty-free imports and good infrastructure, with a view to encouraging exports. In addition to easing the regulatory system or providing direct incentives, such as tax breaks and loan guarantees, safe zones provide targeted security and other public services.

SEZs have been established in several postconflict countries, including Cambodia and Mozambique, where they have helped attract foreign investors and spur job creation. In Cambodia, for example, export processing zones have been associated with the country's impressive job creation performance after the war, especially among women (female employment in industry grew 20 percent a year compared with 7 percent for men) (McLeod and Davalos 2008).

In Sri Lanka, the government has been planning to establish economic zones in conflict-affected areas (Indian Express 2009). Policy makers should think of these zones as an interim step in providing a good business environment, gradually extending benefits such as better regulation and infrastructure to firms throughout the country.

SEZs could be further complemented with "resource corridors," which would more directly link local communities, farmers, and workers to areas with high concentration of natural resources (by, for example, strengthening logistics and infrastructure). Afghanistan's mining sector, for example, has great potential. Although not labor intensive itself, it could be better linked to existing economic activities and livelihoods. This approach has been tested predominantly in nonconflict environments but could also be a promising path in countries recovering from conflict.

Private sector and local community initiatives

The private sector has found innovative ways of alleviating some of the challenges stemming from lack of security in conflict-affected areas by partnering with local entrepreneurs. Firms in conflict areas often hire private security firms or strike deals with warring parties. Foreign firms also take political risk insurance to cover some risks, through, for example, the World Bank's Multilateral Investment Guarantee Agency (MIGA) or the U.S. government's Overseas Private Investment Corporation (OPIC). Respondents to a recent survey of firms in conflict-affected cited engagement with the government in the host country and joint ventures/alliances with local companies as the two main tools they use to mitigate political risks in these countries (MIGA 2011).

Another option is to involve local communities in security arrangements, as Roshan, a telecommunications provider in Afghanistan, has done (box 7.1). The community-based strategy resulted in better security for

---

BOX 7.1   Private sector solutions to the security constraint: Lessons from Afghanistan

Roshan is the largest mobile phone company in Afghanistan. Since beginning operations in 2003 in six major cities, the company has expanded operations to all 34 provinces and more than 230 cities and towns. By 2009, it had more than 3.5 million active subscribers.

Since 2003, the company has invested more than $390 million all over the country. Employing more than 1,000 people directly (and more than 25,000 indirectly, as dealers, distributors, contractors, and suppliers), Roshan is the largest private employer in Afghanistan. One-fifth of its labor force is women, in contrast to a women's workforce participation of 1 percent in Afghanistan. Roshan is also the largest taxpayer in Afghanistan, accounting for about 6 percent of government revenues.

In 2008, Roshan faced a surge in attacks on its cell network towers. These attacks strained Roshan's operating budget, given that the company was already paying $14 million a year to a private company to provide security.

In response, Roshan decided to implement a new community-based security model. The first step was to consult with more than 1,000 local *shuras* (local councils) regarding their views of Roshan. The primary complaint was that Roshan was not providing jobs for locals; communities therefore had no interest in supporting the company.

In response, Roshan signed explicit contracts with each community. The company paid a leasing fee to the community for the use of the tower site, and the local community was required to ensure that the installations were not attacked. Roshan also introduced other incentives, such as bonus payments if the tower remained safe for a given a number of months, and it made significant investments in local infrastructure, based on the community's wishes (in some communities, Roshan provided funds for a local well; in others it funded solar electricity for the local mosque).

Taking this bold experiment a step farther, Roshan implemented it in Kandahar, one of Afghanistan's most conflict-affected regions. Within a few months, the company saw dramatic results and soon expanded the program to all areas of the country. The program is very popular in local communities, where it has generated jobs for local youth and provided much needed infrastructure in a war-torn country. The initiative also reduced the company's security bill for its cell towers from $14 million to $7.5 million.

Roshan's experience highlights three major issues in conflict zones. First, demand for jobs is high. Roshan reported receiving 10,000 applications for every job it filled in the early stages of the program. Second, private sector companies can overcome the disadvantages of operating in a high-risk environment, including security-related ones. Third, the private sector can be a useful source of funding for local infrastructure, without compromising profitability (Roshan has been profitable since its second quarter of operation).

Is Roshan's experience replicable? One key to success appears to be the company's orientation toward social development in addition to profit making. This orientation probably reflects the fact that Roshan's majority shareholder is the Aga Khan Fund for Economic Development, which has a longer-term outlook and a commitment to building sound businesses in the developing world. Ninety percent of Roshan's employees are Afghans, and the expatriate component is being further reduced. As CEO Karim Khoja says, "My proudest moment will be to transfer the company to an Afghan CEO."

Sources: Authors, based on Herman and Dhanani 2010; remarks by CEO Karim Khoja at HBS Social Enterprise Conference, March 2010 and personal communication with Karim Khoja, July 2010; and Roshan web site (http://www.roshan.af).

Roshan's facility, at a significantly lower cost than the alternative of hiring an international private security agency. In addition, it provided important benefits for the local community.

Rebuilding infrastructure

Armed conflict destroys or inflicts heavy damage to physical infrastructure instrumental to providing basic services and connecting communities and firms to markets. Electricity and water supplies, roads, rail networks, bridges, communication systems, and sanitation systems are often destroyed or rendered unusable. Based on the limited evidence from investment climate surveys, lack of access to electricity and transport seem to be a particularly important constraint to job creation in conflict-affected areas. In Afghanistan, for example, more than three decades of war left the country largely in ruins: in 2004, only 16 percent of households in rural Afghanistan had access to electricity, and three-quarters of the population had no access to public transportation in their communities (World Bank 2005). After two decades of violence in Sri Lanka, in 2003 only 64 percent of households in the Northern and Eastern provinces had access to electricity, compared with a national average of 73 percent.[18] Road networks were also considerably inferior in conflict-affected provinces (those located in the north and the east of the island) (figure 7.12).

Infrastructure limitations make it more expensive to do business and create jobs in conflict-affected areas. In Afghanistan, for example, 87 percent of firms have to operate with a private generator (chapter 4).

In Sri Lanka, the end of the conflict in the Northern Province in 2009 provided an opportunity to assess some of the economic benefits associated with improved infrastructure and access to markets, as the A9 highway that connects the north with the rest of the country was reopened. Improved connectivity allowed for more fluid mobility of people and goods, resulting in the rapid convergence of prices. The average price premium in Jaffna compared with Colombo on

FIGURE 7.12 **Sri Lanka infrastructure accessibility index**

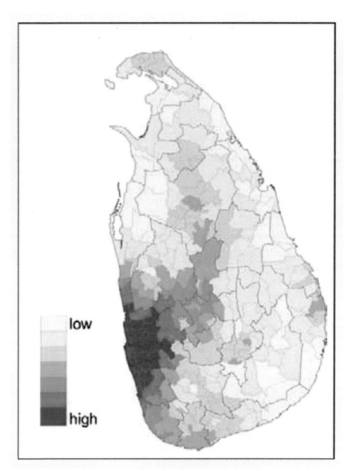

Source: World Bank 2007.
Note: The accessibility index is calculated for every point as the sum of the population totals of surrounding cities and towns inversely weighted by the road network travel time to each town.

10 selected items was 48 percent in May–July 2008; one year later, the price premium on the same products had declined to 24 percent (World Bank 2010c).

Rebuilding much needed infrastructure in the aftermath of violent conflict faces significant challenges. Financing requirements are great, renewed violence could destroy the rebuilt infrastructure, and the vast scale of needs makes it difficult to prioritize.

Private, public, NGO, and international actors have found ways to address some of these challenges. Three complementary approaches are adopted:

- *Providing infrastructure on a limited basis, possibly in SEZs, which are geographically limited and managed separately from the rest of the economy.* SEZs could also help address some of the regulatory and security concerns associated with job creation in conflict-affected areas, as discussed above.

- *In the medium term, tapping into innovative forms of financing.* Conflict-affected countries can use some innovative financing mechanisms—such as diaspora bonds, future-flow securitization, and performance-indexed bonds—to alleviate financing constraints (Ketkar and Ratha 2009). These mechanisms are

likely to be available only in the medium term, however, as they can be very complex and often require a stronger financial and regulatory framework than exists immediately after conflict.

- *Supporting the community-based/decentralized building of infrastructure and service provision.* An innovative experiment in progress in Afghanistan is the National Solidarity Program, which uses a decentralized community-driven mechanism coupled with international funds to execute local infrastructure projects (box 7.2). A similar program in Nepal

---

BOX 7.2   Community-led infrastructure provision: Afghanistan's National Solidarity Program

Afghanistan's National Solidarity Program (NSP), launched in 2003, is a community-led rural development initiative focused mainly on reconstruction and rural infrastructure. The program provides block grants (averaging $32,800 per community) to local governance bodies known as community development councils (CDCs) for infrastructure projects selected by beneficiaries. Grants are disbursed directly to the councils and managed through a bank account with a public bank. Participation of women in the CDCs is mandatory, although they sometimes participate in women-only councils. Communities are also required to contribute 10 percent of the cost of each project, with funds in the form of cash donations, work hours, or construction materials. The program is implemented by Afghanistan's Ministry of Rural Rehabilitation and Development and financed by a consortium of international donors.

The NSP is the only program to have reached all provinces in Afghanistan, affecting the lives of more than 17 million people. As of 2009, some 22,000 communities had successfully elected CDCs, and more than 50,000 community projects had been partially or fully financed (about 31,000 had been completed). Most projects focus on building or restoring irrigation facilities, power supply, roads, and bridges and bringing drinking water to communities.

The program is estimated to have employed some 4,000 Afghan nationals. It has also developed the skills of 600,000 local council members in areas such as conflict resolution, accounting,

and bookkeeping. Average economic rates of return across four sampled sectors (irrigation, power, water supply, and roads) have been estimated at 18.9 percent. An early randomized evaluation shows that the program has led to the creation of functional local councils, thereby decreasing the power of traditional elites. The program has led to greater engagement of women in community life and improved the perception of government figures. The impact of the program on access to services, infrastructure and utilities, economic activities, communities' trust, or the likelihood of violence, however, has been mixed (Beath and others 2010).

The successful roll-out of the NSP shows that community-driven development initiatives can be an important instrument amid conflict, when governments may be in too feeble a position to implement programs. In addition to direct economic benefits, these schemes can serve to foster cohesion and develop local capacities. However, significant challenges remain. Can coverage be extended to the 9,000 communities most affected by conflict, which are currently not part of the scheme? Will the NSP be sustainable without international donor funding? Can these small projects be scaled up? Will the CDCs continue to represent their communities, or will they be captured by the traditional elites over time?

Sources: Authors, based on Beath and others 2010; World Bank 2009a; World Bank Afghanistan National Solidarity Program website (http://web.worldbank.org/WBSITE/ EXTERNAL/COUNTRIES/SOUTHASIAEXT/0,,contentMDK:21166174~pagePK:146736~piPK:146830~theSitePK:223547,00.html).

(the Poverty Alleviation Fund) is a rural development program focused on developing rural community infrastructure linked to communities' priorities. In both programs, local communities identify, plan, build, operate, and maintain infrastructure. Community-based infrastructure development and service provision could help alleviate some security risks and help policy makers prioritize in an environment of tight fiscal constraints and vast needs. This type of intervention is less relevant for large infrastructure projects with cross-regional spillovers (ports, airports, highways), which are better addressed by higher-level government administrations.[19]

Strengthening the regulatory framework and governance

In enterprise surveys, private businesses in South Asia cite lack of effective regulation and governance as a major constraint, especially in conflict-affected areas. Almost 40 percent of firms in the region cite corruption as a major or severe constraint, the third-most-cited obstacle to business after political instability and electricity. Tax administration and policy uncertainty are also among the top constraints. There is some variation across countries in the importance of different elements of regulation and governance, as discussed in chapter 4. Average severity appears higher on all dimensions of regulation and governance in conflict-affected areas (figure 7.11). This finding is consistent with findings from conflict-affected countries outside the region, where political risk—mainly in the form of potential adverse regulatory changes, which are significantly more likely than in other developing countries—are a main concern of investors (MIGA 2011).

Regulatory issues—related to land, for instance—can be at the heart of armed conflict. In India, for example, the Maoist insurgency is heavily concentrated in forest areas,

where land rights are at the center of the dispute. The Indian government has taken steps to address this constraint and source of grievance, enacting, for example, the Scheduled Tribes and Other Traditional Forest Dwellers Act in 2006 (box 7.3). Although it is probably too early to assess the effects of this law, the act is a very positive sign. Land issues also appear to be an important constraint in Afghanistan, where 68 percent of companies that tried to obtain additional land between 2005 and 2008 reported being unable to do so, according to the country's 2008 enterprise survey.

Improving the regulatory environment is key to encouraging private sector job creation in conflict situations. To attract investment, governments can focus on "soft measures," such as reducing barriers to firm registration and operations and cleaning up at least the most blatant pockets of corruption.

There is significant room for improvement. Afghanistan, for example, ranks 160th in the world on the overall ease of doing business and last in the world on protecting investors, trading across borders, and closing a business. But some of the top performers in improving their *Doing Business* rankings in recent years are postconflict countries, such as Liberia (box 7.4) and Rwanda. Given the limited upfront costs, simplification of business regulations is a key first step to attracting the private sector. Other components of the regulatory framework, such as tackling pervasive corruption, are likely to take more time to show improvement.

Three broad lessons for the development of the private sector in conflict-affected areas emerge from the success stories described in this section. First, the state plays an important role as an enabler of private sector activity by rebuilding infrastructure, strengthening the regulatory environment and the legitimacy of institutions like the judiciary, and providing security for the labor force. Second, communities can play a vital role in the success of private companies, sometimes by becoming stakeholders

BOX 7.3 **Improving the land rights framework in India**

The Scheduled Tribes and Other Traditional Forest Dwellers (Recognition of Forest Rights) Act of 2006 represents a departure from past forestry policy in India. The act seeks to address forest dwellers' demands for land rights by granting both individual and communal rights to people living and cultivating land in forested areas. The Ministry of Tribal Affairs, in conjunction with state governments and village councils, is required to verify occupancy and grant titles to forest dwellers that meet the requirements of the law.

Production in forest areas in India is a combination of timber, agriculture, and collection of nontimber forest produce (NTFP). Forestry and logging accounted for about 1 percent of GDP in 2009. Collection of fuelwood employed an estimated 11 million people, generating revenue of about $17 billion in 2001. Although data on forest production are limited, the Ministry of Environment and Forests estimates that 200 million people rely on timber and NTFPs for part or all of their livelihoods.

The Forest Rights Act is therefore expected to have a significant impact on the livelihoods of forest dwelling communities. Increased tenure security should provide incentives for investments in improvements to the land. Granting communities rights and responsibility over nonagricultural land should lead to more efficient forest management and sustainable

collection of NTFPs. Livelihoods in forest areas are severely constrained by a lack of infrastructure and government services. By providing for the administrative transformation of forest villages into revenue villages, the Forest Rights Act should increase the supply of roads, electricity, schools, and other government services to forest-dwelling communities.

Because of slow and partial implementation, many of the benefits of the Forest Rights Act have yet to be realized. According to the Ministry of Tribal Affairs, which periodically publishes data on the status of the implementation of the act, implementation varies widely from state to state. As of September 2010, Chhattisgarh had received more than 16 times the number of claims as Jharkhand and distributed more than 11 times as many titles. Orissa had issued titles for more than half of all claims submitted, whereas Gujarat had issued titles for less than 10 percent of claims. No state had accepted claims or issued titles for a significant number of communal claims. Instead, the focus has been on implementing the individual titles that represent part of the rights granted to forest dwellers under the act. The coming years should prove critical to the success of this act and the livelihoods of the populations dependent on forestry.

Sources: Authors, based on World Bank 2006; Government of India 2007, 2010. The full text of the act is available at http://forestrights.nic.in.

in private firms. Third, in their own interest, successful firms take a holistic approach to business, investing in their core economic activities (by creating jobs and developing human resources), contributing to their communities (by supporting education and health programs), and conducting policy dialogue with and supporting the reforms of the government. Community development initiatives are a way for firms to ensure local ownership, enhance their reputations, and improve security and the profitability and sustainability of their activities.

Although constraints to job creation in conflict-affected areas are severe, there are

ways around some of them. Developing a vibrant private sector takes a long time, however. In Afghanistan, for example, 10 years after the start of the latest armed conflict, domestic firms still produce primarily for the small domestic market, few foreign companies (less than 2 percent of all firms) operate, the quality of jobs remains low (World Bank 2008a). The public sector is therefore called on to play a more active role through labor market programs in conflict-affected areas during the initial phase of the recovery, before the private sector is able to absorb workers and generate jobs.

BOX 7.4   Improving the regulatory framework in a postconflict situation: Lessons from Liberia

Liberia is still recovering from the ravages of 14 years of conflict (1989–2003), during which it experienced one of the largest economic collapses in the world since World War II, with GDP decreasing by more than 90 percent. More than 6 percent of Liberia's population was killed, an estimated 500,000–1 million people were internally displaced (IDMC 2010), and an estimated 70 percent of schools and government buildings were destroyed. Apart from privately owned generators, there was no electricity in most of Liberia from 1991 to 2006 (Radelet 2007).

After the restoration of peace, in 2003, and the election of Ellen Johnson Sirleaf, in 2005, Liberia pursued a private sector–driven growth strategy (World Bank 2008b). A cabinet-level working group was created to think about the nature and sequencing of the reforms needed to attract the private sector. As a first step, the committee identified areas where "quick wins" could be obtained, in the form of simplifications to the business registration process and the establishment of a one-stop-shop to advise potential entrepreneurs of opportunities and provide them with technical support. As a second step, the committee focused on longer-term reforms that required legislative changes, such as the investment and revenue legal codes. In 2007, the Liberia Better Business Forum was established to facilitate public-

private dialogue for further proposals to improve the business environment.

After debuting in the *Doing Business* ranking at number 170 in 2007, Liberia moved to 155th place by 2010. The number of days needed to open a business was reduced from 68 in 2008 to 20 in 2010. Obtaining construction permits was made easier by abolishing the requirement to obtain a tax waiver certificate before submitting documents. As a result, the number of days needed to obtain a permit dropped from 398 in 2008 to 77 in 2010. The trade process was expedited by creating a one-stop shop bringing together various ministries and agencies and streamlining the inspection regime. In 2009, Liberia also committed to the Extractive Industry Transparency Initiative, under which it must comply with the global standard for transparent management of revenues from its extractive industries (iron, ore, diamonds, gold, timber, and rubber).

These reforms appear to be paying off: net inflows of foreign direct investment increased from $21 million in 2002 to $83 million in 2005 and $144 million in 2008. GDP per capita growth was 9.4 percent in 2007 and 7.1 percent in 2008, despite the global financial crisis.

Sources: Radelet 2007; Doing Business Indicators; World Development Indicators.

Education service delivery in conflict situations

Conflict usually forces people to miss out on years of education and training. In South Asia, conflict-affected areas start from a very low skill base, with illiteracy rampant among the workforce. As discussed in chapter 5, improving educational attainment and skills of the future workforce is fundamental if workers are to access more and better jobs. In conflict areas, the education system can also play a critical role in addressing some of the societal divisions associated with violence (World Bank 2011).

Skills provision in conflict situations requires innovative delivery mechanisms. Security concerns and the lack of physical (schools) and human (teachers) infrastructure are three important challenges. The difficulty of providing education and training in conflict-affected areas is compounded by extensive migration and displacement.

Although the public sector is likely to take the lead, NGOs, international aid organizations, private companies, and community initiatives can also be active in providing trained personnel or funds to rebuild, building infrastructure and improving security and access. The diaspora could play a vital role, as its members have the knowledge, ideas, and

BOX 7.5   **Improving schooling despite armed conflict through community schools in Nepal**

The government of Nepal had managed schools in the country since 1971—with poor educational results on average and wide inequalities across wealth categories. In 2001, the nationwide literacy rate was 54 percent, and gross enrollment in primary schools ranged from 22 percent among the poorest fifth of households to 90 percent among the top fifth.

In 2001, the government amended the Education Act, renaming all government-funded schools as community schools. Communities were empowered to take over the management of public schools by applying formally to the government and putting together a school management committee consisting of parents and influential local citizens. The school management transfer option was available to all communities, and the transfer process was voluntary.

The process of transferring the management of schools to communities began in 2002. It accelerated after 2003, when the World Bank provided financial and technical support through the Community School Support Program (CSSP). The CSSP had four main components: incentive grants of $1,500 in the year of transfer and performance grants for increasing enrollment and promotion rates; scholarships for children who were disadvantaged or had never been enrolled in school; training programs for teachers, community members, and supporting organizations; and monitoring and evaluation of strategies and interventions in recently transferred schools.

As of July 2010, more than 10,000 of Nepal's 25,000 public schools had been transferred to community management. A rigorous randomized control trial compared a set of 40 treatment schools that had been encouraged to apply for a transfer of management with 40 control schools, which were not given any such encouragement. Communities whose schools came under community management as a result of this promotion scheme were found to have a smaller share of out-of-school children, particularly among disadvantaged groups. These schools also had better grade progression rates and enhanced community participation and parental involvement. There were no significant differences in teacher absenteeism or student learning levels within the timeframe of the evaluation.

The experience in Nepal provides an example of an alternative service delivery mechanism that could be helpful in times of armed conflict. Community ownership (and the corresponding autonomy from the government) means that schools, students, teachers, and school management are in a better position to avoid altercations with the groups fighting in the war. In fact, progress in school enrollment in conflict-affected areas, where community schools where most prevalent, was more rapid than in the rest of the country. As a result, high-conflict areas had higher primary school enrollment rates than low-conflict areas by 2004. The increase in enrollment rates was particularly pronounced for girls, among whom enrollment rates increased 27 percentage points in high-conflict areas (box figure 7.5.1).

BOX FIGURE 7.5.1   **Primary school enrollment rate in Nepal among children 6–10 years old, 1996–2004**

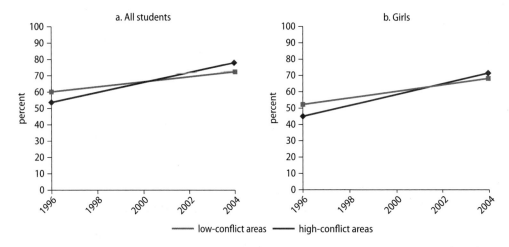

(continues next page)

BOX 7.5 (continued)

Can Nepal's experiment be generalized to other areas? Nepal's government decided to transfer schools to community management not on the basis of objective data but because such management was already prevalent in other places, such as forestry conservation and small irrigation areas. Many schools already had functioning school management committees; it was not clear whether their functioning changed as a result of this initiative. This history of community management may be absent in other settings, making Nepal's experience difficult to replicate.

Sources: Chaudhury and Parajuli 2009; World Bank 2001, 2010b.

market experience obtained while working abroad as well as local knowledge—and possibly still relevant socioeconomic ties—that may allow them to be successful.

Educational services such as "school in a box" kits and mobile educational programming could be useful in camps and settlements for internally displaced people. In the wake of the 2010 earthquake in Haiti, for example, schooling was provided inside buses that moved from community to community or camp to camp.[20] In areas with significant numbers of internally displaced people, temporary suspension of any documentation requirements could ease some of the constraints they face when enrolling in school and allow them to register for school without having to return to their areas of origin.[21]

Other alternatives, such as community delivery of educational services, could be helpful in addressing security issues. Community- and home-based education initiatives are two ways to get around security constraints, especially during the transitional stage. Community-level schemes could be useful by having women in a community, for example, organize themselves to accompany children and women to educational centers. In Afghanistan, many of these programs have been supported by NGOs, both before and after the ousting of the Taliban in 2001. The Ministry of Education has also participated as an official partner (Sigsgaard 2009).

Community- and home-based education initiatives can also facilitate the expansion of educational services into places affected by conflict, which are often difficult to reach

and cut off from population centers. The experience of Nepal's community schools can provide some lessons for the delivery of educational services amidst armed conflict (box 7.5).

Distance education through television, video, and particularly radio is another way of working around security problems. According to the British Broadcasting Corporation (BBC), almost half of the Afghan population listens to its radio dramas every week, suggesting great potential to use this medium as an educational tool, raise awareness, and promote social cohesion.

Labor market policies and programs

Because reforms to improve the business environment take time to bear fruit, labor market institutions, policies, and programs such as those discussed in chapter 6 have a particularly important role to play at the early postconflict stage. DDR programs; public works; training programs; and policies to support self-employment and the informal sector play both an activation (promotion) and a safety net (protection) role. As discussed below, however, the design of these programs is more complex in conflict situations.

Disarmament, demobilization, and reintegration programs

The DDR of excombatants has become a key element of peace building in conflict-affected countries. DDR programs usually target excombatants in three broad phases: disarmament (collecting and disposing of weapons); demobilization (disbanding military structures); and reintegration (the process of facilitating the return of former combatants to civilian life, the armed forces, or the police). The last phase is essentially an activation program. Reintegration packages—including vocational training, formal education, physical and mental health services, incentives for entrepreneurship, employment services, public works, and cash transfers—are at the heart of this phase (UN 2010).

DDR programs are underway in Afghanistan and Nepal. Afghanistan's $141 million demobilization program, which ran from 2003 to 2005, demobilized 63,000 professional soldiers and 7,500 child soldiers. In the reintegration phase, 46 percent of excombatants attended vocational or small business training, and 43 percent opted to go into agriculture. The reintegration phase was to have been completed in 2006 but was extended an additional two years after it was revealed that 56 percent of all demobilized excombatants were earning less than $1 a day (Carames and Sanz 2009). A new reintegration program directed at the entire affected community (not only excombatants), the Afghanistan Peace and Reintegration Program, is now in place. No formal evaluation exists, but by June 2011, 1,700 former fighters had publically joined the program (ISAF 2011).

In Nepal, nearly 20,000 members of the People's Liberation Army have been demobilized, at a cost of about $50 million.[22] These excombatants were to have been gradually reintegrated into the national armed forces, but political disagreements have prevented this phase from being completed.[23]

DDR programs can be costly. In a global survey of programs in 19 countries, researchers found that the average cost per demobilized person was $1,434—about 3.5 times per capita income in these countries (Carames and Sanz 2008). In Afghanistan and Nepal, programs have been more expensive, with costs per demobilized person of $2,278 in Afghanistan and $2,500 in Nepal (Carames and Sanz 2009). The disarmament and demobilization stages usually represent a small share of the budget (less than 10 percent); most of the spending goes toward reinsertion and reintegration. In this phase, excombatants who participate in the reintegration program often receive economic compensation to substitute for some of the income they would have earned by participating in violent activities. Afghanistan paid excombatants a total of $990, on average, to participate ($180–$480 a month over a period of two to four months)—the second-highest payment in the world after Colombia ($2,750). Nepal pays $46 a month (the duration of payments is not clear). DDRs may be unaffordable for many countries, especially when the conflict is nationwide.

Reintegration is the most difficult part of the DDR process. Providing relevant training and helping people find economic opportunities during or after a conflict is always difficult. The task is even harder in the case of excombatants. Reintegration is often about more than just finding new income sources, as excombatants have also lost physical security, political influence, social networks, and prestige with the end of the conflict (Willibald 2006). Failure to address these losses may jeopardize the DDR process and peace more generally (box 7.6).

The extensive use of cash transfers in the reintegration process illustrates some of the risks of such interventions. The effectiveness of the cash transfers is unclear a priori. On the one hand, to the extent that financing is the binding constraint, transfers could encourage compliance with disarmament commitments and help restore livelihoods. On the other hand, transfers, especially in cash, could exacerbate the illicit arms trade and generate resentment in the community. The effectiveness of transfer programs is therefore likely to depend on economic opportunities and the details of the implementation of the program, such as payment location, eligibility criteria, and targeting mechanisms.

BOX 7.6   Lessons from efforts to reintegrate Ugandan youth

In Uganda, a country affected by more than two decades of civil conflict, a group of researchers put together a program in the northern part of the country aimed at reintegrating youth. The program—the Survey of War Affected Youth (SWAY)—included an analysis of the needs and difficulties experienced by youth returning from the Lord Resistance Army (LRA), one of the main rebel groups in the country. It surveyed more than 1,000 households and 741 young men in 2005 and 2006 and 619 young women in 2007.

The program focused on youth who lived in the areas of interest before the escalation of the violence in 1996 and who had recently returned after having been part of the LRA. As the LRA selected and abducted members randomly, outcomes for these youth could be compared with those of youth who were not selected or abducted to serve in the LRA. The idea was to use the results of the survey to inform policy makers who were about to design a full DDR program for excombatants.

Assistance to youth in Northern Uganda took two main forms: reinsertion assistance and longer-term reintegration and development services. Reinsertion assistance included interim counseling; vocational training; basic health care; and a reinsertion package that comprised household items, agricultural tools, seeds, and an unconditional cash payment. Cash payments were provided not only to returnees but also to other families living in affected areas. Interventions included vocational training, cash, and assistance in starting small enterprises and psychosocial care.

Some of the lessons drawn by the team could be helpful in the design of other DDR programs in other parts of the world. Three findings deserve attention:

- Catching up on missed education is a pressing need, requiring a strong focus on secondary school and adult literacy. There is a need to go beyond the usual focus on primary education.
- In part as a consequence of lost education and work experience, excombatants were less than half as likely as noncombatant peers to be engaged in a skilled trade or a business. Their earnings were about a third those of youth who had not served in the LRA. Cash was one of the most crucial inputs needed for new income-generating activities; even the modest amounts of cash associated with the reinsertion package helped excombatants regenerate livelihoods. Interventions such as facilitation or business skills training could have important impacts on the effectiveness of these funds.
- Reinsertion packages for excombatants should be introduced in tandem with larger programs of support for all youth. SWAY researchers identified increased resentment and stigmatization on the part of people not receiving these benefits, making reintegration more difficult. Where cash disbursements are paid, it is crucial that they be designed to minimize the risks of stigmatization, resentment, misuse, and theft.

Source: Annan and others 2007.

Despite the prevalence of DDR programs in postconflict environments, the individual and country-specific factors that lead to successful reintegration are still not well understood. In their study of the highly regarded program in Sierra Leone, Humphreys and Weinstein (2007) find that it was of limited effectiveness in reintegrating more educated people, higher-ranking members of the rebel forces, and people who had been part of military units that had been most abusive of civilians. The fact that the effects of the program varied depending on the characteristics of the individuals calls for more detailed

evaluations of DDR programs, allowing for heterogeneous effects across individuals.

International experience with DDR does suggest some lessons for improving the chances of successful reintegration or activation:

- Because DDR is a long process, a strong commitment to peace from all parties and sufficient financing—often from international donors—is crucial.[24]
- A strong training component seems to be critical. Such training is especially relevant in a country like Nepal, where

---

BOX 7.7   **Training and employing displaced people: The case of Asocolflores in Colombia**

Colombia has suffered from violence for more than two decades. The primary sources of violence are conflicts among the government; right-wing paramilitary groups, such as the Revolutionary Armed Forces of Colombia (FARC); and left-leaning guerillas. By 2008, 2.65–4.36 million people had been displaced by the conflict, the second-largest population of displaced people in the world (after Sudan). A disproportionate number of the displaced are Afro-Colombians or members of indigenous tribal groups, who have low levels of literacy and numeracy.

Colombia is also the second-largest exporter of cut flowers in the world. In 2006, 70 percent of all roses and 97 percent of the carnations sold in the United States came from Colombia.

In 2003, the Colombian Association of Flower Exporters (Asocolflores) established a school of floriculture to enable people displaced by the conflict to find work. It developed a nine-month training course focused on cultivating, harvesting, grading,

and packing flowers. The course was followed by a four-month work period on flower farms, after which participants found permanent employment in the fast-growing flower industry.

The program was funded by Asocolflores and flower farmers; it also received funds and technical support from the U.S. Agency for International Development (USAID) and the Pan-American Development Fund (PADF). Participants were provided with a stipend, lodging, and psychological support to help them recover from displacement. By 2008, with an investment of $1.8 million, the school had benefited more than 1,631 families. A key lesson from the Colombian experience is that the private sector, supported by public funds, can be a useful source of training and jobs for displaced populations, especially in fast-growing industries that employ unskilled labor.

Sources: Caycedo and Mendoza 2008; IDMC 2009; PADF 2008; USAID 2006.

---

the military is already large and there are few prospects for absorbing all demobilized excombatants into it or the police forces.

- Public employment is likely to play an important role for excombatants, who often lack employable skills and are cut off from social networks.
- In certain cases, the private sector can be a useful partner, as it has been in Colombia, where public-private partnerships have created more than 1,800 jobs for internally displaced people (box 7.7). This experience can be extended to excombatants.[25]

Public work programs

Public works programs are often implemented in nonconflict situations (chapter 6).[26] In an analysis of 102 communities in countries affected by conflict in 2005, researchers found that 44 percent of conflict-affected communities had at least one public works project (World Bank 2010a). These

programs have many features that make them well-suited for conflict situations:[27]

- The workforce in conflict and postconflict areas is more likely to be in rural areas, where agriculture is the primary source of income. Most workfare programs target rural areas and involve the building or rehabilitating of community infrastructure, which is likely to increase the productivity of the agricultural sector and rural nonfarm activities.
- People in conflict areas have lower levels of education than people in nonconflict areas. Workfare programs are ideal for such people, because they provide work for unskilled workers (some programs also provide additional vocational training).
- People in conflict and postconflict areas are more likely to work in informal jobs, which provide little or no social protection. By instituting a workfare program, governments can provide informal unemployment insurance.

• Conflict and postconflict areas are characterized by mobile populations. Workfare programs, along with a traditional resettlement campaign, can help ease the transition of internally displaced people to their places of origin by providing them with temporary employment and guaranteed income for a period of time.

Implementing a public work program in conflict and postconflict situations poses certain challenges, however:

• Security is a major concern. In most cases, workfare programs can proceed only when there is sufficient order to provide a secure work environment and transportation to work sites, especially for women. Land mines and other conflict-induced hazards must be removed before a workfare program can begin.
• Most workfare programs use the wage rate as a targeting device, setting it at a level that is high enough to induce people to participate in the program and low enough to attract only the very poor. In conflict-affected areas, setting an appro-

priate wage can be difficult if private labor markets have not functioned for some time. In such situations, practitioners must be creative. In Sierra Leone, for example, preconflict household survey data, along with monthly price data on staple foods and fish, were used to come up with a wage estimate.

• Some communities may be so destroyed that the scope of public works may be broader than usual. In such communities, it could be desirable to include the rebuilding of private homes as part of the workfare program, as was done in Sri Lanka.
• Excombatants may not be able to work with other members of society, given the animosities generated during the conflict. Fearing reprisals, many excombatants in Sierra Leone did not wish to return to their villages, where a workfare program had been established. The solution was to allow such people to work in the workfare program set up in the capital.

Sri Lanka's public works program overcame some of these problems (box 7.8).

BOX 7.8 Implementing public works in a postconflict environment: Sri Lanka's Northern Province Emergency Recovery Project

The decades-long conflict between the Liberation Tigers of Tamil Eelam (LTTE) and the Sri Lanka government ended in May 2009. The conflict had led to the destruction of social and economic infrastructure and the displacement of hundreds of thousands of people from the five northern districts of Jaffna, Kilinochchi, Mannar, Mullaitivu, and Vavuniya. As part of its resettlement plan, the government established a cash-for-work program to repair community infrastructure and provide returning internally displaced populations with short-term income support.

Community leaders and project officers of the five districts identified projects. Community members mobilized returning households to form community cash-for-work committees, which identified projects of immediate need for the communities.

Projects included debris removal and land clearance, well restoration and construction, small-scale irrigation canal rehabilitation, small road rehabilitation and repairs, classroom rehabilitation, health clinic repairs and rehabilitation, and repair and construction of community drinking water facilities.

A maximum of three adults (including the head of household) from each returning household were eligible to participate in the program, with only one member allowed to participate on a given day. This feature of the program was included to encourage participants to seek other work.

In order to encourage only the very poor to self-select into the program, the wage rate was set at 15 percent below the market rate for unskilled labor for the district. The market wage was established by a

(continues next page)

(district) wage-fixing committee that included representatives of the government (who consulted the private sector), NGOs, and donors.

Participants could work for a total of 50 days. Given that the vast majority of internally displaced people returned to homesteads that had been severally damaged during the conflict, participants were allowed to work on their own homes during the first 10 days. The rationale was that they would not be able to work well with the workfare program or

with any other job if their homes remained in disrepair. Repairing one's own home also increased the sense of revival and confidence in the future.

By 2010, about 275,000 internally displaced people had returned to their villages. Participants in the program worked more than 380,000 person-days, repairing 1,500 kilometers of roads and 145 wells and cleaning more than 900 hectares of public spaces.

Source: Government of Sri Lanka 2010.

Training

The considerably lower skill base of the workforce in conflict-affected areas means that reskilling—with an emphasis on promoting literacy, noncognitive skills, and practical skills—is key for postconflict recovery. Given the large informal sectors in these areas, the discussion of training programs in chapter 6 is relevant here.

Public work and DDR programs often include training components, which attempt to cater to the diverse training needs of target groups. In the Afghanistan Peace and Reintegration Program, for instance, training includes not only literacy skills but also practical training in farming, farm equipment maintenance, nursery establishment and management, watershed management, road building and maintenance, and basic electrical work and plumbing.

Initially, the government takes the lead, often in partnership with international aid organizations and NGOs. Over time, the private sector can play an important role, particularly as it is more likely to provide job-related training and an employment pathway for trained workers (see box 7.7).

The difficulty of providing education and training in conflict-affected areas is compounded by extensive migration and displacement. The usual approach is to wait for people to come back to their homes, as evidenced

by the common reallocation packages offered in postconflict situations. Sometimes, however, people do not have the right opportunities at home or fear returning. Following the ceasefire in Sri Lanka, for example, unemployment rates increased significantly for the most educated (especially people who had recently moved back) in the Northern and Eastern provinces. With unemployment at 29 percent, this group became the most likely to be unemployed in the conflict-affected areas—a change from conflict times (World Bank 2007).

Support for self-employment and microenterprise development

Other interventions seek to support self-employment and microenterprise development to help informal sector workers improve their potential for generating income. Particularly relevant are microfinance, the strengthening of business supply chains, and business training in fostering entrepreneurship in the informal sector (World Bank 2011). Much of the discussion of interventions that promote self-employment in chapter 6 is also relevant for conflict-affected areas. It is important to recognize, however, that the presence of a large mobile population, security risks, malfunctioning product and input markets, and the erosion of trust in the community make microcredit and related operations particularly challenging in conflict-affected areas.

One example of a program that tries to tackle these issues in a postconflict environment is the Nepal Poverty Alleviation Fund (PAF), which seeks to promote entrepreneurship through its income-generating component. PAF provides loans, complemented with funds for infrastructure needed to better link products to markets.[28]

Initiatives directed at bringing producers and markets together—such as initiatives in Kosovo and Rwanda in the tourism, coffee, and dairy industries—could also bring early results (World Bank 2011). As with other interventions, programs directed at supporting self-employment need to be further evaluated before more specific lessons can be drawn on what works, when, and where.[29]

Fiscal and capacity constraints to public employment programs

Most conflict-affected areas lack governments with sufficient fiscal resources or capacity to administer large bureaucracies or public employment programs. Both of these constraints are likely to be particularly severe in cases of nationwide conflict.

Conflict-affected countries tend to have high levels of indebtedness (figure 7.13), low tax revenues, and high dependency on foreign aid. Tax revenues are low across South Asia, especially in Afghanistan (6 percent of GDP) and Pakistan (10 percent of GDP) (World Bank 2011b). Moreover, the military takes up a large share of central government expenditures in South Asia, estimated at 10 percent in Afghanistan and Bangladesh, 15 percent in India and Sri Lanka, and 18 percent in Pakistan (the average for conflict-affected countries worldwide is 3.2 percent) (World Bank 2011b).

These fiscal constraints and the considerable capacity constraints in conflict environments suggest an important role for international organizations and foreign governments in funding and capacity building. A risk, however, is that postconflict countries become highly dependent on foreign aid,

especially when the conflict is nationwide. In Afghanistan, for example, official development assistance represented 45.8 percent of gross national income in 2008 (World Bank 2011b). This dependency on foreign aid may pose risks to postconflict recovery by crowding out domestic resource mobilization, making unsustainable expenditure commitments, and raising the exchange rate (Boyce 2007). Moreover, international aid declines significantly after the initial postconflict period (Chen, Loayza, and Reynal-Querol 2007), before local revenue sources have recovered sufficiently. Some postconflict areas also depend heavily on international organizations and NGOs for well-paid jobs, which could further distort labor markets.[30]

Despite these caveats, international organizations have an important role to play, especially in the short term, by ensuring that local firms have the opportunity to participate in aid-financed tenders (in the logistics and construction sectors, for example). The Afghan First initiative by the North Atlantic Treaty Organization is a promising example of how to build capacity and increase the participation of local firms in conflict-affected areas.[31]

FIGURE 7.13 Central government debt as a percentage of GDP in conflict and nonconflict areas of South Asia and the world, 1990s and 2000s

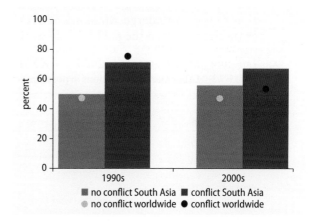

Sources: Authors, based on data from World Bank 2011b and UCDP/PRIO conflict database.
Note: Differences between conflict and nonconflict are significant at the 5 percent level. A country is considered to be in conflict in a given year if it experienced 25 or more battle deaths from confrontations between the military forces of two parties, at least one of which is the government of a state. Results do not change if India is excluded from the analysis.

A jobs transition path in conflict zones

Job-related interventions need to be sequenced depending on the stage and the type of the conflict. The constraints to job creation vary depending on whether the conflict is ongoing or over, nationwide or localized. These constraints will determine the design of all labor market programs discussed in this chapter, from public works and microcredit programs to changes in regulation and the provision of basic services, including education and infrastructure.

Security is a key determinant of the sustainability and desirability of investment in conflict-affected areas. Insecurity is a continuum: even postconflict situations experience a certain degree of violence. A minimum level of security is needed before certain investments can be made in conflict-affected areas; achieving security is likely to drive the sequencing of interventions.[32] There is little private investment in conflict-affected areas, and opportunities for wage employment are restricted. Large infrastructure projects or other fixed investments may not be feasible in areas where violence and insecurity are still rampant; innovative interventions that try to maintain human capital may represent a better investment.

Once a minimum level of security is achieved, job creation efforts in conflict zones need to undergo three major types of transitions: from the public sector as the key provider of jobs to a greater role for the private sector, from low-skilled agricultural jobs to higher-productivity nonfarm jobs, and from targeted programs to broad-based job creation. Table 7.3 summarizes these transitions.

Who creates jobs?

Given the constraints on private business, the public sector is often the main creator of jobs initially after conflict. Direct public employment should be only a transition strategy, however. Fiscal conditions, efficiency considerations, and unintended adverse effects of public employment (such as corruption and politicization of jobs) all caution against maintaining the state as a long-term provider of jobs. Given these concerns, policy makers need to develop a strategy for transitioning to a greater role for the private sector.

What jobs to create?

In the initial stages, it is natural that jobs be created in the agricultural sector, where the bulk of the workforce is already involved, as well as in other unskilled sectors. Sectors such as construction, which have the potential to employ local unskilled labor and help in postconflict rebuilding, should be encouraged, through, for example, public works and training in needed skills. The Pakistan postcrisis needs assessment identified

TABLE 7.3   Labor market transitions in postconflict zones

Key question	Constraints/concerns	Job transition path	
		From	To
Who creates jobs?	Security, infrastructure, poor regulations, fiscal constraints	Public sector, international organizations	Private sector, public-private partnerships
What jobs to create?	Security, rural, unskilled work force	Agricultural, unskilled, casual	Nonfarm, skilled, regular wage or salaried
For whom to create jobs?	Vulnerable populations (excombatants, youth at risk, war victims)	Targeted programs	Broad-based job creation

Source: Authors.

construction as the sector with the greatest immediate potential for job generation in the conflict-affected areas. Yet key sectors are often not prioritized, especially in view of the need for quick gains. In the worldwide community surveys conducted as part of the *Moving out of Poverty* series (World Bank 2010a), for example, only 16 percent of conflict-affected communities reported receiving assistance with agriculture and only 7 percent benefited from a finance/credit project.

The transition plan should seek to move workers toward higher-productivity jobs, which will pay more and result in greater welfare improvements. Initial steps toward doing so can include making the agricultural sector more productive, by, for example, providing better inputs, such as improved seeds, fertilizer, and storage facilities; creating functioning local markets; and rebuilding transport and communication networks to access more distant markets. Longer-term transition plans could include retraining the workforce to participate in manufacturing or services, as well as facilitating the growth of firms in the nonfarm sector. These measures are likely to create more jobs that pay regular wages or salaries. The private sector can be involved, through public-private partnerships, for example.

For whom to create jobs?

In the early stages of the conflict, policy interventions should be directed at managing the risks of renewed conflict and addressing the lack of economic opportunities for the vulnerable. Without credible economic alternatives to people involved in the fighting, an end to the violence is unlikely. Job creation can play an important role in helping address the concerns and grievances that led to the conflict, which is fundamental in buttressing confidence in the peace process.[33] Nepal—where persisting disagreements on how to integrate excombatants have left the country politically unstable almost five years after the peace agreement—illustrates the importance of addressing such concerns.

Job creation efforts in conflict-affected areas have to deal with three types of populations with special needs. The first is excombatants, who need to be integrated into the civilian or military workforce and be given incentives to refrain from violence. The second is at-risk youth and war victims. This group includes families who have lost some of their members; people with physical or mental disabilities; and households that are extremely vulnerable because they have no steady streams of income. The third is people displaced by the conflict, who may wish to return to their homes but need to be able to find jobs and feel secure there.

Targeting is difficult in conflict-affected areas. Identifying and locating beneficiaries often proves difficult. One way to overcome these problems can be to target programs for specific areas rather than specific people, thereby allowing self-selection to determine who receives benefits. This is the approach followed in Afghanistan, for example, under the Peace and Reintegration Program (Islamic Republic of Afghanistan 2010).

Over the longer term, broad-based job creation is needed in these areas. To work toward this goal, government can operate targeted programs for a limited time while encouraging the growth of other activities and firms to provide a broader set of jobs. Table 7.4 summarizes some policies that can be implemented at each step of this transition process.

Because of the violent nature of conflict, the impacts of policy interventions in conflict or postconflict environments have rarely been rigorously analyzed. As a result, policy makers cannot draw on a large body of evidence.[34] Some evidence on World Bank projects suggests that urban development projects are most likely to succeed and that private sector development projects need a longer time horizon for success (Chauvet, Collier, and Duponchel 2010). The quality of supervision is also an important determinant of project success, but evidence remains limited. Piloting some interventions and progressively expanding programs could help shed light on program effectiveness. In many conflicts, governments do not regain control of all conflict areas at the same time. Starting the

TABLE 7.4 Policy interventions in the initial postconflict stages

Goal	Possible interventions
Create some jobs quickly.	• Set up labor-intensive public works, especially in rural areas. • Create employment agencies where needed. • Respond to the needs of the displaced and internally mobile by creating job opportunities outside areas directly affected by conflict. • Distribute tools and inputs for farming and construction (starting with rehabilitation of people's own houses).
Promote agriculture and other informal sector activities, such as jobs in construction and self-employment.	• Rehabilitate complementary infrastructure needed for production and getting products to market (this intervention should be combined with appropriate business services). • Provide credit, funds, and training to foster entrepreneurship (microcredit, cash transfers to start businesses, business development training).
Create the base for better jobs by improving workers' skills.	• Focus on progressively getting children back to school and providing practical training and literacy courses for youth and adults using existing networks, community initiatives, and NGOs when available. • Address security concerns related to accessing schools or training, especially for girls (through mobile schools, community involvement in security). • Focus on the needs of displaced people and internal migrants, allowing for reskilling outside areas directly affected by conflict.
Improve the investment climate.	• Create "safe" zones that provide better regulation, services, and security. • Tap into innovative source of financing, such as diaspora bonds, as well as innovative forms of guarantees for foreign direct investment. • Establish investment information centers that match interested foreign investors with potential local partners. • Create links between firms and local communities to ensure the sustainability and profitability of enterprises. • Improve the overall business environment by simplifying regulations and facilitating processes for entry and exit.

Source: Authors.

piloting of labor market programs and policies in areas where control has been restored and then scaling up to the rest of the conflict-affected areas can improve policy results. The National Solidarity Program in Afghanistan is a case in point: the program was piloted in locations where violence was less pronounced before being progressively extended to the rest of the country. In Sri Lanka, many of the labor market and development programs the government is planning for the Northern Province were first piloted in the Eastern Province.

In short, the employment challenge in conflict-affected areas is larger than just creating jobs. It concerns the fundamental problem of establishing functioning economies, creating occupations different from those that existed in the war economy, promoting growth, generating government revenue, and addressing some of the underlying economic and social grievances that may have led to the armed conflict in the first place and could reinitiate violence if not addressed. There are examples of promising interventions, but achieving these goals is likely to take a long time.

Annex 7A Definitions of high-conflict and low-conflict regions in selected South Asian countries

This annex describes the classification of high- and low-conflict regions in Afghanistan, India, Nepal, and Sri Lanka.

Afghanistan

Classification is at the province level. High-conflict provinces are defined as provinces in which the number of deaths per 1,000 people caused by terrorist incidents in 2007 was greater than 0.1. By this definition, 15 provinces are in high-conflict areas (Baghlan, Ghazni, Farah, Helmand, Kandahar, Khost, Kunarha, Nimroz, Paktika, Paktya, Panjsher, Takhar, Urozgan, Wardak, and Zabul) areas. Data on terrorism deaths were obtained from the National Counterterrorism Center (2008).

India

Classification is at the state level. Low-conflict states are states that recorded no conflict-related fatalities in 2000 or 2007. High-conflict states are states that transitioned to a state of conflict during this period—that is, states that recorded no casualties in 2000 but did record conflict-related casualties in 2007. This means that states in conflict in 2000 are excluded from this analysis. By this definition, 10 states are in high-conflict areas (Bihar, Chhattisgarh, Jharkhand, Karnataka, Maharashtra, Meghalaya, Nagaland, Orissa, Uttar Pradesh, and West Bengal). Conflict-related fatalities are based on data from the RAND-MIPT Terrorism Database, collected by the National Memorial Institute for the Prevention of Terrorism (MIPT), in collaboration with the National Counterterrorism Center (NCTC). Data are available for the period January 1998–April 2007.

Nepal

Classification is at the district level. High-conflict districts are those in which the number of conflict deaths per 1,000 people in 2004 was greater than the median; low-conflict districts are those in which the number of conflict deaths per 1,000 people was less than the median level of 0.67. The time period considered was 1996–2004 (two years before the end of the conflict). By this definition, half of Nepal's 36 districts are classified as high-conflict areas (Achham, Arghakhanchi, Bajura, Banke, Bardiya, Bhojpur, Dadeldhura, Dailekh, Dang, Dhading, Dolakha, Dolpa, Doti, Gorkha, Humla, Jajarkot, Jumla, Kailali, Kalikot, Kanchanpur, Kavrepalanchok, Lamjung, Mugu, Myagdi, Nuwakot, Okhaldhunga, Ramechhap, Rolpa, Rukum, Salyan, Sankhuwasabha, Sindhuli, Sindhupalchok, Solukhumbu, Surkhet, and Taplejung). Data on conflict deaths were obtained from the annual *Human Rights Yearbooks* published by the Informal Sector Service Centre (INSEC), an NGO based in Kathmandu.

Sri Lanka

Classification is at the province level. The Northern Province was not included in the analysis because of lack of data. The Eastern Province is classified as high conflict; all other provinces are classified as low conflict. The analysis for Sri Lanka should be interpreted with caution, however, as the data reflect almost two decades of conflict. In addition, the analysis for Sri Lanka differs from that of other countries in that conflict-affected regions are moving from conflict to peace.

Annex 7B   Labor market characteristics and educational attainment in high-conflict and low-conflict areas of selected South Asian countries

TABLE 7B.1   **Labor market characteristics in high-conflict and low-conflict areas of Afghanistan, 2008**

Afghanistan	2008 Low-conflict areas	2008 High-conflict areas	Difference	Difference (rural)
Percentage of working age population employed	55.67	68.37	12.705***	9.192***
Male	76.09	81.08	4.984***	
Female	35.49	54.76	19.273***	
Unemployment rate	1.96	0.66	−1.305***	−1.008***
Male	2.82	0.83	−1.989***	
Female	1.12	0.47	−0.644***	
Labor force participation rate	57.63	69.03	11.400***	8.184***
Male	78.91	81.90	2.995***	
Female	36.60	55.23	18.629***	
Percentage of workers in urban areas	21.77	5.29	−16.481***	
Percentage of workers by sector of employment				
Agriculture	51.46	70.50	19.038***	9.698***
Manufacturing	6.62	1.43	−5.191***	−4.742***
Construction	9.43	4.90	−4.532***	−4.469***
Commerce	12.65	8.45	−4.195***	−0.502*
Transportation	3.13	2.94	−0.183	0.902***
Public administration	4.87	2.21	−2.664***	−0.440***
Percentage of workers by type of employment				
Regular wage or salaried	11.92	4.24	−7.673***	−2.966***
Casual	16.05	10.33	−5.719***	−7.371***
Employer	0.56	0.39	−0.176**	−0.230***
Self-employment	42.98	44.97	1.986***	3.346***
Unpaid family worker	28.46	40.05	11.590***	7.232***
Percentage of workers who are informal	89.09	96.26	7.170***	1.872***

Source: Authors' calculations, based on household and labor force surveys of Afghanistan.
Note: The "difference" column indicates the difference in labor market characteristics between households residing in high-conflict areas and those in low-conflict areas, as defined in annex 7.A. The "difference (rural)" columns computes the same difference for rural areas only.
*** Significant at the 1% level; ** significant at the 5% level; * significant at the 10% level.

TABLE 7B.2   **Labor market characteristics in high-conflict and low-conflict areas of India, 2000 and 2008**

India	2000 Low-conflict areas	2000 High-conflict areas	2008 Low-conflict areas	2008 High-conflict areas	Difference-in-difference	Difference-in-difference (rural)
Percentage of working age population employed	60.75	55.98	58.25	54.37	0.896**	1.118**
Male	81.00	81.17	80.74	80.88	−0.033	
Female	40.01	29.81	35.36	27.17	2.011***	
Unemployment rate	2.23	2.24	2.11	2.09	−0.024***	0.034***
Male	3.10	3.59	3.09	3.31	−0.260***	
Female	1.34	0.85	1.11	0.83	0.228***	
Labor force participation rate	62.99	58.22	60.35	56.46	0.871***	1.153***
Male	84.11	84.76	83.83	84.19	−0.293***	
Female	41.35	30.65	36.46	28.00	2.238***	
Percentage of workers in urban areas	24.05	21.45	27.87	22.36	−2.902***	

(continues next page)

TABLE 7B.2   Labor market characteristics in high-conflict and low-conflict areas of India, 2000 and 2008 (continued)

	2000		2008			
India	Low-conflict areas	High-conflict areas	Low-conflict areas	High-conflict areas	Difference-in-difference	Difference-in-difference (rural)
Percentage of workers by sector of employment						
Agriculture	58.18	61.35	50.18	56.38	3.027***	2.327***
Manufacturing	11.20	10.65	13.79	11.27	−1.960***	−0.525
Construction	5.71	4.08	8.81	6.46	−0.717***	−1.133***
Commerce	10.77	10.62	11.19	10.66	−0.381	0.061
Transportation	3.84	3.69	4.95	4.40	−0.397*	−0.516**
Public administration	2.79	2.38	1.86	1.97	0.515***	0.010
Percentage of workers by type of employment						
Regular wage or salaried	15.94	13.70	18.94	14.83	−1.865***	−1.312***
Casual	30.73	31.45	29.34	30.55	0.491***	−0.259
Employer	1.03	0.60	1.44	0.96	−0.053	−0.265**
Self-employment	29.61	32.71	30.90	32.92	−1.086**	−1.010*
Unpaid family worker	22.69	21.53	19.38	20.73	2.514***	2.846***
Percentage of workers who are informal	86.37	87.94	91.27	92.07	−0.762**	−1.033***

Source: Authors' calculations, based on household and labor force surveys of India.
Note: The "difference-in-difference" column indicates the difference in labor market trends between households residing in high-conflict areas and households residing low-conflict areas between 2000 (when there was no conflict in any of the areas considered here) and 2007 (when only the conflict group was in conflict). The "difference-in-difference (rural)" columns computes the same difference for rural areas only.
*** Significant at the 1% level; ** significant at the 5% level; * significant at the 10% level.

TABLE 7B.3   Labor market characteristics in high-conflict and low-conflict areas of Nepal, 1996 and 2004

	1996		2004			
Nepal	Low-conflict areas	High-conflict areas	Low-conflict areas	High-conflict areas	Difference-in-difference	Difference-in-difference (rural)
Percentage of working age population employed	73.84	81.92	75.91	86.34	2.352*	0.588
Male	79.16	86.26	83.41	89.50	−1.010	
Female	69.07	78.09	69.59	83.83	5.222***	
Unemployment rate	1.68	1.71	2.32	1.17	−1.181***	−0.788**
Male	2.68	2.23	3.16	1.89	−0.819	
Female	0.79	1.25	1.62	0.59	−1.484***	
Labor force participation rate	75.52	83.62	78.24	87.51	1.172	−0.200
Male	81.84	88.49	86.56	91.39	−1.829	
Female	69.87	79.34	71.21	84.42	3.738**	
Percentage of workers in urban areas	7.34	2.31	17.40	6.16	−6.213***	
Percentage of workers by sector of employment						
Agriculture	77.79	87.16	72.67	84.76	2.726**	−1.946
Manufacturing	4.52	2.65	7.56	3.08	−2.619***	−1.151*
Construction	2.47	2.57	2.99	2.84	−0.247	0.265
Commerce	7.45	3.00	7.30	3.02	0.161	1.267*
Transportation	1.21	0.58	1.64	0.49	−0.521*	−0.530*
Public administration	0.62	0.21	0.76	0.23	−0.121	0.183

(continues next page)

TABLE 7B.3   **Labor market characteristics in high-conflict and low-conflict areas of Nepal, 1996 and 2004** (continued)

Nepal	1996		2004			
	Low-conflict areas	High-conflict areas	Low-conflict areas	High-conflict areas	Difference-in-difference	Difference-in-difference (rural)
Percentage of workers by type of employment						
Regular wage or salaried	7.66	4.80	8.91	3.89	−2.167***	0.485
Casual	17.86	11.66	16.30	7.02	−3.084***	−3.835***
Unpaid family worker	49.35	57.22	47.78	60.08	4.420**	3.048*
Percentage of workers who are informal	92.25	95.75	90.79	95.98	1.685**	−0.831

Source: Authors' calculations, based on household and labor force surveys of Nepal.
Note: The "difference-in-difference" column indicates the difference in labor market trends between households residing in high-conflict areas and households residing low-conflict areas between1996 (before the conflict) and 2004 (after the conflict had begun). The "difference-in-difference (rural)" columns computes the same difference for rural areas only.
*** Significant at the 1% level; ** significant at the 5% level; * significant at the 10% level.

TABLE 7B.4   **Labor market characteristics in high-conflict and low-conflict areas of Sri Lanka, 2004 and 2008**

Sri Lanka	2004		2008			
	Low-conflict areas	High-conflict areas	Low-conflict areas	High-conflict areas	Difference-in-difference	Difference-in-difference (rural)
Percentage of working age population employed	54.70	45.92	56.51	45.95	1.787	1.655
Male	75.55	75.52	77.80	76.27	1.504	
Female	34.96	19.74	37.60	18.99	3.384**	
Unemployment rate	4.73	5.35	3.32	4.03	−0.083	−0.084
Male	4.79	5.68	3.15	4.01	0.032	
Female	4.67	5.06	3.48	4.05	−0.180	
Labor force participation rate	59.43	51.27	59.84	49.98	1.704	1.571
Male	80.33	81.20	80.95	80.28	1.536	
Female	39.64	24.80	41.08	23.03	3.204**	
Percentage of workers in urban areas	12.13	22.75	10.24	21.42	−0.558	
Percentage of workers by sector of employment						
Agriculture	31.66	27.39	30.85	24.03	2.545	3.362*
Manufacturing	18.58	11.75	19.21	12.66	−0.273	−1.876
Construction	5.36	4.42	6.32	10.52	−5.148***	−5.303***
Commerce	14.66	24.55	15.38	19.91	5.362***	5.024***
Transportation	5.82	5.87	6.11	4.63	1.537*	1.750*
Public administration	7.38	9.34	6.78	10.80	−2.059*	−2.340*
Percentage of workers by type of employment						
Regular wage or salaried	37.64	26.59	27.18	20.27	−4.138**	−5.741***
Casual	23.00	28.54	29.84	43.15	−7.758***	−9.203***
Employer	2.79	2.91	2.95	2.11	0.964	1.025
Self-employment	27.27	31.50	29.25	29.42	4.065**	6.078***
Unpaid family worker	9.31	10.45	10.78	5.05	6.868***	7.842***
Percentage of workers who are informal	81.24	79.10	71.13	75.99	−6.992***	−6.556***

Source: Authors' calculations, based on household and labor force surveys of Sri Lanka.
Note: The "difference-in-difference" column indicates the difference in labor market trends between households residing in high-conflict areas and households residing in low-conflict areas between 2008 (after the cease fire) and 2004 (during the cease fire). The "difference-in-difference (rural)" columns computes the same difference for rural areas only.
*** Significant at the 1% level; ** significant at the 5% level; * significant at the 10% level.

TABLE 7B.5 Educational attainment in high-conflict and low-conflict areas of South Asia, by country
(percentage of working-age population)

Country/level of education	Low-conflict areas	High-conflict areas	Low-conflict areas	High-conflict areas	Difference	Difference (rural)	Difference-in-difference	Difference-in-difference (rural)
Afghanistan	2008							
No education	67.87	82.19	n.a	n.a	14.320***	4.500***	n.a	n.a
Some primary school	8.74	4.32	n.a	n.a	-4.418***	-3.450***	n.a	n.a
Completed primary school	10.04	6.73	n.a	n.a	-3.315***	-0.906***	n.a	n.a
Lower-secondary schooling	5.45	3.67	n.a	n.a	-1.786***	0.433***	n.a	n.a
Upper-secondary schooling	5.94	2.59	n.a	n.a	-3.340***	-0.346**	n.a	n.a
Tertiary education	1.96	0.50	n.a	n.a	-1.460***	-0.231***	n.a	n.a
India	2000		2008					
No education	37.48	45.51	28.79	35.80	n.a	n.a	-1.017***	-1.563***
Some primary school	9.23	8.37	8.36	7.66	n.a	n.a	0.162	0.405
Completed primary school	13.92	10.06	15.30	13.53	n.a	n.a	2.094***	2.144***
Lower-secondary schooling	28.08	25.67	31.70	29.49	n.a	n.a	0.202	0.500
Upper-secondary schooling	10.85	9.90	8.96	7.54	n.a	n.a	-0.464*	-1.072***
Tertiary education	0.43	0.49	6.90	5.98	n.a	n.a	-0.975***	-0.414***
Nepal	1996		2004					
No education	61.27	69.90	48.22	57.94	n.a	n.a	1.092	-2.343
Some primary school	7.90	10.49	9.46	11.71	n.a	n.a	-0.340	0.237
Completed primary school	12.69	10.25	13.98	13.93	n.a	n.a	2.387**	1.923*
Lower-secondary schooling	15.58	8.43	22.89	14.69	n.a	n.a	-1.053	0.029
Upper-secondary schooling	1.63	0.58	3.46	1.21	n.a	n.a	-1.214***	0.104
Tertiary education	0.93	0.34	1.99	0.53	n.a	n.a	-0.873***	0.051
Sri Lanka	2004		2008					
No education	4.79	7.56	3.13	5.28	n.a	n.a	0.626	0.145
Some primary school	14.99	22.73	8.36	13.24	n.a	n.a	2.853***	2.543**
Completed primary school	23.02	26.10	19.61	25.95	n.a	n.a	-3.260***	-4.847***
Lower-secondary schooling	43.39	35.58	53.89	43.77	n.a	n.a	2.307*	2.833*
Upper-secondary schooling	11.64	6.04	12.34	9.30	n.a	n.a	-2.549***	-0.381
Tertiary education	2.17	1.97	2.69	2.46	n.a	n.a	0.024	-0.293

Sources: Authors' calculations, based on household surveys and conflict data described in annex 7A.

Note: The "difference" column indicates the difference in labor market characteristics between households residing in high-conflict areas and households residing in low-conflict areas, as defined in annex 7A. The "difference (rural)" column computes the same difference in rural areas only. The "difference-in-difference" column is calculated as in tables 7B.2–7B.4 for the respective countries. The "difference-in-difference (rural)" column computes the same difference in trends in rural areas only. *** Significant at the 1% level; ** significant at the 5% level; * significant at the 10% level. n.a. = Not applicable.

Notes

1. This chapter focuses on internal armed conflict against the state. Although the civil wars in Nepal and Sri Lanka recently ended, both countries are included in the analysis, because many of the challenges addressed—and the policy options discussed—refer to postconflict areas. Moreover, a better understanding of the impact of conflict in these countries can provide insights for the rest of South Asia. With this in mind, throughout this chapter the term *conflict affected* is used to characterize areas that are either experiencing violence from internal armed conflict or recovering from armed conflict.

2. Many of the issues discussed in this chapter could also be relevant for other types of disruptions, such as natural disasters. Asia as a whole is the continent most often hit by natural disasters. Since 1950, it has experienced more than 3,900 disasters, 42 percent of the global disasters in this period. These disasters killed more than 5.6 million people (83 percent of the world total) and affected more than 5.4 billion others (90 percent of the world total) (CRED 2011).

3. Measuring the intensity of armed conflict is very difficult. Due to data limitations and for comparability reasons, the indicator of intensity used here is the number of direct deaths from armed conflict. Data sources and methodology are discussed in annex 7A.

4. Migration can also play an important role as a source of jobs for skilled and unskilled workers from conflict-affected countries, both during and after conflicts (World Bank 2011).

5. This assumption is probably stronger in some cases than in others, given that important differences in labor market indicators in conflict and nonconflict areas often predate the conflict. Lack of data prevents analysis of preconflict trends.

6. In India and Nepal, the earlier year is a year of peace; during the later year, there was conflict in areas of both countries. In Sri Lanka, the year of conflict is 2008; 2004 was a year of relative peace (the middle of a ceasefire). The effect of a few additional years of violence is measured. In Afghanistan, where only one round of household survey data is available, the simple differences in outcomes for high-conflict and low-conflict areas are compared. In Pakistan, household surveys do not

provide enough coverage of conflict-affected areas.

7. Although establishing causality is difficult, there is some evidence that lower economic growth and poor economic performance increase the likelihood of armed conflict. A very robust result in the cross-country literature on conflict is that poorer countries and countries with slower growth are at higher risk of experiencing civil war (Collier and Hoeffler 2004; Fearon and Laitin 2003). Using rainfall as an exogenous determinant of economic growth in Africa yields a similar result, suggesting that there is a causal relationship between a lack of economic growth and the incidence of conflict (Miguel, Satyanath, and Sergenti 2004). Within-country analyses also find a strong link between poverty and economic shocks on the one hand and the subsequent emergence of conflict on the other (see Dube and Vargas 2008 on Colombia; Do and Iyer 2010 on Nepal; and Iyer 2009 on South Asia).

8. In this particular study, definitions of poverty are based on subjective measures and a locally defined poverty line for each community. A "ladder of life" was used to determine who in a community qualified as poor. During a ladder of life exercise, focus group participants describe the steps (or levels) of overall well-being of households in their villages. They then rank up to 150 households in their village/neighborhood according to their step on the ladder of life, currently and in the past. The results of this ranking exercise produce a community mobility matrix for each village that can be used to estimate the evolution of prosperity, including the share of households that moved out of poverty, the share of households that experienced upward mobility of any kind, and the degree of mobility (either up or down).

9. Smuggling and other illegal activities (such as poppy cultivation in Afghanistan) are also a major source of employment in many conflict-affected areas in the region. The scope of these activities is difficult to quantify. In 2005, illegal opium revenues were estimated to reach nearly $3 billion, equivalent to half of Afghanistan's legal economy (UNODC 2005). Households in Afghanistan that cultivate poppy are significantly less likely to be poor (World Bank 2005).

10. The effect of conflict on the employment rate—as on other labor market indicators—is

likely to vary depending on the context and the subgroups of the population considered. The effect may also change in the immediate aftermath of the conflict. In Pakistan, for example, after the first wave of the militancy crisis in the North West Frontier Province (Khyber Pakhtunkhwa), women's movements were severely limited after internally displaced people arrived. As a result, women became less likely to work (World Food Programme 2011).

11. As discussed in chapter 3, the female employment rate in Nepal is more than twice the unweighted average of employment rates of the other South Asian countries (40 percentage points higher). Conflict seems to explain only a small share of this, as the evidence indicates that the conflict led to a 5 percentage point increase in employment rates among women in areas most affected by conflict.

12. In India, the difference in preconflict youth unemployment rates is not statistically significant.

13. Except possibly in Sri Lanka, unemployment is not a very strong indicator of labor market conditions in South Asia, where few people can afford to be unemployed, making these trends difficult to interpret.

14. What look like worse labor market outcomes in conflict environments do not necessarily translate into lower average labor incomes. In Nepal, the median household labor income per capita in low-conflict areas was already 1.5 times that of conflict-affected areas before the conflict; the conflict increased this gap to 1.7 by 2004. In contrast, in Afghanistan and Sri Lanka, labor incomes were higher in conflict-affected areas.

15. For example, school enrollment often falls significantly after natural disasters, as children join the labor force (Jacoby and Skoufias 1997; Jensen 2000; Santos 2007).

16. In India, Maldives, and Sri Lanka, firms were not asked about political instability. Surveys there referred to "government policy instability," which includes both macroeconomic and political instability. In Sri Lanka, government policy instability was cited as the second-most severe constraint; in India and Maldives, it was not among the top five constraints.

17. SEZs have become increasingly popular in the developing world: as of 2008, an estimated 3,000 SEZs in more than 130 countries had created more than 68 million direct jobs (FIAS

2008). Bangladesh, India, Nepal, Pakistan, and Sri Lanka all have SEZs. Afghanistan has no duty-free import zones. It is considering establishing trade facilitation zones, export processing zones, or both to enhance export potential. Legislation before the U.S. Congress would establish special import tax status for certain categories of goods made in reconstruction opportunity zones (http://www.state.gov/e/eeb/rls/othr/ics/2010/138776.htm).

18. Even this figure for the north is likely to be an overestimate, as the survey could not cover the remote districts of Kilinochchi, Mannar, and Mullaitivu, where up to 90 percent of the households may not have power (World Bank 2007).

19. For more information on community-driven development projects in postconflict environments, see Barron (2010).

20. See http://www.clintonfoundation.org/haiti_longstanding/haiti_fact_sheet.php.

21. For a discussion of interventions to provide educational services to displaced populations, see Mooney and French (2005).

22. The program is not officially a DDR program but rather a "campment, UN monitoring, and reintegration" (CMR) program. In the long term, the goals of both programs are essentially the same (Gurung 2006).

23. The Nepal Peace Project also includes activation programs to assist families.

24. The review of DDR programs by Carames and Sanz (2009) finds that the disarmament and demobilization stages take about 16 months on average, ranging from 4 months in Angola to 27 months in Sierra Leone. The reintegration phase usually takes considerably longer, lasting two years on average.

25. For a more detailed discussion on the lessons learned from DDR programs, see Meek and Malan (2004).

26. For a review of experiences with public work programs around the world, see Del Ninno, Subbarao, and Milazzo (2009).

27. The authors are grateful to Ernest Sergenti (World Bank) for his contributions to this section.

28. See the Poverty Alleviation Fund website (www.pafnepal.org.np/index.php).

29. For a more detailed discussion of microfinance, cooperatives, and self-help groups in postconflict situations, see ILO (2003).

30. In conflict-affected communities in Afghanistan, for example, employment by NGOs was rated as highly desirable, and households

with an NGO employee were rated as best off (World Bank 2010a).

31. Afghan First has not been rigorously evaluated, but initial data from a capacity building project for local enterprises suggest that Afghan companies supported by the project over the years are increasingly winning contracts. The increase has become steeper since the introduction of Afghan First in 2009. For more information, see http://www.nato.int/cps/en/SID-BF6A3963-402643FF/natolive/official_texts_62851.htm?mode=pressrelease).

32. Of course, the security situation itself can be influenced by policy—not only by direct security measures like policing but also by other interventions discussed in this chapter.

33. For instance, in countries in which ethnic differences were at the heart of the conflict, postconflict public work programs need to be careful not to favor one group over others. In cases where the conflict arose as a result of issues in the management and distribution of natural resources, such as forests, any postconflict job creation strategy needs to ensure that property rights are strengthened and that the rules of the game for the exploitation of the resources are clear and fair.

34. Some notable exceptions are the ongoing impact evaluation of the National Solidarity Program in Afghanistan (Beath and others 2010) and ongoing work evaluating DDR programs and employment interventions in Uganda (Blattman and Fiala 2009).

References

Akresh, R., and D. de Walque. 2008. "Armed Conflict and Schooling: Evidence from the 1994 Rwandan Genocide." IZA Discussion Paper 3516, Institute for the Study of Labor, Bonn.

Amnesty International. 2003. "No One Listens to Us and No One Treats Us as Human Beings: Justice Denied to Women." Report ASA 11/023/2003, London.

Annan, J., C. Blattman, K. Carlson, and D. Mazurana. 2007. "Making Reintegration Work for Youth in Northern Uganda." Research Brief, *Survey of War Affected Youth (SWAY)*, 11.

Arunatilake, N., S. Jayasuriya, and S. Kelegama. 2001. "The Economic Cost of the War in Sri Lanka." *World Development* 29 (9): 1483–1500.

Barron, P. 2010. "CDD in Post-Conflict and Conflict-Affected Areas: Experiences from East Asia." Background paper for the *World Bank World Development Report 2011*. http://wdr2011.worldbank.org/sites/default/files/pdfs/WDR%20Background%20Paper_Barron_0.pdf.

Beath, A., F. Christia, R. Enikolopov, and S.A. Kabuli. 2010. "Randomized Impact Evaluation of Phase-II of Afghanistan's National Solidarity Programme (NSP): Estimates of Interim Program Impact from First Follow-up Survey." http://www.nsp-ie.org/reports/BCEK-Interim_Estimates_of_Program_Impact_2010_07_25.pdf.

Beber, B., and C. Blattman. 2010. "The Industrial Organization of Rebellion: The Logic of Forced Labor and Child Soldiering." Working paper, Department of Political Science, Yale University, New Haven, CT. http://chrisblattman.com/documents/research/2010.IOofRebellion.pdf.

Bhalotra, S., and M. Umana-Aponte. 2010. "The Dynamics of Women's Labor Supply in Developing Countries." IZA Discussion Paper 4879, Institute for the Study of Labor, Bonn.

Blattman, C., and J. Annan. 2010. "The Consequences of Child Soldiering." *Review of Economics and Statistics* 92 (4): 882–98.

Blattman, C., and N. Fiala. 2009. "Uganda: Post-War Youth Vocational Training." http://chrisblattman.com/projects/nusaf_yo/.

Blattman, C., and E. Miguel. 2010. "Civil War." *Journal of Economic Literature* 48 (1): 3–57.

Boyce, J. 2007. "Public Finance, Aid and Post-Conflict Recovery." Working paper, Department of Economics, University of Massachusetts, Amherst, MA.

Brueck, T. 2004. "Coping Strategies Post-War Rural Mozambique." Working paper, Queen Elizabeth House, University of Oxford, Oxford.

Carames, A., and E. Sanz. 2008. "Analysis of Disarmament, Demobilization and Reintegration. DDR. Programmes in the World during 2007." School for a Culture of Peace, Bellaterra, Spain. http://escolapau.uab.cat/img/programas/desarme/ddr005i.pdf.

———. 2009. "Analysis of Disarmament, Demobilization and Reintegration. DDR. Programmes in the World during 2008." School for a Culture of Peace, Bellaterra, Spain. http://escolapau.uab.es/img/programas/desarme/ddr/ddr2009i.pdf.

Card, D. 1999. "The Causal Effect of Education on Earnings." In *Handbook of Labor Economics*, vol. 3, ed. O. Ashenfelter and D. Card, 1801–63. Amsterdam: Elsevier.

Caycedo, A., and E. Mendoza. 2008. "Colombian Flowers and Floriculture." http://issuu.com/acaycedo/docs/colombian _grown_208_pages_single.

Central Bank of Sri Lanka. Various years. *Annual Reports*. Colombo.

Chaudhury, N., and D. Parajuli. 2009. "Pilot Evaluation: Nepal Community School Support Project." http://siteresources.worldbank.org/ SOUTHASIAEXT/Resources/223546-11924 13140459/4281804-1215548823865/Nepal CSSP.pdf.

Chauvet, L., P. Collier, and M. Duponchel. 2010. "What Explains Aid Project Success in Post-Conflict Situations?" Policy Research Working Paper 5418, World Bank, Washington, DC.

Chen, S., N. Loayza, and M. Reynal-Querol. 2007. "The Aftermath of Civil War." Policy Research Working Paper 4190, World Bank, Washington, DC.

Collier, P., and A. Hoeffler. 2004. "Greed and Grievance in Civil Wars." *Oxford Economic Papers* 56 (4): 563–95.

Collier, P., A. Hoeffler, and N. Sambanis. 2005. "The Collier-Hoeffler Model of Civil War Onset and the Case Study Project Research Design." In *Understanding Civil War: Evidence and Analysis*, ed. P. Collier and N. Sambanis, 1–33. Washington, DC: World Bank.

Collier, P., A. Hoeffler, and M. Söderbom. 2008. "Post-Conflict Risks." *Journal of Peace Research* 45 (4): 461–78.

Collier, P., and N. Sambanis. 2005. *Understanding Civil War: Evidence and Analysis*. Washington, DC: World Bank.

CRED (Centre for Research on the Epidemiology of Disasters). 2011. EM-DAT: The OFDA/ CRED Emergency Disaster Database. Université Catholique de Louvain, Louvain, Belgium. http://www.emdat.be.

Deininger, K. 2003. "Causes and Consequences of Civil Strife: Micro-Level Evidence from Uganda." *Oxford Economic Papers* 55: 579–606.

Del Ninno, C., K. Subbarao, and A. Milazzo. 2009. *How to Make Public Works Work: A Review of the Experiences*. SP Discussion Paper 0905, World Bank, Washington, DC.

Do, Q., and L. Iyer. 2010. "Geography, Poverty and Conflict in Nepal." *Journal of Peace Research* 47 (6): 735–48.

Dube, O., and J. Vargas. 2008. "Commodity Price Shocks and Civil Conflict: Evidence from Colombia." Working Paper 14, Harvard University, Center for International Development, Cambridge, MA.

Fearon, J., and D. Laitin. 2003. "Ethnicity, Insurgency, and Civil War." *American Political Science Review* 97 (1): 75-90.

FIAS (Foreign Investment Advisory Service). 2008. "Special Economic Zones: Performance, Lessons Learned and Implications for Zone Development." World Bank, Washington, DC.

Finegan, T., and R. Margo. 1994. "Work Relief and the Labor Force Participation of Married Women in 1940." *Journal of Economic History* 54 (1): 64-84.

Gardeazabal, J. Forthcoming. "Methods for Measuring Aggregate Costs of Conflict." In *Handbook of the Economics of Peace and Conflict*, ed. M. Garfinkel and S. Skaperdas. Oxford: Oxford University Press.

Glewwe, P. 2002. "Schools and Skills in Developing Countries: Education Policies and Socioeconomic Outcomes." *Journal of Economic Literature* 40 (2): 436–82.

Government of India. 2007. "India's Forests." Ministry of Environment and Forests, New Delhi. http://tribal.nic.in/writereaddata/ mainlinkFile/File1256.pdf.

———. 2010. "Status Report on Implementation of the Scheduled Tribes and Other Traditional Forest Dwellers. Recognition of Forest Rights Act, 2006." Ministry of Tribal Affairs New Delhi. http://tribal.nic.in/writereaddata/ mainlinkFile/File1256.pdf.

Government of Sri Lanka. 2010. "Operational Guidelines for ENReP Cash for Work Program." Ministry of Nation Building and Estate Infrastructure Development (MNBEID), Colombo.

Gurung, C.B. 2006. "So Far, So Good." *Nepali Times*, December 7, Kathmandu.

Herman, L., and Q. Dhanani. 2010. "Roshan: Light at the End of the Tunnel in Afghanistan." Harvard Business School Case Study, Cambridge, MA.

Hoeffler, A. 2011. "On the Causes of Civil War." Forthcoming in *Oxford Handbook of the Economics of Peace and Conflict*, ed. M. Garfinkel and S. Skaperdas. Oxford: Oxford University Press.

Hoeffler, A., and M. Reynal-Querol. 2003. "Measuring the Costs of Conflict." Working paper, Centre for the Study of African Economies and St. Antony's College, University of Oxford,

Oxford. http://www.conflictrecovery.org/bin/2003_Hoeffler_Reynal-Measuring_the_Costs_of_Conflict.pdf.

Humphreys, M., and J. Weinstein. 2007. "Demobilization and Reintegration." *Journal of Conflict Resolution* 51 (4): 531–67.

Indian Express. 2009. "Lanka Plans to Set Up Free Trade Zones in LTTE Bastions." October 23. http://www.indianexpress.com/news/lanka-plans-to-set-up-free-trade-zones-in-ltte-bastions/532356/.

IDMC (Internal Displacement Monitoring Center). 2009. *Internal Displacement: Global Overview of Trends and Developments in 2008.* http://www.internal-displacement.org.

———. 2011. IDP statistics. http://www.internal-displacement.org/8025708F004CE90B/(httpRegionPages.2DE3ACEE54F9A63B802570A6005588C1?OpenDocument.

IISS (International Institute for Strategic Studies). 2010. Armed conflict database. http://www.iiss.org/publications/armed-conflict-database/.

ILO (International Labour Office). 2003. *Jobs after War: A Critical Challenge in the Peace and Reconstruction Puzzle,* ed. E. Date-Bah. Geneva. Geneva: International Labour Office.

INSEC (Informal Sector Service Center). 2008. *Human Rights Yearbook 2008.* Kathmandu.

———. 2010. "Number of Victims Killed by State and Maoists in Connection with the People's War." http://www.insec.org.np/pics/1247467500.pdf.

ISAF (International Security Assistance Force). 2011. Afghanistan Peace and Reintegration Program website. http://www.isaf.nato.int/article/focus/afghanistan-peace-and-reconciliation-program.htm.

Islamic Republic of Afghanistan. 2010. *Afghanistan Peace and Reintegration Program.* National Security Council, Kabul. http://www.sipri.org/blogs/Afghanistan/Afghan%20Peace%20and%20Reconciliation%20Programme-%20draft-%20Apr%2010%20.pdf.

Iyer, L. 2009. "The Bloody Millennium: Internal Conflict in South Asia." Working Paper 09-086, Harvard Business School, Cambridge, MA.

Jacoby, H., and E. Skoufias. 1997. "Risk, Financial Markets, and Human Capital in a Developing Country." *Review of Economic Studies* 64 (3): 311–35.

Jensen, R. 2000. "Agricultural Volatility and Investments in Children." *American Economic Review, Papers and Proceedings* 90 (2): 399–404.

Jones, N., R. Holmes, H. Marsden, S. Mitra, and D. Walker. 2009. "Gender and Social Protection in Asia: What Does the Crisis Change?" Background paper for the Conference on the Impact of the Global Economic Slowdown on Poverty and Sustainable Development in Asia and the Pacific, Overseas Development Institute, London.

Ketkar, S., and D. Ratha. 2009. "New Paths to Funding." *Finance and Development* 46 (2). http://www.imf.org/external/pubs/ft/fandd/2009/06/ketkar.htm.

Lopez, H., and Q. Wodon. 2005. "The Economic Impact of Armed Conflict in Rwanda." *Journal of African Economies* 14 (4): 586–602.

McKay, A., and S. Loveridge. 2005. "Exploring the Paradox of Rwandan Agricultural Household Income and Nutritional Outcomes in 1990 and 2000." Staff Paper 2005–2006, Department of Agricultural Economics, Michigan State University, East Lansing, MI.

McLeod, D., and M. Davalos. 2008. "Sustainable Post-Conflict Employment Creation: From Stabilization to Poverty Reduction." Working paper, Department of Economics, Fordham University, New York. http://www.fordham.edu/economics/mcleod/PostConflictEmployment10.pdf.

Meek, S., and M. Malan, eds. 2004. *Identifying Lessons from DDR Experiences in Africa.* Institute for Security Studies Monograph 106, Pretoria, South Africa.

Menon, N., and Y. van der Meulen. 2010. "Gender and Conflict in Nepal: Testing for 'Added Worker' Effects." Working paper, Rutgers University, Department of Economics, New Brunswick, NJ.

MIGA (Multilateral Investment Guarantee Agency). 2011. *World Investment and Political Risk.* Washington, DC.

Miguel, E., S. Satyanath, and E. Sergenti. 2004. "Economic Shocks and Civil Conflict: An Instrumental Variables Approach." *Journal of Political Economy* 112 (4): 725–53.

Mooney, E., and C. French. 2005. "Barriers and Bridges: Access to Education for Internally Displaced Children." Working paper, Brookings Institution, Washington, DC.

National Counterterrorism Center. 2008. *2007 NCTC Report on Terrorism.* www.nctc.gov.

———. 2009. *2008 NCTC Report on Terrorism.* www.nctc.gov.

PADF (Pan-American Development Foundation). 2008. "Socially-Conscious Flowers: Flowers Help to Support Displaced Colombian Families through the School of Floriculture." http://www.padf.org/DOCUMENTS/News Stories/080204_asocolflores_prnewswire .pdf.

Radelet, S. 2007. "Reviving Economic Growth in Liberia." Working Paper 133, Center for Global Development, Washington, DC.

Santos, I. 2007. "Disentangling the Effects of Natural Disasters on Children: 2001 Earthquakes in El Salvador." Ph.D. dissertation, Kennedy School of Government, Harvard University, Cambridge, MA.

Schweitzer, M. 1980. "World War II and Female Labor Force Participation Rates." *Journal of Economic History* 40 (1) 89–95.

Shemyakina, O. 2011. "The Effect of Armed Conflict on Accumulation of Schooling: Results from Tajikistan." *Journal of Development Economics* 95 (2): 186–200.

Sigsgaard, M. 2009. *Education and Fragility in Afghanistan: A Situational Analysis.* International Institute for Educational Planning, United Nations Educational, Scientific and Cultural Organization (UNESCO), Paris.

Smith, D. 2004. "Trends and Causes of Armed Conflict." In *The Berghof Handbook for Conflict Transformation* ed. D. Bloomfeld, M. Fischer, and B. Schmelzle. Berlin: Berghof Research Centre for Constructive Conflict Management. http://www.berghofhandbook .net/articles/smith_handbook.pdf.

Stewart, F., C. Huang, and M. Wang. 2001. "Internal Wars in Developing Countries: An Empirical Overview of Economic and Social Consequences." In *War and Underdevelopment*, vol. 1, ed. F. Stewart and V. Fitzgerald, 67–103. Oxford: Oxford University Press.

UN (United Nations). 2010. *Integrated Disarmament, Demobilization, and Reintegration Standards.* http://www.unddr .org/iddrs/framework.php.

UNODC (United Nations Office on Drugs and Crime). 2005. *Afghanistan Opium Survey.* Kabul.

Urdal, H. 2006. "A Clash of Generations? Youth Bulges and Political Violence." *International Studies Quarterly* 50 (3): 607–30.

———. 2008. "Population, Resources and Violent Conflict: A Sub-National Study of India 1956–2002." *Journal of Conflict Resolution* 52 (4): 590–617.

USAID (U.S. Agency for International Development). 2006. *Success Story: Flower Industry Gives Jobs to Displaced.* http://www .usaid.gov/stories/colombia/ss_co_flowers .html.

Verwimp, P., and J. Van Bavel. 2010. "Violent Conflict, Gender, and Schooling: Micro-Level Evidence from Burundi." Paper presented at a workshop on gender and conflict, World Bank, Washington, DC, June 9.

Willibald, S. 2006. "Does Money Work? Cash Transfers to Ex-Combatants in Disarmament, Demobilization and Reintegration Processes." *Disasters* 30 (3): 316–39.

World Bank. 2001. "Nepal: Priorities and Strategies for Education Reform." Report 26509-NEP, Washington, DC.

———. 2005. *Afghanistan Poverty, Vulnerability and Social Protection: An Initial Assessment.* Washington, DC.

———. 2006. *India: Unlocking Opportunities for Forest-Dependent People in India.* Main Report, vol. 1, Washington, DC.

———. 2007. "Sri Lanka Poverty Assessment. Engendering Growth and Equity: Opportunities and Challenges." South Asia Region, Poverty Reduction and Economic Management Sector Unit, Washington, DC.

———.2008a. "The Afghanistan Investment Climate in 2008." http://siteresources.world bank.org/AFGHANISTANEXTN/Resources/ 305984-1237085035526/5919769-1258729 848597/1AFInvestmentClimatesurveyReport Final.pdf.

———. 2008b. "Liberia Poverty Reduction Strategy Paper." June, Washington, DC.

———. 2009a. "Emergency Project Paper on a Proposed Additional Grant in the Amount of SDR 50.9 Million." April. Washington, DC.

———. 2009b. "*Pakistan: Preliminary Damage and Needs Assessment: Immediate Restoration and Medium Term Reconstruction in Crisis Affected Areas.* Washington, DC.

———. 2010a. *Moving out of Poverty: Rising from the Ashes of Conflict,* ed. D. Narayan and P. Petesch. Washington, DC.

———. 2010b. "Nepal Community School Support Project: Project Performance Assessment Report." Report 55407, Washington, DC.

———. 2010c. "Sri Lanka: Reshaping Economic Geography." South Asia Region, Poverty Reduction and Economic Management Department and Sri Lanka Country Management Unit, Washington, DC.

———. 2011a. *Doing Business Database*. Washington, DC: World Bank.

———. 2011b. *World Development Indicators*. Washington, DC: World Bank.

———. 2011c. *World Development Report 2011: Conflict, Security, and Development*. Washington, DC.

World Bank and ADB (Asian Development Bank). 2010. *Post Crisis Needs Assessment*. Islamabad.

World Food Programme. 2011. "Pakistan-Food Security and Market Assessment in Crisis-Affected Areas of NWFP and FATA." Working paper, Rome.

Appendix A

Household surveys used

Table A.1 summarizes the labor force and living standards surveys used throughout this book. In countries where both types of data are available (Bangladesh, Nepal, and Pakistan), labor force surveys were the primary source of data, as they tend to be better suited for the analysis of the labor market. For these countries, living standards surveys were used to complement labor force survey data and to analyze poverty and employment (household consumption is not available in most labor force surveys). These living standard surveys were also used for examining specific issues for which they were better suited, such as education provision or educational attainment by socio-economic group. The most recent labor survey in Bangladesh is a welfare-monitoring survey, which differs from a typical labor force survey. It was used in order provide the latest estimates. This survey does not allow for the calculation of all indicators used in this book. Finally, either due to coverage or year of surveys, only particular national surveys were suitable for the analysis of labor market outcomes and conflict. Table A.1 provides a summary of the different national surveys used, and identifies when a particular survey was used to examine selected issues only.

TABLE A.1   **Labor force and living standards surveys used**

Country	Survey	Year	Comments
Afghanistan	National Risk and Vulnerability Assessment	2007/08	
Bangladesh	Labor Force Survey	2002/03	
	Labor Force Survey	2005/06	
	Monitoring of Employment Survey (MES)	2009	Core indicators only
	Household Income and Expenditure Survey	2000	Poverty analysis and education analysis only
	Household Income and Expenditure Survey	2005	Poverty analysis only
	Household Income and Expenditure Survey	2010	Poverty analysis and education analysis only
Bhutan	Living Standards Survey	2003	
	Living Standards Survey	2007	
India	National Sample Survey (Employment Schedule)	1983	
	National Sample Survey (Employment Schedule)	1993/94	
	National Sample Survey (Employment Schedule)	1999/2000	
	National Sample Survey (Employment Schedule)	2004/05	
	National Sample Survey (Employment Schedule) (Thin Round)	2007/08	
	National Sample Survey (Employment Schedule)	2009/10	
Maldives	Vulnerability and Poverty Assessment	1998	
	Vulnerability and Poverty Assessment	2004	
Nepal	Labor Force Survey	1998/99	
	Labor Force Survey	2007/08	
	Living Standards Survey	1995/96	Poverty analysis, education analysis, and conflict analysis only
	Living Standards Survey	2003/04	Poverty analysis, education analysis, and conflict analysis only
Pakistan	Labor Force Survey	1999/2000	
	Labor Force Survey	2007/08	
	Labor Force Survey	2008/09	
	Social and Living Standards Measurement Survey	2001/02	Poverty analysis and education analysis only
	Social and Living Standards Measurement Survey	2007/08	Poverty analysis and education analysis only
Sri Lanka	Labor Force Survey	2000	
	Labor Force Survey	2004	Education analysis and conflict analysis only
	Labor Force Survey	2006	Education analysis only
	Labor Force Survey	2008	
	Household Income and Expenditure Survey	1995/96	Poverty analysis only
	Household Income and Expenditure Survey	2006/07	Poverty analysis and education analysis only

Source: Authors' compilation.

Appendix B

Methodology used to analyze labor transitions

The book is interested in labor transitions—specifically, the ability of workers to move across sectors and types of employment over time and the extent to which they move from less desirable to more desirable jobs (and vice versa). Such transitions are typically measured with panel data on individuals or households over time. Such panel data are only rarely available in South Asia, however. To compensate for the absence of true panel data, the authors constructed synthetic panel data from multiple rounds of cross-sectional surveys for Bangladesh, India, and Nepal, adapting a technique developed by Lanjouw, Luoto, and Mckenzie (2011) for studying poverty transitions.

The key idea behind the method is to exploit the relationship between an individual's employment status, which varies from period to period, and time-invariant individual and household characteristics in order to examine labor transitions over time. Individual time-invariant characteristics can be obtained from cross-sectional surveys (with certain assumptions). They thus form the connectors that help convert cross-sectional data into synthetic panel data.

The following (minimal) econometric expression illustrates the method. Let y_{ij} be binary variables that represent the various labor outcomes of interest for individual i, $i = 1,\ldots, N$, in survey round (or period) j, where $j = 1$ or 2. The main labor outcomes of interest are the employment statuses of individuals: for workers in rural areas, being employed in the rural nonfarm sector (versus agriculture); for workers in urban areas, being employed as casual or low-end self-employed workers (versus regular wage or salaried workers or high-end self-employed workers). Although the same subscript i is used to index individuals, the only data available are cross-sectional.

The labor transitions of interest can be represented by

$$P(y_{i1} < z_1 | y_{i2} < z_2) \qquad \text{(B.1)}$$

$$P(y_{i1} < z_1 | y_{i2} > z_2) \qquad \text{(B.2)}$$

$$P(y_{i1} > z_1 | y_{i2} < z_2) \qquad \text{(B.3)}$$

$$P(y_{i1} > z_1 | y_{i2} > z_2) \qquad \text{(B.4)}$$

The first quantity represents the probability that individual i stays in the same employment status (for example, working in agriculture) in both survey rounds (that is, no labor transition takes place over the time spanned by the two survey rounds). The second quantity represents the probability that individual i improves his or her employment status in the second time period (for example, by moving from agriculture in the first survey round to the rural nonfarm sector in the second survey round). The cut-off point is z_j, set at 0.5. Below this point (indicated by <), workers are in the less desirable employment status; above this point indicated by >), they are in the more desirable employment status. An analogy can be made to poverty analysis, where a similar cut-off point is known as the poverty line: households are considered poor if their consumption falls below this cut-off point.

The synthetic panel data are constructed from repeated rounds of cross-sectional data by applying estimated coefficients and error terms obtained from the regressions of individual labor outcomes on individual time-invariant characteristics in one survey round to a second round. These data can then be used to predict lower-bound and upper-bound estimates of labor transitions (B.1–B.4) overall and for various population groups. Estimates are made using both nonparametric and parametric methods.

The method for analyzing poverty transitions was validated with true panel data (including data on Bosnia-Herzegovina, Lao People's Democratic Republic, Peru, and Vietnam). The method for labor transitions was validated with true panel data from Nepal. The estimates of the lower and upper bounds for poverty and labor transition rates largely encompass the true rates, providing empirical support for the validity of this method. (For more technical details on the methodology used to construct pseudo-panel data, see Dang and Lanjouw 2011 and Lanjouw, Luoto, and McKenzie 2011.)

References

Dang, H.-A., and P. Lanjouw. 2011. "Measuring Poverty Dynamics with Pseudo-Panels Based on Cross-Sections: An Application to Vietnam." Working paper, Development Research Group, World Bank, Washington, DC.

Lanjouw, P., J. Luoto, and D. McKenzie. 2011. "Using Repeated Cross-Sections to Explore Movements in and Out of Poverty." Policy Research Working Paper 5550, World Bank, Washington, DC.